# NORTH AMERICAN SUBURBS

THE GLENDESSARY PRESS — Berkeley

Consulting Editor:
Donald A. Hansen  *University of California, Berkeley*

# NORTH AMERICAN SUBURBS

## Politics, Diversity, and Change

Edited by
### John Kramer
State University
of New York,
Brockport

The Glendessary Press, Inc.
2512 Grove, Berkeley, California
94704

Copyright © 1972 by The Glendessary Press, Inc., Berkeley. All rights reserved. No part of this book may be reproduced in any form, by mimeograph or any other means, without permission in writing from the publisher. Printed in the United States of America.

Library of Congress Card Catalog No.: 70-178881

ISBN: 0-87709-717-8 clothbound;   0-87709-217-6 paperback

# CONTENTS

PREFACE  *ix*

INTRODUCTION  *xi*

PART ONE: BEYOND THE SUBURBAN MYTH  *1*

    INTRODUCTION  *3*

1. THE MYTH OF SUBURBIA  *5*
Bennett M. Berger

2. THE PROCESS OF SUBURBAN DEVELOPMENT  *19*
S. D. Clark

3. URBANISM AND SUBURBANISM AS WAYS OF LIFE: A RE-EVALUATION OF DEFINITIONS  *31*
Herbert J. Gans

    SUGGESTIONS FOR FURTHER READING  *51*

PART TWO: SUBURBIA PAST AND PRESENT  *53*

    INTRODUCTION  *55*

4. THE BIG CHANGE IN SUBURBIA  *57*
Frederick Lewis Allen

5. THE SUBURBAN BOOM  *71*
Ben J. Wattenberg with Richard M. Scammon

6   SUBURBAN PERSISTENCE   82
    Reynolds Farley

7   THE SOCIAL AND ECONOMIC
    CHARACTERISTICS OF AMERICAN SUBURBS   97
    Leo F. Schnore

    SUGGESTIONS FOR FURTHER READING   109

PART THREE: SUBURBAN DIVERSITY EXAMINED   111

    INTRODUCTION   113

8   THE HOME IN CRESTWOOD HEIGHTS   116
    John R. Seeley, R. Alexander Sim,
    and Elizabeth W. Loosley

9   AN ANATOMY OF SUBURBIA   137
    Herbert J. Gans

10  THE NATURAL HISTORY
    OF A RELUCTANT SUBURB   160
    William M. Dobriner

11  JEWISH-GENTILE RELATIONS IN LAKEVILLE   174
    Benjamin B. Ringer

12  THE OTHER MAYOR LEE   185
    John Kramer

13  MOBILE HOMES: INSTANT SUBURBIA
    OR TRANSPORTABLE SLUMS?   201
    Robert Mills French and Jeffrey K. Hadden

    SUGGESTIONS FOR FURTHER READING   212

# Contents

## PART FOUR: POLITICS IN SUBURBIA  213

### INTRODUCTION  215

**14** THE POLITICAL SOCIOLOGY OF AMERICAN SUBURBIA: A REINTERPRETATION  218
Frederick M. Wirt

**15** POLITICAL PERSPECTIVES OF SUBURBAN PARTY LEADERS  237
Dennis S. Ippolito

**16** POLITICAL PARTICIPATION IN AN UPPER-MIDDLE-CLASS SUBURB  256
Joseph Zikmund II and Robert Smith

SUGGESTIONS FOR FURTHER READING  270

## PART FIVE: TOWARD SUBURBIA'S FUTURE  271

### INTRODUCTION  273

**17** THE METROPOLITAN GOVERNMENT APPROACH: SHOULD, CAN, AND WILL IT PREVAIL?  276
Daniel R. Grant

**18** SUBURBAN ACTION: ADVOCATE PLANNING FOR AN OPEN SOCIETY  284
Paul and Linda Davidoff and Neil Newton Gold

**19** THE CASE FOR CROWDING  306
William H. Whyte

SUGGESTIONS FOR FURTHER READING  322

REFERENCES  323

# PREFACE

For six years now I have taught undergraduate courses in urban sociology. Six years is not a particularly long period of time, as academic careers go, but it is of sufficient duration to identify some of the problems which commonly arise in the "urban course." Foremost among these, in my view, is the difficulty of generating realistic discussion about the North American suburbs.

The problem of creating a suburban component in an urban sociology curriculum has, in my experience, two dimensions. First, many of the students entering my classes are confirmed believers in the whole or in portions of "the suburban myth." They tend to see suburbia as an immense sea of sameness in which one set of suburbanites (all are presumed to be drawn from that stolid mass of humanity known as the "middle class") is entirely interchangeable with another. Second, I have found that the readily assignable reading material in urban sociology gives suburbia such cursory treatment that my students' stereotypical preconceptions seldom are challenged. Only by placing on reserve a set of fugitive selections, drawn from an assortment of recent professional journals and excerpted from the book-length studies of the past decade, can I effectively dissuade them from their oversimplified views.

The exasperations of the reserve room, well known to every college student and instructor, have led me to edit this "reader." It brings together nineteen of the selections I have found most productive in making the structure of suburban society an open rather than a closed question. Because the book is designed to be employed as supplementary reading, no attempt has been made to duplicate the basic theoretical materials found in the standard urban texts. Moreover, the selections have been kept to a reasonable number, to make the volume supplementary in price as well as in context, and much has been left out. Only a few of the many different types of suburban communities are treated, and many of the usual suburban subject areas (such as the family and school) receive only indirect coverage. Nevertheless, I consider the collection a proven commodity. The intent of the book is to stimulate meaningful discussion, and each of the selections has served this purpose in my own classrooms. I hope these readings will prove as useful for others as they have been for me and for my students.

Readers, by definition, are the work of many. The authors of these selections deserve thanks for creating the substance of this book, and their publishers warrant appreciation for their permissions to reprint. Thanks, also, must be given to the staff of the Glendessary Press for their encouragement and cooperation, in particular to C. H. Gustafson for his assiduous but never belligerent editing of my own contributions.

# INTRODUCTION

This reader deals with the suburbs of North America. Within this impossibly broad topic, however, it has a guiding theme. Through its nineteen selections, the volume seeks to explore the suburbs' variety. This introduction attempts to create a perspective. It summarizes the nature of suburban diversity in North America. It reviews the genesis of that pervasive but misleading body of folklore ("the suburban myth") which suggests that suburbia is unidimensional. And, it speaks briefly to the relevance of "suburban study" in an age when it often seems as though our full attentions should be directed inside city limits, toward the crushing problems of those who have not made the suburban trek.

In the lexicon of the urban sciences, "suburbanization" represents a particular form of metropolitan deconcentration. Like its parent process, suburbanization involves the movement of people and institutional agencies outward from an urban core. Its special quality relates to the location of cities' political boundaries. When deconcentration extends beyond these boundaries, so that a densely settled milieu begins to take shape upon what in a legal sense is extra-city landscape, the phenomenon is known as suburbanization and the settlements are called suburbs.[1]

---

1. By defining suburbanization and suburbs in this very general way, a number of extra-city areas sometimes referred to by more specialized terminology are subsumed under the "suburban" designation. In particular, the "rural-urban fringe" and "satellite cities" often are treated as separate and sociologically distinct units. For an exposition of the areal concepts applicable to the territory immediately outside of North American cities see Murphy 1966, especially chapter 3.

Metropolitan deconcentration is a ubiquitous process. All urban growth, past and present, has involved expansion outward from central places, but only under certain conditions can a significant amount of suburbanization occur. At a minimum, people must feel free to live immediately beyond the borders of cities. (City walls once protected urban inhabitants and, at the same time, acted as barriers to suburban growth.) Adequate transportation and communications technology must link cities and suburbs together in systems of economic and cultural interchanges; and, in a purely mechanical sense, the political borders of cities must be relatively fixed, so that they may not be extended arbitrarily to encapsulate new growth at the urban periphery.

In North America, since the first trolley and commuter railway lines were extended beyond city limits shortly before the turn of this century the minimal conditions for suburbanization have been met. Furthermore, additional stimuli have been present. Under the impact of industrialization the continent's urban areas have undergone massive population increases, and deconcentration thereby has been impelled. Deconcentration into suburbia has been facilitated by an economic system emphasizing continual growth. The construction of new housing units (in the suburbs) and the decentralization of business and industry (into suburban sectors) have been basic components of the growth syndrome. Large segments of the urban population have acquired financial resources sufficient to exercise deliberate choice of residential locale, and the direction of this choice obviously has been toward the suburbs. The coming of the automobile has provided an individualized mechanism for reducing the time–distance ratio in urban areas. And finally, in the United States, a massive "invasion and succession" phenomenon has occurred. Many rural blacks have moved to the cities; many urban whites have fled to the racial sanctity of suburban soil. The result of all of these factors in combination has been suburbanization at its zenith. In 1900 the cities of North America stood in virtual isolation. Today each is surrounded by a vast suburban ring, which grows more populous and extends further into the hinterland with each passing year.

United States Census Bureau figures, covering the decade between 1960 and 1970, reveal suburbanization's continuing force. In these ten years the overall population of the nation's Standard Metropolitan Statistical Areas (SMSAs) grew by seventeen percent.

# Introduction

But ninety-five percent of this metropolitan growth, in turn, occurred outside of the area's central cities. From 1960 to 1970 the United States' suburban population—operationally defined by the Census Bureau as those living in SMSAs but outside of central cities—rose from fifty-four million to seventy-three million. (See Wattenberg and Scammon, selection five, for a résumé of the SMSA-derived "suburban" designation, and for a discussion of its advantages and disadvantages.) Indeed, by 1970, suburbia had become the modal American address. A higher percentage of the United States' citizenry lived in "the suburbs" (thirty-six percent) than in cities (twenty-nine percent) or in non-metropolitan areas (thirty-five percent).[2,3]

As suburbanization has proceeded, it has brought to the extra-city environs a myriad of socially distinct populations and a wide array of industrial, business, and commercial facilities. In 1925 a rural sociologist—Harlan P. Douglass—made the first detailed examination of the suburbs and found, even then, that the suburban terrain was occupied by people and institutional agencies of every description (1925, chapters 3 and 4). He wrote of "workers' suburbs and bosses' suburbs" and of "children's suburbs and old people's suburbs," to cite just two of his many paired comparisons. The suburbs, as Douglass saw them, represented the city spilled over into the countryside. Individual suburban communities, like city neighborhoods, tended to be specialized and to have socially homogeneous citizenries. But the suburban territory as a whole was used for many different purposes and, in that regard,

---

2. The 1970 United States population figures are drawn from the U.S. Bureau of the Census, *Current Population Reports,* Series P-23, No. 37, "Social and Economic Characteristics of the Population in Metropolitan and Nonmetropolitan Areas: 1970 and 1960" (Washington, D.C.: U.S. Government Printing Office, 1971). Data for this report were obtained from the March 1970 Current Population Survey, not from the April 1970 census. Moreover, to facilitate 1960 to 1970 comparisons, the report assumes that the number and geographical size of the nation's SMSAs did not change in the ten-year interval. In reality, the number of SMSAs increased from 212 to 243 and the Census Bureau also added counties to many of the existing SMSAs during the decade. The result, then, is that the report somewhat understates the actual 1970 United States "suburban" population. Final reports of the 1970 census undoubtedly will show that approximately thirty-eight percent of the United States populace lived in "The Suburbs."

3. Measuring the suburban population of Canada by roughly the same technique—i.e., residents of the Dominion's twenty-one metropolitan areas who live outside of those areas' central cities—there were 4,396,866 Canadian "suburbanites" in 1966. This figure represents twenty-two percent of the 1966 Canadian population of 20,014,880. The data are from *The World Almanac 1970 Edition* (Garden City: Doubleday, 1970), p. 497. For a more extensive review of urbanization and suburbanization in Canada see Kasahara 1968.

Douglass perceived it to be an urban area in its early stages of development.

Since Douglass's day, the "urbanization" of the suburbs has continued. The suburban sectors of North America now are highly variegated areas. They have drawn into their many settings persons from all of the continent's major ethnic, racial, and religious groups and from all points along the socio-economic spectrum. They also have attracted an ever-growing collection of business and industrial concerns. The scenario has been one of reciprocal reaction. People have moved to the suburbs for residential purposes; business and industry have come to feed upon the lush suburban consumer and labor markets; more people have been attracted by suburbia's indigenous employment opportunities, and so on. Contrary to popular wisdom, the suburbs cannot be characterized merely as "dormitories" for the central cities. The number of suburbanites working in suburban territories is more than twice the total of suburb-to-city commuters.[4]

Visually, and in terms of land-use patterns, most suburban sectors now resemble the outer portions of cities. Residential neighborhoods stand side by side with industrial installations and with clusters of slick commercial emporia. Apartment houses and high-rise office buildings are beginning to create multi-level suburban skylines which blend with those of the cities themselves. And, on many demographic indices (as Wattenberg and Scammon point out) suburbia and cities are not radically distinct although, in aggregate, the suburbs are somewhat more affluent and considerably whiter.

But even suburbia's whiteness can be overstated. By 1970, in the United States, over 3.5 million blacks lived in suburban sectors and in the preceding ten years the nation's black suburban populace grew by more than 1.1 million.[5] The recent influx of blacks to suburbia does not necessarily mean that white suburbs are easing their traditional practices of racial and class exclusion. Most suburban blacks live in mini-ghettos wedged between the more usual white suburban places (see Kramer, selection twelve). The

---

4. For a variety of suburban versus central-city employment data, as of 1968, see *Changes in Urban America*, United States Department of Labor, Bureau of Labor Statistics, BLS Report No. 353, April 1969.

5. Data about the United States' 1970 black suburban population are from the U.S. Bureau of the Census, *Current Population Reports*, Series P-23, No. 37, 1971. The recent black migration to suburbia is discussed in detail by Birch (1970).

addition of more than one million black "suburbanites" in the last decade, however, and the arrival of more than eighteen million new whites—many of them "blue collar" workers residing in "working class" suburbia—has intensified the already heterogeneous character of the wide suburban expanse.

Applied to the richly varied character of the extra-city setting in North America, the concept of suburban diversity refers to the disparity between types of suburban settlements. The separate localities often are categorized according to the basic role they play in the economy of metropolitan areas. At the most general level there are residential suburbs, employing suburbs (those dominated by large-scale industrial facilities or commercial complexes), and those with "mixed" formats. Yet economic function is only one of the many dimensions upon which suburbs differ. The residential-employing-mixed trichotomy barely begins to suggest the actual range of contemporary suburban places. There are new tract suburban communities, for example, and stately old suburban towns. There are incorporated suburbs, in which local rights of self-determination are jealously guarded, and there are unincorporated suburbs which exist as place names but not as political entities. Many suburbs remain homogeneous in a racial, ethnic, or socio-economic sense. Others have become decidedly heterogeneous on one or more of these important qualities. Indeed, the suburban settlements of North America are so diverse that they defy the creation of a realistic and exhaustive typology.

The contextual features which differentiate suburbs also serve to differentiate their internal social organizations. Because individual suburban places possess dissimilar functional, historical, political, and demographic attributes, they also possess dissimilar social environments. Many of the selections to follow deal explicitly with this issue. In this introduction only one point about the diversity of suburban social organization need be stressed. From the standpoint of sociology, the term "suburb" has relatively little meaning. It refers only to a locality nearby and somehow interdependent with a city. To employ the term to suggest a single type of place, or to imply that there is an overarching pattern of "suburban" social organization, is to engage in an overgeneralization of serious proportions.

And yet that is precisely what all of us do as a matter of

everyday routine. In conversation, and more than occasionally in otherwise quite sophisticated writing, the word "suburb" and its derivatives ("suburban" and "suburbia") are used to evoke an image. The picture is one of identical houses occupied by similar people. In addition, a none-too-flattering social climate is suggested, one of complacency and conformity. The image is not entirely false. Suburban settlements approximating the image do exist, but the totality of suburbia is much more. The net effect of the overgeneralization is to obscure the suburbs' diverse essence.

In recent years, social scientists have labeled the notion of suburban homogeneity "the suburban myth" and have traced it to its source. It stems from the era immediately following World War II when, in the countryside close by North America's major cities, huge tracts of mass-produced homes and apartments began to arise with what seemed to be the speed of light. To the eye, according to S. D. Clark (selection two), the scene was a "great and undifferentiated mass of dwellings, street blocks, and subdivisions, beginning and ending nowhere that could be seen clearly." For a short period of time the nature of the social arrangements in these new and chaotic places, and the effects of the new suburbs upon the social fabric of North America, were open and intriguing questions.

Answers to these questions were not long in coming. In part, they were the product of North America's sociologists, some of whom studied postwar suburbia from afar by means of census data, and some of whom actually took to the uncharted suburban byways and cul-de-sacs with clipboards and questionnaires in hand. The former discovered that the new suburbanites were younger, better-educated, and more likely to be recently married than might be expected by random selection. Researchers in the field searched for more qualitative characteristics and, to note a few of their many findings, discovered that the new suburbs were unusually "family-centered," possessed atypically high levels of "neighboring," and contained a surprising abundance of well-subscribed voluntary associations. Most of the sociologists' reports were of the usual academic sort, however. Filled with jargon and statistics, often ending with hesitant statements calling for further research, they by no means filled the need for a definitive suburban portrait. Into the breach rushed an array of journalists, novelists, and intrepid social critics who began to bombard the

# Introduction

American public with an easily comprehended summary of suburbia's ethos.

By all odds, the most influential treatise on the new suburbs was William H. Whyte's best-selling *The Organization Man* (1956). Then the editor of *Fortune*, Whyte observed and interviewed the residents of a small number of mass-produced postwar suburbs, most notably Park Forest, Illinois, and Drexelbrook, Pennsylvania. He detected in these places an "unmistakable similarity in the way of life," one which seemed to be unique in the annals of North American history.

At the root of Whyte's analysis was his in-depth demographic finding that the new suburbs were occupied by young, geographically and socially mobile corporation executives and the members of their nuclear families. The corporations, Whyte observed, imbued their managerial employees with "the social ethic"—a mindset emphasizing teamwork as the optimum device for progress. Individuality, according to this philosophy, was at best inefficient and at worst seditious. The new suburbs were the corporation brought home. They were socially engineered by their residents according to management principles learned at work. The major problem in these rootless places was to reduce the potentially devastating uncertainties which could accrue to such a transient population. And so, in the new suburbs, the social arrangements were structured purposefully to enroll everyone into group activities. A process of mass socialization took place, creating a psychologically protective communal spirit. Families could move in or out, as corporation transfers dictated, but new arrivals quickly became the functional equivalents of those who had just left. For the human entities involved, each inter-city move usually meant residence in another suburb, often in another suburb of the "package" variety. The marked similarities between these settlements minimized the stress of adjustment to the new locality and to the new job.

In Whyte's new suburbia, life was frenetic. Father traveled daily to his office in the central city. He returned each evening to a schedule of PTA meetings, church socials, and informal gatherings of neighbors. Mother spent her day in an endless round of kaffeeklatsches with the girls. The children, encouraged by their parents to develop social skills even at the expense of their own identities, were being molded unerringly into precious little images of Mom and Dad. Clearly, on a continent where rugged individuality had been valued for centuries, the smothering homogeneity of life in the suburbs was something to view with alarm.

In fairness to Whyte, he never claimed that his descriptions could be applied to all North American suburbs. He self-consciously dealt with a particular type of suburb and with one occupied by a particular type of resident. But his book became a source of literary inspiration. It spawned a host of even more "penetrating" suburban assessments, many of which purported to describe suburbia as a whole. The distinctions between the instant suburbia of Whyte's focus and the other types of suburban settlements often were ignored. By the late 1950s there was a voluminous body of descriptive suburban literature on the popular market. In sum, suburbia was all of a piece. In a word, suburbia was conformity. Then, from conformity, an almost endless series of suburban social pathologies was projected.

The total list of supposed suburban maladies is too lengthy to recount in this introduction, but a few of them can be mentioned for illustrative purposes. Suburbia was found to be pervaded by a kind of melancholia because, after all, the human spirit is not easily confined to a lock-step system of compulsive fellowship. The melancholia often times became identifiable as actual mental illness, usually of the latent sort, but more than occasionally it flared into overt disequilibrium. Suburbanites flocked to their churches for solace. They concentrated upon their families and their homes and upon their material goods as islands of personal property amidst widespread social sharing. Conformity produced its own spiral in the form of status-striving. Later, in the more sensational accounts of suburban life, the extra-city landscape came to be described as a veritable hotbed of sexual wanderings. Sex, so it seemed, was an antidote to the innate meaninglessness of suburban existence. Worst of all, to some of suburbia's antagonists, the suburbs were resistant to change. Politically they were bastions of conservatism and those who migrated to them, no matter what their former political leanings, inevitably succumbed to that most dreaded disease of all—creeping Republicanism.

Even as the popular stereotypes were being purveyed, however, there were iconoclasts at work. For the most part these doubters were social scientists. They objected to the idea that the suburbs were "carbon duplicates" of one another, and found no validity

## Introduction

in the premise that suburbia was uniquely nefarious. As early as 1957, at the height of the boom in popular suburban criticism, sociologists Thomas Ktsanes and Leonard Reissman (1959) argued that suburbs, even those populated by the fabled junior captains of American industry and their families, were merely "new homes for old values."[6] Ktsanes and Reissman contended that new suburbanites brought with them from the city established ways of viewing the world and well-ingrained behavior patterns. To the extent that suburbia was attracting a socially diverse flow of immigrants, it was to be expected that the different suburban communities would exhibit different systems of social organization.

A year later, sociologist William M. Dobriner called for research in a wide variety of suburban settings.[7] He suggested that the social class composition of suburban settlements, the length of time since their founding, and the conditions of their creation were more crucial influences upon social organization than suburban location itself. Observing the considerable interest in suburbia at that time, and noting the obvious need for further suburban research, Dobriner predicted "bright" prospects "for a vigorous sociology of the suburbs." Time has proven him only partially correct.

By the early 1960s there was a modicum of corrective suburban study under way. The notion that the suburbs of North America possessed similar populations with similar modes of social organization was scrutinized and quickly dismissed under the derogatory "suburban myth" title. A modest number of social scientists began to use the myth as a hypothesis-to-be-rejected, comparing the actual forms of suburban social behavior, as found in a small but varied set of suburban communities, against its tenets. Out of these corrective studies, some of which are included in this volume, came the general recognition of suburban diversity. Out of these studies, too, came the explicit realization that suburbia is a dynamic setting, its social and institutional structure constantly becoming more complex and urban. By the mid-1960s,

---

6. Ktsanes and Reissman's seminal attack on the suburban myth was first presented in 1957 as a paper before the American Studies Association of the Lower Mississippi. Two years later the paper was published as "Suburbia--New Homes for Old Values."

7. *The Suburban Community* (1958). Dobriner's evaluation of "suburban study" to that time, and his call for additional research, is contained in the introduction. The remainder of the book consists of suburban readings. *The Suburban Community* was the first and, prior to this volume, the only "reader" devoted exclusively to suburbia.

the intellectual groundwork had been laid for an objective effort to chart and to explain the changing intricacies of suburban society.

Unfortunately, the actual volume of suburban study during the 1960s was relatively small. In 1967 sociologist Dennis Wrong could note, with telling accuracy, that "suburbia is no longer a very fashionable topic" (1967, p. 358). During the 1960s social scientists as well as the creators of popular imagery turned their attentions in unison to the central cities, where ghetto disturbances and other manifestations of social inequality captured the conscience and the imagination. Sociologists, in particular, wound up much of their suburban business and concentrated upon the issues of poverty and frustration downtown. Only a small number continued to conduct suburban research. Now, more than a decade after Dobriner's optimistic prediction, the potential of suburban study is unfulfilled. Few of its heuristic opportunities have been exploited. The social environments in many of the non-middle-class and non-dormitory portions of suburbia remain to be investigated. Moreover, there is a pressing need to restudy middle-class suburbs, especially those of the mass-produced variety built shortly after World War II. As Herbert Gans's study of Levittown indicates (selection nine) all may not be what it once was in these enclaves, or even what it once seemed to be.

Of course, the relatively low estate of suburban study is understandable. On the surface, suburban inquiry would appear to be an activity deserving only limited priority. Most of our compelling domestic problems seem to be centered within city borders. But many of the cities' ills are, in fact, consequences of suburbanization and, as Paul and Linda Davidoff and Neil Newton Gold conclude (in selection eighteen), their remedies are as properly sought in suburbia as in the cities themselves. It is imperative that ways be found to bring suburban resources to bear in the struggle to revitalize our urban cores. Yet we know so little about the varieties of suburban social organization that it has been impossible thus far to develop sophisticated problem-solving programs with metropolitan scope. One fact is clear: to be content with sloganizing about suburbia, as if it were a single-tracked setting, is to foredoom any attempts to deal with our complex urban dilemmas.

On another level, as well, suburban study is needed. In keeping with its growing urban character, suburbia is fast attracting its

## Introduction

own battery of "urban" problems. Suburban crime rates are rising. Highways are congested. Municipal revenues in many of the multitude of small suburban political jurisdictions are insufficient to meet the mounting demand for services. Blight and decay are becoming suburban afflictions, particularly in the "inner ring" suburbs which stand closest to the city. Meanwhile, suburbia continues to expand, wreaking havoc upon the natural environment in its wake. North America's urban future is being created, largely without plan and largely unobserved. As that urban savant Robert Moses has lamented:

> I worry more about the suburbs than about the cities. In the cities we are at least aware of and are trying to undo the errors of the past. In the suburbs these felonies are being compounded and perpetuated. (1956, p. 88)

Of the nineteen selections in this reader, seventeen bear original publication dates of 1960 or later. Many of the writings overtly confute elements of the suburban myth, and the remainder serve to illustrate the suburbs' changing variety. To create points of reference the inclusions are divided into five parts. Part one contains three selections that directly criticize the myth and place suburban study in its current intellectual context. The first of the four articles in part two briefly reviews the history of suburbanization in North America. The remaining three examine some of the statistical dimensions of contemporary suburban diversity (as of 1960). These articles employ different approaches, but all of them use United States census data as their source of information. Part three contains descriptive insights into six different suburban social settings. The three inclusions of part four examine aspects of suburbia's varied political structure. Finally, in part five, three selections deal with some of the crucial forces which undoubtedly will influence suburban society in the coming generations.

Again, the theme of this volume is suburban diversity. If the collection serves to drive another nail in the suburban myth's figurative coffin, and if its readers develop an increased awareness of North America's actual suburban variety, it will have achieved its purpose.

# PART I: BEYOND THE SUBURBAN MYTH

# INTRODUCTION

Among the most influential critics of the "suburban myth" have been Bennett Berger, Samuel D. Clark, and Herbert Gans. Each conducted an empirical study in the North American suburbs, and each found the myth an inadequate and misleading device for understanding suburban society.

Berger's suburban research took place in a tract of new single-family dwellings occupied by automobile assembly-line workers in California. The workers had moved—from the city of Richmond, some fifty miles distant—to the suburban community of Milpitas when the Ford Motor Company closed its in-city plant and opened a new one a few miles north of San Jose. Berger was impressed with the superficial trappings of this new residential enclave and expected to find that its inhabitants would exhibit the kinds of "behavior, beliefs, and aspirations" which reportedly characterized suburban life. Instead, he found that the workers' life styles had not changed appreciably in the two and one-half years since the move. With only minor discrepancies, these blue-collar suburbanites had merely transported their working-class ways from a city location to what, from physical appearances, seemed to be suburbia unmitigated. In "The Myth of Suburbia" Berger describes the popular stereotypes about the suburbs which led him to his incorrect prediction, and he suggests some of the functions that these stereotypes served (and continue to serve) in North American self-criticism.

Clark's study focused upon fifteen suburban residential areas outside of Toronto. No two of these areas were alike in housing or in demographic characteristics. The research was conducted during the late 1950s and early 1960s, when the Toronto suburban area was growing at a pace rivaling that of any suburban zone in the United States. The aim of the research was to make a preliminary assessment of the social organization emerging in what seemed to be a formless and chaotic environment. From his study, reported in *The Suburban Society*, Clark concluded that suburbia begins almost without social structure, but as it matures an urban society gradually comes into being. Reprinted here is Clark's initial statement of the problem (taken from the introductory chapter of *The Suburban Society*), in which he criticizes elements of the suburban myth and eloquently states the model of urban evolution in the suburbs.

The final selection in this part is Gans's noted essay entitled "Urbanism and Suburbanism as Ways of Life." It was written while Gans was completing his study of Levittown, New Jersey (see selection seven). The suburbs, Gans argues, are not unique worlds unto themselves. They resemble the outer areas of cities in the fact of their quasi-primary social relationships. Suburban social organization, he suggests, is a product of the social and cultural orientation brought to suburbia by its residents. The most important factors shaping suburban society are the social class and life-cycle positions of the suburban inhabitants. If the purely ecological placement of suburban settlements acts as an independent influence upon social structure, we lack as yet the information to draw the connection.

# The Myth of Suburbia

BENNETT M. BERGER

In recent years a veritable myth of suburbia has developed in the United States. I am not referring to the physical facts of large-scale population movement to the suburbs: these are beyond dispute. But the social and cultural "revolution" that suburban life supposedly represents is far from being an established fact. Nevertheless, newspapers and magazines repeatedly characterize suburbia as "a new way of life," and one recent textbook refers to the rise of suburbia as "one of the major social changes of the twentieth century."

To urban sociologists, "suburbs" is an ecological term, distinguishing these settlements from cities, rural villages, and other kinds of communities. "Suburbia," on the other hand, is a cultural term, intended to connote a way of life, or, rather, the intent of those who use it is to connote a way of life. The ubiquity of the term in current discourse suggests that its meaning is well on the way to standardization—that what it is supposed to connote is widely enough accepted and implicitly enough shared to permit free use of the term with a reasonable amount of certainty that it will convey the image or images it intends. Over the last dozen years, these images have coalesced into a full-blown myth, complete with its articles of faith, its sacred symbols, its rituals, its promise for the future, and its resolution of ultimate questions.

---

*Reprinted from the* Journal of Social Issues *17 (1961), pp. 38–49, by permission of the author and the publisher, the Society for the Psychological Study of Social Issues.*

The details of the myth are rife in many popular magazines as well as in more highbrow periodicals and books; and although the details should be familiar to almost everyone interested in contemporary cultural trends, it may be well to summarize them briefly.

## THE ELEMENTS OF THE MYTH

Approaching the myth of suburbia from the outside, one is immediately struck by rows of new "ranch-type" houses either identical in design or with minor variations built into a basic plan, winding streets, neat lawns, two-car garages, infant trees, and bicycles and tricycles lining the sidewalks. Nearby is the modern ranch-type school and the even more modern shopping center dominated by the department store branch or the giant supermarket, itself flanked by a pastel-dotted expanse of parking lot. Beneath the television antenna and behind the modestly but charmingly landscaped entrance to the tract home resides the suburbanite and his family. I should say *"temporarily* resides" because perhaps the most prominent element of the myth is that residence in a tract suburb is temporary; suburbia is a "transient center" because its breadwinners are upwardly mobile, and live there only until a promotion or a company transfer permits or requires something more opulent in the way of a home. The suburbanites are upwardly mobile because they are predominantly young (most commentators seem to agree that they are almost all between 25 and 35), well educated, and have a promising place in some organizational hierarchy—promising because of a continuing expansion of the economy and with no serious slowdown in sight. They are engineers, middle-management men, young lawyers, salesmen, insurance agents, teachers, civil service bureaucrats—groups sometimes designated as Organization Men, and sometimes as "the new middle class." Most such occupations require some college education, so it comes as no surprise to hear and read that the suburbanites are well educated. Their wives too seem well educated; their reported conversation, their patois, and especially there apparently avid interest in theories of child development all suggest exposure to higher education.

According to the myth, a new kind of hyperactive social life has developed in suburbia. Not only is informal visiting or

# The Myth of Suburbia

"neighboring" said to be rife, but a lively organizational life also goes on. Clubs, associations, and organizations allegedly exist for almost every conceivable hobby, interest, or preoccupation. An equally active participation in local civic affairs is encouraged by the absence of an older generation who, in other communities, would normally be the leaders.

This rich social and civic life is fostered by the homogeneity of the suburbanites; they are in the same age range, have similar jobs and incomes; their children are around the same age, their problems of housing and furnishing are similar. In short, a large number of similar interests and preoccupations promotes their solidarity. This very solidarity and homogeneity, on top of the physical uniformities of the suburb itself, is often perceived as the source of the problem of "conformity" in suburbia; aloofness or detachment is frowned upon. The "involvement of everyone in everyone else's life" submits one to the constant scrutiny of the community, and everything from an unclipped lawn to an unclipped head of hair may be cause for invidious comment. On the other hand, the uniformity and homogeneity make suburbia classless, or one-class (variously designated as middle or upper-middle class). For those interlopers who arrive in the suburbs bearing the unmistakable marks of a more deprived upbringing, suburbia is said to serve as a kind of "second melting pot" in which those who are on the way up learn to take on the appropriate folkways of the milieu to which they aspire.

During the day, suburbia is almost wholly given over to the business of child-rearing. Manless during the day, suburbia is a female society in which the young mothers, well educated and without the interference of tradition (represented by doting grandparents), can rear their children according to the best modern methods. "In the absence of older people, the top authorities on child guidance (in suburbia) are two books: Spock's *Infant Care*, and Gesell's *The First Five Years of Life*. You hear frequent references to them."

The widely commented upon "return to religion" is said to be most visible in suburbia. Clergymen are swamped, not only with their religious duties but with problems of marriage counseling and other family problems as well. The revivified religious life in suburbia is not merely a matter of the increasing size of Sunday congregations, for the church is not only a house of worship but a local civic institution also. As such it benefits from the generally active civic life of the suburbanites.

Part of the myth of suburbia is the image of suburbanites as commuters. Much has been deduced about suburbia from the fact of commuting. For father, commuting means an extra hour or two away from the family—with debilitating effects upon the relationship between father and children. Sometimes this means that Dad leaves for work before the children are up and comes home after they are put to bed. Naturally, these extra hours put a greater burden upon the mother, and have implications for the relationship between husband and wife.

The commuter returns in the morning to the place where he was bred, for the residents of suburbia are apparently former city people who "escaped" to the suburbs. By moving to suburbia, however, the erstwhile Democrat from the "urban ward"[1] becomes the suburban Republican. The voting shift has been commented on or worried about at length; there seems to be something about suburbia that makes Republicans out of people who were Democrats while they lived in the city. But the political life of suburbia is characterized not only by the voting shift, but by the vigor with which it is carried on. Political *activity* takes its place beside other civic and organizational activity, intense and spirited.

## THE SOURCES OF THE MYTH

This brief characterization is intended neither as ethnography nor as caricature, but it does not, I think, misrepresent the image of suburbia that has come to dominate the minds of most Americans, including the intellectuals. Immediately, however, a perplexing question arises: why should a group of tract houses, mass produced and quickly thrown up on the outskirts of a large city, apparently generate so unique and distinctive a way of life? What is the logic that links tract living with suburbia as a way of life?

If suburban homes were all within a limited price range, then one might expect them to be occupied by families of similar income, and this might account for some of the homogeneity of the

---
1. William Whyte has a way of making the phrase "urban ward" resound with connotations of poverty, deprivation, soot, and brick—as if "urban ward" were a synonym for "slum."

neighborhood ethos. But suburban developments are themselves quite heterogeneous. The term "suburbia" has not only been used to refer to tract housing developments as low as $8,000 per unit and as high as $65,000 per unit, but also to rental developments whose occupants do not think of themselves as homeowners. The same term has been used to cover old rural towns (such as those in the Westchester-Fairfield County complex around New York City) which, because of the expansion of the city and improvements in transportation, have only gradually become suburban in character. It has been applied also to gradually developing residential neighborhoods on the edges of the city itself. The ecological nature of the suburbs cannot justify so undifferentiated an image as that of "suburbia."

If we limit the image of suburbia to the mass-produced tract developments, we might regard the fact of commuting as the link between suburban residence and "suburbanism as a way of life." Clearly, the demands of daily commuting create certain common conditions which might go far to explain some of the ostensible uniformities of suburban living. But certainly commuting is not a unique feature of suburban living; many suburbanites are not commuters; many urban residents are. It may be true that the occupations of most suburbanites presently require a daily trip to and from the central business district of the city, but it is likely to be decreasingly true with the passage of time. For the pioneers to the suburban residential frontier have been followed not only by masses of retail trade outlets, but by industry also. Modern mass production technology has made obsolete many two- and three-story plants in urban areas. Today's modern factories are vast one-story operations which require wide expanses of land, which are either unavailable or too expensive in the city itself. With the passage of time, "industrial parks" will increasingly dot suburban areas, and the proportions of suburbanites commuting to the city each day will decrease.

If the occupations of most suburbanites were similar in their demands, then this might help account for the development of a generic way of life in the suburbs. And, indeed, if suburbia were populated largely by Organization Men and their families, then one could understand more readily the style of life that is ascribed to it. Or, lacking this, if Organization Men, as Whyte puts it, give the prevailing *tone* to life in suburbia, then one could more readily understand the prevalence of his model in the writing on suburbia. But there is no real reason to believe that the Organization Man dominates the suburbs. Perhaps the typical Organization Man is a suburbanite. But it is one thing to assert this and quite another thing to assert that the typical tract suburb is populated by Organization Men and their families or dominated by an Organization way of life.

Clearly then one suburb (or *kind* of suburb) is likely to differ from another not only in terms of the cost of its homes, the income of its residents, their occupations and commuting patterns, but also in terms of its educational levels, the character of the region, the size of the suburb, the social and geographical origin of its residents, and countless more indices—all of which, presumably, may be expected to lead to differences in "way of life."

But we not only have good reason to expect suburbs to *differ* markedly from one another; we have reason to expect striking *similarities* between life in urban residential neighborhoods and tract suburbs of a similar social cast. In large cities many men "commute" to work, that is, take subways, buses, or other forms of public transportation to their jobs, which may be over on the other side of town. There are thousands of blocks in American cities with rows of identical or similar houses in them within a limited rental or price range, and presumably occupied by families in a similar income bracket. The same fears for massification and conformity were felt regarding these urban neighborhoods as are now felt for the mass-produced suburbs. Certainly, urban neighborhoods have always had a class character and a "way of life" associated with them. Certainly, too, the whole image of the problem of "conformity" in suburbia closely parallels the older image of the tyranny of gossip in the American small town.

In continually referring to "the myth of suburbia" I do not mean to imply that the reports on the culture of suburban life have been falsified; and it would be a mistake to interpret the tone of my remarks as a debunking one. *I mean only to say that the reports of suburbia we have had so far have been extremely selective.* They are based, for the most part, upon life in Levittown, New York; Park Forest, Illinois; Lakewood, near Los Angeles; and most recently (the best study so far) a fashionable suburb of Toronto, Canada. The studies that have given rise to the myth of suburbia have been studies of *white-collar suburbs* of large cities.

## The Myth of Suburbia

If the phrase "middle-class suburb" or "white-collar suburb" strikes the eye as redundant, it is testimony to the efficacy of the myth. Large tracts of suburban housing, in many respects indistinguishable from those in Levittown and Park Forest, have gone up and are continuing to go up all over the country, not only near large cities, but near middle-sized and small ones as well. In many of these tracts, the homes fall within the $12,000 to $16,000 price range, a range well within the purchasing abilities of large numbers of semi-skilled and skilled factory workers in unionized heavy industry. Many of these working-class people are migrating to these new suburbs—which are not immediately and visibly characterizable as "working class," but which, to all intents and purposes, look from the outside like the fulfillment of the "promise of America" symbolized in the myth. Even more of them will be migrating to new suburbs as increasing numbers of factories move out of the city to the hinterlands. Many of these people are either rural bred or urban-working-class bred, with relatively little education, and innocent of white-collar status or aspiration. And where this is true, as it is in many low-price tracts, then one may expect sharp differences between their social and cultural life and that of their more sophisticated counterparts in white-collar suburbs.

This should be no surprise; indeed, the fact that it should have to be asserted at all is still further testimony to the vitality of the myth I have been describing. My own research among auto workers in a new, predominantly "working class" suburb in California demonstrates how far removed their style of life is from that suggested by the myth of suburbia. The group I interviewed still vote eighty-one percent Democratic; there has been no "return to religion" among them—more than half of the people I spoke to said they went to church rarely or not at all. On the whole, they have no great hopes of getting ahead in their jobs, and an enormous majority regard their new suburban homes not as a temporary resting place, but as paradise permanently gained. Of the group I interviewed, seventy percent belonged to not a single club, organization, or association (with the exception of the union), and their mutual visiting or "neighboring" was quite rare except if relatives lived nearby. The details of the findings are available in another place (Berger 1960); let me summarize them by saying that the group of auto workers I interviewed has, for the most part, maintained its working-class attitudes and style of life intact in the context of the bright new suburb.

## THE FUNCTIONS OF THE MYTH

Similar conditions probably prevail in many of the less expensive suburbs; in any case, semi-skilled "working class" suburbs probably constitute a substantial segment of the reality of suburban life. Why, then, is the myth still so potent in our popular culture? Suburbia today is a public issue—something to talk about, everywhere from the pages of learned journals to best sellers, from academic halls to smoke-filled political rooms, from the pulpits of local churches to Hollywood production lots.[2]

One source of the peculiar susceptibility of "suburbia" to the manufacture of myth is the fact that a large supply of visible symbols are ready at hand. Picture windows, patios and barbecues, power lawn mowers, the problems of commuting, and the armies of children manning their mechanized vehicles down the sidewalks, are only secondarily facts; primarily they are symbols whose function is to evoke an image of a way of life for the non-suburban public. These symbols of suburbia can be fitted neatly into the total pattern of the "spirit" of this "age." Suburbia is the locus of gadgetry, shopping centers, and "station-wagon culture"; its grass grows greener, its chrome shines brighter, its lines are clean and new and modern. Suburbia is America in its drip-dry Sunday clothes, standing before the bar of history fulfilled, waiting for its judgment. But like Mr. Dooley's court, which kept its eyes on the election returns, the "judgments of history" are also affected by contemporary ideological currents, and the myth of suburbia is enabled to flourish precisely because it fits into the general outlook of at least four otherwise divergent schools of opinion whose function it is to shape the "judgment of history."

---

2. In the movie version of the novel *No Down Payment,* ostensibly a fictional account of life in the new suburbia, Hollywood makes a pointed comment on social stratification. The sequence of violence, rape, and accidental death is set in motion by the only important character in the story who is not a white-collar man: the rural Tennessee-bred service station manager. Frustrated at being denied the job of police chief (because of his lack of education), he drinks himself into a stupor, rapes his upper-middle-class, college-educated neighbor, and then is accidentally killed (symbolically enough) under the wheels of his new Ford. The film closes with his blonde, nymphomaniacal widow leaving the suburb for good on a Sunday morning, while the white-collar people are seen leaving the Protestant church (denomination ambiguous) with looks of quiet illumination on their faces.

## The Myth of Suburbia

To realtor-chamber of commerce defenders of the American Way of Life suburbia represents the fulfillment of the American middle-class dream; it is identified with the continuing possibility of upward mobility, with expanding opportunities in middle-class occupations, with rising standards of living and real incomes, and the gadgeted good life as it is represented in the full-color ads in the mass-circulation magazines.

To a somewhat less sanguine group, for example architects, city planners, aestheticians, and designers, suburbia represents a dreary blight on the American landscape, the epitome of American standardization and vulgarization, with its row upon monotonous row of mass-produced cheerfulness masquerading as homes, whole agglomerations or "scatterations" of them masquerading as communities. To these eyes, the new tract suburbs of today are the urban slums of tomorrow.

Third, the myth of suburbia seems important to sociologists and other students of contemporary social and cultural trends. David Riesman says of the authors of *Crestwood Heights* that they "collide, like Whyte, with a problem their predecessors only brushed against, for they are writing about *us*, about the professional upper middle class and its businessmen allies. . . . They are writing, as they are almost too aware, about themselves, their friends, their 'type.'" There are, obviously, personal pleasures in professionally studying people who are much like oneself; more important, the myth of suburbia conceptualizes for sociologists a microcosm in which some of the apparently major social and cultural trends of our time (other-direction, social mobility, neoconservatism, status anxiety, etc.) flow together, and may be conveniently studied.

Finally, for a group consisting largely of left-wing and formerly left-wing critics of American society, the myth of suburbia provides an up-to-date polemical vocabulary. "Suburb" and "suburban" have replaced the now embarrassingly obsolete "bourgeois" as a packaged rebuke to the whole tenor of American life. What used to be condemned as "bourgeois style," "bourgeois values," and "bourgeois hypocrisy," are now simply designated as "suburban."

But while the myth of suburbia is useful to each of these four groups, it cannot be written off simply as "ruling-class propaganda," or as an attempt to see only the sunny side of things, or, for that matter, as an attempt to see only the darker side of things—or even as a furtive attempt to peer into a mirror. Too many responsible intellectuals, while uncritically accepting the *myth* of suburbia, are nevertheless extremely critical of what they "see" in it.

But precisely *what* is it that they are critical of? Is it conformity? status anxiety? chrome? tail fins? gadgetry? gray flannel suits? No doubt, these are symbols powerful enough to evoke images of an enemy. But the nature of this "enemy" remains peculiarly elusive. Surely, there is nothing specifically "suburban" about conformity, status anxiety and the rest; nor is there anything necessarily diabolical about mass-produced domestic comfort and conservatively cut clothes. It is extraordinary that, with the single exception of William H. Whyte's attempt to trace the "web of friendship" on the basis of the physical structure of the Park Forest "courts," no one, to my knowledge, has come to grips with the problem of defining what is specifically *suburban* about suburbia. Instead, most writers are reduced to the use of hackneyed stereotypes not of suburbia, but of the upper middle class. When most commentators say "suburbia," they really mean "middle class."

The sources of this way of life, however, lie far deeper than mere residence in a suburb. These sources have been much discussed in recent years, most notably, perhaps, by Mills, Riesman, Fromm, and Galbraith. They go beyond suburbs to questions of wealth, social status, and corporate organization. Even Whyte's famous discussion of suburbia (upon which so much of the myth is founded) was undertaken in the context of his larger discussion of the Organization Man, a social type created by the structure of corporate opportunity in the United States—something a good deal more profound than the folkways of suburbanites. Seen in this light, suburbia may be nothing but a scapegoat; by blaming "it" for the consequences of our commitment to chrome idols, we achieve ritual purity without really threatening anything or anyone—except perhaps the poor suburbanites, who can't understand why they're always being satirized.

But heaping abuse on suburbia instead of on the classic targets of American social criticism ("success," individual and corporate greed, corruption in high and low places, illegitimate power, etc.) has its advantages for the not-quite-completely-critical intellectual. His critical stance places him comfortably in the great tradition of

# The Myth of Suburbia

American social criticism, and at the same time his targets render him respectable and harmless—because, after all, the critique of suburbia is essentially a "cultural" critique; unlike a political or economic one, it threatens no entrenched interests, and contains no direct implications for agitation or concerned action. Indeed, it may be, as Edward Shils has suggested, that a "cultural" critique is all that is possible today from a left-wing point of view; the American economy and political process stand up fairly well under international comparisons, but American "culture" is fair game for anyone.

Despite the epithets that identify suburbia as the citadel of standardization and vulgarization and conformity, suburbia is also testimony to the fact that Americans are living better than ever before. What needs emphasis is that this is true not only for the traditionally comfortable white-collar classes, but for the blue-collar, frayed-collar, and turned-collar classes also. Even families in urban slums are likely to be paying upward of $85 a month in rent these days, and for this or only slightly more they can "buy" a new tract home in the suburbs. There is an irony, therefore, in the venom that left-wing critics inject into their discussions of suburbia, because the criticism of suburbia tends to become a criticism of industrialization, "rationality," and "progress," and thus brings these critics quite close to the classic conservatives, whose critique of industrialization was also made in terms of its cultural consequences. It is almost as if left-wing critics feared the seduction of the working class by pie—not in the sky, not even on the table, but right in the freezer.

## WHAT MIDDLE CLASS?

The "achievement" of suburbia by the working class is a *collective* achievement made possible by prosperity and the labor movement. As such, it does not constitute evidence of individual social mobility. In a prosperous society there occurs not only individual mobility between strata in a relatively stable hierarchy; the entire hierarchy is pushed up by prolonged widespread prosperity, and rearranged by changes in the distribution of occupations and income. The function of a system of social stratification is to maintain viable, hierarchical distinctions between different categories of people, and when symbols which formerly distinguished rank no longer can, because they have become available to all, we should expect a change in the symbolic aspects of social stratification—if, that is, symbols are to retain the power to make distinctions.

It is perhaps for this reason that in recent years there has been such a relative de-emphasis on economic criteria of stratification in favor of the distinctly cultural ones—that is, those having to do with style of life. For in a society in which even a semi-skilled factory worker can earn $5,000 a year and own two cars, a ranch house, and a TV set, it should perhaps be no surprise that groups with higher prestige (but perhaps without considerably greater income) should defend themselves against the potential threat posed by widespread material abundance to their "prestige" by designating such economic possessions "vulgar" and by asserting the indispensability of a certain style of life—that is, something that cannot be immediately purchased with no down payment. Like universities, which respond to the clamor for higher education by tightening their entrance requirements, prestige groups respond to the clamor by money for prestige by tightening *their* entrance requirements. This has been common enough among aristocratic groups for a long time; money and possessions have rarely been sufficient to admit one to the select circles of old wealth; and the increasingly sharp symbolic distinction between the upper middle class and the lower middle class (not only distinctions of income) suggest that something similar may be occurring on lower levels of society.

Whereas at one time in recent history the phrase "middle class" evoked images of Sinclair Lewis, Main Street, *Saturday Evening Post* families of smiling faces around brown-turkeyed dinner tables, and a concern with "respectability," today the phrase is just as likely to evoke images of cocktail parties, country clubs, other-directedness, the *Atlantic Monthly*, Van Gogh prints in wide, deep mats, and a hypersensitivity to considerations of status. Sociologists recognize this ambiguity by designating the style suggested by the former series of images as "lower" middle class, and the style suggested by the latter series of images as "upper" middle class, and tend to think the issue has been clarified. But the real problem implicit in the terminological need to break the middle class into an upper and a lower stratum is too complex to be solved by a simple linguistic device. The problem is not only one of drawing a line between two contemporary "middle class" styles of life; the immense difference between the life-styles of the lower middle class and that of the upper middle class also involves a historical dimension.

Nineteenth-century America was a middle-class society in the sense that its typical (if not its statistically modal) individuals were shoestring entrepreneurs, and the covers of the *Saturday Evening Post* are a testimony to their former hegemony and to the continuing power of the myth they created. Today, we designate the style of those who follow the lead of the "old" middle class, as "lower" middle class, in order to make room for the style of the burgeoning "new" middle class, which we designate as "upper" middle class because this latter style is a tailored, truncated version of an older upper-class model emphasizing "taste" and "grace," and made possible—even necessary—by the bright vistas looming before the increasing numbers of college-educated people with a promising place in our burgeoning bureaucratic hierarchies. We have no clear images of American "working-class style" precisely because the lowest positions on our socio-economic ladder were traditionally occupied by the most recent groups of European immigrants, each of which, as they arrived, pushed earlier groups of immigrants up. Our images of working-class life, consequently, are dominated by ethnic motifs. But with the end of mass immigration from Europe, it is possible that an indigenous urban working-class culture may develop in the United States in the near future. In its visible manifestations, however, this style is likely to approximate the style of the "old" middle class, *without*, however, inheriting the mantle of social mobility. In short, the lowest native stratum of substantial size in the American industrial order today (excluding Negroes, New York's Puerto Ricans, and marginal workers) probably lives in the style we call "lower middle class."

It is only in this sense that America can be called a middle-class society and, to be sure, a substantial minority of the people I interviewed identified themselves as "middle class." But our society approves of this usage as synonymous with "homeowner," or "respectable standard of living," and the myth of suburbia itself may reinforce the propensity to identify oneself with "America" because America is increasingly characterized in the mass media as a "middle-class society" and the new suburbs are submitted as strong evidence of this. "Anybody with a steady job and income is middle class," one of my respondents told me, and certainly this is true if we conceive of lower-middle-class people as upper-middle-class people with slightly lower incomes. For although it is true that these suburbanites I studied do have only slightly lower incomes than a young insurance salesman or a junior engineer, it illumines nothing to call them middle class because their style (whether it be designated as lower middle class or working class) is a *terminal* one; they live in the present, mostly in the solid, respectable style their income permits, but mobility is something that is possible only for their children. With a house in the suburbs, two cars, a TV set, a wife and two children, and many "major" and "minor" kitchen appliances, one respondent, explaining why he didn't want to be foreman, said, "I'm a working man; I don't like to be sitting down or walking up and down all the time." Another, explaining why he quit being a foreman after six months, said, "I got nothing against guys in white shirts, but I just ain't cut out for work like that." These are the statements of working-class (or, if one insists, lower-middle-class) men, who because of prosperity and the labor movement have been able to achieve a material standard of living never before possible on any large scale for manual workers. But the element of social mobility is missing; aspiration and anticipation as well as "status anxiety" and "conformity" are things for educated people with a fluid position in an organizational hierarchy, and it is this which makes suburban domesticity in a $12,000 house a *final* fulfillment.

Nothing I have said about suburbs gives us the right to doubt the truth of what many observers have said about places like Park Forest and Levittown. I do, however, question the right of others to generalize about "suburbia" on the basis of a few studies of selected suburbs whose representative character has yet to be demonstrated. It is remarkable how, despite the efflorescence of the mass-produced suburbs in post–World War II America, references to "suburbia" more often than not cite the examples of Park Forest and Levittown—as if these two communities could represent a nationwide phenomenon that has occurred at all but the very lowest income levels and among most occupational classifications. If "suburbia" is anything at all unique, we'll never know it until we have a lot more information about a lot more suburbs than we now, unfortunately, have.

# The Process of Suburban Development

S. D. CLARK

A book having to do with the suburbs can scarcely lay claim to uniqueness. For the past quarter-century in America there has been perhaps no social phenomenon more in the news. A mounting flow of popular magazine articles and paperbacks has appeared, devoted to an examination of the way of life of the suburban resident. Particular suburban areas have been intensively scrutinized; the whole general phenomenon of suburbanism has been brought under review. It would seem there could be little more about the suburbs to be said.

Yet there is little attempt in the extensive literature which has grown up about the suburbs to examine how the suburban society comes into being and develops. Emphasis has tended to be placed upon those characteristics of social organization, patterns of social life, which appear to be distinctive to a suburban society. What has been sought are the outlines and internal structuring of an ordered social system which can be described in much the same way as urban or rural society is described. Underlying a good many of the efforts which have been made to analyze the suburban society is the assumption that it is a new kind of social creation, a product of forces in American social life which only recently have come into play. Thus has developed, however much there may be differences in matters of detail, the image or stereotype of suburbia.

---

*Reprinted from* The Suburban Society, *by S. D. Clark, by permission of University of Toronto Press. © University of Toronto Press, 1966, and the author.*

Unwittingly, suburban residents have contributed to the building up of the suburbia image. The mass movement of population into the suburbs suddenly created for publishers a vast new reading public to be exploited, and suburban residents, whatever else they may be, are egotistical enough to want to read about themselves. A good deal of the literature on suburbia has been of a sort bordering on the sensational. The more the facts about suburban life have been distorted the more certain has been the interest in what was written. Myths tended to become built on to myths to produce a caricature of the suburban dweller so grotesque that few people living in suburban areas have been able to resist the temptation of seeking to discover what they are supposed to be like. If lurid details about the sexual misdemeanors of the population could be related a lively reading public was that much more assured.

Not everything written about suburbia has been designed to appeal to the suburban housewife seeking amusement or instruction in light reading. Suburbanism as a social phenomenon has had its serious students. Yet the suburbia myth, which has served so well the writer seeking a popular appeal, has served no less well the writer seeking an appeal to that large and growing body of readers pleased to go by the title of intellectuals. Here the object has been to shock not the lone miserable suburban housewife but the American Public as a whole. What is happening in suburbia has been made to appear symptomatic of what is happening in American society generally. The suburban dweller, it is claimed, gives expression in stark form to a way of life or attitude of mind becoming increasingly characteristic of the North American wherever he may reside. Thus it was in suburbia that David Riesman could most readily find his "other-directed" and William H. Whyte his "organization" man. By his escape from the city, and from the country, the suburbanite is believed to have let himself become exposed to the full force of certain changes taking place in the society of North America.

In such an interpretation of present-day trends and tendencies in American society, certain very decided value judgments are apparent. "I speak in this paper," Riesman wrote, in the opening sentence of a paper entitled "The Suburban Sadness," "from the perspective of one who loves city and country, but not the suburbs" (Riesman 1958, p. 375). A generation ago, the student of American society, then in background truly a man of the country, could find in the big city all that was evil, depraved, and corrupt in the American way of life. A highly romantic picture of rural society, the product of not a little nostalgia, served to bring into sharp relief the undesirable qualities of urban society. In the quarter-century or so that has since passed, the student of American society has learned to love the city in the manner in which he has long loved the country, and now it is suburbia, portrayed in terms of a slavish conformity, fetish of togetherness, and craze for organization, which is set over against a romantic image of the city with its narrow and cluttered streets, its quaint shops and picturesque tenements, its strange and ever-changing assortment of people of many colors, nationalities, and languages, producing a way of life which seemingly brings out all that is best in man.

It is difficult to believe that some of those writers who have been prepared to pass judgment on the character of American society know any better the suburbs they profess to dislike than "the country" they profess to love. Yet the suburbia myth cannot be dismissed as the product simply of the imagination of urban-bred intellectuals intent on finding in the suburban way of life the symptoms of "the sickness of our times." Interest in the phenomenon of suburbanism has led to much research and faithful reporting of research findings. So deeply imbedded in sociological thinking, however, is the suburbia myth that it has determined the very design of much of the research undertaken. Students of suburbia have gone from reading Riesman to reading Fromm and Whyte, and nothing to them appears more sociologically righteous than the effort to discover in the suburban society a basic personality type, a dominant ethos or outlook on life, a distinctive structure of social relationships. Here, indeed, is a society which seems to exemplify to a high degree the character of the socializing process at work in all societies. The very emphasis upon values of child-rearing in the suburban society appears to reflect the underlying concern of the population for conformity and the creation of the conditions for social consensus and integration.

By concentrating attention upon certain suburban areas, it has not been difficult to build up a particular image or stereotype of suburbia, or, indeed, of a suburban personality. For instance, from the picture presented in *Crestwood Heights* of what was reputed to be a North American suburb, much could be made of the suburbanite's overwhelming concern for conformity, his enslavement to the values of a society which placed prime emphasis upon the future welfare of the child, his deeply rooted social and political conservatism and distrust of anything which threatened his accepted way of life (Seeley, Sim, and Loosley 1956). The Crestwood Heighter appeared very much to be an other-directed organization man.

Had those students of suburbia who have thus used the Crestwood Heights study, however, known Toronto better, known something about the hundreds of subdivisions spreading east to Whitby, north to Newmarket, and west to Brampton and beyond, known even more that Crestwood Heights at the time it was being studied had been settled for twenty-five years or more and was made up of an upper-middle- or upper-class population half Gentile and half Jewish, they would have realized how little typical of a suburban community this community was, if, indeed, in any sociological sense it could be considered suburban at all. What was really being studied in Crestwood Heights was not the social process of suburbanism but the culture of a particular urban social class and, in large degree, a particular ethnic group.

A good many of those residential areas selected for investigation by the student of suburbia have possessed characteristics not unlike those of Crestwood Heights. Though they may not have had as wealthy a population, they have been areas which tended to attract people rising in the social scale and highly conscious of their social status. Very often, they have been heavily populated by middle-class or upper-middle-class Jewish people anxious to find in the suburbs a social world where they could be sheltered from the assimilative or culturally disintegrative forces of a Gentile urban environment. Almost all of them have had something of a ready-made quality. Residential communities like Park Forest and the Levittowns (or in the Toronto area Don Mills and Thorncrest Village) did not simply grow up. They were created, often on the initiative or under the direction of one man. They were "packaged" suburbs, residential developments which were designed to offer the family settling in them everything that was required to live a full community life. Suburban communities such as these thus had something of the character of social oases, residential areas created outside the city and sharply set off not only from old established urban areas but as well from other suburban residential areas growing up about.

Why it is residential areas of the packaged type which so often have been selected for study is not at all hard to understand. The very isolation of such areas from the built-up sections of the urban community, their physical compactness, and their development around well-defined centers make them easy to study. They have clear-cut boundaries and there is an orderliness in the structure of their social life. They appear to have some sort of ethos or character and they appear to produce a distinctive personality type. Such can scarcely fail to be the case in view of the fact that only certain kinds of people choose to settle in them.

In such areas the sociologist finds a society which can be described and analyzed in the same way the anthropologist describes and analyzes the primitive society. The characteristics of the population can be readily determined, sampling techniques employed where necessary, patterns of behavior searched out and meaningfully related to the values and goals of the group as a whole, processes of socialization identified and measured, and the major institutions of the society fitted together into something that appears to have the characteristics of a social system. In methodological terms, indeed, the packaged suburban community offers an almost perfect sociological laboratory for investigation and analysis within a functional theoretical framework.

In the very selection made of suburban communities for study, however, a bias becomes built into the sociological conception of suburbanism. A high degree of order is found characteristic of suburban society, but it is those suburban societies displaying a high degree of order which have tended to be selected for study and investigation. With theoretical tools borrowed largely from the anthropologist and psychologist, what the sociologist has been looking for in suburban society is a system of order and nowhere can he find such a system better than in the packaged type.

Where, of course, the sociological interest is in the examination of such social processes as those of socialization, integration, and the creation of social consensus, there can be no quarrel with the selection that has been made. There is an order in suburban society as there is an order in all societies and the nature of this order can be most clearly discerned in those suburban communities which are a product of planning and direction. But suburbanism is not only an order, it is also a process, and an understanding of suburbanism as a process involves looking at those suburban areas not where a sense of order is the most prominent but where it is the least. It is in these latter areas, not in those which are a product of planning and direction, that are to be discovered the dynamics of suburban growth. There is a pattern of suburban development, but it is a pattern in the direction away from as well as towards a state of order. The suburban society is not something created whole and complete, to be examined primarily in terms of the way it is structured. Rather, it is something which grows up, develops, and it can therefore only be understood in terms of the process of its growth. What suburban development essentially means is the process of transformation of the country into the city. It is in the nature of this transformation that are to be found the distinctive characteristics of the suburban society.

Had there been after the Second World War no sudden mass movement of population beyond urban boundaries but rather a steady, continuous spreading of urban residents outwards, suburbanism as a social phenomenon would have attracted little attention. The suburbs gained their social significance because they were areas into which great masses of people suddenly moved. Throughout the development of society on the North American continent there have been long intervals when economic, political, and other conditions (war, in particular) discouraged any great movement of population. When conditions developed favorable to such movement, it tended as a result to take place in the form of a great "rush." In such manner were the Western Canadian Prairies occupied in the years after the turn of the century and in such manner has the countryside surrounding such cities as Toronto become occupied in the years since the Second World War.

Census figures, which do nothing more than indicate the overall increase of population, reveal nevertheless in striking fashion the nature of the development which took place in the Toronto area. Between 1941 and 1961, while the population of the City of Toronto grew only from 667,457 to 672,407 (it declined in the decade 1951-61), that of the twelve surrounding municipalities which were to become a part of Metropolitan Toronto grew from 242,534 to 946,380. More significant still was the fact that of this 703,846 increase of population in the twelve surrounding municipalities, eighty-two percent of it, 577,036, occurred in the three outer municipalities of Etobicoke, North York, and Scarborough. By 1951 the nine inner municipalities had become almost fully occupied. Indeed, in the years 1951-61, these municipalities increased in population by only 57,352, from 245,748 to 303,100 (see Table 1). It was not here, in these older built-up areas, but in the countryside beyond that occurred the phenomenal growth of population in the years after the Second World War.

TABLE 1
POPULATION OF THE NINE INNER MUNICIPALITIES

|  | 1941 | 1951 | 1961 |
|---|---|---|---|
| York | 81,052 | 101,582 | 129,645 |
| East York | 41,821 | 64,616 | 72,409 |
| Leaside | 6,183 | 16,233 | 18,579 |
| Mimico | 8,073 | 11,342 | 18,212 |
| New Toronto | 9,504 | 11,194 | 13,384 |
| Weston | 5,740 | 8,677 | 9,715 |
| Forest Hill | 11,757 | 15,305 | 20,489 |
| Long Branch | 5,172 | 8,727 | 11,039 |
| Swansea | 6,988 | 8,072 | 9,628 |

In 1941 the combined population of the three townships of Etobicoke, Scarborough, and North York was 66,244. By 1956 it was 413,475. Five years later it had become 643,280 (see Table 2).

TABLE 2
POPULATION OF THE THREE OUTER MUNICIPALITIES

|  | 1941 | 1951 | 1961 |
|---|---|---|---|
| Etobicoke | 18,973 | 53,779 | 156,035 |
| Scarborough | 24,303 | 56,292 | 217,286 |
| North York | 22,968 | 85,897 | 269,959 |

Beyond these townships, in areas reaching out twenty-five miles or more from the City of Toronto, the growth of population was almost as phenomenal, but here census figures can provide no accurate measure. The increase in the population of such townships as Toronto, Vaughan, Markham, and Pickering, and, further out still, Chinguacousy, Nelson, Trafalgar, King, Whitchurch, East Gwillimbury, and Whitby was striking enough (see Table 3), but it was in certain specially favored parts of these townships that the real increase occurred. By the end of the 1950s places like Port Credit, Brampton, Georgetown, Woodbridge, Markham, Richmond Hill, Aurora, and Newmarket had lost their character of small-town communities in becoming the centers of large urban concentrations of population (see Table 4).

TABLE 3
POPULATION OF TOWNSHIPS BEYOND METROPOLITAN TORONTO

|  | 1941 | 1951 | 1961 |
|---|---|---|---|
| Toronto | 12,481 | 28,528 | 62,616 |
| Vaughan | 5,829 | 9,766 | 16,701 |
| Markham | 7,134 | 10,625 | 13,426 |
| Pickering | 6,602 | 10,371 | 17,201 |
| Chinguacousy | 3,716 | 5,225 | 7,571 |
| Nelson | 4,169 | 8,193 | Annexed |
| Trafalgar | 4,585 | 8,118 | 31,743 |
| King | 5,357 | 7,469 | 12,845 |
| Whitchurch | 3,294 | 5,157 | 7,391 |
| East Gwillimbury | 3,647 | 4,400 | 10,357 |
| Whitby | 2,310 | 2,972 | 6,312 |

TABLE 4
POPULATION OF TOWNS BEYOND METROPOLITAN TORONTO

|  | 1941 | 1951 | 1961 |
|---|---|---|---|
| Port Credit | 2,160 | 3,643 | 7,203 |
| Brampton | 6,020 | 8,389 | 18,467 |
| Georgetown | 2,562 | 3,452 | 10,298 |
| Woodbridge | 1,044 | 1,699 | 2,315 |
| Markham | 1,204 | 1,606 | 4,294 |
| Richmond Hill | 1,345 | 2,164 | 16,446 |
| Aurora | 2,726 | 3,358 | 8,791 |
| Newmarket | 4,026 | 5,356 | 8,932 |

However much allowance may be made for population increase resulting from local economic growth, it would seem apparent that by 1961 the population of what was in a very real sense the Toronto urban community had grown to about two million, over one-half of which was to be found beyond the borders of the city and the nine inner municipalities. What this growth meant was that for every person living in an old built-up residential area in 1961, one other was living in a residential area at the very most not more than fifteen years old. Indeed, considering that the main increase in the population of the suburbs took place after 1953, there probably was at least one person out of four in the Toronto urban community at the end of the 1950s who was living within a residential area not more than five years old. What clearly had occurred was a great mass movement of population out of the city into the country. In terms of how particular areas of the countryside were occupied, the movement, indeed, assumed the character of a "rush." Where in many areas there had been only three or four scattered rural families, a year later as many as five hundred or a thousand suburban families could be located.[1] The country was suddenly taken over and made into a part of the urban community. It was this sudden taking over of the country by an urban population which was the dominant feature of suburban development as it took place in the Toronto area in the years after the Second World War.

Though what resulted was a suburban society, it was a suburban society which did not conform to any stereotype of suburbia. It had no structure; indeed, it had no boundaries which could be readily determined. It could not be mapped in the way a Park Forest or Thorncrest Village could. It consisted of little more than a great and undifferentiated mass of dwellings, street blocks, and subdivisions, beginning and ending nowhere that could be seen clearly. Where the new residential developments crowded down on the immediate borders of older established residential areas, what was suburban became almost completely indistinguishable from what was urban. Where, on the other hand, urban residents had spread themselves out in areas far distant from the city, there was no easy telling where the suburban left off and the rural began. Clearly, the city was taking over the country but in a manner that produced no readily recognizable form or structure of community life. Conspicuous because of the type of people they attracted, their well-defined boundaries, and their distinctive forms of community life were those suburban residential developments of the packaged type, and little less conspicuous were those cottage-type communities far out from the city developing as havens for the urban poor. But these were residential developments providing housing for only an insignificant proportion of the total suburban population. Stretching for miles beyond the city, and with boundaries which had little meaning other than marking the limits of particular subdivision developments, were residential areas which had no clear or distinctive qualities about them. If the plans of subdividers, or history, gave them a name, they seemingly

---

1. There is no end of examples of subdivision developments which illustrate the pattern of growth in particular areas. In East Gwillimbury Heights outside the town of Newmarket, for instance, the first houses were ready for occupancy in the midwinter of 1957-58. By the autumn of 1958 virtually all of the approximately five hundred homes in this subdivision were occupied. Though more than one subdivision was involved, the increase in population of census tract 162 in Scarborough, an area bounded by Victoria Park, Lawrence Avenue, Birchmount Road, and Highway 401, illustrates the same process of rapid growth. In 1951 the population of this tract was 321. In 1956 it was 14,995!

possessed nothing which could identify them as suburban except that they lay beyond the community that was urban.

If the term suburban is to be used to describe all such residential areas developing beyond urban borders it can be given sociological meaning only by being made to apply to a type of society which while not yet urban is in the process of becoming urban. The suburban is a society coming into being. It is its lack of a form or structure which gives it its distinctive character. When it comes to possess a form or structure it has to that extent lost its suburban character and taken on a character that is urban.

Only as a theoretical construct, of course, can such a "pure" suburban society be conceived. In any suburban residential area there is in fact from the very beginning something of the established urban society built into its social structure. People cannot move from the city to the country without bringing with them at least some of the equipment necessary for building an urban society. As well, there are few suburban communities which in their beginnings did not take over and transform for their purposes some part of the society which was there before the occupation by an urban population began. Urban and rural are not so far apart, in the structure of their social life or in their social values, that the making over of the country into the city leads to the complete dissolution of the society of the one in the establishment of the society of the other. If no suburban society can come into being, and take a shape sufficient for it to be recognized as a suburban society, without its already having become something of an urban society, there is no suburban society, on the other hand, which is not in a small degree at least a rural society as well.

Any examination of the process of suburban development must necessarily take account of those forces which secure the easy and almost imperceptible transformation of the society of the country into the society of the city. The packaged residential development is only one example of how the country is made into the city without serious disturbance to the values and ways of life of the people involved. The growth of the rural village into a community urban in character is another example. Certainly, where the movement of population to the suburbs involves people of different social classes, religions, and ethnic backgrounds these differences are reflected in the character of the residential areas which develop. A working-class suburb, as Bennett Berger (1960) has convincingly demonstrated, is not the same as an upper-middle-class suburb. Some of the new society is simply a re-creation of the old society long known.

Yet this does not mean that suburban society is only a projection, as William M. Dobriner (1963) tends to argue, of the forms and ways of life of the urban society. If a working-class suburb is not the same as an upper-middle-class suburb, neither is it the same as an old established working-class residential area. What is important is not what gets carried over from the urban to the suburban society but what fails to get carried over. Something happens to the way people live, to the social structure in which they participate, when they move out of the city to the suburbs.

Given the character of suburban development, it would be hard to imagine how such could fail to be the case. The very act of moving involves some upset of established ways of life, social attachments, and values. Even the packaged suburban community does not come into being without disturbance in the manner of life of the residents. Where suburban development involves the movement all at once of great masses of people from the city to the country the disturbance can be very great.

Thus the study of suburbanism is a study of social change. What results in the end is an urban society. But the suburban society is made into an urban society only after an interval of time. It differs from the urban society in that it is an urban society not yet complete. Much of what makes up a society is carried with them by people moving from the city to the country but much is left behind. What emerges is a simpler society, a society less elaborately structured, less socially differentiated, less ordered. Indeed, at that point in time when settlement in the suburban community has just taken place, the society is one almost totally lacking in structure and form.

In methodological terms, what such a conception of suburbanism means is that there can be no easy determining the boundaries and limits of the society being analyzed. Where the form and structure of this society can be perceived, it has to that extent lost its suburban character. It is the society without form and structure—and thus without identifiable boundaries—which is truly suburban. Yet, of course, no social analysis is possible if the limits of what is being analyzed cannot be determined. It is this fact which justifies the emphasis in sociology upon order and structure and leads to the effort to construct, however it may be defined, some sort of boundary-maintaining social system. The suburban society must be talked about as if it really were a society with identifiable boundaries.

To talk about the suburban society in this manner does not mean, however, that analysis has to proceed in terms of one model only of the society. If the way the suburban society comes into being and develops is to be analyzed, what is required is a model of the society as it was and a model of the society as it has become or is becoming. The suburban society must be distinguished from the urban society even though it may be nothing more than a less perfect form of this society. As well, one suburban society must be distinguished from another in terms of the degree to which it conforms to the model of the urban—or "pure" suburban—society. Within such a framework of analysis interest shifts from an examination of those forces in the suburban society securing its character as an ordered social system to an examination of those forces bringing about its change from one kind of social system to another.

In the study here undertaken of the Toronto suburban community it was not possible to find a social creation, of course, which fully conformed to any analytical model of the suburban society. What was inevitably required were a number of compromises with actuality. Not only was there no "typical" suburban society to be found, there were to be found no clearly demarcated types of suburban societies. The population of the city, in truth, had spilled itself out in the country in every conceivable manner. In the overall view, it was this formlessness which was the most distinctive characteristic of the suburban community.

Yet, while form may have appeared to be lacking, it was lacking in different degrees in different suburban areas. There could be no mistaking the suburb which had grown up as a result of careful planning and direction—the "packaged" suburb—from the suburb which had grown up without any planning or direction at all. However treacherous the effort to classify suburban areas into broad types, only by such classifying can the pattern of suburban development be perceived and analyzed. There is a pattern of development of suburban society as there is a pattern of development of any society. It is the recognition of such a pattern which distinguishes comparative sociological from historical analysis.

# Urbanism and Suburbanism as Ways of Life
## A Re-evaluation of Definitions

HERBERT J. GANS

The contemporary sociological conception of cities and of urban life is based largely on the work of the Chicago School, and its summary statement in Louis Wirth's essay, "Urbanism as a Way of Life" (1938). In that paper, Wirth developed "a minimum sociological definition of the city" as a "relatively large, dense and permanent settlement of socially heterogeneous individuals" (p. 50). From these prerequisites, he then deduced the major outlines of the urban way of life. As he saw it, number, density, and heterogeneity created a social structure in which primary-group relationships were inevitably replaced by secondary contacts that were impersonal, segmental, superficial, transitory, and often predatory in nature. As a result, the city dweller became anonymous, isolated, secular, relativistic, rational, and sophisticated. In order to function in the urban society, he was forced to combine with others to organize corporations, voluntary associations, representative forms of government, and the impersonal mass media of communications (pp. 54–60). These replaced the primary groups and the integrated way of life found in rural and other pre-industrial settlements.

Wirth's paper has become a classic in urban sociology, and most texts have followed his definition and description faithfully (Dewey 1960). In recent years, however, a considerable number

---

*Reprinted from Arnold Rose, ed.,* Human Behavior and Social Processes *(Boston: Houghton-Mifflin Co., 1962), pp. 625–648, by permission of the publisher.*

of studies and essays have questioned his formulations (Axelrod 1956; Dewey 1960; Form et al. 1954; Gans 1959; Greer 1956; Greer and Kube 1959; Janowitz 1952; Reiss 1955; Reiss 1959; Seeley 1959; Smith, Form, and Stone 1954; Stone 1954; Whyte 1955; Wilensky and Lebeaux 1958; Young and Willmott 1957).[1] In addition, a number of changes have taken place in cities since the article was published in 1938, notably the exodus of white residents to low- and medium-priced houses in the suburbs, and the decentralization of industry. The evidence from these studies and the changes in American cities suggest that Wirth's statement must be revised.

There is yet another, and more important reason for such a revision. Despite its title and intent, Wirth's paper deals with urban-industrial society, rather than with the city. This is evident from his approach. Like other urban sociologists, Wirth based his analysis on a comparison of settlement types, but unlike his colleagues, who pursued urban–rural comparisons, Wirth contrasted the city to the folk society. Thus, he compared settlement types of pre-industrial and industrial society. This allowed him to include in his theory of urbanism the entire range of modern institutions which are not found in the folk society, even though many such groups (e.g., voluntary associations) are by no means exclusively urban. Moreover, Wirth's conception of the city dweller as depersonalized, atomized, and susceptible to mass movements suggests that his paper is based on, and contributes to, the theory of the mass society.

Many of Wirth's conclusions may be relevant to the understanding of ways of life in modern society. However, since the theory argues that all of society is now urban, *his analysis does not distinguish ways of life in the city from those in other settlements within modern society*. In Wirth's time, the comparison of urban and pre-urban settlement types was still fruitful, but today, the primary task for urban (or community) sociology seems to me to be the analysis of the similarities and differences between contemporary settlement types.

This paper is an attempt at such an analysis; it limits itself to distinguishing ways of life in the modern city and the modern suburb. A re-analysis of Wirth's conclusions from this perspective

---

1. I shall not attempt to summarize these studies, for this task has already been performed by Dewey (1960), Reiss (1955), Wilensky (1961), and others.

# Urbanism and Suburbanism as Ways of Life

suggests that his characterization of the urban way of life applies only—and not too accurately—to the residents of the inner city. The remaining city dwellers, as well as most suburbanites, pursue a different way of life, which I shall call "quasi-primary." This proposition raises some doubt about the mutual exclusiveness of the concepts of city and suburb and leads to a yet broader question: whether settlement concepts and other ecological concepts are useful for explaining ways of life.

## THE INNER CITY

Wirth argues that number, density, and heterogeneity had two social consequences which explain the major features of urban life. On the one hand, the crowding of diverse types of people into a small area led to the segregation of homogeneous types of people into separate neighborhoods (p. 56). On the other hand, the lack of physical distance between city dwellers resulted in social contact between them, which broke down existing social and cultural patterns and encouraged assimilation as well as acculturation—the melting pot effect (p. 52). Wirth implied that the melting pot effect was far more powerful than the tendency toward segregation and concluded that, sooner or later, the pressures engendered by the dominant social, economic, and political institutions of the city would destroy the remaining pockets of primary-group relationships (pp. 60–62). Eventually, the social system of the city would resemble Tönnies's *Gesellschaft*—a way of life which Wirth considered undesirable.

Because Wirth had come to see the city as the prototype of mass society, and because he examined the city from the distant vantage point of the folk society—from the wrong end of the telescope, so to speak—his view of urban life is not surprising. In addition, Wirth found support for his theory in the empirical work of his Chicago colleagues. As Greer and Kube (1959, p. 112) and Wilensky (Wilensky and Lebeaux 1958, p. 121) have pointed out, the Chicago sociologists conducted their most intensive studies in the inner city.[2] At that time, these were slums recently invaded by new waves of European immigrants and rooming house and skid

---

2. By the *inner city*, I mean the transient residential areas, the Gold Coasts and the slums that generally surround the central business district, although in some communities they may continue for miles beyond that district. The *outer city* includes the stable

row districts, as well as the habitat of Bohemians and well-to-do Gold Coast apartment dwellers. Wirth himself studied the Maxwell Street Ghetto, an inner-city Jewish neighborhood then being dispersed by the acculturation and mobility of its inhabitants (Wirth 1928). Some of the characteristics of urbanism which Wirth stressed in his essay abounded in these areas.

Wirth's diagnosis of the city as *Gesellschaft* must be questioned on three counts. First, the conclusions derived from a study of the inner city cannot be generalized to the entire urban area. Second, there is as yet not enough evidence to prove—nor, admittedly, to deny—that number, density, and heterogeneity result in the social consequences which Wirth proposed. Finally, even if the causal relationships could be verified, it can be shown that a significant proportion of the city's inhabitants were, and are, isolated from these consequences by social structures and cultural patterns which they either brought to the city, or developed by living in it. Wirth conceived the urban population as consisting of heterogeneous individuals torn from past social systems, unable to develop new ones, and therefore prey to social anarchy in the city. While it is true that a not insignificant proportion of the inner-city population was, and still is, made up of unattached individuals (Rose 1947), Wirth's formulation ignores the fact that this population consists mainly of relatively homogeneous groups, with social and cultural moorings that shield it fairly effectively from the suggested consequences of number, density, and heterogeneity. This applies even more to the residents of the outer city, who constitute a majority of the total city population.

The social and cultural moorings of the inner-city population are best described by a brief analysis of the five types of inner-city residents. These are:

1. the "cosmopolites";
2. the unmarried or childless;
3. the "ethnic villagers";
4. the "deprived"; and
5. the "trapped" and downward mobile.

The "cosmopolites" include students, artists, writers, musicians,

---

residential areas that house the working- and middle-class tenant and owner. The *suburbs* I conceive as the latest and most modern ring of the outer city, distinguished from it only by yet lower densities, and by the often irrelevant fact of the ring's location outside the city limits.

## Urbanism and Suburbanism as Ways of Life

and entertainers, as well as other intellectuals and professionals. They live in the city in order to be near the special "cultural" facilities that can only be located near the center of the city. Many cosmopolites are unmarried or childless. Others rear children in the city, especially if they have the income to afford the aid of servants and governesses. The less affluent ones may move to the suburbs to raise their children, continuing to live as cosmopolites under considerable handicaps, especially in the lower-middle-class suburbs. Many of the very rich and powerful are also cosmopolites, although they are likely to have at least two residences, one of which is suburban or exurban.

The unmarried or childless must be divided into two subtypes, depending on the permanence or transience of their status. The temporarily unmarried or childless live in the inner city for only a limited time. Young adults may team up to rent an apartment away from their parents and close to job or entertainment opportunities. When they marry, they may move first to an apartment in a transient neighborhood, but if they can afford to do so, they leave for the outer city or the suburbs with the arrival of the first or second child. The permanently unmarried may stay in the inner city for the remainder of their lives, their housing depending on their income.

The "ethnic villagers" are ethnic groups which are found in such inner-city neighborhoods as New York's Lower East Side, living in some ways as they did when they were peasants in European or Puerto Rican villages (Gans 1959). Although they reside in the city, they isolate themselves from significant contact with most city facilities, aside from workplaces. Their way of life differs sharply from Wirth's urbanism in its emphasis on kinship and the primary group, the lack of anonymity and secondary-group contacts, the weakness of formal organizations, and the suspicion of anything and anyone outside their neighborhood.

The first two types live in the inner city by choice; the third is there partly because of necessity, partly because of tradition. The final two types are in the inner city because they have no other choice. One is the "deprived" population: the very poor; the emotionally disturbed or otherwise handicapped; broken families, and, most important, the non-white population. These urban dwellers must take the dilapidated housing and blighted neighborhoods to which the housing market relegates them, although among them are some for whom the slum is a hiding place, or a temporary stop-over to save money for a house in the outer city or the suburbs (Seeley 1959).

The "trapped" are the people who stay behind when a neighborhood is invaded by non-residential land uses or lower-status immigrants, because they cannot afford to move, or are otherwise bound to their present location (Seeley 1959).[3] The "downward mobiles" are a related type; they may have started life in a higher class position, but have been forced down in the socio-economic hierarchy and in the quality of their accommodations. Many of them are old people, living out their existence on small pensions.

These five types all live in dense and heterogeneous surroundings, yet they have such diverse ways of life that it is hard to see how density and heterogeneity could exert a common influence. Moreover, all but the last two types are isolated or detached from their neighborhood and thus from the social consequences which Wirth described.

When people who live together have social ties based on criteria other than mere common occupancy, they can set up social barriers regardless of the physical closeness or the heterogeneity of their neighbors. The ethnic villagers are the best illustration. While a number of ethnic groups are usually found living together in the same neighborhood, they are able to *isolate* themselves from each other through a variety of social devices. Wirth himself recognized this when he wrote that "two groups can occupy a given area without losing their separate identity because each side is permitted to live its own inner life and each somehow fears or idealizes the other" (1928, p. 283). Although it is true that the children in these areas were often oblivious to the social barriers set up by their parents, at least until adolescence, it is doubtful whether their acculturation can be traced to the melting pot effect as much as to the pervasive influence of the American culture that flowed into these areas from the outside.[4]

The cosmopolites, the unmarried, and the childless are *detached* from neighborhood life. The cosmopolites possess a distinct

---

[3]. The trapped are not very visible, but I suspect that they are a significant element in what Raymond Vernon has described as the "gray areas" of the city (1959).

[4]. If the melting pot has resulted from propinquity and high density, one would have expected second-generation Italians, Irish, Jews, Greeks, Slavs, etc. to have developed a single "pan-ethnic culture," consisting of a synthesis of the cultural patterns of the propinquitous national groups.

subculture which causes them to be disinterested in all but the most superficial contacts with their neighbors, somewhat like the ethnic villagers. The unmarried and childless are detached from neighborhood because of their life-cycle stage, which frees them from the routine family responsibilities that entail some relationship to the local area. In their choice of residence, the two types are therefore not concerned about their neighbors, or the availability and quality of local community facilities. Even the well-to-do can choose expensive apartments in or near poor neighborhoods, because if they have children, these are sent to special schools and summer camps which effectively isolate them from neighbors. In addition, both types, but especially the childless and unmarried, are transient. Therefore, they tend to live in areas marked by high population turnover, where their own mobility and that of their neighbors creates a universal detachment from the neighborhood.[5]

The deprived and the trapped do seem to be affected by some of the consequences of number, density, and heterogeneity. The deprived population suffers considerably from overcrowding, but this is a consequence of low income, racial discrimination, and other handicaps, and cannot be considered an inevitable result of the ecological make-up of the city.[6] Because the deprived have no residential choice, they are also forced to live amid neighbors not of their own choosing, with ways of life different and even contradictory to their own. If familial defenses against the neighborhood climate are weak, as is the case among broken families and downward mobile people, parents may lose their children to the culture of "the street." The trapped are the unhappy people who remain behind when their more advantaged neighbors move on; they must endure the heterogeneity which results from neighborhood change.

Wirth's description of the urban way of life fits best the transient areas of the inner city. Such areas are typically heterogeneous in population, partly because they are inhabited by transient types

---

5. The corporation transients (Whyte 1956; Wilensky and Lebeaux 1958), who provide a new source of residential instability to the suburb, differ from city transients. Since they are raising families, they want to integrate themselves into neighborhood life, and are usually able to do so, mainly because they tend to move into similar types of communities wherever they go.

6. The negative social consequences of overcrowding are a result of high room and floor density, not of the land coverage or population density which Wirth discussed. Park Avenue residents live under conditions of high land density, but do not seem to suffer visibly from overcrowding.

who do not require homogeneous neighbors or by deprived people who have no choice, or may themselves be quite mobile. Under conditions of transience and heterogeneity, people interact only in terms of the segmental roles necessary for obtaining local services. Their social relationships thus display anonymity, impersonality, and superficiality.[7]

The social features of Wirth's concept of urbanism seem therefore to be a result of residential instability, rather than of number, density, or heterogeneity. In fact, heterogeneity is itself an effect of residential instability, resulting when the influx of transients causes landlords and realtors to stop acting as gatekeepers—that is, wardens of neighborhood homogeneity.[8] Residential instability is found in all types of settlements, and, presumably, its social consequences are everywhere similar. These consequences cannot therefore be identified with the ways of life of the city.

## THE OUTER CITY AND THE SUBURBS

The second effect which Wirth ascribed to number, density, and heterogeneity was the segregation of homogeneous people into distinct neighborhoods,[9] on the basis of "place and nature of work, income, racial and ethnic characteristics, social status, custom, habit, taste, preference and prejudice" (1938, p. 56). This description fits the residential districts of the *outer city*.[10] Although these districts contain the majority of the city's inhabitants, Wirth went into little detail about them. He made it clear, however, that the socio-psychological aspects of urbanism were prevalent there as well (p. 56).

Because existing neighborhood studies deal primarily with the

---

7. Whether or not these social phenomena have the psychological consequences Wirth suggested depends on the people who live in the area. Those who are detached from the neighborhood by choice are probably immune, but those who depend on the neighborhood for their social relationships—the unattached individuals, for example—may suffer greatly from loneliness.

8. Needless to say, residential instability must ultimately be traced back to the fact that, as Wirth pointed out, the city and its economy attract transient—and, depending on the sources of outmigration, heterogeneous—people. However, this is a characteristic of urban-industrial society, not of the city specifically.

9. By neighborhoods or residential districts I mean areas demarcated from others by distinctive physical boundaries or by social characteristics, some of which may be perceived only by the residents. However, these areas are not necessarily socially self-sufficient or culturally distinctive.

10. For the definition of *outer city*, see footnote 2.

exotic sections of the inner city, very little is known about the more typical residential neighborhoods of the outer city. However, it is evident that the way of life in these areas bears little resemblance to Wirth's urbanism. Both the studies which question Wirth's formulation and my own observations suggest that the common element in the ways of life of these neighborhoods is best described as *quasi-primary*. I use this term to characterize relationships between neighbors. Whatever the intensity or frequency of these relationships, the interaction is more intimate than a secondary contact, but more guarded than a primary one.[11]

There are actually few secondary relationships, because of the isolation of residential neighborhoods from economic institutions and workplaces. Even shopkeepers, store managers, and other local functionaries who live in the area are treated as acquaintances or friends, unless they are of a vastly different social status or are forced by their corporate employers to treat their customers as economic units (Stone 1954). Voluntary associations attract only a minority of the population. Moreover, much of the organizational activity is of a sociable nature, and it is often difficult to accomplish the association's "business" because of the members' preference for sociability. Thus, it would appear that interactions in organizations, or between neighbors generally, do not fit the secondary-relationship model of urban life. As anyone who has lived in these neighborhoods knows, there is little anonymity, impersonality or privacy.[12] In fact, American cities have sometimes been described as collections of small towns.[13] There is some truth to this description, especially if the city is compared to the actual small town, rather than to the romantic construct of anti-urban critics (Vidich and Bensman 1958).

Postwar suburbia represents the most contemporary version of the quasi-primary way of life. Owing to increases in real income

---

11. Because neighborly relations are not quite primary, and not quite secondary, they can also become *pseudo-primary;* that is, secondary ones disguised with false affect to make them appear primary. Critics have often described suburban life in this fashion, although the actual prevalence of pseudo-primary relationships has not been studied systematically in cities or suburbs.

12. These neighborhoods cannot, however, be considered as urban folk societies. People go out of the area for many of their friendships, and their allegiance to the neighborhood is neither intense nor all-encompassing. Janowitz has aptly described the relationship between resident and neighborhood as one of "limited liability." (1952, chap. 7).

13. Were I not arguing that ecological concepts cannot double as sociological ones, this way of life might best be described as small-townish.

and the encouragement of home ownership provided by the FHA, families in the lower middle class and upper working class can now live in modern single-family homes in low-density subdivisions, an opportunity previously available only to the upper and upper middle classes (Wattell 1958).

The popular literature describes the new suburbs as communities in which conformity, homogeneity, and other-direction are unusually rampant (Berger 1960; Vernon 1959). The implication is that the move from city to suburb initiates a new way of life which causes considerable behavior and personality change in previous urbanites. A preliminary analysis of data which I am now collecting in Levittown, New Jersey, suggests, however, that the move from the city to this predominantly lower-middle-class suburb does not result in any major behavioral changes for most people. Moreover, the changes which do occur reflect the move from the social isolation of a transient city or suburban apartment building to the quasi-primary life of a neighborhood of single-family homes. Also, many of the people whose life has changed reported that the changes were intended. They existed as aspirations before the move, or as reasons for it. In other words, the suburb itself creates few changes in ways of life. Similar conclusions have been reported by Berger in his excellent study (1960) of a working-class population newly moved to a suburban subdivision.

## A COMPARISON OF CITY AND SUBURB

If urban and suburban areas are similar in that the way of life in both is quasi-primary, and if urban residents who move out to the suburbs do not undergo any significant changes in behavior, it would be fair to argue that the differences in ways of life between the two types of settlements have been overestimated. Yet the fact remains that a variety of physical and demographic differences exist between the city and the suburb. However, upon closer examination, many of these differences turn out to be either spurious or of little significance for the way of life of the inhabitants (Wattell 1958).[14]

The differences between the residential areas of cities and suburbs which have been cited most frequently are:

---
14. They may, of course, be significant for the welfare of the total metropolitan area.

## Urbanism and Suburbanism as Ways of Life

1. Suburbs are more likely to be dormitories.
2. They are further away from the work and play facilities of the central business districts.
3. They are newer and more modern than city residential areas and are designed for the automobile rather than for pedestrian and mass-transit forms of movement.
4. They are built up with single-family rather than multifamily structures and are therefore less dense.
5. Their populations are more homogeneous.
6. Their populations differ demographically: they are younger; more of them are married; they have higher incomes; and they hold proportionately more white-collar jobs (Duncan and Reiss 1956, p. 131).

Most urban neighborhoods are as much dormitories as the suburbs. Only in a few older inner-city areas are factories and offices still located in the middle of residential blocks, and even here many of the employees do not live in the neighborhood.

The fact that the suburbs are farther from the central business district is often true only in terms of distance, not travel time. Moreover, most people make relatively little use of downtown facilities, other than workplaces (Foley 1957; Jonassen 1955). The downtown stores seem to hold their greatest attraction for the upper middle class (Jonassen 1955, pp. 91–92); the same is probably true of typically urban entertainment facilities. Teen-agers and young adults may take their dates to first-run movie theaters, but the museums, concert halls, and lecture rooms attract mainly upper-middle-class ticket-buyers, many of them suburban.[15]

The suburban reliance on the train and the automobile has given rise to an imaginative folklore about the consequences of commuting on alcohol consumption, sex life, and parental duties. Many of these conclusions are, however, drawn from selected high-income suburbs and exurbs, and reflect job tensions in such hectic occupations as advertising and show business more than the effects of residence (Spectorsky 1955). It is true that the upper-middle-class housewife must become a chauffeur in order to expose her children to the proper educational facilities, but such differences as walking to the corner drug store and driving to its suburban

---

15. A 1958 study of New York theatergoers showed a median income of close to $10,000, and thirty-five percent were reported as living in the suburbs (Enders, undated).

equivalent seem to me of little emotional, social, or cultural import.[16] In addition, the continuing shrinkages in the number of mass-transit users suggests that even in the city many younger people are now living a wholly auto-based way of life.

The fact that suburbs are smaller is primarily a function of political boundaries drawn long before the communities were suburban. This affects the kinds of political issues which develop and provides somewhat greater opportunity for citizen participation. Even so, in the suburbs as in the city, the minority who participate are the professional politicians, the economically concerned businessmen, lawyers and salesmen, and the ideologically motivated middle- and upper-middle-class people with better than average education.

The social consequences of differences in density and house type also seem overrated. Single-family houses on quiet streets facilitate the supervision of children; this is one reason why middle-class women who want to keep an eye on their children move to the suburbs. House type also has some effects on relationships between neighbors, insofar as there are more opportunities for visual contact between adjacent homeowners than between people on different floors of an apartment house. However, if occupants' characteristics are also held constant, the differences in actual social contact are less marked. Homogeneity of residents turns out to be more important as a determinant of sociability than proximity. If the population is heterogeneous, there is little social contact between neighbors, either on apartment-house floors or in single-family-house blocks; if people are homogeneous, there is likely to be considerable social contact in both house types. One need only contrast the apartment house located in a transient, heterogeneous neighborhood and exactly the same structure in a neighborhood occupied by a single ethnic group. The former is a lonely, anonymous building; the latter, a bustling micro-society. I have observed similar patterns in suburban areas: on blocks where people are homogeneous, they socialize; where they are heterogeneous, they do little more than exchange polite greetings (Gans 1961).

Suburbs are usually described as being more homogeneous in house type than the city, but if they are compared to the outer

---

16. I am thinking here of adults; teen-agers do suffer from the lack of informal meeting places within walking or bicycling distance.

city, the differences are small. Most inhabitants of the outer city, other than well-to-do homeowners, live on blocks of uniform structures as well—for example, the endless streets of rowhouses in Philadelphia and Baltimore or of two-story duplexes and six-flat apartment houses in Chicago. They differ from the new suburbs only in that they were erected through more primitive methods of mass production. Suburbs are of course more predominantly areas of owner-occupied single homes, though in the outer districts of most American cities home ownership is also extremely high.

Demographically, suburbs as a whole are clearly more homogeneous than cities as a whole, though probably not more so than outer cities. However, people do not live in cities or suburbs as a whole, but in specific neighborhoods. An analysis of ways of life would require a determination of the degree of population homogeneity within the boundaries of areas defined as neighborhoods by residents' social contacts. Such an analysis would no doubt indicate that many neighborhoods in the city as well as the suburbs are homogeneous. Neighborhood homogeneity is actually a result of factors having little or nothing to do with the house type, density, or location of the area relative to the city limits. Brand-new neighborhoods are more homogeneous than older ones, because they have not yet experienced resident turnover, which frequently results in population heterogeneity. Neighborhoods of low- and medium-priced housing are usually less homogeneous than those with expensive dwellings because they attract families who have reached the peak of occupational and residential mobility, as well as young families who are just starting their climb and will eventually move to neighborhoods of higher status. The latter, being accessible only to high-income people, are therefore more homogeneous with respect to other resident characteristics as well. Moreover, such areas have the economic and political power to slow down or prevent invasion. Finally, neighborhoods located in the path of ethnic or religious group movement are likely to be extremely homogeneous.

The demographic differences between cities and suburbs cannot be questioned, especially since the suburbs have attracted a large number of middle-class child-rearing families. The differences are, however, much reduced if suburbs are compared only to the outer city. In addition, a detailed comparison of suburban and outer city residential areas would show that neighborhoods with the same kinds of people can be found in the city as well as the suburbs. Once again, the age of the area and the cost of housing are more important determinants of demographic characteristics than the location of the area with respect to the city limits.

## CHARACTERISTICS, SOCIAL ORGANIZATION, AND ECOLOGY

The preceding sections of the paper may be summarized in three propositions:

1. As concerns ways of life, the inner city must be distinguished from the outer city and the suburbs; and the latter two exhibit a way of life bearing little resemblance to Wirth's urbanism.
2. Even in the inner city, ways of life resemble Wirth's description only to a limited extent. Moreover, economic condition, cultural characteristics, life-cycle stage, and residential instability explain ways of life more satisfactorily than number, density, or heterogeneity.
3. Physical and other differences between city and suburb are often spurious or without much meaning for ways of life.

These propositions suggest that the concepts urban and suburban are neither mutually exclusive, nor especially relevant for understanding ways of life. They—and number, density, and heterogeneity as well—are ecological concepts which describe human adaptation to the environment. However, they are not sufficient to explain social phenomena, because these phenomena cannot be understood solely as the consequences of ecological processes. Therefore, other explanations must be considered.

Ecological explanations of social life are most applicable if the subjects under study lack the ability to *make choices*, be they plants, animals, or human beings. Thus, if there is a housing shortage, people will live almost anywhere, and under extreme conditions of no choice, as in a disaster, married and single, old and young, middle and working class, stable and transient will be found side by side in whatever accommodations are available. At that time, their ways of life represent an almost direct adaptation to the environment. If the supply of housing and of neighborhoods is such that alternatives are available, however, people will make choices, and if the housing market is responsive, they can even make and satisfy explicit *demands.*

Choices and demands do not develop independently or at random; they are functions of the roles people play in the social system. These can best be understood in terms of the *characteristics* of the people involved; that is, characteristics can be used as indices to choices and demands made in the roles that constitute ways of life. Although many characteristics affect the choices and demands people make with respect to housing and neighborhoods, the most important ones seem to be *class*—in all its economic, social and cultural ramifications—and *life-cycle stage.*[17] If people have an opportunity to choose, these two characteristics will go far in explaining the kinds of housing and neighborhoods they will occupy and the ways of life they will try to establish within them.

Many of the previous assertions about ways of life in cities and suburbs can be analyzed in terms of class and life-cycle characteristics. Thus, in the inner city, the unmarried and childless live as they do, detached from neighborhood, because of their life-cycle stage; the cosmopolites, because of a combination of life-cycle stage and a distinctive but class-based subculture. The way of life of the deprived and trapped can be explained by low socio-economic level and related handicaps. The quasi-primary way of life is associated with the family stage of the life-cycle, and the norms of child-rearing and parental role found in the upper working class, the lower middle class, and the non-cosmopolite portions of the upper middle and upper classes.

The attributes of the so-called suburban way of life can also be understood largely in terms of these characteristics. The new suburbia is nothing more than a highly visible showcase for the ways of life of young, upper-working-class and lower-middle-class people. Ktsanes and Reissman have aptly described it as "new homes for old values" (1959). Much of the descriptive and critical writing about suburbia assumes that as long as the new suburbanites lived in the city, they behaved like upper-middle-class cosmopolites and that suburban living has mysteriously transformed them (Duhl 1956; Fromm 1955, pp. 154–62; Riesman 1958; Whyte 1956). The critics fail to see that the behavior and personality patterns ascribed to suburbia are in reality those of class and age

---
17. These must be defined in dynamic terms. Thus, class includes also the process of social mobility, stage in the life-cycle, and the processes of socialization and aging.

(Dobriner 1958). These patterns could have been found among the new suburbanites when they still lived in the city and could now be observed among their peers who still reside there—if the latter were as visible to critics and researchers as are the suburbanites.

Needless to say, the concept of "characteristics" cannot explain all aspects of ways of life, either among urban or suburban residents. Some aspects must be explained by concepts of social organization that are independent of characteristics. For example, some features of the quasi-primary way of life are independent of class and age, because they evolve from the roles and situations created by joint and adjacent occupancy of land and dwellings. Likewise, residential instability is a universal process which has a number of invariate consequences. In each case, however, the way in which people react varies with their characteristics. So it is with ecological processes. Thus, there are undoubtedly differences between ways of life in urban and suburban settlements which remain after behavior patterns based on residents' characteristics have been analyzed, and which must therefore be attributed to features of the settlement (Fava 1958).

Characteristics do not explain the causes of behavior; rather, they are clues to socially created and culturally defined roles, choices, and demands. A causal analysis must trace them back to the larger social, economic, and political systems which determine the situations in which roles are played and the cultural content of choices and demands, as well as the opportunities for their achievement.[18] These systems determine income distributions, educational and occupational opportunities, and in turn, fertility patterns, child-rearing methods, as well as the entire range of consumer behavior. Thus, a complete analysis of the way of life of the deprived residents of the inner city cannot stop by indicating the influence of low income, lack of education, or family instability. These must be related to such conditions as the urban economy's "need" for low-wage workers, and the housing market practices which restrict residential choice. The urban economy is in turn shaped by national economic and social systems, as well as by local and regional ecological processes. Some phenomena can be explained exclusively by reference to these ecological processes.

---

18. This formulation may answer some of Duncan and Schnore's objections to sociopsychological and cultural explanations of community ways of life (1959).

However, it must also be recognized that as man gains greater control over the natural environment, he has been able to free himself from many of the determining and limiting effects of that environment. Thus, changes in local transportation technology, the ability of industries to be footloose, and the relative affluence of American society have given ever larger numbers of people increasing amounts of residential choice. The greater the amount of choice available, the more important does the concept of characteristics become in understanding behavior.

Consequently, the study of ways of life in communities must begin with an analysis of characteristics. If characteristics are dealt with first and held constant, we may be able to discover which behavior patterns can be attributed to features of the settlement and its natural environment.[19] Only then will it be possible to discover to what extent city and suburb are independent—rather than dependent or intervening—variables in the explanation of ways of life.

This kind of analysis might help to reconcile the ecological point of view with the behavioral and cultural one, and possibly put an end to the conflict between conceptual positions which insist on one explanation or the other (Duncan and Schnore 1959). Both explanations have some relevance, and future research and theory must clarify the role of each in the analysis of ways of life in various types of settlement (Dobriner 1958, p. xxii). Another important rationale for this approach is its usefulness for applied sociology—for example, city planning. The planner can recommend changes in the spatial and physical arrangements of the city. Frequently, he seeks to achieve social goals or to change social conditions through physical solutions. He has been attracted to ecological explanations because these relate behavior to phenomena which he can affect. For example, most planners tend to agree with Wirth's formulations, because they stress number and density, over which the planner has some control. If the undesirable social conditions of the inner city could be traced to

---

19. The ecologically oriented researchers who developed the Shevsky-Bell social area analysis scale have worked on the assumption that "social differences between the populations of urban neighborhoods can conveniently be summarized into differences of economic level, family characteristics and ethnicity" (Bell and Force 1956). However, they have equated "urbanization" with a concept of life-cycle stage by using family characteristics to define the index of urbanization (Bell and Force 1956; Greer 1960; Greer and Kube 1959). In fact, Bell has identified suburbanism with familism (1958).

these two factors, the planner could propose large-scale clearance projects which would reduce the size of the urban population, and lower residential densities. Experience with public housing projects has, however, made it apparent that low densities, new buildings, or modern site plans do not eliminate anti-social or self-destructive behavior. The analysis of characteristics will call attention to the fact that this behavior is lodged in the deprivations of low socio-economic status and racial discrimination, and that it can be changed only through the removal of these deprivations. Conversely, if such an analysis suggests residues of behavior that can be attributed to ecological processes or physical aspects of housing and neighborhoods, the planner can recommend physical changes that can really affect behavior.

A RE-EVALUATION OF DEFINITIONS

The argument presented here has implications for the sociological definition of the city. Such a definition relates ways of life to environmental features of the city qua settlement type. But if ways of life do not coincide with settlement types, and if these ways are functions of class and life-cycle stage rather than of the ecological attributes of the settlement, a sociological definition of the city cannot be formulated.[20] Concepts such as city and suburb allow us to distinguish settlement types from each other physically and demographically, but the ecological processes and conditions which they synthesize have no direct or invariate consequences for ways of life. The sociologist cannot, therefore, speak of an urban or suburban way of life.

CONCLUSION

Many of the descriptive statements made here are as time-bound as Wirth's.[21] Twenty years ago, Wirth concluded that some form

---

20. Because of the distinctiveness of the ways of life found in the inner city, some writers propose definitions that refer only to these ways, ignoring those found in the outer city. For example, popular writers sometimes identify "urban" with "urbanity," i.e., "cosmopolitanism." However, such a definition ignores the other ways of life found in the inner city. Moreover, I have tried to show that these ways have few common elements, and that the ecological features of the inner city have little or no influence in shaping them.

21. Even more than Wirth's they are based on data and impressions gathered in the large Eastern and Midwestern cities of the United States.

of urbanism would eventually predominate in all settlement types. He was, however, writing during a time of immigrant acculturation and at the end of a serious depression, an era of minimal choice. Today, it is apparent that high-density, heterogeneous surroundings are for most people a temporary place of residence; other than for the Park Avenue or Greenwich Village cosmopolites, they are a result of necessity rather than choice. As soon as they can afford to do so, most Americans head for the single-family house and the quasi-primary way of life of the low-density neighborhood, in the outer city or the suburbs.[22]

Changes in the national economy and in government housing policy can affect many of the variables that make up housing supply and demand. For example, urban sprawl may eventually outdistance the ability of present and proposed transportation systems to move workers into the city; further industrial decentralization can forestall it and alter the entire relationship between work and residence. The expansion of present urban renewal activities can perhaps lure a significant number of cosmopolites back from the suburbs, while a drastic change in renewal policy might begin to ameliorate the housing conditions of the deprived population. A serious depression could once again make America a nation of doubled-up tenants.

These events will affect housing supply and residential choice; they will frustrate but not suppress demands for the quasi-primary way of life. However, changes in the national economy, society, and culture can affect people's characteristics—family size, educational level, and various other concomitants of life-cycle stage and class. These in turn will stimulate changes in demands and choices. The rising number of college graduates, for example, is likely to increase the cosmopolite ranks. This might in turn create a new set of city dwellers, although it will probably do no more than encourage the development of cosmopolite facilities in some suburban areas.

The current revival of interest in urban sociology and in community studies, as well as the sociologist's increasing curiosity about city planning, suggest that data may soon be available to formulate

---

22. Personal discussions with European planners and sociologists suggest that many European apartment dwellers have similar preferences, although economic conditions, high building costs, and the scarcity of land make it impossible for them to achieve their desires.

a more adequate theory of the relationship between settlements and the ways of life within them. The speculations presented in this paper are intended to raise questions; they can only be answered by more systematic data collection and theorizing.

## SUGGESTIONS FOR FURTHER READING

The most exhaustive catalogue of the suburban myth's tenets, and the most thorough refutation of these propositions, is Scott Donaldson's *The Suburban Myth* (New York: Columbia University Press, 1969). An earlier attack on the idea of suburban sameness can be found in William M. Dobriner's *Class in Suburbia* (Englewood Cliffs, N.J.: Prentice-Hall, 1963). Among the more readable article-length works bearing upon the myth are: Richard Stauber, "The Swampy Science of Suburbia: A Case for the Sociology of Knowledge" (*Kansas Journal of Sociology*, vol. 1, 1965, pp. 137-154); Anselm Strauss, "The Changing Imagery of American City and Suburb" (*Sociological Quarterly*, vol. 1, 1960, pp. 15-24); and Dennis Wrong, "Suburbs and Myths of Suburbia" in Dennis Wrong and Harry Gracey (eds.), *Readings in Introductory Sociology* (New York: MacMillan, 1967).

# PART II: SUBURBIA PAST AND PRESENT

# INTRODUCTION

One of the principal shortcomings of the suburban myth is its ahistorical tendency. Many who wrote about the North American suburbs in the 1950s explicitly suggested that suburbanization was a unique postwar phenomenon. Others implied that the social arrangements they found in the postwar suburbs were likely to endure in perpetuity. The current orientation of suburban study stresses the premise of social evolution. The social organization of suburbs, like that of any other kind of communities, changes over time. Therefore, it is important to know what the suburbs used to be, so that their present condition—or, more precisely, their present conditions—might better be understood.

"The Big Change in Suburbia," the first selection in this part, represents one of the initial recapitulations of the American suburban past. Its author, the late Frederick Lewis Allen, was the editor of *Harper's*. Even at the peak of the suburban myth's hold upon the popular imagination he attempted to place postwar suburban growth in a historical context. Included in his article is a good deal of over-generalization about the suburbs as they existed in 1954. But Allen's lucid five-stage schema of American suburban history (from the "horse and buggy era" to the period when "business discovers the suburbs") remains a valuable overview of suburban development in North America.

The second selection is drawn from the book *This U.S.A.*, by Ben J. Wattenberg and Richard Scammon. Wattenberg is the author of many books and articles about contemporary America, and Scammon served as director of the United States Bureau of the Census from 1961 to 1965. Using census data, the authors attacked many of the myths about United States society. The section reprinted here focuses on the suburban myth in particular and the discussion is both historical and contemporary in approach. As part of their presentation, Wattenberg and Scammon review the Census Bureau's measures of "suburban" and discuss their applications. Though the selection employs the 1960 census as its primary source, data from the 1970 census, when they are available, are certain to reinforce the authors' basic arguments.

The third selection, "Suburban Persistence," is an extremely provocative article. Its author, Reynolds Farley, contends that some suburbs do not change in terms of socio-economic composition despite rapid rates of population growth. If this is a characteristic of certain types of suburbs (and Farley acknowledges the selective nature of his data) the implications for comprehending suburban diversity are enormous. As Farley concludes, it is clear that "continued research in the dynamics of suburbanization is needed."

No sociologist has been more active in studying suburban variety than Leo Schnore. In the final selection in part two, "The Social and Economic Characteristics of American Suburbs," Schnore addresses the issue of contemporary suburban diversity (as of 1960). He observes the differences in fifteen social and economic characteristics as they are found in two sets of residential, employing, and mixed suburbs. Careful reading of this article, and a little imagination, should suggest other research designs through which additional inter-suburban demographic comparisons might be conducted.

# The Big Change in Suburbia

## FREDERICK LEWIS ALLEN

A few months ago the editors of *Fortune* went into a huddle and, after elaborate calculations, produced the statement that as many as nine million people have moved to the suburbs of American cities since 1947, and that as a result there are now thirty million suburbanites in the United States; a record number, and by a large margin. The growth of Suburbia, said the editors, "is portentous even in a country accustomed to talking of growth in superlatives."

The accuracy of their count may be open to challenge, but there can be little doubt that they put their finger on one of the major changes of our time, which seems destined to alter the face of the land and affect our national way of life for generations to come.

The editors of *Fortune* did not classify as suburbanites everybody who lives on the outskirts of our big cities, or their figures would have been much larger. They included only those who work in the city but "prefer to live where there is more open space": those who are attempting to enjoy, if not the best of two worlds, at least something of the respective blessings of two worlds, the world of the city and the world of the country.

In our modern civilization, the metropolis is an almost irresistible magnet. For generations there has been a continuing drift of men and women from the countryside to the cities, and especially

*Reprinted from "The Big Change in Suburbia: Part One," Harpers 108 (June 1954), pp. 21-28, by permission of the publisher, Harper's Magazine, Inc., and Agnes Rogers Lewis.*

to the biggest ones. For the metropolis is where, by and large, the big money, the big decisions, and the big reputations are made. It is the nucleus of power. It is GHQ. It is the place to go for shows, crowds, dazzle, and adventure. And so, decade after decade, it pulls toward it the restless, the ambitious, the energetic, the lovers of excitement, the young men and women who want to be at the center of things, where opportunity may be around the next corner and there is a feeling in the air that anything may happen. "Bam, whang, whang goes the drum, tootle-te-tootle the fife. Oh for a day in the city square, there is no such pleasure in life!" And also, because of its very size and anonymity, it offers that comparative privacy which to some wears the face of loneliness, but to the independent-minded offers freedom to choose their own kind of living.

But likewise—and especially since the beginning of the automobile age—the metropolis has repelled a considerable number of those whom it drew to it: repelled them with its noise, soot, fumes, barren pavements, traffic tie-ups, nervous pressures, and inhuman dimensions, and especially with the apparent unsuitability of the life it imposes upon small children. It has not repelled many of these people all the way back to the countryside, for its magnetic power is too strong for that: what it has done has been to hold them within its sphere of influence like so many planets—or, more literally, to drive them part way out of town, to attempt to live *by* the city and yet *in* the country; to enjoy the power and glory of the city and yet at the same time, by daily travel, to enjoy quiet in place of its noise, clean fresh air and uninhibited sunshine in place of its soot and fumes, greenery and gardens in place of its barren pavements, living space in place of its congestion, peace in place of its nervous pressures, a neighborly village life in place of its vast anonymity, and an environment in which children will be able to work and play naturally.

Such a combination of contrasting values seems temptingly easy. Rapid transit systems, good commuter service on the railroads, and above all the automobile make it, for the time being, at least physically possible. But for his effort the commuter pays a high price—in fact, many prices.

The most obvious one is the sheer cost, in time and energy, of commuting, of repetitive, self-canceling travel. Suppose a man lives twenty-five miles from his office (not an excessive distance for a

# The Big Change in Suburbia

commuter): that means some fifty miles of travel a day, two hundred fifty miles a week, twelve thousand miles a year—perhaps nearly half a million miles in a lifetime of commuting, without getting anywhere he has not been before. Or to put the cost in terms of time, a man who puts in three hours a day in transit, over a period of forty years, will have devoted considerably over three of those forty years to the mere business of getting there and back. He may have utilized much of this time in reading the paper, or looking over reports, or enjoying bridge games; but these are mitigations of an interminable slavery to the 7:59 and the 5:25.

And there is a curious spiritual cost, too, in that his life is strongly divided. He belongs to the city, but not quite; only as a non-resident, non-dues-paying, and therefore only partly responsible member. He belongs to his suburb, but only as a part-time person who spends the best of his daylight hours, and of his energies, in exile from it. As my wife once put it, his heart and his treasure are twenty miles apart. He becomes something like a split personality, playing one role by day and another by night and over the weekends.

And even his wife, though she may spend nearly all her time in the suburb, is subconsciously aware that during the day it is only half a community, an unnatural manless matriarchy. No wonder she busies herself furiously in organizations of all sorts, as if to rid herself of the frustrating feeling that the place where things are really going on is somewhere else, and that meanwhile she is condemned to play the part of a conscientious and hard-working waiting-room attendant.

## THE UNBALANCED SUBURB

Not only is the life of a suburban community out of balance during the day; there are respects in which it is likely to be out of balance all the time. Take, for instance, the make-up of its population. The standard, traditional pattern has been for young couples to move to Suburbia after marriage—most likely when their first child approaches the active age and they are confronted with the problems of play-space and schooling. When the children are grown, the parents in some cases return to the city. If they do not, their unmarried daughters seem more likely to remain with them than do their sons. Perhaps, too, widows and divorcees are more likely to remain than their male equivalents. Anyhow, the result is likely to be a shortage of young and middle-aged males in Suburbia.

This, of course, is by no means a uniform phenomenon. A careful study of the 1950 population figures for the areas where the Census Bureau has broken these down by age groups, shows no heavy preponderance of young women in some towns which had a considerable semi-independent life of their own before thay attracted commuters in quantity. Most of the Boston suburbs belong in this class. In the Walpole, Massachusetts, census tract, for example, women in the 20-to-45-year bracket outnumber men in the same age group only slightly—1,768 women to 1,588 men: for the Lincoln, Massachusetts, census tract the figures are 476 women to 380 men; in Cohasset, there are 683 women to 603 men; and in Weston the numbers are almost even—921 women to 885 men. But in some of the long-established suburbs outside other cities the preponderance of young women is striking: in Winnetka and Highland Park outside Chicago, for instance, and in Shaker Heights outside Cleveland. In the four census tracts in Shaker Heights, for example, women between 20 and 45 outnumber men by 2,250 to 1,567.

But it is in some of the New York suburbs—prosperous communities which have been almost completely suburban in character for a generation or more—that the disparity in numbers between the young people of the two sexes tends to be most acute. In Bronxville, for instance, according to the 1950 figures, women between 20 and 45 outnumbered men in the same age group almost three to two; in Scarsdale and Bedford, more than three to two; and there was actually one census tract in Scarsdale—lying between the Bronx River and the White Plains Post Road—in which, between the ages of 20 and 45, there were 842 women and only 453 men! Polygamy not being in good repute there, the situation of the surplus women might seem a little unfavorable.

(Where, you may ask, are the men? Well, some are at college or doing graduate work; for the first time, the census of 1950 listed such people at their places of study rather than at their home addresses. Some are in the armed forces. Some are at work in far places, or in industrial areas; some simply prefer the independence of the city, though not in sufficient numbers to prevent women from outnumbering men in every one of the five boroughs of New

## The Big Change in Suburbia

York. In any case, the shortage of unmarried men in many a suburb produces a curious imbalance in its social life.)

And in at least one other respect Suburbia tends to be out of balance: it tends to bring together in large communities people of similar economic status, if not of similar occupation. Many things conspire to bring about this result: the mass-production principle in housing, which invites real-estate developers to make money by building a lot of similar houses which appeal to people in the same income bracket; and also zoning regulations; and also, of course, the natural preference of most commuters, who feel more comfortable when surrounded by people of more or less similar status. We all enjoy, naturally, having the bulk of our intimate, day-to-day contacts with those who look at things with eyes like our own; but the tendency, today, to group together large numbers of people of the same economic status in housing projects, housing developments, and suburban areas may tend to insulate them from the problems and preferences of those in other sections of the population, and thus hinder that approach to the classless civilization which is such a source of American strength.

Another special characteristic of Suburbia is that the suburban region inevitably is always changing. Now of course change is everywhere in American life—in the city and in the countryside as well as in the suburb. But it is especially disturbing in Suburbia because in most cases the commuter chose his place of residence with a hopeful eye to peace, space, and stability, and all these values are threatened by the changes about him; and also, of course, because the transformation of Suburbia is so particularly rapid. Men and women who bought houses with delightful prospects over hill and dale find the prospects cut off by new housing developments; the grove of trees beyond the garden becomes Woodmere Acres or Colonial Estates. Men and women who wanted to live in a settled community find neighbors moving away and new ones coming in. Parents who join the Parent-Teacher Association and go diligently to school meetings, and who think before long that they are acquainted with the leading dramatis personae of the village disputes, discover, the next year, that a new group of people they've never heard of have organized a new attack upon the school problems. And the change is continuous and relentless. The more families flee the city for the deep tangled wildwood, the less deep, tangled, and wild does the wood become.

No wonder the suburbanite embraces zoning regulations with all his heart. They represent, it is true, a kind of governmental interference with private enterprise which in another context he might regard with black disfavor; but in fact they appeal to the most conservative instincts in his nature, as protectors of the status quo. And it is fortunate that they do appeal to him; for zoning is one of the few effective instruments available to impose some sort of orderly restraint upon the otherwise disorderly growth of Suburbia.

Yet even zoning regulations cannot stop the influx of newcomers, though they can divert and channel it; and in one way or another the process of change continues, placing new and unexpected difficulties in the way of the family which moved out in the hope of being able to combine the opportunities of the city with the peace of the country.

FIVE CHAPTERS OF CHANGE

The headlong changes of today have had their antecedents. I think we might divide the story of Suburbia to date into five chapters—overlapping chapters, as we shall see.

The first chapter, or period, began late in the nineteenth century, when the number of year-round commuters first became considerable. Up to that time, many well-to-do people had had country places outside the city to which they repaired for at least part of the year, and of course some of them had had large estates on the outskirts; but it was not until the latter years of the century, generally speaking, that numerous people who had lived part of the year at, let us say, Milton outside Boston, or on the Main Line outside Philadelphia, or at Lake Forest, or at Webster Groves, began to remain in such places for the winter; that, contrariwise, the sons and daughters of the outlying villages began in large numbers to take city jobs to which they traveled daily; and that the regular commuters, who chose to live "forty-five minutes from Broadway," invaded these outlying villages in such numbers as to give them a truly suburban quality. (The date was later for the younger cities than for the older ones, and in the case of both Los Angeles and Detroit the pattern—especially the subsequent pattern—was distorted: in Los Angeles several suburbs came to rival the city nucleus in importance, and in Detroit the outlying

## The Big Change in Suburbia

industrial areas likewise became the tail that wagged the dog.)

The first period we might call the horse-and-buggy era of Suburbia, for the commuters were pretty well confined to the narrow belts of land within walking distance of railroad stations and trolley lines, except for those fortunate few who could afford a coachman to harness the horse and drive them to the station, and, after the turn of the century, the growing number of those who could swing the cost of that unreliable luxury, the automobile.

The second chapter brought a striking change. It began at about the close of World War I—say about 1919 or 1920—and covered roughly the 1920s—the era of the automobile revolution, during which the number of cars registered in the United States, which had been less than 2½ million in 1915 and had increased to 9 million by 1920, took a leap all the way to 26½ million in 1930. When the automobile became something that almost anybody might own, and the open car gave way to the closed one which you could leave at the station in any weather, and there was a terrific spate of road-building and road-improving, all at once large areas of previously inaccessible land were opened up for suburban living. The subdivider appeared in force; farmer Jones's pasture was crisscrossed with paved streets to become Lakehurst Gardens; the short platform at the railroad station was lengthened, and lengthened yet again, to make room for the growing army of candidates for the 8:10 train; and community after community began the long stern chase to keep up with the parking problem. Many a town which had previously regarded itself as partly independent of the city suddenly found its original inhabitants outnumbered by the "city people," who—to the rage of these original inhabitants in some cases—captured control of the school system and imposed new-fangled zoning regulations upon the community. Suburbia was growing at a headlong pace.

When the new commuters of the 1920s built houses, they tended to be romantic about it, and what their architects and builders produced for them was, by and large, eclectic: an English-type half-timbered house would rise alongside a Spanish villa with an American federal-type mansion or a Dutch colonial one cheek by jowl. Could the owners of those houses have better expressed their wish to get away, by night, from the ugliness of the commercial world that supported them by day, and to recapture gracious ways of living that they associated with English country houses, or

European estates, or the mansions of an earlier, supposedly unspoiled America—with, of course, up-to-date plumbing?

In the minds of some of the commuters the suburban dream included something else, too; they wanted to be able to put their roots down. When a man built an ample English country house in an American suburb and carved the date 1922 over the front door, wasn't it part of his dream that he was founding an estate that would go down from generation to generation, without very much change in the surroundings? Yet already the automobile age was beginning to frustrate that dream, for every new subdivions that was opened up was destined to change those surroundings beyond repair.

After the panic of 1929 the process of change slowed down, and presently, as the Great Depression deepened, it came almost to a halt as we entered the third of our five periods, the fifteen-year period of Depression and World War II, which we might call the era of fringe development and of filling in the chinks. During the early 1930s the economic paralysis of the nation brought new building nearly to a standstill. During the latter 1930s there was considerable construction of modest houses and of suburban apartment houses (where these were permitted by zoning regulations); the more outlying parts of the cities themselves tended to spread until the gaps were almost closed; and there was continuing activity along those interurban highways which Lewis Mumford and Benton Mackaye once called "Roadtown," with their filling stations, used-car lots, hamburger stands, bar-and-grill joints, neon lights, and ramshackle dwellings. The government meanwhile poured money into the construction of majestic parkways, bridges, tunnels, trunk highways, and cloverleaf intersections. Then again the process of change was slowed by the wartime shortages of the early 1940s, except where the government built clusters of war workers' housing. The net result was that between 1930 and 1945 the change in Suburbia was less than sensational, and the growth of the suburban population just about kept pace with the growth of the population at large.

But since World War II the change has been swift. We have entered the fourth and fifth chapters of the history of Suburbia. These are overlapping chapters in point of time, but they represent two such strikingly different kinds of change that I should like to discuss them separately. Chapter IV is the postwar boom in

# The Big Change in Suburbia

housing for GI veterans and other young families, which may have passed its peak though it is still continuing; Chapter V is the discovery of the suburbs by business, which began a long time ago but is now apparently just going into high gear.

## THE MASS-PRODUCED SUBURBS

The postwar boom in GI housing has been a nationwide phenomenon, comprising developments both large and small; but to see it on the grand scale you should visit one of the new mass-produced suburbs such as Park Forest outside Chicago, or Lakewood outside Los Angeles, or Levittown, Long Island. These have been observed and described with such faithful care by W. H. Whyte, Jr., writing in *Fortune*, and by Harry Henderson, writing in *Harper's*, that I shall not attempt here a long account of them. Suffice it to say that they are wholly astonishing places. Finding a large, almost unoccupied piece of land within striking distance of a city, the developer has built on it a whole town of very similar houses, applying the economies of mass production to the fierce demand for housing which was caused by the halt in building during the war and by the rising marriage rate and birthrate of the 1940s. These suburbs were built for the young people of an intensely domestic generation, who want to have babies, and take their parental duties seriously; who cannot afford servants and would not know what to do with them if they had them; who enjoy sharing the work in and about the house; who fully subscribe to the do-it-yourself credo of a generation of household tinkerers; and who subscribe equally fully to the current cult of informality, getting into slacks or shorts as soon as they reach the suburb and continuing to wear them until they leave for town.

These new towns have been laid out with a more thoughtful eye to the realities of the automobile age than most of their predecessors. Levittown, for instance, has wide boulevards for through traffic, well separated from the houses, which stand along narrower, curving roads; the houses themselves are not severely crowded, having ample front grass-plots and room in the rear for gardens; and there is a commendable variety in exterior design and especially in texture and color, so as to mitigate the endless monotony of thousands upon thousands of basically similar houses on flat land.

The standard form of architecture in such developments is ranch-type, of which the latest variant is "split-level"; they tend to be one-story or story-and-a-half houses, with agreeably long roof lines. One that I went through in an outlying part of New Rochelle, New York, was selling for $25,750, a rather high price for such communities; it had, typically, a picture window for the living room, a dining area off the living room, a kitchen waiting for the latest mechanical equipment, and, up a few steps (above the garage), three bedrooms and two baths. The garage was built for two cars, not one. The walls were shingled, and prospective purchasers were informed that they might have "optional brick front on living-room panel."

To a visitor from another area, or from an earlier decade, such houses would seem very small but pleasantly simple and unpretentions, and extraordinarily mechanized: I noted that by paying some $1,250 extra one could get the house I looked at fully air-conditioned. Physically, they represent a characteristically American response to an era of high building costs and abundant machinery; spiritually, they represent an abandonment of the dream of old-world charm that flourished in the twenties, and of the dream of old-fashioned American cottage living that accompanied it and then tended to supersede it in the thirties.

Today's dream looks westward to California, and—even on Long Island—envisions a happy family in Technicolor slacks and Hawaiian shirts having a barbecue feast on the terrace, all smiling as in the latest ads.

These are very gregarious communities, in which people wander in and out of one another's houses without invitation, and organize themselves into everything from car pools to PTAs and hobby clubs of numerous sorts; and in which the churches are much more important institutions than anyone who was brought up in the twenties or thirties would have imagined they would be. Such gregarious communities are paradises for the well-adjusted; by the same token, they are less inviting to residents who prefer a modicum of seclusion and resist being expected to live up to—or down to—the Joneses. And they are not only built for people who, for the time being at least, are on one economic level—according to Mr. Henderson, the incomes range mostly from $4,000 to $7,000 a year—but are occupied by people who, again for the time being, nearly all belong to the same age group.

## The Big Change in Suburbia

The passage of years will undoubtedly modify somewhat this latter peculiarity; but at present these new suburbs tend to combine that segregation by income level, which I have already referred to as a somewhat dubious suburban tendency, with a segregation by age group, which has become at least a temporary feature of much recent mass housing. A firm believer in diversity, who would like to see more, not less, mixing together on easy terms of people of different economic fortunes, different age groups, and different occupations and preoccupations, cannot help wondering if these larger new suburbs can escape being natural breeding grounds for conformity.

### BUSINESS DISCOVERS THE SUBURBS

Simultaneously with the postwar boom in housing we have been witnessing another phenomenon which I call Chapter V of the story of Suburbia—the discovery of the suburbs by business.

Always, of course, suburbanites have been served by local markets, local grocery and supply stores, and other local enterprises for their day-to-day needs; but in earlier days they went to the city for their major purchases. In the 1930s, however, some of the major department stores and luxury stores began to establish suburban branches to snare out-of-town shoppers in at least the neighborhoods of their own lairs. The movement became successful, was interrupted by World War II, and then was resumed at an even faster pace, especially in the New York area; so that as long ago as the end of 1951, when the Regional Plan Association compiled a list of suburban branch stores in the environs of New York, it was able to count as many as eighty—thirty of them in Westchester and Fairfield counties, twenty-one in northern New Jersey, and twenty-nine on Long Island. And presently the movement took on a new and portentous shape with the advent of regional shopping centers.

The idea of the regional shopping center has a complex ancestry. It owes much, for instance, to the experience of Sears Roebuck and Montgomery Ward with their outside-the-center-of-town retail stores, built in the 1930s, and to the success of small shopping centers in southern California, which had demonstrated that plenty of room to park was more of a magnet for shoppers than proximity to the glitter—and congestion—of crowded urban centers. These successes led to the location of Bullock's department store at the edge of Pasadena, and to the building of the Crenshaw shopping center and others in the Los Angeles area. But as embodied at Shoppers' World near Framingham, outside Boston, and at Northgate outside Seattle, the regional shopping center is really something quite new: a group of stores, usually including one or more big department stores, situated all by themselves, remote from any city center—even sometimes in otherwise open country—but provided with convenient access from highways, very ample and convenient parking space, and facilities for rest and festivity. (Victor Gruen, one of the leading architects of regional shopping centers, has even suggested that they might include "greenhouses, play areas, band shells, outdoor theaters, outdoor fashion shows, miniature zoos, outdoor shows of painting and sculpture, flower shows, picnic grounds.")

By now the idea has become so epidemic that it would be wearisome to list all the regional shopping centers which are under construction or in contemplation outside one or another of our major cities. Suffice it to mention the biggest one in immediate prospect, which may have opened before these words see print: Northland, outside Detroit. Its principal feature is a department store operated by the J. L. Hudson Company, but according to the plans it will include also some seventy other stores, will cover in all over four hundred fifty acres, and will be able to park seven thousand cars!

Here, surely, is a revolutionary step toward that urban decentralization" which the regional plan experts have been hopefully talking about for a generation. And now still another step, of another sort, is being taken, however uncertainly. Branch stores and shopping centers represent service to the consumer who is supposed to be already there; but the movement of business headquarters to the suburbs is something else again. And this, too, is under way, especially in Westchester County outside New York, where the county association has reported that sixty-nine corporations, employing more than twenty thousand persons, are establishing new buildings in the area.

Here again there are precedents for what is happening. There have always been major businesses which did not think it necessary to have their focus of operations in a big city. Nevertheless it is news when such a big national outfit as the General Foods

## The Big Change in Suburbia

Corporation decides to move its headquarters—with twelve hundred people—from New York to White Plains, some twenty-three miles to the north; when the American Telephone Company decides that its long-distance lines shall be managed from White Plains; when Union Carbide & Carbon at least acquires land for a move, although the move is now stalled; when General Electric buys a tract of territory north of White Plains; and when a long list of other concerns of varying sizes are either planning to settle in Westchester or are flirting with the idea.

Drive east from White Plains toward Port Chester along Westchester Avenue and you can see the portents of the change. On your right, on a hillside, stands the severe brick triple building which will house General Foods. Across the way, in the woods of the former Whitelaw Reid estate, the trucks roll in with materials for the rising headquarters of Allstate Insurance; and deeper in those woods we are told that we may find, later, the central offices of Standard Vacuum Oil Company.

How far will this new movement go? That is anybody's guess. Clearly a move to a suburban location would be folly for a business whose chief officials need to be in frequent contact with bankers, lawyers, advertising agencies, news sources, buyers, or other visitors to the metropolitan crossroads. (Clearly, too, the movement is so young that some of the problems which will emerge cannot now be envisioned: some of the social problems for the personnel, for instance, such as the marriage prospects for young women employees in regions where there may be shortages of eligible men.) But there are types of concerns which do not need to live at the crossroads—such as experimental laboratories, which may need to receive only occasional contracts, or insurance companies, which build their businesses largely through agents. For such concerns the potential advantages are clear; clean air, light, quiet, and agreeable places to live within easy motoring distance. And in the thinking of some executives, comparative safety from atomic bombing is an undeniable element. Guess as you will about the future of this trend; I would venture to say only that I think it is more likely to continue than to come to an early end.

Well, there you have the five chapters of the story of Suburbia: first, the horse-and-buggy era of settlements along the railroads and trolley lines; second, the opening of new areas, by the automobile revolution of the 1920s; third, the era of fringe development and filling in the chinks during the thirties and early forties; fourth, the postwar era of mass-produced housing for young couples; and fifth, the discovery of the suburbs for business, for branch stores, for regional shopping centers, and for business headquarters.

These latter changes, since 1945, are bringing about, at full gallop, a transformation which seems bound to alter profoundly the living conditions of those who now inhabit the suburbs, and even to affect strikingly all the rest of us wherever we may live.

# The Suburban Boom

BEN J. WATTENBERG
with RICHARD M. SCAMMON

A suburb, as everyone knows from popular fiction, is a place where all houses are alike except for those which are very different ("starkly modern"); where all the husbands travel to the big city in the early morning and return late at night, scarcely seeing their children at all from Monday to Friday, and only through a martini haze on Saturday and Sunday; where crabgrass is king; where elementary-school children change twenty-dollar bills at the school lunch counter; where mothers are chauffeurs and body servants, not mothers at all; and where local government is chaotic, inefficient, corrupt, and generally haphazard.

So at least we were led to believe after the big suburban sprawl following World War II, and much of the half-truth has tenaciously hung on.

What is interesting to note is that so many of our social stories in recent years have centered on the suburb. Our guess is that this has not happened accidentally or coincidentally; rather, story locale seems to conform directly to national movement—in this case the surge of the American population to a place loosely described as the suburb. Consequently, we note that "farmer's daughter" stories and "city slicker" tales have lost popular favor in direct proportion to the ongoing exodus from farms and cities. Today we hear yarns about suburban wife-swapping.

---

*From* This U.S.A. *by Ben J. Wattenberg in collaboration with Richard M. Scammon, copyright © 1965 by Ben J. Wattenberg. Reprinted by permission of Doubleday & Company, Inc., and the author.*

We have seen so far in this chapter that Americans are leaving farms and rural regions, and that the central city population is declining. Yet we know that the American population grew by 18.5 percent over the decade. The immediate question then, is a simple one: Where are we going? And the answer, equally simple, is this: to the suburbs, of course.

Once more, terms must be defined, for location terminology is among the most complex in the entire census operation.

It takes delicate statistical maneuvering to isolate and measure what we call "suburban"—and, in truth, the final statistical result is still a long way from total accuracy. However, as in many statistical situations, the measure is still meaningful because its inaccuracy remains constant from year to year. In other words, if we are wrong by the same amount and percentage each time we count, the wrongness (unless flagrant) tends to cancel out and the resultant information is important. So it is with our measurement of the suburb as presented here; it is not fully accurate, but it is highly relevant.

The statistical problem is this: suburban residents are a part of a wider category known as "urban." How then do we distinguish between all urban peoples—i.e., those living in cities, towns, or villages of more than 2500 population—and those living in what we choose to call the suburbs?

The first task is to list the general characteristics of suburbanites:

1. They do not live in rural dwellings.
2. They do, therefore, live in cities or towns ("urban").

Further,

3. They do not live in large central cities (of, say, over 50,000 population).

Finally,

4. They do live *near* large central cities of over 50,000.

We must, then, measure the number of people who live in the smallish city or town near or adjoining the big city, but not including dwellers of smallish cities or towns not close to big ones.

One way in which this sifting is accomplished is through a valuable statistical concept called the Standard Metropolitan Statistical Area, or the SMSA. Briefly, an SMSA is comprised of a central city of more than 50,000 plus the adjacent counties which

## The Suburban Boom

are "socially and economically integrated" with that central city.[1] In other words, an SMSA is an inexact attempt to define an area that encompasses a socio-economic whole; in transcending city lines it includes the city and its environs (e.g., Greater Pittsburgh, Greater St. Louis). The SMSA includes, in short, both urbia and suburbia (and, unfortunately for statistical purposes, at the outer edges of its furthest counties, often some ruralia as well).[2,3]

By using the SMSA we can furnish a rough measure of suburbia in this manner: if a person lives within an SMSA, but outside of that SMSA's central city, he is in the suburbs. He fulfills all our earlier characteristics—he's not likely to be rural, he is likely to be urban, he does not live in the central city, he does live near the central city.

Using the SMSA sifter, we can now note the vast rise in the suburban species:

TABLE 1
PERCENTAGE DISTRIBUTION OF THE POPULATION BY RESIDENCE

|  | Total | Living in SMSAs — In central cities (big-city dwellers) | Living in SMSAs — Outside central cities (suburban) | Outside SMSAs (rural dwellers and urban dwellers living away from big cities) |
|---|---|---|---|---|
| 1960 | 63% | 32% | 31%(!) | 37% |
| 1950 | 56 | 33 | 23 | 44 |
| 1940 | 51 | 32 | 19 | 49 |
| 1930 | 50 | 33 | 18 | 50 |
| 1920 | 44 | 30 | 14 | 56 |
| 1910 | 38 | 26 | 12 | 62 |

A still more sophisticated measuring device is the Census Bureau's one of the Urbanized Area. This can give a more accurate definition to suburbia but has a drawback in that it is a relatively new census tool that goes back only to 1950. The UA, like the

---

1. The basic determinant of whether an outlying county is "integrated" into a central-city SMSA complex is the percentage of county dwellers who work in or around the central city or the percentage of the county's workers who live in the city. Where these criteria are not conclusive, an analysis may be made of newspaper circulation figures, percentage of inter-county phone calls, traffic counts and county charge account sales by retail stores of that central city.

2. The Duluth-Superior SMSA, for example, encompasses the whole "iron range" of Minnesota including a dozen or so small mining towns located fifty or sixty miles north of Duluth. This is not a typical SMSA structure—but neither is it a completely isolated case. As mentioned, the statistical tools involved in measuring suburbia are imperfect.

3. In New England, where the states have generally different county structures, the SMSA lines follow town lines rather than county lines.

SMSA, measures a socio-economic area surrounding and including a large central city. The UA, however, does not follow the arbitrary legal boundaries of the county as does the SMSA; rather, it extends only to the end of the central cities' "urban fringe."[4] By ignoring county lines, the UA avoids counting as urban the rural dwellings on the outskirts of distant counties. Generally, the concept of Urbanized Area is a more accurate one for computing suburban development than is the SMSA. Here is what the pinpoint UA measurement reveals:

TABLE 2

PERCENTAGE OF POPULATION BY RESIDENCE
IN AND OUTSIDE URBANIZED AREAS

|  | 1950 | 1960 |
|---|---|---|
| In UAs | 46% | 54% |
| Central cities | 32 | 32 |
| Urban fringe (suburban) | 14 | 21 |
| Outside UAs | 54 | 47 |

Before going on to analyze these UA and SMSA figures, let us recall two considerations:

1. that the accuracy of these figures lies in the consistency of their inaccuracy. For example, some suburban areas have become large enough to qualify as central cities even though they are essentially suburban by nature. Conversely, there are high-rise apartment house colonies in suburban areas, and their occupants are counted as suburbanites although we might normally view them as city dwellers.

2. that the SMSA and UA figures must not be confused with the "total urban" figures—which are much higher (almost seventy percent in 1960). "Urban" population includes everyone living in towns over 1500; SMSAs and UAs deal only with areas including and surrounding large cities.

Now, with these qualifications out of the way, a look at the dizzying pattern of the figures:

The 1960 Census tells us that we are rapidly becoming a suburban nation. When we take the 1970 Census it is probable that, by the SMSA definition of "suburban," more of our people will

---

4. Which is determined basically by population density as computed from census enumeration districts.

# The Suburban Boom

be living in suburbs than in either central cities or in non-SMSA areas.

We are becoming, then, a society of people who live near, but not in, big cities.

But this trend, as mentioned earlier, is not a new one; Americans have been migrating from downtown central-city areas to suburbs for well over a hundred years, and it is not only an American trend: it has happened in London, Paris, Berlin, Hong Kong, and Bombay.

Despite this historical continuum, the tendency is to observe the present move outward as a new phenomenon. And indeed, there are plenty of new *forms* that suburbia today depends upon:

—The suburban shopping center.
—The new detached "development" private home.
—New super-highways and new roads.
—The automobile and, increasingly, on the two-car family.
—Mass transportation to the central city.
—New political units divorced from central-city politics.

It is easy, then, to postulate that the suburban way of life in the 1960s is an inherently new way of American existence, and indeed, many have said as much. Suburbia, we can gather from both fiction and non-fiction, is an America wrapped in cellophane, or perhaps encased in polyethylene film: its newness has been stamped out on a gargantuan twentieth-century social punch press—a different world. The people in it are new too (they are Organization Men), the houses are of new design ("ranches," "split-levels"), and the moral values, too, we're told, are quite new and split-level ("Teen-Age Boy from Good Family Found with Heroin"). We are asked to believe, in short, that everything is new and different in the new places of residence, the American suburb. But is it?

Consider first those new forms:

—The shopping center was preceded by the "uptown" or "local" department store. It served its in-city neighborhood in much the same way that today's suburban shopping center serves its neighborhood. There are certain differences: rarely did the older type of shopping center have actual branches of the prestige downtown stores, and the older shopping areas were not primarily designed to be reached by automobile. These differences are of importance to the retailer today, but the shopper today has much the same as before: large neighborhood department stores.

—Today's new "development" private home outside the city limits was preceded by the in-city "row houses." These, incidentally, were even more "alike" than today's suburban development houses, which are criticized so severely for their conformity. There is a nice irony in the *chutzpah* of the social critic living in a multistoried cellular apartment house damning suburban homes for being alike and conforming. In New York the same school of criticism goes further; the suburban life is belittled because it consumes so much time each day to commute; then, when a builder puts a large office building right on top of the railroad station (cutting the commutation time), the building is scorned as being unaesthetically set down on top of another.

—It is true that the new suburbia is dependent on the new highways and parkways and, somewhat desperately, on the automobile. It is true that it can wither without the lifeline of mass transit to the central city. But what of the old in-city suburbia? It also grew outward along the spokes of transport facilities: trolley, railroad, bus, and subway; and it was, if anything, even more dependent on mass commuter transit. The automobile, of course, was less conspicuous in old suburbia, but then again, the automobile was less conspicuous everywhere only a few decades ago; it is, after all, a relatively new invention.

—There are new suburban political units today, and these are most typically divorced from any central city government. But history indicates that there were new suburban political units back in the old in-city suburbia and that they too were rather free of downtown control. One such situation is described with vigor and candor in the memoirs of New York's "Boss" Ed Flynn (*You're the Boss*, Viking, 1947). Flynn vividly recalls the political formation of the Bronx some years after the turn of the century. Although the borough was then already incorporated into New York City, its politics were a small-town affair. The "towns" involved at that time were Mott Haven, Melrose, Fordham, Tremont (all now only names on a subway map). The in-city suburb of the Bronx had its own strong political machine. It warred mightily with downtown Tammany rule and had, perhaps, as little to do with

## The Suburban Boom

New York City politics as does the politics of Westchester County today.

We had mentioned before that the move *from* the downtown central city is nothing new. Now we can go a half-step further: if the suburban destination of the central-city migrant is perhaps somewhat new and farther away, it is certainly not brand-new, for suburbs have been with us for a long time. If its forms are different, its people are not—for they still come from the central city for the same reasons as before: a little more open space, a smaller community, fresh air.

What about the pejorative aspects of suburbia? Organization Men do live in the suburbs. So do many other Americans. Organization Man also lives in the city apartment, the small company town, or, when he is especially rewarded, in what has been called the exurb. Organization-mindedness is a condition of the mind, not of real estate.

The new suburban houses are indeed ranch houses and split-levels. Some of them are dreary, but many are exceptionally comfortable. Suburbanites have no monopoly on either drab uniformity or creature comforts. And it is emphatically *not* true that Teen-Age Boys from Good Suburbs Take Heroin—at least not any more of them than the minority of teen-agers of good families who get into trouble anywhere. All these problems and many more are found today in suburbia only because that's where so many Americans live, not because of a flaw in the structure of suburbia. Those famous "coddled kids" are there because that is where middle-class American families now live. The suburban scandals we read about occur with frequency today because it takes people to generate scandal, and the suburbs have more people in them than ever before.

For all this, however, there is at least one new aspect to our suburban life today: the suburbs are increasingly available. The time-honored move from the central city to the suburb has always been a direct function of personal income, for it nearly always costs more money to live on a quarter of an acre in a private home in suburbia than it does to live in a middle-class dwelling in the city. Today, more than ever before, Americans *have* that extra money to make the long-cherished move. This is clearly observable from the historical SMSA chart (Table 1). Note that the rate of suburbanization was far faster from 1950 to 1960 than at any earlier time. It was a perfect decade for the suburbanization process: consumers had more money than ever before and the materials and manpower for home construction were at last available. In actual numbers, there were *seventeen million* new urban-fringe residents added over that decade.

The newest aspect of suburbia, then, is not the direction of the geographical move, for we've been taking that trip away from the city for a long time. The destination, too, has always been the same—a better place to live. The important newness in suburbia today is that so many of us can make the trip. Soon the comfortable suburban life will stand as the *plurality* way of American life—and that is a truly new and impressive fact not only in the story of suburbia but in the whole history of humankind. This is a newness more far-reaching than the difference between a ranch house and a row house. There *is*, in short, a basically "new way of life" in the suburbs, as we have been told; but the newest characteristic is that so many people are able to enjoy the benefits of an old, attractive way of life.

This is not to sell short or bypass or ignore the importance or pitfalls of the new forms: the shopping centers, the automotive society, the roads, some ticky-tacky houses. Nor is it meant to imply that nothing but quantity and forms are new in the suburban way of life—for there are undoubtedly important new social forces at work in suburbia. Rather, the effort here is to see things in an adjusted perspective. American suburbs have been built rather solidly on an earlier and sturdy way of life. The United States did not invent the suburb; it was not created by Turnpike out of PTA and Power Lawnmower. The dominant American contribution to suburban life is a simple one: here and now, for the first time, masses of people are able to enjoy its fruits.

What happens to us statistically with suburbanization? What does the Census reveal about the urban fringe in relation to other areas? In what quantitative ways are suburbanites different from central city dwellers? How do they differ from rural dwellers?

—Suburbanites are richer. Family median income in the urban fringe: $7114; in the city: $5945; on the farm: $3228. More families earn $10,000 or more in the suburbs (24%) than in the city (17%). There are fewer families with incomes under $3000 in the suburb (10%) than in the city (18%).

—There are more families with children in the suburbs. In the fringe: 62%; in the city: 52%; on the farm: 55%.

—Suburbanites stay in school longer. Median number of school years completed for persons over 25: suburbs, 12.0; city, 10.7; farm, 8.8.

—Suburbanites are more likely to be employed. Unemployment rates: fringe, 4.6%; city, 5.5%; farm, 4.8% (in 1960).

—More suburbanites are employed as professionals, managers, and in white-collar work generally. White-collar rates: fringe, 50%; city, 45%.

—Suburbanites are marginally more "native" than city dwellers —but farmers are most likely to be native-born:

|  | Suburbs | City | Farm |
|---|---|---|---|
| Native born of native parentage | 75% | 74% | 90% |
| Native born of foreign parentage | 18% | 17% | 8% |
| Foreign born | 6% | 9% | 2% |

—Suburbanites are more likely to be owners, not renters. 67% of suburban dwelling units are owner-occupied versus 47% of central city units.

—Suburbanites have more bathrooms per dwelling. 21% have "more than one" versus 12% in central cities.

—Suburbanites have more rooms per dwelling: 5.1 to 4.6 in the central city.

—Suburbanites live in newer dwellings: 70% of the city dwellings were built prior to 1940, only 42% of the suburban dwellings are that old.

—Suburban homeowners are younger than city homeowners: 47% in the suburbs are between 25 and 44; in the city only 34% are between 25 and 44.

—Suburbanites are more likely to be from someplace else. In 1960, 21% of the suburban residents had made a move across county lines during the past five years. The corresponding central city percentage was 14%.

—Suburbia has many fewer non-whites. Only 8% of all Negroes live in suburban areas, while 51% live in central cities. (The comparative white figures: 23% in suburbia, 30% in central cities.)

These items on income, housing, occupation, education, nativity, and race conform fairly closely to the general view of contemporary suburbia: a richer place to live, with the trappings of middle-class wealth and semi-exclusivity. On the other hand, there are a number of areas where the popular notion does not conform closely to the facts. For example:

The Notion: Suburbia is America's breeding ground.

The Fact: The suburban fertility rate is only fractionally higher than that of the central city (suburb 1985; city 1956). The highest fertility rate is found on the farm (2377).

The Notion: Suburbanites are always moving. They come from someplace else, soon they'll be going someplace else.

The Fact: Although as noted previously, suburbanites do make inter-county moves somewhat more often, they do not move more often from house to house (suburban rate cumulative for five years from 1955 to 1960: 50% moved, versus city rate of 48%). Furthermore, suburbanites are not much more likely to be from out of state (suburban rate: 33% versus central city rate of 29%). Typically, then, suburban mobility is different only in the original move from the city to the suburb, which is often in the same state, but across county lines.

The Notion: Suburbs are bedroom communities. Their people work in the city.

The Fact: Only about a fifth (22%) of the employed workers who reside in the urban fringe work outside the county of residence. This is an inexact measurement because the urban fringe and the central city are often located in the same county. However, for fringe areas where a cross-county trip is necessary to reach the central city, the numbers seem to stand up. In the urban fringe of New York City, where a cross-county trip is necessary to get into Manhattan, 36% of the employed persons work across county lines. In San Mateo County, immediately adjacent to San Francisco, 46% worked outside the county. There is considerable evidence, then, that suburban towns, by and large, are developing their own jobs rather than merely milking the big city for big pay checks.

One of the interesting things to speculate upon is the *range* of differences between city and suburb. As noted, in many fields this difference is small: unemployment within one percent, nativity within a point or two, house-to-house moving within two points.

In other fields, of course, the differences are greater, but the general impression one receives on examining many figures is one of similarity rather than difference. Statistically, one gets the feeling that the suburb is quite like the city, only more so, and the suburbanite has not become a new person since leaving the city.

A breed apart? Our new breed of American is not new because he lives near rather than in the big city. He is new, rather, because he is a participant in the silent social revolutions discussed earlier and elsewhere. He is a new American because he is better educated than his father was, because he earns more money at a better job. Thise are the factors that allow him to move from the city to the suburban quarter-acre. Suburbia, accordingly, would seem to be one of the effects, not the cause of what might be called the Better America.

# Suburban Persistence

REYNOLDS FARLEY

Rapid suburban growth combined with declines in central city population is often assumed to be a post–World War II pattern of urban growth. Theodore White (1960) noted:

> For just as the census of 1890 announced the passing of the frontier, the census of 1960 announced the passing of the great city. For half a century the great urban centers had dominated American culture and politics. Decade by decade, as if by some irrevocable law of history, the great cities had steadily increased in size at every count.
>
> But in 1960 the crest has passed and they were dwindling.... Two-thirds of the stupendous 28,000,000 (1950 to 1960) growth of the nation had taken place in suburbia. (p. 217)

The recent pattern of suburban growth supposedly has implications for the socio-economic structuring of urban areas. The college-educated white-collar workers, it is thought, have moved to suburbia in large numbers, leaving cities to be populated by non-whites and lower-status whites. Such a process is congruent with the Burgess hypothesis of urban growth. His model suggested that the highest-status residents live on the periphery of the settled area while the central portions contain the newest in-migrants and those whose earning powers condemn them to inexpensive or run-down residences (Park, Burgess, and McKenzie 1925).

---

*Reprinted from the* American Sociological Review *29 (1964), pp. 38–47, by permission of the publisher, the American Sociological Association, and the author; originally published as paper 19 in the series "Comparative Urban Research" by the Population Research and Training Center, University of Chicago.*

Schnore (1963) attempted to rephrase the Burgess hypothesis and to suggest an evolutionary model for city growth:

> With growth and expansion of the center and with radical improvements in transportation and communication technology, the upper strata have shifted from central to peripheral residence, and the lower classes have increasingly taken up occupancy in the central areas abandoned by the elite. (p. 84)

But if this model for city growth is to be validated and if the process of suburbanization is to be understood it will be necessary to describe the dynamics of the growth process. Numerous studies, such as those by McKenzie (1934, pp. 180ff.), Ogburn (1937), Kish (1954), Dornbusch (1952), and Duncan and Reiss (1956, ch. 11), have demonstrated that cities and their suburbs differ in composition at one point in time, yet this cross-sectional approach does not reveal how these differences developed nor does it indicate whether cities and suburbs are becoming more alike or dissimilar in composition.

This paper attempts to analyze change over time in city–suburban status differentials, using census data for 1950 and 1960. Changes in seventeen of the twenty-five largest urbanized areas, all those for which comparisons were feasible, suggest that these cities and the suburban areas are becoming more dissimilar in composition. Generally the suburban areas have shown not only more rapid growth in total numbers but proportionally greater increases in population of higher socio-economic status.

One of the major reasons for increasing city–suburban differentiation is the growth of suburbs. Yet suburbs are not new nor is the flight to suburbia a recent development. As early as the 1760s suburban areas near Boston and Philadelphia were populated and in 1910 one-quarter of the population of the twenty-five metropolitan districts defined by the Census Bureau lived in suburban zones rather than in central cities.[1] These suburban areas have recently experienced rapid growth, but the Burgess model does not suggest what the relation between the characteristics of suburban areas and population growth might be. Have some types of suburbs experienced more rapid growth than others? Does rapid population growth alter the socio-economic characteristics of a

---
1. Bridenbaugh, 1955, pp. 25, 231; Bureau of the Census, *Thirteenth Census of the United States, 1910, Population*, vol. 1, p. 75.

suburb or do suburban places retain their peculiar characteristics even after great population increases?

Two groups of suburbs are analyzed in an attempt to answer questions of this nature. For a group of 137 suburbs of twenty-four central cities it was possible to relate 1920 and 1960 measures of socio-economic composition and growth. Smaller and newer suburbs are included in a description of change for the period 1940 to 1960—the years of postwar suburbanization. Although growth was common to almost all of these suburbs, the suburbs that grew most rapidly were those that had the characteristics of highest social status in 1960. Population growth, however, did not greatly change the composition of many suburbs. A sound prediction of the 1960 socio-economic characteristics of a particular suburb could be made merely by knowing that suburb's characteristics in 1920. When the shorter time span—1940 to 1960—is used there is even greater evidence for persistence of suburban characteristics.

As aggregates, central cities and suburban areas have become increasingly dissimilar in socio-economic composition. This finding suggests that the recent growth of suburbs fits the traditional model of city expansion, since the suburban areas have shown the largest gains in higher-status population. Yet as individual entities, suburbs demonstrate a stability of characteristics relatively little affected by population growth. This suggests that the characteristics of a suburb may be fixed relatively early in that suburb's history and subsequent growth reinforces existing socio-economic residential patterns.

## CENTRAL CITY-SUBURBAN AGGREGATE DIFFERENCES

How have cities and suburban areas changed in population size and composition during the recent decade of rapid suburbanization? To answer this question cities were compared with their suburban areas on the basis of census data for 1950 and 1960 urbanized areas. Boundaries for these areas were not restricted to corporation limits but rather were chosen by means of density and land use criteria.[2] The urbanized area for a city in 1960 may not include exactly the same area as the 1950 urbanized area, since

---

2. U.S. Bureau of the Census, *Census of Population, 1960*, vol. 1, part A, p. xix.

changes in land use or density may have qualified some fringe areas to be included in 1960 which were excluded in 1950. Nevertheless at both dates the urban fringe—that portion of an urbanized area exterior to the city—represents the suburban area since it includes the densely settled land area outside but near a central city.

City-suburban comparisons were made for seventeen of the twenty-five most populous 1960 cities. Eight of the largest cities (Atlanta, Dallas, Houston, Memphis, Milwaukee, San Antonio, San Diego and Seattle) were excluded because, between 1950 and 1960, each city annexed an area containing a large population in 1960, thus complicating any interannual city-suburban comparisons. Although only 17 of the 213 urbanized areas defined in 1960 were used in this analysis, these 17 areas contained fifty-four percent of the total population living in urbanized areas in 1960.[3]

The pattern of population loss in the central city and population increase in the suburban ring appeared in fourteen of the seventeen areas examined. None of the cities grew as rapidly as its suburban area. One of the most striking changes was the central cities' gain of non-white population. In 1950 about fourteen percent of the total population of these cities was non-white but by 1960 the non-white population had increased to twenty-one percent. These suburban areas, however, generally had little non-white population at both dates; about five percent of their aggregate population was non-white in both 1950 and 1960.[4]

In the aggregate the suburban population became more sharply differentiated from central city population in socio-economic status during the 1950s. The proportion of adult males who were high school graduates, for example, increased by 6.2 percentage points in the suburbs but only by 1.6 points in the central cities. The proportion of white-collar workers in the male labor force increased by 3.6 points in the suburbs compared with 0.9 points in central cities.[5]

---

3. Ibid., Table 22.

4. Ibid. and PC(1)-B, Table 13.

5. The percentage of the male population ages 25 and over with a complete high school education increased from 36.5 in 1950 to 38.1 in 1960 in the cities and from 44.0 to 50.2 in the suburbs. The percentage of the civilian male labor force in white-collar occupations increased from 38.0 in 1950 to 38.9 in 1960 in the cities and from 41.4 to 45.0 in the suburbs. U.S. Bureau of the Census, *Census of Population, 1960*, PC(1)-C, Tables 73 and 74.

Because much of the discussion of city-suburban differentiation has been based on the residential patterns of well-educated adults and white-collar workers, city-suburban differences in the distributions of education and occupation are examined in detail for each urbanized area. To determine in a concise manner whether a city and its suburban area became more similar or more dissimilar in composition from 1950 to 1960, indices of occupational dissimilarity were computed using the Census Bureau's nine non-agricultural occupational categories plus the category "unemployed." The numerical value of this index of dissimilarity states the percentage of the labor force in either area that would have to change occupations for the occupational distributions of both areas to be identical (Duncan and Duncan 1955, p. 494).

The index of occupational dissimilarity for a city and its fringe in 1950 may be contrasted to the same index comparing the two areas in 1960. If the index for 1960 has a larger numerical value than the index for 1950, the two areas have become more dissimilar in occupational composition. Educational dissimilarity indices were computed in an analogous manner, using eight educational attainment levels. These indices are presented in Table 1.

TABLE 1
INDICES OF DISSIMILARITY COMPARING CENTRAL CITIES
WITH THE REMAINDER OF THE URBANIZED AREA

| Urbanized Area | Indices of Educational Dissimilarity 1950 | 1960 | Difference | Indices of Occupational Dissimilarity 1950 | 1960 | Difference |
|---|---|---|---|---|---|---|
| Detroit | 7.0 | 14.2 | 7.2 | 7.2 | 14.9 | 7.7 |
| St. Louis | 11.6 | 18.4 | 6.8 | 13.1 | 20.6 | 7.5 |
| Chicago | 9.8 | 16.2 | 6.4 | 11.5 | 17.4 | 5.9 |
| Washington | 17.7 | 23.7 | 6.0 | 21.9 | 28.5 | 6.6 |
| Minneapolis-St. Paul | 8.1 | 14.0 | 5.9 | 9.3 | 13.4 | 4.1 |
| Pittsburgh | 4.6 | 10.2 | 5.6 | 9.0 | 10.5 | 1.5 |
| New Orleans | 5.0 | 9.7 | 4.7 | 9.2 | 12.4 | 3.2 |
| Denver | 8.3 | 12.7 | 4.4 | 11.6 | 9.3 | -2.3 |
| Buffalo | 9.8 | 14.0 | 4.2 | 9.7 | 14.6 | 4.9 |
| Cincinnati | 6.0 | 9.7 | 3.7 | 8.9 | 9.6 | 0.7 |
| Philadelphia | 13.8 | 17.4 | 3.6 | 13.0 | 17.1 | 4.1 |
| New York | 5.3 | 8.2 | 2.9 | 8.4 | 11.2 | 2.8 |
| Boston | 8.8 | 11.5 | 2.7 | 11.8 | 15.3 | 3.5 |
| San Francisco-Oakland | 8.6 | 9.7 | 1.1 | 9.4 | 11.3 | 1.9 |
| Los Angeles | 4.6 | 5.6 | 1.0 | 8.5 | 8.5 | 0.0 |
| Baltimore | 15.7 | 16.5 | 0.8 | 12.5 | 16.4 | 3.9 |
| Cleveland | 25.6 | 26.2 | 0.6 | 27.4 | 27.0 | -0.4 |

Sources: U.S. Bureau of the Census, *Census of Population, 1950*, vol. 2, Tables 34 and 35; U.S. Bureau of the Census, *Census of Population, 1960*, PC(1)-C, Tables 73 and 74.

## Suburban Persistence

A general pattern of increasing dissimilarity clearly appears. Considering educational dissimilarity, the 1960 index for each area exceeded the 1950 index. For many of the urbanized areas the increase was sizable; for instance, the value for the Detroit area doubled. Considering occupational composition, in each urbanized

TABLE 2
COMPARISON OF EDUCATIONAL AND OCCUPATIONAL
COMPOSITION OF CENTRAL CITIES AND THEIR URBAN
FRINGE AREAS, 1950 AND 1960 (MALE POPULATION ONLY)

| Urbanized Area | Year | Percent High School Graduate ||| Percent White-collar Workers* |||
| | | City | Fringe | Difference | City | Fringe | Difference |
|---|---|---|---|---|---|---|---|
| Baltimore | 1950 | 26.6 | 39.7 | 13.1 | 34.4 | 37.8 | 3.4 |
| | 1960 | 27.4 | 42.3 | 14.9 | 34.6 | 42.8 | 8.2 |
| Boston | 1950 | 42.5 | 50.1 | 7.6 | 34.9 | 42.1 | 7.2 |
| | 1960 | 42.8 | 54.3 | 11.5 | 36.4 | 46.9 | 10.5 |
| Buffalo | 1950 | 29.5 | 39.0 | 9.5 | 30.4 | 36.8 | 6.4 |
| | 1960 | 29.9 | 43.6 | 13.7 | 29.3 | 38.5 | 9.2 |
| Chicago | 1950 | 35.8 | 45.5 | 9.7 | 36.1 | 41.4 | 5.3 |
| | 1960 | 35.7 | 53.9 | 18.2 | 34.9 | 45.3 | 10.4 |
| Cincinnati | 1950 | 32.9 | 32.4 | -0.5 | 37.4 | 37.6 | 0.2 |
| | 1960 | 33.6 | 43.3 | 9.7 | 37.9 | 45.1 | 7.2 |
| Cleveland | 1950 | 30.2 | 55.8 | 25.6 | 26.5 | 53.9 | 27.4 |
| | 1960 | 28.9 | 55.1 | 26.2 | 24.5 | 50.2 | 25.7 |
| Denver | 1950 | 50.5 | 48.1 | -2.4 | 47.3 | 30.3 | -17.0 |
| | 1960 | 51.6 | 62.3 | 10.7 | 46.6 | 48.5 | 1.9 |
| Detroit | 1950 | 33.3 | 39.1 | 5.8 | 30.3 | 30.9 | 0.6 |
| | 1960 | 32.8 | 45.9 | 13.1 | 30.5 | 39.1 | 8.6 |
| Los Angeles | 1950 | 50.4 | 51.4 | 1.0 | 42.2 | 40.6 | -1.6 |
| | 1960 | 53.7 | 53.0 | -0.7 | 45.6 | 41.7 | -3.9 |
| Minneapolis– St. Paul | 1950 | 43.7 | 51.7 | 8.0 | 42.6 | 47.5 | 4.9 |
| | 1960 | 46.1 | 60.1 | 14.0 | 42.2 | 50.9 | 8.7 |
| New Orleans | 1950 | 29.9 | 29.2 | -0.7 | 39.0 | 36.8 | -2.2 |
| | 1960 | 33.4 | 44.8 | 11.4 | 39.5 | 42.9 | 3.4 |
| New York | 1950 | 35.7 | 40.1 | 4.4 | 42.4 | 42.1 | -0.3 |
| | 1960 | 37.8 | 45.6 | 7.8 | 43.5 | 46.0 | 2.5 |
| Philadelphia | 1950 | 29.8 | 43.5 | 13.7 | 33.6 | 43.3 | 9.7 |
| | 1960 | 30.7 | 48.1 | 17.4 | 35.0 | 46.1 | 11.1 |
| Pittsburgh | 1950 | 33.0 | 37.6 | 4.6 | 32.8 | 32.0 | -0.8 |
| | 1960 | 34.4 | 53.1 | 18.7 | 33.8 | 37.2 | 3.4 |
| St. Louis | 1950 | 25.9 | 37.5 | 11.6 | 34.4 | 43.4 | 9.0 |
| | 1960 | 26.2 | 44.1 | 17.9 | 31.4 | 46.7 | 15.3 |
| San Francisco– Oakland | 1950 | 45.6 | 54.2 | 8.6 | 39.8 | 42.5 | 2.7 |
| | 1960 | 47.7 | 56.6 | 8.9 | 41.3 | 44.9 | 3.6 |
| Washington | 1950 | 48.3 | 66.0 | 17.7 | 46.2 | 60.5 | 14.3 |
| | 1960 | 45.8 | 67.4 | 21.6 | 45.6 | 63.3 | 17.7 |

* The percent white collar equals the sum of male professional, managerial, clerical and sales workers divided by the total male civilian labor force.
Sources: U.S. Bureau of the Census, *Census of Population, 1960*, PC(1)–C, Tables 73 and 74; U.S. Bureau of the Census, *Census of Population, 1950*, vol. 2, Tables 34 and 35.

area except Cleveland, Denver, and Los Angeles, the city and urban fringe became more dissimilar in occupational composition.

The distributions of educational attainment and occupational composition are summarized by the percentage of the male population aged 25 and over with a high school education and the percentage of the male labor force holding white-collar jobs. Table 2 presents these figures for each city and its fringe.

In both years the suburban areas generally exceeded the cities in percentage of high school graduates. During this decade city-suburban differences increased because the suburban areas showed greater increases in high school-educated population than did central cities. In fact in the central cities of Chicago, Cleveland, Detroit, and Washington the proportion with a high school education declined. A similar pattern of change emerges for occupational composition. In 1950 five of the central cities had a larger percentage of the male labor force in white-collar occupations than their suburban areas. In 1960 only one city—Los Angeles—had a larger percentage of its male labor force in white-collar jobs than its suburban area.

The indices of dissimilarity with respect to socio-economic status (Table 1) and the city-suburban differences in the proportion of well-educated adult males and white-collar workers (Table 2) both point to increasing differentiation between the city and suburban populations in socio-economic status. Inspection of Table 2 suggests that this has come about because suburban areas gained high-status population at a faster rate than central cities. From 1950 to 1960 suburban areas have grown faster than cities and have undergone compositional changes which make these areas increasingly dissimilar to cities.

## SUBURBAN PERSISTENCE, 1920 TO 1960

Suburbs have long surrounded central cities. At the turn of this century Adna Weber wrote: "The movement toward the suburbs, which is stronger in America than elsewhere with the exception of Australia, not only necessitates frequent annexations of territory, but even then baffles the statistician" (Weber 1899, p. 36). Ample research has shown that population decentralization has been occurring at least since 1920, that there are blue-collar as well as white-collar, industrial as well as dormitory and heterogeneous as well as homogeneous suburbs. And yet the relations between suburban growth and compositional change have not been explored. The following analysis attempts to elucidate the role of growth in the process of suburbanization.

Measures of a suburb's socio-economic status may be compared at different points in time to analyze changes in the composition of individual suburbs. The Census of 1920 tabulated school enrollment for sixteen- and seventeen-year-olds in cities of population 10,000 or more. In suburbs such as Cleveland Heights, Ohio, and Newton, Massachusetts, typical exclusive residential areas, large percentages of the teen-age population were enrolled in school, while in industrial suburbs such as Hoboken and Hamtramck low percentages were enrolled. The percentage of sixteen- and seventeen-year-olds attending school in 1920 may be considered a measure of a suburb's socio-economic status, and for 1960 the percentage of the population twenty-five years of age or older with a high school diploma may be regarded as a roughly comparable measure.

A comparison of these status measures for 1920 and 1960 was possible for 137 suburbs of twenty-four central cities. To be included a suburb had to be within a 1920 metropolitan district, be within a 1960 urbanized area, and have retained its corporate identity for this period.

Table 3 presents the regression of the 1960 measure on the 1920 measure. A high degree of persistence in relative position is apparent, the zero order correlation coefficient being .81. Suburbs high or low on the measure for 1920 tended to retain the same position in 1960. This forty-year persistence of socio-economic characteristics contrasts surprisingly with the apparent fact of rapid change in suburbia.

Population growth is one of the distinctive features of suburban areas. Although the 137 suburbs examined are relatively old—the minimum population was 10,000 in 1920—they did experience rapid growth between 1920 and 1960. Their total population increased from 4.2 million in 1920 to 6.8 million in 1960, an increase of sixty-three percent, which is almost as large as the nation's increase of sixty-eight percent for this period.[6] To analyze the relation between growth and the status measures for 1920

---

6. U.S. Bureau of the Census, *Fourteenth Census of the United States, 1920, Population*, vol. 3, Table 10; U.S. Bureau of the Census, *Census of Population, 1960*, vol. 1, part A, Table 3 and PC(1)-A, Table 5.

## TABLE 3
### SUMMARY OF REGRESSION ANALYSIS
### FOR 137 SUBURBS OF 24 CENTRAL CITIES

*Variables:*

Education, 1960—Percent of a suburb's 25 and over population with a high school education in 1960. (Mean = 41.46, Standard Deviation = 12.94)

Education, 1920—Percent of the 16- and 17-year-old population of a suburb enrolled in school in 1920. (Mean = 38.24, Standard Deviation = 15.42)

Growth—One minus the proportion of a suburb's 1960 population accounted for by its 1920 population. (Mean = 28.58, Standard Deviation = 37.41)

| *Zero order regressions:* | Education, 1960 on Education, 1920 | Education, 1960 on Growth |
|---|---|---|
| Slope | .682±.053 | .174±.071 |
| Intercept | 15.18 | 36.50 |
| Correlation coefficient | .812 | .501 |

| *Multiple regression:* | |
|---|---|
| Intercept | 16.08 |
| Partial regression coefficients: | |
|   Free variable: Education, 1920 | .610±.022 |
|   Free variable: Growth | .072±.018 |
| Partial correlation coefficients: | |
|   Free variable: Education, 1920 | .779 |
|   Free variable: Growth | .355 |
| Multiple correlation coefficient | .839 |

| *Percentage of variance explained:* | |
|---|---|
| Explained by zero order regression of Education, 1920 on Education, 1960 | 65.9 |
| Additional with growth | 4.4* |
| Unexplained | 29.7 |
| Total | 100.0 |

\* Significant by F test at .01 level.

Sources: U.S. Bureau of the Census, *Fourteenth Census of the United States, 1920, Population*, vol. 3, Table 10; U.S. Bureau of the Census, *Census of Population, 1960*, PC(1)–C, Tables 32 and 81.

and 1960 multiple regression was used and the results are presented in Table 3.

The measure of growth used in this analysis is somewhat unusual. The measure is equivalent to 1.00 minus the proportion of the suburb's 1960 population accounted for by its 1920 population. Thus a suburb whose population tripled during the forty-year period is scored .67 on this measure, that is, 1.00 minus .33. A place losing population during the interim receives a score of less than zero. These growth scores for the 137 suburbs are distributed more or less normally and are, therefore, more appropriate for regression analysis than the conventional measure, percentage change in population.

The association of growth and socio-economic level over the forty-year span was explored with two questions as guides. First, did growth occur indiscriminately throughout the suburban area or was it related to the characteristics of the suburbs? Second, did rapid growth produce substantial compositional change and lessen persistence of socio-economic characteristics?

To answer the first question we note the positive association of socio-economic level in 1960 and growth during the years 1920 to 1960 ($r=.50$). This indicates that growth did not occur indiscriminately among suburbs but that suburbs with high growth rates were those with high-status characteristics in 1960. This relationship is consistent with the notion that the more exclusive suburbs have absorbed the spill-over of higher status residents from the central city as well as attracted higher-status immigrants to the area.

Second, a comparison of the zero order correlation coefficients indicates that initial (1920) educational level is a far more powerful predictor of current (1960) educational level than is growth during the intervening years. The educational characteristics of these suburbs have generally persisted from 1920 to 1960. A comparison based on the partial correlation coefficients leads to the same conclusion. Persistence of educational level, irrespective of differential growth, is a powerful factor accounting for current educational level, while differential growth, irrespective of initial educational level, is a much weaker explanatory factor.

The partial regression coefficient relating 1960 educational level to growth during the years 1920 to 1960 is significantly different from zero. When variance among suburbs in current educational level is partitioned, as in Table 3, it can be seen that the use of a growth variable adds a small but significant increase to the variance explained by initial educational level alone. A high initial educational level coupled with rapid growth represents the combination most favorable to a high current educational level, though the influence population growth exerts is relatively small, as illustrated by a hypothetical comparison of two suburbs. Consider two suburbs, each having one-half of the sixteen- and seventeen-year-old population enrolled in school in 1920. Assume that the population of one suburb triples from 1920 to 1960 while that of the other suburb remains constant. Using the regression equations described in Table 3, we would predict that in the rapidly growing suburb the percentage of high school graduates in 1960 would be 51.4, while in the suburb that experienced no growth it would be 46.6

## SUBURBAN PERSISTENCE, 1940 TO 1960

Suburbs described in the analysis of change from 1920 to 1960 had populations exceeding 10,000 in 1920 and might be expected to undergo less change than suburbs that started with smaller populations and grew more rapidly. Little socio-economic information for cities of under 10,000 population in 1920 was given by the Census. As an alternative, suburban persistence and growth will be described for the period 1940 to 1960 for suburbs of Boston, Chicago, and Cleveland. Since a shorter time span is involved, greater persistence might be expected, but the rapid postwar suburban growth may have introduced new patterns of compositional change.

All suburbs of Chicago and Cleveland within the 1940 metropolitan district and within the 1960 Standard Metropolitan Statistical Area, which had populations in 1940 exceeding 2500, and which retained their identity for this period were included. Towns within the 1940 Boston metropolitan district and 1960 Standard Metropolitan Statistical Area for which 1940 and 1960 figures were tabulated were also used.

Percentage of the population aged 25 and over with a high school education was used as a socio-economic measure at both dates. The growth measure described above was also employed in this analysis. Mean values for these measures are:

TABLE 4
MEAN VALUES: SUBURBS OF BOSTON, CLEVELAND, AND CHICAGO

|  | Boston | Chicago | Cleveland |
|---|---|---|---|
| Number of suburbs | 50 | 61 | 25 |
| 1940 % H.S. graduate | 40.0 | 33.6 | 39.1 |
| 1960 % H.S. graduate | 57.6 | 53.1 | 55.6 |
| Mean 1940 population | 29,100 | 15,700 | 13,200 |
| Mean 1960 population | 36,000 | 27,100 | 26,100 |
| Mean growth measure | 26.8 | 45.5 | 51.0 |

Table 5 presents the results of the regression exercise for the three sets of suburbs.

## TABLE 5
### SUMMARY OF REGRESSION ANALYSIS FOR SUBURBS OF BOSTON, CLEVELAND, AND CHICAGO

*Variables:*

Education, 1940—Percent of a suburb's 25 and over population with a high school education in 1940.

Education, 1960—Percent of a suburb's 25 and over population with a high school education in 1960.

Growth—One minus proportion of a suburb's 1960 population accounted for by its 1940 population.

| *Zero order regressions:* | Intercept | Slope | Correlation Coefficient |
|---|---|---|---|
| Boston: | | | |
| Education, 1960 on Education, 1940 | 12.15 | .886±.105 | .888 |
| Education, 1960 on Growth | 41.44 | .352±.176 | .602 |
| Chicago: | | | |
| Education, 1960 on Education, 1940 | 22.55 | .909±.094 | .917 |
| Education, 1960 on Growth | 49.56 | .078±.145 | .127 |
| Cleveland: | | | |
| Education, 1960 on Education, 1940 | 26.92 | .733±.165 | .858 |
| Education, 1960 on Growth | 39.06 | .131±.242 | .324 |

| | Boston | Chicago | Cleveland |
|---|---|---|---|
| *Multiple regressions:* | | | |
| Intercept | 16.87 | 15.75 | 27.21 |
| Partial regression coefficients: | | | |
| Free variable: Education, 1940 | .782±.016 | .930±.033 | .751±.035 |
| Free variable: Growth | .231±.008 | .134±.021 | .151±.025 |
| Partial correlation coefficients | | | |
| Free variable: Education, 1940 | .944 | .941 | .926 |
| Free variable: Growth | .821 | .548 | .728 |
| Multiple regression coefficient | .964 | .942 | .936 |
| *Percentage of variance explained:* | | | |
| Explained by zero order regression of Education, 1960 on Education, 1940 | 78.8 | 84.0 | 73.5 |
| Additional with growth | 14.4* | 4.7* | 14.1* |
| Unexplained | 6.8 | 11.3 | 12.4 |
| Total | 100.0 | 100.0 | 100.0 |

* Significant by F test at .01 level.

Sources: U.S. Bureau of the Census, *Sixteenth Census of the United States, Population*, vol. 2, Tables 30 and 31; U.S. Bureau of the Census, *Census of Population, 1960*, PC(1)-C, Tables 32 and 81.

Turning again to the questions posed earlier about the relations of initial and current socio-economic level and growth, we note first the association of growth and high current socio-economic level. Although these correlation coefficients are not extremely high, they indicate that the suburbs that had grown most rapidly were those with higher-status characteristics in 1960. Second, the results indicate that initial socio-economic level is a far more powerful predictor of current socio-economic level than growth in Chicago and Cleveland and a somewhat more powerful predictor in Boston. These results are consistent with those obtained from the analysis of 1920 to 1960 change.

When the partial correlation coefficients are examined, however, it becomes clear that growth is relatively more important in respect to initial level when smaller suburbs are included and when the time span is shortened. Together initial level and growth account for about ninety percent of the variance in current educational level among the suburbs of these three cities, and in each case, the growth factor contributes a significant increment to the explained variance. Such a growth pattern indicates that in the last twenty years, population growth has upgraded the relative socio-economic position of a suburb.

This can be illustrated by a comparison of suburbs assumed to have similar percentages of high school graduates in 1940 but different growth rates. Assume that two Cleveland suburbs both had forty percent of the adult population high school graduates in 1940 but that the population of one suburb doubled while that of the other neither increased nor declined. The regression model predicts that sixty-five percent would be high school graduates in 1960 in the growing suburb and fifty-seven percent in the other suburb. This is consistent with the notion that the higher-status members of the community have increasingly chosen suburban residences in the more exclusive suburbs. But the persistence of suburban characteristics, even among these rapidly growing suburbs, cannot be overlooked. For each set of suburbs the initial educational level served as a powerful predictor of current educational level, indicating that even rapid population growth did not greatly shift the relative socio-economic positions of these suburbs.

## CONCLUSIONS AND SUMMARY

The pattern of urban development indicated by the analyses presented in this paper is consistent with the Burgess model. The central parts of the area are built up first; over time as the housing quality in the center deteriorates the resident population is made up of lower status and in-migrant groups unable to afford the newer, more desirable housing on the periphery. During the 1950s the proportion non-white rose sharply in central cities, but remained constant in suburban areas. The proportions of white-collar workers and high school graduates, although rising in urbanized areas as aggregates, remained nearly constant in central cities but increased substantially in the suburbs.

Population growth between 1920 and 1960 tended to flow to the higher-status suburbs. As suggested earlier the movement from central cities to suburbs may be selective of higher-status population leaving the city in search of more desirable residential areas. It has been shown that occupational groups tend to live near their jobs but that the top white-collar groups depart from this rule to choose low-density communities even if these communities are not readily accessible (Hoover and Vernon 1959, p. 157; Duncan and Duncan 1956). Thus growth may have occurred in more exclusive suburbs as the higher-status workers who could afford commuting costs sought residence in high-status suburbs while the growth of lower-status suburbs may have been dependent upon the expansion of employment opportunities proximate to these suburbs and the large-scale decentralization of manufacturing that has occurred only recently (Bogue and Kitagawa 1954, p. 128). This type of differential suburban growth would foster increasing city–suburban differences.

Individual suburbs, however, rank in much the same way with respect to status level in 1960 as they did twenty or forty years earlier. In fact a sound prediction of the current educational level of a suburb's adult population can be made by knowing the school attendance rate of its adolescent population forty years earlier.

What reasons can be given for suburban persistence? Why shouldn't population growth within a suburb change the compositional characteristics of that suburb? Consider some examples:

Evanston and Hammond are approximately equal in population size, at the same distance from Chicago's Loop, comparable in age, and both have Lake Michigan frontage. Yet the inhabitants of these suburbs have quite different characteristics. A meat packing plant was the first establishment to attract residents to Hammond, and excellent rail facilities fostered later industrial growth, while the history of Evanston was dependent upon Methodist institutions including Northwestern University.

Parma and Shaker Heights, two of Cleveland's largest suburbs, were settled at approximately the same time and are the same distance from Cleveland. Census figures for 1960 show that college graduates and professional workers formed a sizably larger percentage of Shaker Heights' population than of Parma's.[7] When these suburbs were laid out, real-estate promoters planned numerous small homes in Parma and large expensive homes in Shaker Heights (Schauffler 1941, p. 67).

The specialization involved in the origin of a suburb may have implications for its distinctive socio-economic composition, so that once a suburb is established, the population that moves into that suburb tends to resemble the population already living there.

The feasibility of analyzing longitudinally compositional changes within urban areas has been demonstrated. Yet from an analysis based on measurements made at two or three points in time processes can only be inferred. Characteristics of migrants to and from cities and suburban areas and rates of migration flow need to be studied. For example, Goldstein (1963) suggests that the growth pattern of many American metropolitan areas may be similar to that of Copenhagen. He discovered that a movement of persons with high incomes to Copenhagen was countered by a movement of persons with low incomes out of suburbs and into the central city. Net figures concealed a much greater gross movement which had the effect of raising the socio-economic characteristics of suburban areas and lowering these characteristics for the central city. Clearly continued research in the dynamics of suburbanization is needed.

---

7. In 1960 the percentage of the male labor force holding professional jobs was 13.6 in Parma and 26.8 in Shaker Heights. The percentage of the population 25 and older having completed four or more years of college was 7.0 in Parma and 31.7 in Shaker Heights. U.S. Bureau of the Census, *Census of Population, 1960*, PC(1)-C, Table 72.

# The Social and Economic Characteristics of American Suburbs

LEO F. SCHNORE

In the traditional popular image, "the suburb" is nothing more than the dwelling place of commuters who work in the nearby central city. While it is certainly correct to characterize many outlying subcenters as little more than "bedroom cities," a realistic portrayal must reflect the fact that "dormitory towns are only one species of suburb" (Woodbury 1955). Some suburbs are literally manufacturing centers, devoted to light or heavy industry, while others are given over to the provision of such specialized services as education or recreation; as such, they represent significant centers of employment, drawing workers from other subcenters and even from the central city itself. Indeed, the range of economic specialization that can be discerned among suburbs is virtually as wide as that observable among other cities.

Despite the great variety of suburban functions, however, it has proved useful to distinguish two main types of suburb—employing and residential. This distinction made an early appearance in the literature of urban sociology, notably in the work of Taylor (1915) and that of Douglass (1925; 1934). Subsequent research has demonstrated the utility of this simple dichotomy. Harris (1943) has shown that "the commonest types of suburb are housing or dormitory suburbs and manufacturing or industrial suburbs," and it has been further shown that these two basic types differ with respect to a number of important social, economic, and demographic characteristics, including their rates of population growth (Schnore 1956; 1957a). It is the purpose of this study to discover whether or not systematic differences existed between suburbs according to functional type as of 1960, and (if so) to delineate suburban profiles by reference to characteristics enumerated in the 1960 Censuses of Population and Housing. In short, it is our intention to retest one of the more neglected hypotheses advanced by Louis Wirth in his well-known essay, "Urbanism as a Way of Life":

> An industrial city will differ significantly in social respects from a commercial, mining, fishing, resort, university, and capital city. A one-industry city will present different sets of social characteristics from a multi-industry city, as will an industrially balanced from an unbalanced city, a suburb from a satellite, a residential suburb from an industrial suburb.... (Wirth 1938, p. 49)

One of the new questions in the 1960 Census concerned the workplace of each employed person. Initially, we had hoped to make use of this item in order to make a precise identification of individual suburbs according to type. Unfortunately, the tabulation and publication of information on workplace makes use of such gross categories that it proved impossible to use these materials in the way that was originally contemplated. Workplaces are simply classified as lying inside or outside the worker's county of residence, and the only individual incorporated places that are recognized are those of 50,000 or more inhabitants—essentially the central cities of the Standard Metropolitan Statistical Areas and Urbanized Areas. In a few of these areas, however, workplace data can be used to characterize suburbs in a very rough fashion. In those few cases in which the central city is a separate county (e.g., San Francisco) or a quasi-county (e.g., St. Louis) it is possible to estimate the number of suburban commuters who work there. A person living in a New York suburb and working in the city itself, for example, will have to cross a county line, since the five boroughs making up the city are themselves separate counties. As a consequence, the proportion of a particular New York suburb's working population that is registered as "working in a county other than the county of residence" includes all those who travel to other employing centers in different counties. Thus the proportion working outside the county of residence serves as a rough index of the suburb's functional status, i.e., as an employing or a residential subcenter. A suburb with a high proportion of its employed population working outside the county is very probably a residential suburb. At the same time, a suburb with a very low proportion working in another county is quite likely to be an employing subcenter providing jobs for its own residents, if not for others as well. In any event, close inspection of the data for New York's suburbs indicated that this proportion would serve as a useful basis of classification. Let us examine the results.

TABLE 1
SOCIAL AND ECONOMIC CHARACTERISTICS OF SUBURBS
IN THE NEW YORK URBANIZED AREA, 1960

|  | Employing | Type of Suburb Intermediate | Residential |
|---|---|---|---|
| **A. AGE AND ETHNIC COMPOSITION** | | | |
| 1. Percentage foreign-born | 12.9 | 12.7 | 11.9 |
| 2. Percentage non-white | 10.6 | 7.8 | 1.5 |
| 3. Percentage aged 65 or more | 10.2 | 9.6 | 9.4 |
| **B. FERTILITY AND DEPENDENCY** | | | |
| 4. Non-worker–worker ratio | 1.27 | 1.33 | 1.41 |
| 5. Fertility ratio | 391 | 401 | 376 |
| 6. Percentage with children under 6 | 26.0 | 27.6 | 25.9 |
| **C. SOCIO-ECONOMIC STATUS** | | | |
| 7. Percentage completed high school | 40.9 | 42.9 | 50.6 |
| 8. Percentage in white-collar occupations | 44.9 | 47.2 | 58.0 |
| 9. Median family income | $7,051 | $7,337 | $8,994 |
| **D. POPULATION GROWTH** | | | |
| 10. Median rate of increase | 5.7 | 17.5 | 32.1 |
| 11. Percentage of places losing population | 24.0 | 25.0 | 8.0 |
| 12. Percent migrant 1955–60 | 11.8 | 14.0 | 20.1 |
| **E. HOUSING CHARACTERISTICS** | | | |
| 13. Percentage built between 1950 and 1960 | 16.8 | 20.8 | 24.4 |
| 14. Percentage owner-occupied units | 50.3 | 55.0 | 67.7 |
| 15. Percentage one-family units | 48.5 | 50.1 | 63.9 |
| Number of suburbs | 25 | 24 | 25 |

## THE SUBURBS OF NEW YORK

In Table 1, seventy-four incorporated places of 10,000 or more inhabitants lying within the New York–Northeastern New Jersey Urbanized Area have been classified as belonging to one of three types of suburb. Places with less than 25 percent of their employed populations working outside the county of residence are labeled "employing" suburbs. At the other extreme, places with 37.5

percent or more workers commuting across a county line are characterized as "residential" suburbs; on average, a place in this category sends almost 50 percent of its employed labor force into another county. Finally, a third "intermediate" or "mixed" category is recognized, wherein intercounty commuters make up 25 to 37 percent of its resident working population. Recognition of this third category permits a more rigorous text of the hypothesis to the effect that there exist systematic differences between employing and residential suburbs; if such differences exist, the values registered for the intermediate type should fall somewhere between those found for the two polar types.[1] In fact, Table 1 shows that a number of systematic differences according to type do characterize the suburbs of New York.

*Age and ethnic composition.* Panel A in Table 1 shows that the three types of suburb differ in population composition. Employing suburbs contain larger proportions of foreign-born and non-white inhabitants. In particular, the proportion non-white in residential suburbs is notably lower than in the two other types. Finally, the proportion of the population aged sixty-five or more tends to vary systematically from one suburban type to the next, although the differences tend to be rather small.[2]

*Fertility and dependency.* Panel B shows the non-worker–worker ratio for the three types of suburb; this is the ratio of the number of persons not in the labor force (including children under fourteen years of age) to the number within the labor force. On average, it can be seen that residential suburbs have a heavier burden of dependency. This ratio is mainly a function of two factors—age composition and labor force participation. Suburbs with large numbers of dependent old and young persons can be expected to

---

[1]. The "intermediate" type recognized in this paper should not be confused with the "balanced" type of suburb identified by Douglass, wherein jobs and workers are approximately equal in number.

[2]. The proportions non-white and aged 65 and over were taken from U.S. Bureau of the Census, *U.S. Census of Population: 1960, General Population Characteristics* (Washington, D.C.: U.S. Government Printing Office, 1961), Table 13 for each state. Unless otherwise indicated, the remaining characteristics were taken from U.S. Bureau of the Census, *U.S. Census of Population: 1960, General Social and Economic Characteristics* (Washington, D.C.: U.S. Government Printing Office, 1961), Tables 32 and 33 for each state. These two publications are Chapters "B" and "C" respectively, and will be so identified in subsequent references. Unless otherwise indicated, the values shown are unweighted means for the type of suburb in question.

## Social and Economic Characteristics

exhibit higher ratios, as can those in which labor force participation rates are lower. The second and third lines suggest that the variations in dependency between types of suburb are not simply the result of variations in levels of fertility. The fertility ratio (children under five years old per thousand women fifteen to forty-nine years old) proves to be highest in the intermediate type, with lower values in the two polar types of suburb.[3] Similarly, the proportion of married couples with children under six years of age is highest in the intermediate type. It is interesting to note that these are the only two characteristics in which the values for the intermediate type do not fall between those for the two polar types of suburb.

*Socio-economic status.* Perhaps the clearest differences between New York suburbs emerge when three measures of socio-economic status are considered. Among persons aged twenty-five years and older, Panel C reveals that residential suburbs have clearly higher proportions who completed twelve or more years of education. Similarly, among members of the employed labor force, comparable differences between suburban types appear with respect to the proportions engaged in white-collar pursuits—those in professional, managerial, clerical, and sales occupations. Finally, systematic variations can be observed with respect to median family income. The relatively self-contained suburbs (employing sub-centers) have the lowest average income, while residential suburbs register substantially higher income. These differences are clearly in accordance with earlier findings (Schnore 1957b).

*Population growth.* Still another series of differences between employing and residential suburbs that has been subjected to some prior research concerns population change. Two earlier studies have suggested that residential suburbs tended to grow faster than employing suburbs in the thirties and the forties.[4] Panel D

---

3. The source of the fertility ratio was Chapter "B," Table 13. This measure is also commonly known as "the child-woman ratio."

4. For growth rates between 1930 and 1940, see Harris 1943. Suburban growth between 1940 and 1950 is examined in Schnore 1957a; and Schnore 1958. The growth rates for 1950–1960 were computed on the basis of data taken from U.S. Bureau of the Census, *U.S. Census of Population: 1960*, vol. 1, *Characteristics of the Population*, Part A, "Number of Inhabitants" (Washington, D.C.: U.S. Government Printing Office, 1961), Table 8 for each state. The rates of growth were adjusted for annexations of territory and population between 1950 and 1960 by reference to Table 9. For the importance of this adjustment, see Schnore 1962.

indicates that these growth differentials persisted in the fifties, at least among the New York suburbs under examination. While employing suburbs were growing at a rate that averaged less than six percent over the decade, residential suburbs increased by over thirty percent in the same interval. The second line shows that less than one out of every ten residential suburbs lost numbers during the decade, while one out of every four registered population losses in the other two types. That these growth differentials were brought about mainly by variations in migration is suggested by the last line in Panel D, where it can be seen that one out of every five inhabitants of residential suburbs was an in-migrant, i.e., lived in a different county in 1955 and 1960. Intermediate and employing types of suburb had notably lower proportions migrant according to this measure.

*Housing characteristics.* The last set of characteristics examined here has to do with certain features of the housing stock found in different types of suburb.[5] In accordance with the growth differentials previously observed, it can be seen that the housing stock of residential suburbs is much newer than that of other types; almost one out of every four housing units in New York's residential suburbs is to be found in a structure built between 1950 and 1960. Similarly, occupancy by owners is much more frequent in residential suburbs, for over two out of every three occupied units is inhabited by the owner. In contrast, almost half the units found in New York's employing suburbs are occupied by renters. Finally, clear-cut differentials may be observed with respect to type of residential structure. Over six out of every ten housing units in the residential suburbs of New York are in "one-housing-unit structures," i.e., single-family residences. This contrasts with the situation in employing and intermediate suburbs, where roughly half the dwelling units are found in multiple-family structures.

## THE EMPLOYMENT–RESIDENCE RATIO

Unfortunately, the procedures used in classifying New York's suburbs cannot be employed in other areas. In most cases, the

---

5. All of the housing data were taken from U.S. Bureau of the Census, *U.S. Census of Housing: 1960*, vol. 1, *States and Small Areas* (Washington, D.C.: U.S. Government Printing Office, 1962), Table 1 for each state.

TABLE 2

NUMBER OF SUBURBS IN EACH OF 25 URBANIZED AREAS
OF MORE THAN 750,000 INHABITANTS, 1960

| Urbanized Area | Population 1960 | Number of Suburbs in Study |
|---|---|---|
| New York–Northeastern New Jersey | 14,114,927 | 74 |
| Los Angeles–Long Beach, Calif. | 6,488,791 | 34 |
| Chicago–Northwestern Indiana | 5,959,213 | 30 |
| Philadelphia, Pa.–N.J. | 3,635,228 | 14 |
| Detroit, Mich. | 3,537,709 | 22 |
| San Francisco–Oakland, Calif. | 2,430,663 | 18 |
| Boston, Mass. | 2,413,236 | 16 |
| Washington, D.C.–Md.–Va. | 1,808,423 | 4 |
| Pittsburgh, Pa. | 1,804,400 | 22 |
| Cleveland, Ohio | 1,784,991 | 12 |
| St. Louis, Mo.–Ill. | 1,667,693 | 12 |
| Baltimore, Md. | 1,418,948 | 0 |
| Minneapolis–St. Paul, Minn. | 1,377,143 | 4 |
| Milwaukee, Wis. | 1,149,997 | 7 |
| Houston, Texas | 1,139,678 | 3 |
| Buffalo, N.Y. | 1,054,370 | 5 |
| Cincinnati, Ohio–Ky. | 993,568 | 4 |
| Dallas, Texas | 932,349 | 4 |
| Kansas City, Mo.–Kans. | 921,121 | 1 |
| Seattle, Wash. | 864,109 | 1 |
| Miami, Fla. | 852,705 | 4 |
| New Orleans, La. | 845,237 | 1 |
| San Diego, Calif. | 836,175 | 3 |
| Denver, Colo. | 803,624 | 2 |
| Atlanta, Ga. | 768,125 | 3 |

central city is located in the same county as the suburbs surrounding it. As a consequence, these suburbs cannot be readily characterized as "employing" and "residential" in accordance with the census data on workplace. Even the detailed tabulations of workplace—wherein commuter trips to central cities of 50,000 and over will be separately identified—will not permit an exact classification of suburbs according to type, since work trips to places other than central cities will not be separately reported.

For these reasons, we have turned to another source of information as a means of classifying suburbs according to functional type. We have used the "employment-residence" ratio computed by Jones and Collver (1959, p. 72) for all incorporated places of 10,000 or more inhabitants in 1950; as they indicate, "the employment-residence ratio was obtained by comparing the number of workers employed in the city in 1954 in manufacturing and trade with the number of employed residents reporting these same occupations." Cities are differentiated, then, on the basis of the net daily movement of workers into and out of them. A place with a high ratio tends to have many more jobs than employed workers, and can be fairly characterized as an employing subcenter. On the other hand, a place with a low employment–residence ratio has more workers than jobs available locally, and can be aptly categorized as a residential subcenter.

In all, the twenty-five largest Urbanized Areas contain exactly 300 suburbs for which employment–residence ratios have been calculated. The list in Table 2, ordered by population size, shows the number of suburbs found in each of the twenty-five Urbanized Areas of more than 750,000 inhabitants in 1960.

Once again there is the problem of establishing "cutting points." For present purposes, suburbs with employment–residence ratios of 101 or more were classified as "employing" subcenters. Those with ratios falling between 51 and 100 are termed "intermediate," and those with ratios of 50 or less are treated as "residential" suburbs.[6] As it happens, this procedure yields three groups of approximately equal size.

TABLE 3
ECONOMIC BASE OF SUBURB BY TYPE

| Economic Base | Employing | Intermediate | Residential |
|---|---|---|---|
| Percentage Mm (manufacturing) | 70.6 | 33.3 | 2.0 |
| Percentage M (industrial) | 3.9 | 7.1 | 2.0 |
| Percentage Mr (diversified, with manufacturing predominant) | 7.8 | 16.2 | 13.1 |
| Percentage S (service) | 2.9 | 2.0 | 5.1 |
| Percentage Rm (diversified, with retail trade predominant) | 5.9 | 23.2 | 23.2 |
| Percentage Rr (retail trade) | 8.9 | 18.2 | 54.6 |
| Total | 100.0 | 100.0 | 100.0 |
| Number of suburbs | 102 | 99 | 99 |

Table 3 shows the economic base of each suburb according to functional type. It will be seen that the employing suburbs are heavily specialized in manufacturing; in fact, if one adds together the first three categories—manufacturing, industrial, and diversified suburbs in which manufacturing predominates—one finds

---
6. Jones and Collver suggest that cities with ratios below 50 should be treated as "dormitory suburbs," and they point out that "all but three of these cities are located within SMA's and only four are manufacturing or industrial cities" (1956, p. 71).

four out of every five employing suburbs represented. At the other extreme, residential suburbs are heavily specialized in the provision of retail trade and services. Over half these places are retail trade centers, and if one combines the last three categories—retail trade centers, diversified centers in which retail trade predominates, and service centers—one finds four out of every five of the residential suburbs so classified. As expected, the intermediate suburbs represent a greater mixture of places from the standpoint of their economic bases. These materials suggest that in working with subcenters classified according to their employment-residence ratios we are dealing with more or less distinctive types of suburb which play dissimilar roles in the metropolitan economy.

## SOCIAL AND ECONOMIC CHARACTERISTICS OF 300 SUBURBS

Table 4 provides summary profiles of 300 employing, intermediate, and residential suburbs, using the employment-residence ratios as the basis of the typological distinction. The characteristics shown include all those previously analyzed for the suburbs of New York.

*Age and ethnic composition.* As in the case of New York, suburbs generally appear to vary systematically with respect to certain compositional features. Employing suburbs contain not only higher proportions of foreign-born inhabitants, but they also contain larger percentages of non-whites. The non-white representation in residential suburbs is again notably lower than in the other types. With respect to age composition, employing suburbs tend to have larger proportions of older inhabitants, but the other two types do not differ much in this respect.

*Fertility and dependency.* Similarly, residential and intermediate types of suburb are not clearly distinguished with respect to dependency, for their non-worker-worker ratios are identical. This ratio, seen in Panel B, is only slightly lower for employing suburbs. These findings represent a departure from the patterns exhibited by New York's suburbs, where a rather clear gradient was in evidence. Like New York's suburbs, however, the larger sample reveals the highest fertility ratios in the intermediate type of suburb; employing and residential suburbs have child-woman ratios

TABLE 4

SOCIAL AND ECONOMIC CHARACTERISTICS OF SUBURBS
IN THE 25 LARGEST URBANIZED AREAS, 1960

|  | Type of Suburb | | |
|---|---|---|---|
|  | Employing | Intermediate | Residential |
| A. AGE AND ETHNIC COMPOSITION | | | |
| 1. Percentage foreign-born | 10.5 | 8.5 | 7.7 |
| 2. Percentage non-white | 7.0 | 6.2 | 2.4 |
| 3. Percentage aged 65 or more | 9.7 | 9.0 | 9.1 |
| B. FERTILITY AND DEPENDENCY | | | |
| 4. Non-worker–worker ratio | 1.41 | 1.44 | 1.44 |
| 5. Fertility ratio | 421 | 437 | 422 |
| 6. Percentage with children under 6 | 27.8 | 29.2 | 28.2 |
| C. SOCIO-ECONOMIC STATUS | | | |
| 7. Percentage completed high school | 43.2 | 48.2 | 55.8 |
| 8. Percentage in white-collar occupations | 44.6 | 49.8 | 58.5 |
| 9. Median family income | $6,869 | $7,510 | $8,210 |
| D. POPULATION GROWTH, 1950–60 | | | |
| 10. Median rate of increase | 6.0 | 18.1 | 26.9 |
| 11. Percentage of places losing population | 30.4 | 24.2 | 16.2 |
| 12. Percentage migrant 1955–60 | 13.8 | 16.7 | 17.4 |
| E. HOUSING CHARACTERISTICS | | | |
| 13. Percentage built between 1950 and 1960 | 24.1 | 29.4 | 31.6 |
| 14. Percentage owner-occupied units | 57.7 | 63.1 | 71.4 |
| 15. Percentage one-family units | 62.3 | 68.2 | 75.9 |
| Number of suburbs | 102 | 99 | 99 |

that are lower and virtually identical. Similarly, the proportions of married couples with children under six years of age are lower in the two polar types of suburb, with a higher proportion found in the suburbs of the intermediate type. Again, these findings reproduce the patterns observed when only the seventy-four New York suburbs were under scrutiny.

*Socio-economic status.* The New York sample also proved to be typical with respect to differentials in socio-economic status between suburbs of varying type. Panel C in Table 4 shows that the highest proportion completing high school is found in the residential suburbs. Similarly, the largest relative number of employed persons in white-collar occupations is found in this same type of suburb. Finally, income differentials are again very pronounced. A gap in excess of $1,300 separates the median incomes of employing and residential suburbs, with the latter type clearly favored.

*Population growth.* We have already referred to evidence to the effect that the growth of residential suburbs outstripped that of employing suburbs during the 1930s and 1940s. During the 1950s, according to Panel D, this differential clearly persisted. While employing subcenters grew an average of only six percent over the 1950–1960 decade, residential suburbs grew by almost twenty-seven percent. Again, suburbs of intermediate type registered intermediate gains. We also see that three out of every ten employing suburbs actually lost population during the decade, while only half as many residential suburbs registered losses during the same interval. Again, as in the case of the New York sample, residential suburbs were generally more likely to contain migrants, i.e., people who lived in different counties in 1955 and 1960.

*Housing characteristics.* The final array of characteristics examined here refers to housing in employing, intermediate, and residential suburbs. Panel E reveals higher proportions of new housing (built between 1950 and 1960) in residential suburbs; this finding, of course, is in accordance with the expectation formed on the basis of examining differentials in population growth. Another set of differences that was anticipated—largely on the basis of New York suburban experience—has to do with housing tenure. Panel E shows that dwelling units in residential suburbs are more likely to be occupied by owners than by renters. Finally, the three types of suburb differ systematically with respect to type of residential structure. While lower proportions of dwelling units are of the one-family style in employing and intermediate suburbs, fully three out of every four units are designed for single-family occupancy in residential suburbs. As in most of the preceding comparisons, then, the housing data for all 300 suburbs reflect the patterns observed in the more limited sample drawn from the environs of New York.

## SUMMARY AND CONCLUSIONS

The massive shifts in population denoted by the concept of "suburbanization" have been thoroughly documented in demographic research.[7] Moreover, detailed case studies have reminded us of the diversity of suburbs in America.[8] As Riesman has observed, however, "we cannot link nation-wide data on changes in

---

7. See, for example, Hawley 1956.

8. See, for example, Whyte 1956, Part 7, "The Transients"; Seeley, Sim, and Loosley 1956; and Berger 1960.

metropolitan areas with Whyte's descriptions of how Park Forest feels toward its pro tem inhabitants. This is the characteristic situation in sociology today—that research in the macrocosmic and in the microcosmic scarcely connect, scarcely inform each other" (Riesman 1957, p. 125). This study represents an effort at portraying what is typical in contemporary suburbia while simultaneously giving attention to variations within the broad category "suburb."

We have followed the sociological tradition by identifying two major types of suburb—employing and residential. For purposes of analysis, however, we have recognized a third—an intermediate type. Some fifteen social and economic characteristics were then examined, first in a sample of 74 suburbs surrounding New York City and subsequently in a group of 300 suburbs found within the twenty-five largest Urbanized Areas.

The values observed for thirteen of these fifteen characteristics tended to increase or decrease systematically as one moved from one type of suburb to the next. In other words, the characteristics of the intermediate class of suburbs tended to fall somewhere between those of employing and residential suburbs. The exceptions to this pattern both involved characteristics reflecting suburban fertility—the child-woman ratio and the proportion of married couples with children under six years of age. Both of these measures turned out to be higher (in both samples) for intermediate suburbs than in employing or residential subcenters.

Perhaps the most clear-cut set of differences were those having to do with socio-economic status. Measures of income, education, and occupational standing all showed the same results in both samples, i.e., the highest values were registered in the residential suburbs, somewhat lower values in the intermediate class, and the lowest values in the employing category. Other measures with a "status" connotation—proportions foreign-born and non-white, and proportions in owner-occupied and single-family dwelling units—showed similar patterns.

Finally, this study has demonstrated the continuation of a long-term trend with respect to population growth. Growth differentials favoring residential suburbs continue to characterize the fifties, just as they did the thirties and the forties. While it is undeniable that suburbs vary in many respects, it is equally clear that these variations are quite systematic and predictable.

## SUGGESTIONS FOR FURTHER READING

The most detailed case-study of early suburbanization in America is Sam B. Warner's *Streetcar Suburbs* (Cambridge: Harvard University and The M.I.T. Presses, 1962). In this book Warner documents and describes the growth of metropolitan Boston—especially the growth of the towns of Roxbury, Dorchester, and West Roxbury—between 1870 and 1900. For an entertaining vignette about turn-of-the-century life, written as it occurred, see Richard Harding Davis, "Our Suburban Friends" (*Harpers*, vol. 89, June 1894, pp. 155-157). Harlan Douglass's *The Suburban Trend* (New York: The Century Press, 1925) can also be read for its historically significant data, but many of Douglass's arguments are quite contemporary in nature.

As the data from the 1970 United States Census becomes available there is certain to be an eclectic series of books and articles delineating suburbia's present social demography. For a review of the studies based on 1960 and earlier data see James R. Pinkerton, "City-Suburban Residential Patterns by Social Class" (*Urban Affairs Quarterly*, vol. 4, June 1969, pp. 499-519). This article ends with an excellent bibliography. A later, more technical article, which critically examines the theoretical and conceptual bases of previous studies of metropolitan social differentiation, is Joel Smith's "Another Look at Socioeconomic Status Distributions in Urbanized Areas" (*Urban Affairs Quarterly*, vol. 5, June 1970, pp. 423-453). For a collection of many of Leo Schnore's articles dealing with the metropolitan expanse, see *The Urban Scene* (New York: The Free Press, 1965).

The terminology and methodological aspects of demographic research in the suburbs are well explored in the following articles: Richard Kurtz and Joanna B. Eicher, "Fringe and Suburb: A Confusion of Concepts" (*Social Forces*, vol. 37, October 1958, pp. 32-37); Robin Pryor, "Defining the Rural-Urban Fringe" (*Social Forces*, vol. 47, December 1968, pp. 212-215); and Ira Rosenwaike, "A Critical Examination of the Designation of Standard Metropolitan Statistical Areas" (*Social Forces*, vol. 48, March 1970, pp. 322-333).

# PART III: SUBURBAN DIVERSITY EXAMINED

# INTRODUCTION

The aim of part three is to provide a series of glimpses into dissimilar suburban settings. The six selections are not comparable in method nor in institutional focus, but each deals with a separate type of contemporary suburban settlement.

The first selection is taken from the classic study *Crestwood Heights*. In the research for this volume, authors John Seeley, R. Alexander Sim, and Elizabeth W. Loosley exhaustively surveyed the social-psychological milieu in an upper-middle-class, suburban area in metropolitan Toronto. (Crestwood Heights actually is a residential borough within the city limits—see S. D. Clark's criticism of the study in selection two.) Included here is a particularly graphic description of the Crestwood Heights home and its various functions in the lives of that community's affluent residents.

The next selection is "An Anatomy of Suburbia" by Herbert Gans. Originally published as an article, it is in fact a partial précis of *The Levittowners*, which describes aspects of the social organization in New Jersey's Levittown during the two years immediately following its founding in 1958. With data gathered through participant and non-participant observation, Gans examines portions of the suburban myth in the very type of "package" suburb from which the myth was generated. His conclusions are well-reasoned and non-belligerent (notice that not all aspects of the suburban myth are discarded out of hand). *The Levittowners* was perhaps the most comprehensive and sophisticated suburban study published during the 1960s.

The third selection describes still another type of suburban setting, the "sacked village." Old Harbor, studied by William Dobriner, once was a quiet rural town. By the mid-1950s, however, it had been occupied by suburbanites coming outward from the city. As these new residents came to Old Harbor and superimposed their style of life upon an already existing social structure, the village became "two communities" in one. Dobriner, in "The Natural History of a Reluctant Suburb," describes the interplay between the contending forces.

Another type of heterogeneous suburban settlement, a community populated by persons with diverse ethno-religious backgrounds, is the subject of the fourth selection. Lakeville is a Midwestern suburb with more than twenty-five thousand residents. It is an older, elite, town with a suburban history dating back to the 1920s. After World War II a heavy migration of Jews from "Lake City" occurred until, by the mid-1950s, approximately one-third of the community was Jewish and two-thirds Gentile. In *The Edge of Friendliness*, from which this selection comes, Benjamin Ringer notes the changes in Lakeville which have resulted from the Jewish migration. Reprinted here is the book's concluding chapter, in which Ringer describes the general atmosphere of the Jewish–Gentile relationships in the community. On the surface, tranquillity seems to be the overriding characteristic. Beneath the surface, however, animosities and separatism still linger.

The fifth selection, "The Other Mayor Lee," deals with the political life of Kinloch, Missouri, a poverty-level and totally black enclave locked between two middle-class suburban towns in St. Louis County. As a politically autonomous municipality with an all-black local government, Kinloch is atypical of the black settlements that now dot the suburban landscape. Most are politically unincorporated or portions of larger, predominantly white, political jurisdictions. Furthermore, when I investigated the community I did not view my research as "suburban study"; thus the article ignores some of the issues commonly treated in suburban research. Nevertheless, through its focus on local politics, the article describes a significant component of the town's social organization and suggests that Kinloch, even though racially homogeneous, is not without its sources of community conflict. In addition, it makes the often overlooked point that poverty and frustration (and blacks) are not absent from the suburban scene.

## Introduction

The final selection in part three explores a new mode of suburban residence—the mobile home, a type of domicile quite different from the relatively sumptuous homes found in Crestwood Heights. With the increasing movement of industry into the suburbs, and the rising cost of permanent suburban dwellings, mobile homes are likely to house growing numbers of lower-status workers on the urban periphery. In "Mobile Homes: Instant Suburbia or Transportable Slums," Robert French and Jeffrey Hadden discuss the social implications of the trend toward "wheel estate" living, and raise a number of considerations for metropolitan planning.

# The Home in Crestwood Heights

JOHN R. SEELEY, R. ALEXANDER SIM,
and ELIZABETH W. LOOSLEY

The primary significance of the house from the viewpoint of child-rearing, then, does not lie in its architecture, or in the artifacts with which it is furnished, or in its devices for the satisfaction of basic physiological needs. It is the body of attachments and meanings that are associated with the house which are in this connection important. In this role the house is a valuable means of ensuring privacy in a crowded city; a vehicle for enforcing family solidarity and conformity; a place to practice and perfect consumption skills; a major item of personal property, which, for the head of the family (and, to a less degree, for his wife and children), stands as a concrete symbol of his status and visible sign of his success. It is in terms like these that the significance of the house must be stated.

THE HOUSE AS PROPERTY

Property is an essential component of status in Crestwood Heights. The Crestwooder who owns an adequate house has become a substantial member of the community and, as such, is respected and admired by his peers. The house and its furnishings;

*Excerpted from Chapter 3 of* Crestwood Heights, *by John R. Seeley, R. Alexander Sim, and Elizabeth W. Loosley, © 1956 by Basic Books, Inc., New York. Reprinted by permission of the publisher and John R. Seeley.*

## The Home in Crestwood Heights

the street and the street number; the location in Crestwood—all are acquired items which make up the total property complex of the house.

It is on these items, and other similar ones, that the competitive struggle of the Crestwooder for power focuses. These are the symbols around which he must center his efforts to realize the "good life," and organize the strivings which lend a meaning to his existence. Property does not, then, acquire its value directly from its intrinsic monetary worth, or from narrow utilitarian considerations, but from the public evaluations of things as they evolve in the markets of exchange and in the rialto of status.[1] It is the attributes imputed to broadloom, or a particular style of architecture, or the work of a fashionable artist, or a street and number, which give them an edge as weapons wielded in the battle for social position. Utility is secondary to social acceptability.

Typically, a Crestwood man announced at dinner, "Well, today I have satisfied a life-long ambition." After breathless inquiry from the family, he revealed the fact that he had purchased a new Cadillac. He had, he said, bought the automobile for personal gratification; but the spread of excitement to the whole family suggested that the aura of his success enveloped them also. Other articles— especially large and expensive ones—also evidently conferred status, for example, a new, deluxe model, electric stove and refrigerator, a television set, broadloom for the second floor. In another family, the husband would repeatedly suggest the purchase of a new refrigerator. Each time his wife would demur: she liked the one she had; she did not need a new one. Her reluctance was not motivated by economy, nor was his insistence based on technical need. His rationalization of the purchase was "I like pampering you." When he bought the refrigerator "as a surprise" she "loved it." If the wife wants something the husband does not wish to buy, the roles may be reversed, although the cajolery remains the same. The husband gives in; the wife is delighted; she likes being "spoiled"; he is endlessly pleased with the new gadget, the acquisition of which has, incidentally, raised the prestige of the home. Similarly the children receive or secure for distribution artifacts for general use or for individual consumption.

---

1. Cf. Hallowell 1943; and Benedict 1934, pp. 181 et seq.

The new item is accepted into the family circle and incorporated into its life pattern. But it is not fully integrated until display has brought about its validation as property. The rug, or the painting, or the drapes are "shelter," not at the margin between bodily exposure and survival, but on the dividing line between discomfort and psychological well-being. The acclaim which the new article receives directly or indirectly spells out its value as "shelter" in the psychological sense; though a poised consumer who knows what will eventually be acclaimed needs less overt recognition, pleasant as well-modulated praise may be.

The owner tends to become deeply—but not irrevocably—identified with his house and its contents. This emotional tie is well known to real-estate dealers and prospective buyers and is played upon in the course of all property transactions. One woman informant, who had lived away from home for many years, tells of the sale of the family house after her mother's death. In her account (as in the accounts of others) one may sense something close to an identification of the house with the body—somewhat the same fear of violation, somewhat the same defenses against attack.

> We had a beautiful house, one of the "showplaces" of the district. Mother had wanted a house like that almost all her married life. When she had the chance to get it, she planned it down to the last detail with the architect. Of course, it wasn't the kind of architecture I would have chosen, pure Georgian, but it was very good of its type and Mother loved it. We moved into it just when I went away to college and I never really lived in it. Several times the house was broken into while we were away in the summer and, although nothing valuable was ever stolen, it upset Mother almost as much as if some accident had happened to one of us. She just couldn't bear "strangers" going through her belongings and treating them so roughly.
>
> I was there with Dad when some people came to look over the house after Mother died. He was a Mr. X who had just come from the States to take some important executive position in the T.W. plant. His wife came with him. She went over every inch of the house, running everything down: said the woodwork would all have to be bleached and that the place needed to be redecorated completely. Mr. X tried to beat Dad down about the price, very rudely, as if money could buy everything. I had no idea I would feel it so much. After all, it was very much Mother's house and I hadn't ever lived there for any length of time. But I finally just had to go away and leave Dad to deal with them.

Into this world of things the child enters almost, it would seem, prenatally. The nursery is equipped in advance of the first confinement, and is often refurnished before succeeding confinements. Many Crestwood nurseries approach the streamlined efficiency of those appearing in the advertisements featured by women's journals. It is little wonder that some parents regard the sense of property as instinctive, for the child's earliest sensory experience may be, not at his mother's breast, but through contact with a set of lifeless objects: bottles, cloth, sides of the crib, and the like. Further indoctrination into the world of things follows: gift giving, the placing of bright objects in the crib and playpen for the child to manipulate. Finally, behavior is learned in which private possession and protective personal modesty are closely linked. The parents may play with the child, taking away a rattle, at the same time saying "mine," then returning it to its rightful "owner." It is not surprising that "mine" becomes a dominant word, not only in the games and quarrels of peer groups, but also in later life when the purchase of the largest house possible filled with the finest and most appropriate objects money can buy, betokens success in the struggle to acquire prestige and power.

Before this stage is reached, a lengthy series of subtle behavior patterns, centering around property, must be learned and practiced, reminiscent to some degree of the more primitive potlatch.[2] Never must this behavior become extreme or obvious, however. The young child likes, and is encouraged, to show off a new kiddie-car or article of clothing. Adults at first consider such behavior amusing because of its naive enthusiasm. Later, the same tolerance is not forthcoming; for, in display, the child must learn nonchalance, as well as delicacy.

Unlike the young child, the Crestwood adult automatically watches for the quick appraising glance which will tell him that the recently acquired property-item is acceptable and desirable. He knows that the artifact is ultimately valuable not in itself but if it assures him of continued acceptance by his peers or prompts, what is even more esteemed, an invitation to join a group of higher status. Thus property, in which the house is all-important, is manipulated to confirm status and enforce prerogatives in Crestwood Heights.

---

2. For a description of the potlatch as a primitive ceremonial, see Benedict 1934, pp. 184-211.

## THE HOUSE AS STAGE

The Crestwood House is adapted for the "staging" of "productions," and this characteristic is brought to the fore especially whenever formal hospitality is practiced. On such occasions, the space which has been purchased at great price, lends itself to the gracious reception of guests. Indeed space is essential to permit the inclusion of a sufficiently impressive number of visitors. Space thus allows the ritual destruction of the privacy it has also created; for it is only as the symbols of status—acquired, presumably, for private enjoyment—are revealed to selected groups and individuals, that their ultimate cultural value can be determined.[3]

Since the guests play the role of audience, their attention and presence are concentrated upon the center of the stage, on those areas reserved for display and hospitality: the living room, dining room, and (a more recent accession) the recreation or "rumpus" room. In the wings, food and other symbols of hospitality are prepared, to be introduced as needed. The hall or reception room is unusually important. Here the opening scene is played, with its seldom remembered but inevitably significant opening verbal exchanges. Here also the finale is enacted, following which the family, with the curtain new drawn, resumes, sometimes with a little embarrassment, relationships at a less theatrical or "staged" level.

The Crestwood preparations for hospitality and the behavior appropriate to such occasions are noted in a statement submitted by a university student:

> The entertainment of the middle middle class is almost exclusively within the family residence. It is exceptional to find a guest being taken to the hotel for dinner, for example. It would be considered very poor taste, and suggest that the host and hostess did not consider their guest worthy of the trouble of entertaining him at home.
>
> A person takes his "cue" from the individuals he is entertaining. When a woman has a tea or bridge party, how she patterns her behavior depends upon who is present. There are definite norms governing actions if members either of a lower or a higher class status have been invited because, in both cases, the hostess must use all her resources in

---

3. The house is not the only stage on which hospitality is enacted but techniques of entertaining are much the same whether the home, the club, or the exclusive restaurant is the chosen field of display. Moreover, decorative features of the one may carry over to the other. The bar, for instance, which is an increasingly prominent feature of restaurant and club, is often reproduced, in miniature, as part of the rumpus room. In the club setting, however, it is the fact of membership which is brought into prominence; in the case of the home, it is the amenities of the house.

# The Home in Crestwood Heights

an effort to impress her own position upon the guests. In such a case the best china is dusted and brought forth, the lace cloth and silver tea service come into use; even the topics of conversation are closely regulated by convention. Any controversial issues are carefully avoided; true inner feelings are repressed, else interaction among the individuals would be impossible. Conversation is maintained at a "sociable" level: talk for the sake of talking, being witty, amusing, amiable but never really saying anything. We may compare the house, in the situation, to a *stage* and the people present to characters who are displaying the parts they play in the community at large.

The staging or "display" orientation is illustrated also in the use of "picture windows." They are most frequently located in the front of the house overlooking the street—rather than in the back where they would afford a view of the garden. The purpose seems less to give the occupants a view of the outside, for which a much smaller window would suffice, and more to extend an invitation to the outsider to look in. Through these windows, the mildly curious passing observer may identify, where the drapes permit, the owner of a grand piano, a valuable crystal chandelier, or a striking red brocade chair. There is an air here not only of display but of coquetry as well. The window is spacious, but it will not open; it is large, but it is often hooded by heavy drapes; it reveals an interesting room, but the revelation merely encourages the imagination to speculate on all the others.

The theatrical or staged appearance is not equally evident in all houses; some are more artless or conventional than others. Even children are aware of these differences and discuss them freely, especially after parties, when they comment with considerable candor on the homes they have visited. Said a five-year-old in a home known for its avant-garde taste, and very self-conscious about colorful display: "Mummie, aren't you afraid when people come to our house that they'll think they are coming to a furniture store?" One house may give a definite impression of "night club" décor, showing the pronounced influence of mass communication media, movies, and house decorating magazines. On the other hand, drabness in the decoration of some homes appeared to be quite as studied and self-conscious as the color in the examples cited above. In the former, however, the nonchalance of slip-covered furniture and the mute testimony of prestige-laden family heirlooms effectively indicate the status of the family which had arranged these props.

Entering one of the more patently theatrical abodes may produce an unusual effect upon the guest. Criticism may be hostile:

> She uses pink a lot. That's her attempt to make the place warm and give it life, but she can't quite bring it off. Actually she doesn't live in that house at all, she's someplace else altogether; and when I visit her, I feel I'm in an empty house.

Or:

> Everything is exceedingly studied in every detail. The décor is refined to the point where . . . well, the other day when I called there, I was afraid to lay down my green gloves because they clashed with everything. The walls and rugs are matching powder blue. This blends with the Wedgwood. The brass around the fireplace gives a dash of brightness, but the fire itself is seldom lit. When it is, the blaze is deeply shadowed. There is no thought of it giving warmth, but only an added, moving subdued light.

The Crestwood house seemed often oddly reminiscent of a series of department store windows, charmingly arranged, harmoniously matched in color, but rather cold and empty of life. On more than one occasion an interviewer had the experience of waiting while his hostess whisked the plastic covering off the furniture. In such a home one did not find children's toys on the living-room rug, or a piece of sewing dropped on the chesterfield or table, with the needle sticking in it and thread or thimble nearby. There was no homely litter to proclaim that family activity went on amidst the inanimate objects, chosen with such care. In some houses one was almost driven to ask, "But where do they *live?*" In others, the piled magazines and the evidences of hard use indicated that a room, though tidy at the moment, was indubitably a "living room." In still other cases, it was found that the so-called living room, like the rural parlor, was spared daily wear—this is possible in a large house—while a small den or breakfast nook served the purpose.

For the outsider, the stage must always be set and ready. Intimates can be brought into a disordered house with the simple explanation: "This place is a shambles"; the wider circle of acquaintances cannot be received so casually. Certain articles are reserved for the most formal display only: in one house, a handsome silver tea service on an ornate Sheffield tray was enveloped in plastic, and the covering would not be removed for an outsider dining informally with the family.

The furnishing of this elaborate stage is an arduous undertaking. The people of Crestwood Heights appear to occupy a middle position, not only in the class structure, but also in the hierarchy of taste. The majority of them are not in a position to acquire the prestige-giving objects commonly found in upper-class homes. They lack the excess wealth, the judgment, the contacts, and, often, the desire, to secure them; yet they are compelled to collect material possessions from which they can derive pleasure and status. Rather than a Renoir, Crestwooders will buy an Emily Carr, a William Winter, an Arthur Lismer; or, at a lower economic level, good reproductions of modern artists. But these purchases pose nagging questions. Is the object still in style? Is it *passé?* Or is it already "coming back"? Crestwooders are not in a position to confer respectability upon an item simply because they have given it their patronage, since they themselves still hope to derive status from their purchase. Thus, in a changing, unstable society, there is, for those who are its most mobile members, a continuing need to revalidate the material objects with which the house has been "dressed."

Upon the stage of the Crestwood home the family plays out, then, several endless dramas, public and private, which include numerous characters, enacting many roles at different times and for different purposes. These dramas allow varying degrees of privacy and display. An area of privacy is never completely absent, even during a New Year's Eve party. Display is also never absent, even through the darkest hours of the night, for the family is solidly located in one particular street, in one particular section, and in one particular style of house. This backdrop of the house is, in the minds of all those who are intimate with or know of its owners, as permanent a symbol of status as is the husband's position and income, or the wife's beauty, accent, and clothing. Thus the central theme of all the dramas the house supports becomes competition for social status; hope of success or chance of failure provide suspense, but the dénouement is never final, since in Crestwood Heights standards of style and taste shift and change in bewildering complexity.

THE HOUSE AS HOME

Although Crestwooders attach great importance to the house as a vehicle for competitive display, they also call it "home." The terms "house" and "home" point up the fundamental differentiation between the technological item and its emotional connotations.

The Crestwooder, like his contemporaries, builds or buys a house; but he "makes" a home. He sells a house, it burns down, or it is broken into; but a home is "broken up." Adjectives like "happy" and "harmonious" go with home. One hears of an unhappy home; but a house *is* empty, or bleak, or noisy, or gaudy. Yet there is a great deal of ambiguity in Crestwood Heights about the "hominess" of the house. On the one hand, it is a quality which is taken for granted by many Crestwooders. One woman, in an interview, said:

> I've never once thought about the house that way [an effect to be achieved]. I live here; I came here as a young married woman; I had my children here. They grew up and my husband and I have grown old here, so I just accept it.

On the other hand, this "old shoe" attitude towards the house is not universal; and, even when present, it often coexists with anxiety about the acceptability of the house and with concern for the preservation of its contents, relieved perhaps by rather bitter remarks about neighbors who are over-ostentatious, and whose house "can never be a home because they are afraid of marring the theatrical arrangements prescribed by the decorator." With perhaps a trifle too much protestation, some residents repeatedly pointed to the fact that, in contrast to many others, their house is a home. Said one informant:

> The whole neighborhood plays in this house. They are in and out all the time. We had a party here with girls. One boy said to my son, "Gee, you're lucky. My mother never allows me to take anyone home." One girl said to him, "Why, you live in a palace!" The boy said, "Yeah, I know; it's the best house I have ever been in, but I have to take my shoes off before I go into my bedroom."

Another Crestwood mother reported that she liked having the house full of people; but when a researcher visited her, she seemed nervous, and she fussed about the furniture. In a routine psychological test given at school, this woman's child replied negatively to the question, "Do you like to have parties at your home?" When it is a question of the house being used as a home, in the

## The Home in Crestwood Heights

sense that children, for example, might wish to use it, there is much evidence that parents are very protective of contents; and that they fear and resent boisterous behavior of their own or neighbors' children within the house. Yet the fiction is preserved that the home is one place where each member of the family may be himself, even though the house is designed by adults chiefly to suit their ambitions, comforts, and purposes. This is one point at which the focus on the child is blurred. The rumpus room and the children's rooms are, however, meticulously fitted to what decorators and the furniture trade consider the taste of a child.

Crestwooders make a definite distinction between behavior at home and the behavior appropriate to other forms of shelter, such as the club. While the club may afford the Crestwooder certain facilities and an atmosphere of privacy, which he may associate with the comforts of the ideal home, he still differentiates between the two. To him, the club and home not synonymous terms. And yet the hostess often finds the club more convenient than her own home as a place to entertain; perhaps because, as one woman revealed with some asperity, "if service is wrong or the food is off, you can blame the management of the club." The club, as this informant said, was not just more convenient; the anxious hostess felt more comfortable there than she did at home. The man in describing the joys of club life—"getting together with the boys," "putting your feet up"—seemed to be describing homey forms of relaxation.

The privacy which the house as home offers (or "should" offer) is highly prized by the Crestwooder. In a culture which, on the surface, has largely abandoned the Victorian concept of a carefully graded intimacy, free admittance to the home may still stand as one criterion of intimate friendship.[4] The home tends to become the only or primary means of guarding any inviolability of the private self. This self he may be forced increasingly to deny in the outside social, business, and professional contacts of his daily life, but the home can serve as psychological shelter for whatever fragment of it remains. The Crestwooder may not know of the abstract distinction, but his behavior with regard to admitting

---

4. There are certain situations of ungraded intimacy, for instance service club meetings, office parties, and community rallies, but these are rare and of a ceremonial nature. A man's work downtown, even though he may be guarded by a secretary, does expose him to jostling in elevators and the importunities of salesmen and colleagues.

people to his home tends to make important its function as the citadel of the private self.

The behavior around doors, which control access from the outside world to all the areas of the house, is strongly differentiated. The back, or side door, exists for service deliveries. Honored guests are introduced into the house through a formal front entrance. Only a very intimate friend, usually a close neighbor, would think of entering through the side door, perhaps unannounced. Since Crestwood Heights is part of a large city, outside doors are customarily locked, and even children must learn very early to ring or knock for entrance at the appropriate door. In the case of the child, this may well mean the back, or side door, since the living and dining areas with their expensive furnishings must be well guarded from muddy feet and dirty hands. The Crestwood householder, therefore, recognizes that there are infinite gradations among people, and his judgments of these are manifested in their free or controlled entrance to the home.

The same screening process goes on within the home. In the second floor area (the most closely guarded, where outsiders are concerned), the cleansing of the body and the renewing of life in sleep or sexual intercourse take place. Here the human body is carefully groomed and clothed for public view; here the vestments of public life are removed, so that the body can shape itself to the contours of private existence.

Many parents boast of the freedom of movement permitted and encouraged at this upper level. "We don't care what we wear up here." "Our children know what the human body looks like." This decrease in intrafamilial "modesty" increases, in one sense, the private nature of the sleeping, toileting area of the second floor, since freedom is limited as yet only to the family of procreation. Because of this new intimacy, the first-floor "powder room" becomes more necessary than ever. The child, too, must learn at an early age the bathroom behavior which is fitting for family members and for guests. The door that was usually left open or ajar is, in the presence of the guest, locked. Similarly, the spacious manner of allowing doors to remain open on the hall is altered. When strangers are about, they are shut, or almost shut—but not locked.[5]

---

5. These gradients of privacy are clearly recognized by all. The door of the bathroom, to which the visitor has right of access, is locked, even though the occupant may be

## The Home in Crestwood Heights

Doors within the home should be clearly distinguishable. The guest venturing aloft, in a house where there is no ground-floor powder room, will be escorted on his first trip, or carefully instructed "It's the first door on the right." The visitor may be spared the embarrassment of either walking into a bedroom or having to knock on the bathroom door. He should be able to go directly into the bathroom without pause. The bedroom doors are so hung that they can be left ajar, for the tightly closed door in the emancipated home should not be necessary, but at the same time they should screen the bed and dressing table from the casual glance. Similarly the kitchen, basement, and laundry doors should be so placed that the guest will not enter these more private areas unwittingly.

While the house is an expensive device to permit and enforce privacy, it is also true that the superior purchasing power of the Crestwood resident is used to secure more and more mechanical devices that constantly invade this privacy: radio, television, and the telephone are almost universal. The telephone, which the more affluent place beside beds, and even occasionally in the bathroom, allows the invasion at any hour by a casual caller of the private areas that are regularly denied the nearest of kin and the dearest of friends. The automobile, which continues to grow sturdily in size and cost, seems to be only slightly less successful in gaining access to the home. The older houses in Crestwood Heights kept their garages (like the old coach house) discreetly out of sight. In the newer houses, however, the garage has entered into the essential design and rationale. The immense slab which serves as a single door for the two-car garage dominates the smaller, less pretentions door used by the human beings. The space devoted to the car is often greater than that occupied by the living room.

The house not only serves as a means of separating the family from the outside world and even from its closest friends; it is also a device for separating members or the family from each other, thus preparing the child, and its parent, for ultimate separation when the child establishes his own home.

When interviewed about their houses, residents frequently give as their reason for moving to Crestwood Heights, the desire for

---

innocently washing his hands. The bedroom which the visitor has no right to enter is less tightly sealed, although the body is more likely to be naked and interpersonal intimacies are more likely to occur here than in the bathroom.

more space. "The children were growing up, and needed separate bedrooms"; or "they needed a basement recreation room as a place to entertain their friends." Increased income always offers the possibility of buying more space. Privacy for each member of the family is the ideal—but not the isolation of anonymous shelter as offered by a hotel. The essence of the desired privacy is its very presence within the family unit.

> One young matron, recently established in Crestwood, admitted quite frankly that, during the years she had lived in a small apartment, her dream had been to have a bedroom of her own, sacred to herself, which the children could not enter. After the long-contemplated move to Crestwood Heights, this woman with sincere delight planned the decoration of the master bedroom for her sole occupancy, stating that no one else, not even her husband, would use its bathroom.

The Crestwood home must, ideally, provide ample space for separate sleeping and working quarters for each member of the family. There should be a desk or its equivalent in a well-demarcated area for each member of the family "old enough." These areas may be rooms, or merely corners, shelves, or drawers within a larger room; and little pressure is put on the individual to keep this area tidy. When occupying "his" space, the individual should not be disturbed; when absent, his possessions are not to be rearranged. A place for the mother may be the entire kitchen with a still more private corner where she keeps household bills, personal correspondence, recipes, receipts, and money; the boy may have a lab, or a darkroom, and a place for skates, skis, and other gear; the father will have a spot to keep his tobacco, pipes, golf clubs, bridge set, and he may possibly also have a workshop; the girl, similarly, will screen cherished items—letters, photos, diary, cosmetics—from the eyes of other family members. The bedroom is often the repository of most of these items of personal property around which the individual builds his own satisfactions, and which help to differentiate him from the other members of the inner circle of his life—indeed he will often reveal them more freely to a peer in age and sex than to a member of his own family.[6] If he leaves home, he will take these possessions with him.

One Crestwood mother, contrasting the difference between the

---

6. Even the stranger has easier access to some aspects of this private area than another member of the family. For instance, the milkman may know where the household money is kept, and be better aware than the father how much is left in the "kitty" at the end of the month, precisely because the information means very little to him.

## The Home in Crestwood Heights

contemporary house and the house of her girlhood, which was of comparable size, said:

> When I was a girl, we all worked of an evening around the dining room table. We had a warm fire in the room and we all worked quietly or read in the same room. Now, we scatter throughout the house to follow our interests.

The hot stove and the oil lamp drew the family together; now, electric light and warmth, which are equally spread to all corners of the house, also disperse the members of the family. The description well underlines the difference between the activities of the Victorian family and the new individualistic pursuits of the family in Crestwood Heights, pursuits which the type of house encourages.

The material objects which fill the space bought at such a price illumine another important facet of the Crestwood house as home. The Crestwood house, in this context, is not the home celebrated even to recent times in folklore and song, the "home sweet home" which has a peasant meaning—a modest spot, fixed immovably in one locality through several generations, the only symbol of stability in a shifting, cruel world, an abode that is always "there" to "come back to." The dwelling-place does not have this traditional stability in Crestwood Heights, since the family takes for granted the fact that its members will live in a succession of houses. The Crestwooder, therefore, cannot cherish a single image of the home, fixed in time and rooted in space. Nevertheless it is important that the Crestwood resident have a current image of home, a spot to which he may return at the moment, and an object of which he may be proud. The home image may change in the course of time; and it is confidently expected that to those who fashion it this image will become increasingly satisfactory. In Crestwood Heights there is, for example, hardly a trace of looking back, of nostalgia for a "little grey home in the West"—but rather an anticipation of a bigger and better home for the future in some other environment altogether.

Yet the people of Crestwood Heights do not lack sentiment, and are far from nomadic. Although members of the family may belong to clubs, own a summer cottage in the North, patronize a ski lodge, or vacation in Florida during the winter, a relatively permanent deposit of material goods remains in that house which at any particular time they call "home." Indeed, the presence of these objects in a succession of houses is probably the most important factor in the Crestwood concept of the home. It is really the movables which create the air of homeliness, and which are psychologically immovable, rather than the physically rooted house, which is there to be moved into, grown into, moved out of and left behind—an outmoded shell to be reoccupied by another mobile family. The Crestwood house in this aspect impresses the observer again with the constant flux of paradox and compromise which characterizes life in the Heights. It serves as a vehicle for display in an atmosphere of uneasy aspiration; but, at the same time, it must also serve as a defense against the uncertainties created by rapid social change at this class level.

Different attitudes towards these material family possessions may be noted between ethnic groups, between old families and those with newly acquired wealth. The solid, well-established family, when it moves, will take its familiar relics with it; when a child marries, some of these objects are transferred by gift or loan to the new household. Others regard these treasures with bewilderment, and with a mixture of awe and disdain, as the following excerpt from an interview reveals:

> There is no new furniture in the house and not a single piece less than forty-five years old. Everything is slipcovered and very genteel. The fireplace is the focal point in the house. It is used! It is a real living room. They keep fresh flowers in it even when they should be buying food with the money. Appearances are awfully important to them. Pictures on the walls are photographs of the children—one of F.R. himself in palmier days—and a very costly miniature of Junior. There must be at least a dozen pictures of Junior downstairs. He is "prince elect." . . . The house is full of inherited stuff. One piece of furniture will be from an aunt, another from a cousin, and so on. A lot of the furniture is sleazy maple and the rugs are threadbare broadloom. The dining room suite is very old; it was a gift and it's stunning. They eat every day with very old sterling; and they put their napkins in a ring. She bakes her own bread and does her own laundry—even his shirts—with an old electric washing machine and an ordinary electric iron. She has no new labor-saving gadgets. All their electric equipment is old. The furniture has an air of decadent gentility. They even say to us "We're not rich like you! Our place is old. Everything is old, but we rather like it." The colors are faded grays. They had a couple of pictures—old paintings—but they belonged to someone else and the person who owned them borrowed them back.

This same informant also had comments to make on a home where

## The Home in Crestwood Heights

these values did not obtain: "Every time they move, she has to have a new outfit: furniture, drapes, broadloom, and pictures." For such people, taste or selection of an interior decorator becomes all-important in the creation of a home. "They always have a beautiful place, but for them, *getting* the furnishings rather than maintaining and embellishing them, is the home-making adventure."

Thus, while each Crestwooder has different notions as to what collection of material objects constitutes a home, all are agreed that a home is necessary in their scheme of values: the indispensable screen for the functioning of the private selves which in interaction constitute the family unit. As home, the house must satisfy the personal emotional needs of parents and children, needs which are intensified by the varied, and sometimes conflicting, roles of family members.

To the father, the house as home may mean, not the material and visible sign of his success as breadwinner, but the one place he may be himself, relieved of pressing responsibilities, free of competition, sure of warmth and companionship. For the mother, the house as home tends to represent her major task, "the creation, for husband and children, of an environment in which security and understanding are paramount"—an effort, in turn, complicated by the obligation to oversee the complex mechanism for which she is frequently wholly responsible.

For the young child, the home acts, as it does for the woman, as the center and hub of this universe. This attitude gradually changes until the child, in his teens, may regard the home merely as a place to eat and to recuperate from a continuous round of activities outside its orbit; indeed, he may behave towards the parental home as if it were a well-run club, depending on its facilities to entertain his friends at no cost in money or in effort to himself.[7] The attitude changes again when the young adult prepares for marriage. The value of a home then again becomes paramount, since the individual's readiness to finance one of his own is the symbol that he is accepted as a full and functioning adult in his culture.

The house, then, as a focus for family life, becomes a most

---

7. The lack of "responsibility" in and towards the home on the part of the teen-ager is a common topic for discussion among Crestwood parents.

cherished possession. Male and female, at a certain stage of physical maturity, must acquire a house and in this process of proclaiming their social maturity, must further transform the house into a home. Within its walls, the wife plays her role as best she can, alternately maternal, seductive, efficient, but always sustaining husband and children. The house as home symbolizes the lifelong social and biological union between a Crestwood man and woman, which must be maintained through and beyond the period of child-bearing and rearing. This requires sexual compatibility and a broad emotional adjustment—which are often mutually dependent; these, in large part, make possible and are made possible by the home, now no longer merely a house.

The attainment of these favorable conditions is made difficult both by the wife's interest in maintaining and exercising extra-familial interests (or even her former vocational skills) and in preserving her physical attractiveness, and by the high cost of child-rearing in Crestwood Heights. Even with a moderately high income, the Crestwooder is severely taxed to keep up a four-bedroom house and, at the same time, clothe, feed, and rear several children in an "appropriate" way. Yet a smaller house, if it is felt to be "overcrowded," cannot provide the space which is an essential aspect of the ideal home.[8] Should the tension for the family become too great, the only alternative might be to leave Crestwood Heights.

To meet the demands made on the home, the house is deliberately designed to be flexible. Even though certain members of the family may frequently be absent, and all are seldom in the house at the same time, the house must provide maximum service on demand. Indeed, as the children grow and leave home, the parents often maintain this large plant throughout the year, so that all the children may, if they choose, come home with their families on festive occasions. Although the husband may keep up club membership purely for the sake of entertaining, his house must, nevertheless, be designed and equipped to offer comparable hospitality.

To the Crestwooder, the term "home" conveys a special meaning. He does not expect his home to remain constant in time and space, but he does assume that, in whatever house he may occupy,

---

8. A casual survey of the "better homes" type of magazine will reveal that more than one or two children are seldom shown in the advertisements or in the illustrated stories.

*The Home in Crestwood Heights*

he will be surrounded by his primary group and at least a minimum of familiar objects. In these expectations he does not differ too greatly from the Australian aborigine who, on his return from a field trip with an American anthropologist, touched a stone on the edge of the desert, saying, with great emotion, "This—home."

THE HOUSE AS NURSERY

The Crestwood house and alternative forms of shelter have not been examined for a routine catalogue of items in a material culture. Our catalogue is not sufficiently detailed or exact; and moreover, such an undertaking hardly falls within the scope of this inquiry. Our concern, primarily, has been with the effect of this complex of artifacts upon the person, most especially the child; what are the ways in which this apparatus helps to define for him his world, his place in that world—in short, his self?

With growing consciousness of himself and his world, the child learns to recognize the house as his own. Unlike his parents, many of whom have known humbler surroundings, this place is *his* locale. He looks out on this locale and on other people from his playpen and later from his picture window, or from the windows of the family's late-model car. Not only does the child first take for granted, and then accept the objects he sees, just as he does his mother, but they remain even more constantly within his vision, for his mother's community life does go on concurrently with child-rearing. He must learn to respect, to use, and, finally, to want such things enough to become the ambitious person idealized in the culture.

The Crestwood child, born into a world of fine houses and expensive gadgets, must learn, almost before he walks and talks, that some of the objects surrounding him are precious almost beyond telling. From word, facial expression, and gesture, he finally learns not to touch the fragile stemware, should it come within his reach; just as the farm child learns, when beginning to walk, not to fall against the kitchen range; or as the Manus child who lives in a pile-supported hut on a lagoon avoids drowning by learning to swim, with adult help and insistence, as soon as he learns to walk. Parental solicitude about things continues into the child's adolescence, culminating when he wishes to drive the automobile and to secure his own place of abode. In both cases, the parents express anxiety about the child's ability to use and to manage these things.

Within the house, the child must learn the difference between utility and display, and the methods appropriate to each. The protective preoccupation of the adults with the broadloom (and with the equally svelte, almost equally sacred, lawn outside) helps him to differentiate between a useful floor covering, a pleasant tactile sensation, and a valuable item of property which could be ruined by unsteady bladder control in child or dog, if either were allowed upon this surface. Some Crestwood children are given unlimited access to the house, but many others are not. For them the spaciousness of the Crestwood house is somewhat illusory. In a similar way, the child learns that a fountain pen is something to write with, but that it is also an object precious beyond its function. Losing it, or breaking it, is "wrong." All this is doubly puzzling, because there are other things, cigarettes, for instance, which are bought simply to be destroyed. The display attributes of any item in the house are not at first appreciated by the child. To him, they "are," that is all. But the child does learn, very early, to follow his parents' lead, and a corresponding pattern of concern, pride, and display is built up around clothing and toys. Non-familial newness, shininess, and smells merely put a special edge on appreciation.

By its very nature, the Crestwood house with its separate areas for work and leisure is markedly different from the large, inclusive farm kitchen, for example; from the one-room dwelling in the slums; or from the crowded five-room bungalow of the lower middle classes; and it is by means of these differences that the impact of the type of house upon the structure of the family and the formation of personality must be assessed. The Crestwood child is never integrated into a kinship group to anything like the degree that children in these other environments are identified with their kinship groups. The Crestwood child sleeps alone; usually he has his own room. He may be left in the charge of various functionaries and experts for lengthy periods or, more casually, with "baby-sitters" for shorter periods. His mother is still his mother, but he shares her with the community and with his father's professional, business, and social activities.[9] He goes to

---

9. See Lewis 1946.

camp and has experiences in which his family need not be included and from which they can be excluded. The personality norm held up in gradually increased detail before the Crestwood child is that of the individuated person who can and wants to separate himself from his kinship group and establish a new family unit. The child is prepared for this process of psychic separation in part by the very nature of the house in which he lives.

The Crestwood house, where the child is concerned, may be responsible in great part for his later feeling of near-omnipotence as an adult, for his expectation that he should be able (or is able) to control and to plan his destiny in virtually every detail. Shelter, it has already been noted, is considerably above the subsistence level in Crestwood Heights. Life is sufficiently complex, sufficiently well engineered, that the periodic arrival of a truck to pump fuel oil into the basement furnace-tank is almost as automatic a phenomenon as the flow of water always available at the faucet, or of energy at the flick of an electric switch. The child may be well aware of hot and cold weather, but the vagaries of weather are not likely to do more than spoil his plans to play outside (just as rain might merely frustrate his father's intention to have a round of golf).

The weather, then, does not threaten the family livelihood in Crestwood Heights as it does that of the farmer; nor does it involve bodily survival, as it may in the case of the fisherman. The thermostat of the Crestwood house maintains an even temperature within the house, and the child is protected from the elements when he is outside by raincoat, snowsuit, station-wagon coat, and the like—which are provided for him without effort on his part. The Crestwood child never experiences physical peril from the elements in the sense that the child of the prairie farm feels it when exposed to the terror of being lost with his family in a January blizzard. He must, it is true, learn the hazards of automobile traffic, but these are gadget-derived threats, and hence, to him, ultimately controllable. To this child, nature is seldom either beneficent or threatening. His milk comes out of a bottle; his fruit out of a basket. "Roughing it" is never a way of life for him, but a course offered at a summer camp with the implicit guarantee, in the parents' absence, not only of safety, but of benefit to character as well.

Crestwood Heights is only a few hours' drive from the frontier, and the ancestors of many of the residents knew actual physical peril in pioneer days. Consequently there is an often verbalized feeling of guilt that life is now too soft, and that everything is "too easy" for the children. Yet the Crestwood house represents a major preoccupation with protection of both children and adults, with shelter as lavish as family income will permit. It is an apparatus, which, when capably manipulated, secures the occupants against all the principal vagaries of existence—except only those stemming from the behavior of men themselves.

# An Anatomy of Suburbia

HERBERT J. GANS

This article is about a much maligned part of America, suburbia, and reports on a study conducted by an equally maligned method, sociology.

Postwar suburban developments have been blamed for many of the country's alleged and real ills, from destroying its farmland to emasculating its husbands. Sociology is accused of jargony or statistical elaboration of the obvious and of reporting unpopular truths; of usurping the novelist's function and being too impersonal; and most often, of making studies which uphold the conventional wisdom.

My study is not a defense of suburbia, but a study of a single new suburb, Levittown, New Jersey, in which I lived as a "participant-observer" for the first two years of its existence to find out how a new community comes into being, how people change when they leave the city, and how they live and politic in suburbia. (The politics side is omitted from this article.) Nor is it a defense of sociology, but an application of my own conception of it and its methods. The essence of sociology, it seems to me, is that it observes what people really do and say. It looks at the world from their perspective, unlike much literary writing, which often boils

---

Reprinted from New Society 6 (September 28, 1967), pp. 423-431. "An Anatomy of Suburbia" is an edited version of part of Herbert J. Gans, The Levittowners (New York: Pantheon Books, 1967). The article is reprinted with the permission of New Society, Pantheon Books, and the author.

down to cataloguing their shortcomings from the author's perspective. Sociology is a democratic method of inquiry; it assumes that people have some right to be what they are.

Levittown, New Jersey, was built by Levitt and Sons, the largest building firm in the eastern United States. There were two previous Levittowns, in Long Island and in Pennsylvania, and they are the prototype of American postwar suburbia.

Many of my findings on Levittown's impact on its residents are based on interviews with two sets of Levittowners, one a nearly random sample of forty-five buyers in Somerset Park, the first neighborhood to be settled, and the second, of fifty-five others in that neighborhood who had moved there from Philadelphia, here called the Philadelphia or city sample. The two samples were interviewed during 1960 and 1961, after they had lived in Levittown two to three years, and this determines the period on which the cross-sectional analysis is reporting. (The random sample was also interviewed just after its arrival in Levittown, thus providing data on the immediate impact of the move as well.)

Perhaps the most frequent indictment of suburban life had been leveled against the quality of social relationships. The critics charge that the suburbs are socially hyperactive and have made people so outgoing that they have little time or inclination for the development of personal autonomy. The pervasive homogeneity of the population has depressed the vitality of social life, and the absence of more heterogeneous neighbors and friends has imposed a conformity which further reduces the suburbanite's individuality. Indeed, studies showing the importance of physical propinquity in the choice of friends have been interpreted to suggest that physical layout, rather than people, determines the choice of friends. Because many suburbanites are transient or mobile, they have been accused of wanting social companions only for the duration of their stay, disabling them for more intimate friendship.

Evidence from Levittown suggests quite the opposite. People report an accelerated social life, and in fact looked forward to it before moving to Levittown. The major reason for the upswing is indeed homogeneity, but an equally appropriate term might be "compatibility." Propinquity may initiate social contact but it does not determine friendship. Many relationships are indeed transient, but this is no reflection on their intensity. Finally, conformity prevails, although less as malicious or passive copying than

## An Anatomy of Suburbia

as sharing of useful ideas. In short, many of the phenomena identified by the critics occur in Levittown but their alleged consequences do not follow. Levittowners have not become outgoing, mindless conformers; they remain individuals, fulfilling the social aspirations with which they came. To be sure, social life in Levittown has its costs, but these seem minor compared to its rewards.

About half the Levittowners interviewed said that they visited neighbors more than in their former residence; about a quarter said less, and the remaining quarter reported no change. The greatest increase was reported by the people who said they had wanted to do more visiting, particularly those who had had little opportunity for it in their previous residence. As one Philadelphian said, "We used to be with the in-laws and with my mother; we didn't bother with the neighbors before."

In addition to the desire to do more neighboring, the increase resulted initially from the newness of the community and the lack of shopping facilities and other places for daytime activities. But these reasons were mentioned far less often than the "friendliness" of the neighbors, and this in turn was a function of population homogeneity. One Levittowner, describing her next-door neighbor, said, "We see eye to eye on things, about raising kids, doing things together with your husband, living the same way; we have practically the same identical background."

Of course, some friendliness was built into the neighbor relationship, for people needed each other for mutual aid. In a community far from the city, women are cut off from relatives and old friends—as well as from commuting husbands—so that readiness to provide mutual aid is the first criterion of being a good neighbor. This includes not only helping out in emergencies, but ameliorating periodic loneliness by being available for occasional coffee-klatsching and offering informal therapy by being willing to listen to another's troubles when necessary.

The mutual observation that makes the block a goldfish bowl goes on mainly among adjacent neighbors, for with houses only ten feet apart, they see each other frequently and have to maintain friendly relations if that is at all possible. More distant neighbors could be ignored, however.

Even propinquity did not require visiting. Although a number of studies have shown that social relationships are influenced and even determined by the site plan, this was not the case in

Levittown. Since Levittown was laid out with curved blocks, houses facing each other across front and back, there were relatively few neighbors with whom one had constant and involuntary visual contact. Sometimes, even relationships with directly adjacent neighbors could be restricted to an exchange of hellos. For example, it took more than a year for me to meet the occupants of a house diagonally across the street from mine, even though we had been saying hello since the first weeks of occupancy Another person told me he had never even met his next-door neighbor.

Neighbor relations among adults were affected by the children, for children are neighbors too, and their mingling was determined almost entirely by age and propinquity. The relatively traffic-free streets and the large supply of young children enabled mothers to limit their supervision of the children's outdoor play; and the overall compatibility, to give youngsters a free choice of playmates. But children were likely to quarrel and when this led to fights and childish violence their quarrels involved the parents. Half the random sample had heard of quarrels among neighbors on their block, and eighty-one percent of these were over the children.

One type of adult quarrel involved physical disciplining of children by neighbors. Some people believe that only parents should spank their children; others, that neighbors have the right to do so if the child misbehaves out of sight of the parents. When a neighbor punishes another's child, he not only takes on a quasi-parental role but, by implication, accuses the parents of not raising and watching their children properly. In one such case, where a neighbor punished a little boy for sexual exhibitionism, the parents never spoke to him again.

Basically, differences over discipline reflect class differences in child-rearing. Middle-class parents tend to be somewhat more permissive than working-class ones, and when two children play together, the middle-class child may be allowed to act in ways not permitted to the working-class one. Also, working-class parents administer physical punishment more freely, since this is not interpreted as a withdrawal of affection, whereas middle-class families reserve spankings for extreme misbehavior. Then, as children get older, practices change. The working-class child is given more freedom, and by comparison, the middle-class child is given much less. He is expected to do his homework while his working-class peers may be playing on the streets. Middle-class people who observe this freedom, as well as the working-class parents' tolerance of childish profanity, interpret it as neglect. In some cases, middle-class families even prohibit their children from playing with working-class children.

The importance of compatibility is extended also to relationships that do not involve children, and is underscored by the problems encountered by neighbors who differ significantly. One potential trouble spot was age. Class differences also expressed themselves in areas other than child-rearing. Ethnic differences were also a barrier between neighbors. Groups without a strong subcommunity were isolated, notably a handful of Japanese, Chinese and Greek families.

A final barrier was sexual, and this affected the women whose husbands worked irregular schedules and might be home during the day. A woman neighbor did not visit another when her husband was home, partly because of the belief that a husband has first call on his wife's companionship, partly to prevent suspicion that her visit might be interpreted as a sexual interest in the husband. This practice is strongest among working-class women, reflecting the traditional class norm that people of the opposite sex come together only for sexual reasons, and becomes weaker at higher class levels; in the upper middle class there are enough shared interests between men and women to discourage suspicion.

There is no question that Levittown is quite homogeneous in age and income as compared to established cities and small towns, but such comparisons are in many ways irrelevant. People do not live in the political units we call "cities" or "small towns"; often their social life takes place in areas even smaller than a census tract. Many such areas in the city are about as homogeneous in class as Levittown, and slum and high-income areas, whether urban or suburban, are even more so. Small towns are notoriously rigid in their separation of rich and poor, and only appear to be more heterogeneous because individual neighborhoods are so small.

All these considerations effectively question the belief that before the advent of modern suburbs Americans of all classes lived together. Admittedly, statistics compiled for cities and suburbs as a whole show that residential segregation by class and by race is on the increase, but these trends also reflect the breakdown of rigid class and caste systems in which low-status people "knew their place," and which made residential segregation unnecessary.

Even class homogeneity is not as great as community-wide statistics would indicate. Of three families earning $7,000 a year, one might be a skilled worker at the peak of his earning power and dependent on union activity for further raises; another, a white-collar worker with some hope for a higher income; and the third, a young executive or professional at the start of his career. Their occupational and educational differences express themselves in many variations in life-style, and if they are neighbors, each is likely to look elsewhere for companionship.

Most Levittowners were pleased with the diversity they found among their neighbors, primarily because regional, ethnic, and religious differences are today almost innocuous and provide variety to spice the flow of conversation and the exchange of ideas. For example, a Southern neighbor of mine discovered pizza at the home of an Italian-American neighbor and developed a passion for it, and I learned much about the personal rewards of Catholicism from Catholic convert neighbors. At the same time, however, Levittowners wanted homogeneity of age and income—or rather, they wanted neighbors and friends with common interests and sufficient consensus of values to make for informal and uninhibited relations. Their reasons were motivated neither by anti-democratic feelings nor by an interest in conformity. Children need playmates of the same age, and because child-rearing problems vary with age, mothers like to be near women who have children of similar age. And because these problems also fluctuate with class, they want some similarity of that factor—not homogeneity of occupation and education so much as agreement on the ends and means of caring for child, husband, and home.

Income similarity is valued by the less affluent, not as an end in itself, but because people who must watch every penny cannot long be comfortable with more affluent neighbors, particularly when children come home demanding toys or clothes they have seen next door.

The alleged costs of homogeneity were more unreal than the critics claim. It is probably true that Levittowners had less contact with old people than some suburbanites (now rather rare) who still live in three-generation households. It is doubtful, however, that they had less contact with the older generation than urban and suburban residents of similar age and class, with the exception of the occupational transients, who are far from home and may

## An Anatomy of Suburbia

return only once a year. Whether or not this lack of contact with grandparents affects children negatively can only be discovered by systematic studies among them. My observations of children's relations with grandparents suggest that the older generation is strange to them and vice versa, less as a result of lack of contact than of the vastness of generational change.

This is also more or less true of adult relationships with the older generation. Social change in America has been so rapid that the ideas and experiences of the elderly are often anachronistic, especially so for young mobile Levittowners whose parents are first- or second-generation Americans. Philadelphia women who lived with their parents before they moved to Levittown complained at length about the difficulties of raising children and running a household under those conditions, even though some missed their mothers sorely after moving to Levittown. A few found surrogate mothers among friends or neighbors, but chose women only slightly older than themselves and rarely consulted elderly neighbors. As for the husbands, they were, to a man, glad that they had moved away from parents and in-laws.

That suburban homogeneity deprives children of contact with pluralism and "reality" is also dubious. Critics assume that urban children experience heterogeneity, but middle-class parents—and working-class ones, too—try hard to shield them from contact with conditions and people of lower status. Upper-middle-class children may be taken on tours of the city, but to museums and shopping districts rather than to slums. Indeed, slum children, who are freer of parental supervision, probably see more of urban diversity than anyone else, although they do not often get into middle-class areas.

The homogeneity of Levittown is not so pervasive that children are shielded from such unpleasant realities as alcoholism, mental illness, family strife, sexual aberration, or juvenile delinquency. which exist everywhere. The one element missing on most Levittown blocks—though, of course, in many city neighborhoods too—is the presence of Negro families.

The suburban critique is especially strident on the prevalence of conformity. It argues that relationships between neighbors and friends are regulated by the desire to copy each other to achieve uniformity. At the same time, the critics also see suburbanites as competitive, trying to keep up or down with the Joneses to satisfy the desire for status. Conforming (or copying) and competing are not the same—indeed, they are contradictory—but they are lumped together in the critique because they are based on the common assumption that, in the suburbs, behavior and opinion are determined by what the neighbors do and think, and individualism is found only in the city. Both competition and copying exist in Levittown, but not for the reasons suggested by the critics. They are ways of coping with heterogeneity and of retaining individuality while being part of the group.

Enough of the suburban critique has seeped into the reading matter of Levittowners to make "conformity" a pejorative term, and interview questions about it would have produced only denials. Competition is talked about in Levittown, however, and sixty percent of the random sample reported competition among their neighbors. The examples they gave, however, not only included copying, but half the respondents described it positively. "I don't know what competition is," said one man. "Perhaps when we see the neighbors repairing the house, and we figure our own repairs would be a good idea."

The observer's perspective is shaped principally by his relative class position, or by his estimate of his position. If the observer is of higher status than the observed, he will interpret the latter's attempt to share higher-status ideas as competing and his sharing of lower-status ways as copying. If the observer is of lower status than the observed, his ideas will not be shared, of course, but he will consider the more affluent life-style of the higher-status neighbor as motivated by status-striving or "keeping up with the Joneses."

Instances of overt status-striving, carried out to show up the lower status of neighbors, are rare. "Keeping up" takes place, but mainly out of the need to maintain self-respect, to "put the best face forward" or not to be considered inferior and "fall behind." Indeed, the social control norms of block life encourage "keeping down with the Joneses," and criticize display of unusual affluence, so that people who can afford a higher standard of living than the rest and who show it publicly are unpopular and are sometimes ostracized.

Conforming and copying occur more frequently than competition, mostly to secure the proper appearance of the block to impress strangers. A pervasive system of social control develops to enforce standards of appearance on the block, mainly concerning

# An Anatomy of Suburbia

lawn care. The primary technique for social control is humor. Wisecracks are made to show up deviant behavior, and overt criticism surfaces only when the message behind the wisecracks does not get across. Humor is used to keep relations friendly and because people feel that demands for conformity are not entirely proper; they realize that such demands sometimes require a difficult compromise between individual and group standards. When it comes to lawn care, however, most people either have no hard-and-fast personal standards, or they value friendly relations more. Since the block norms and the compromises they require are usually worked out soon after the block is occupied—when everyone is striving to prove he will be a good neighbor—they are taken for granted by the time the block has settled down.

What accounts for the critics' preoccupation with suburban conformity, and their tendency to see status competition as a dominant theme in suburban life? For one thing, many of these critics live in city apartments, where the concern for block status preservation is minimal. Also, they are largely upper-middle-class professionals, dedicated to cosmopolitan values and urban life and disdainful of the local and anti-urban values of lower-middle-class and working-class people.

The new suburbs, being more visible than other lower-middle- and working-class residential areas, have become newsworthy, and during the 1950s they replaced "mass culture" as the scapegoat and most convenient target for the fear and distaste that upper-middle-class people feel for the rest of the American population. Affluent suburbs became false targets of dissatisfaction with the upper middle class's own status-consciousness and competition. The rat race it experiences in career and social striving is projected on life beyond the city limits.

Part of the fear of mass society theorists and suburban critics alike is the transience of the new suburban communities and the feelings of rootlessness that allegedly result. About twenty percent of Levittown's first purchasers were transients, who knew even when they came that their employers—national corporations or the armed services—would require them to move elsewhere some years hence. Their impermanency is reflected in residential turnover figures which showed that in 1964, ten percent of the houses were resold and another five percent rented, and that annual turnover was likely to reach twenty percent in the future. Not all houses change hands that often, of course; a small proportion are sold and rented over and over again.

Whether or not the fifteen percent turnover figure is "normal" is difficult to say. National estimates of mobility suggest that twenty percent of the population moves annually, but this figure includes renters. Levittown's rate is probably high in comparison to older communities of homeowners, fairly typical of newer ones, and low in comparison to apartment areas. Conventional standards of "normal" turnover are so old, and communities like Levittown still so new on the American scene, that it is impossible to determine a normal turnover rate. Indeed, the need to judge turnover stems from the assumption that it is undesirable.

Despite the belief that transients do not participate in community life, in Levittown they belonged to community organizations in considerably larger numbers than "settlers" did, partly because of their higher status.

One way in which transients maintain the feeling of rootedness is to preserve the term "home" for the place in which they grew up. When Levittowners talk of "going home," they mean trips to visit parents. People whose parents have left the community in which they grew up may, however, feel homeless. I remember a discussion with a Levittowner who explained that he was going "home to Ohio" to visit his mother, and his wife said somewhat sadly, "My parents no longer live where I grew up, and I never lived with them where they live now. So I have only Sudberry Street in Levittown; I have no other home."

Frequent moving usually hurts other family members more than the breadwinner. For wives and adolescents transience is essentially an involuntary move, which, like the forced relocation of slum dwellers under urban renewal, may result in depression and other deleterious effects. Studies among children of army personnel, who move more often than corporation transients, have found that geographical mobility per se did not result in emotional disturbance, except among children whose fathers had risen from working-class origins to become officers. These findings would suggest that transience has its most serious effects on people with identity problems.

When the Levittowners were asked whether they considered their community dull, just twenty percent of the random sample said yes, and of Philadelphians (who might have been expected to

## An Anatomy of Suburbia

find it dull after living in a big city), only fourteen percent. Many respondents were surprised at the very question, for they thought there was a great deal to do in the community, and all that was needed was a desire to participate. "It's up to you," was a common reaction. "If a person is not the friendly type or does not become active, it's their own fault." "I don't think it's dull here," explained another, "there are so many organizations to join." The only people who thought Levittown was indeed dull were the socially isolated, and upper-middle-class people who had tasted the town's organizational life and found it wanting.

Lower-middle-class life does not take place either on the street or in meetings and parties; it is home-centered and private. But when all is said and done, something is different: less exuberance than is found in the working class, a more provincial outlook than in the upper middle class, and a somewhat greater concern with respectability than in either. In part, this is a function of religious background: being largely Protestant, the lower middle class is still affected by the puritan ethos.

If "blandness" is the word for this quality, it stems from the transition in which the lower middle class finds itself between the familial life of the working class and the cosmopolitanism of the upper middle class. If left to themselves, lower-middle-class people do what they have always done: put their energies into home and family, seeking to make life as comfortable as possible, and supporting, broadening, and varying it with friends, neighbors, church, and a voluntary association. This world view (if one can endow it with so philosophical a name) is best seen in the pictures that amateur painters exhibited at Parent-Teacher Association meetings in Levittown: bright, cheerful landscapes, or portraits of children and pets painted in primary colors, reflecting the wish that the world be hopeful, humorous, and above all, simple. Most important, their paintings insisted that life can be happy.

Of course, life is not really like this, for almost everyone must live with some disappointment: an unruly child, a poor student, an unsatisfied husband, a bored wife, a bad job, a chronic illness, or financial worry. These realities are accepted because they cannot be avoided; it is the norms of the larger society which frustrate. Partly desired and partly rejected, they produce an ambivalence which appears to the outsider as the blandness of lower-middle-class life.

This ambivalence can be illustrated by the way Levittown

women reacted to my wife's paintings. Since her studio was at home, they had an opportunity to see her work and talk to her about being a painter. They did not like her abstract expressionist style, but they knew it was "art" and so could not ignore it. They responded with anxiety, some hostility, and particularly with envy of her ability to be "creative." But even this response was overlaid with ambivalence. As teen-agers they had learned that creativity was desirable, and many had had some cursory training in drawing, piano, or needlework. Once they had learned to be wives and mothers and had enough sociability, the urge for creativity returned—but not the opportunity.

The adult conception of Levittown's vitality is not shared by its adolescents. Essays which schoolchildren wrote for me early in 1961 suggest that most children are satisfied with Levittown until adolescence. Sixty-eight percent of the sixth graders liked Levittown, but only forty-five percent of the eighth graders, thirty-seven percent of the tenth graders, and thirty-nine percent of the twelfth graders did. In comparison, eighty-five percent of the adults responded positively to a similar question. Dislikes revolve around "nothing to do."

But the commonest gripe is the shortage of ready transportation, which makes not only facilities, but (more important) other teen-agers, inaccessible. A car, then, becomes in a way as essential to teen-agers as to adults. Moreover, many small-town teen-agers like to meet outside the community, for it is easier to "have fun" where one's parents and other known adults cannot disapprove. The adults have provided some facilities for teen-age activities, but not always successfully. One problem is that "teen-age" is an adult tag; adolescents grade themselves by age. Older ones refused to attend dances with the younger set, considering forced association with their juniors insulting.

Specifically, adolescent malcontent stems from two sources: Levittown was not designed for them, and adults are reluctant to provide the recreational facilities and gathering places they want. Like most suburban communities, Levittown was planned for families with young children. The bedrooms are too small to permit an adolescent to do anything but study or sleep; they lack the privacy and soundproofing to allow him to invite his friends over. Unfortunately, the community is equally inhospitable. Shopping centers are intended for car-owning adults, and in accord with the

## An Anatomy of Suburbia

desire of property owners, are kept away from residential areas.

Being new, Levittown lacks low-rent shopping areas which can afford to subsist on the marginal purchases made by adolescents. In 1961, a few luncheonettes in neighborhood shopping centers and a candy store and a bowling alley in the big center were the only places for adolescents to congregate. Coming in droves, they overwhelmed those places and upset the merchants. Not only do teen-agers occupy space without making significant purchases, but they also discourage adult customers. Merchants faced with high rent cannot subsist on teen-age spending and complain to the police if teen-agers "hang out" at their places.

The schools were not designed for after-hour use, except for adults and for student activities which entertain adults, such as varsity athletics. The auditoriums were made available for dances, although when these began, the school administration promptly complained about scuffed floors and damaged fixtures. Only at the swimming pool are teen-agers not in the way of adult priorities, and during the day, when adults are not using it, it is their major gathering place. But even here, smoking and noisy activities are prohibited.

The suburban critique considers life beyond the city limits harmful both to family life and to the happiness and mental health of the individual. The findings from Levittown suggest just the opposite—that suburban life has produced more family cohesion and a significant boost in morale through the reduction of boredom and loneliness. Some problems remain, and since this study is not intended as a eulogy for suburban living, I will emphasize them. Even so, most Levittowners have adapted positively to their new community.

Since people move to the suburbs as families, it is difficult to separate individual from family adaptation, and maladaptation often affects people in their family roles. Obviously, many Levittowners came partly to facilitate family life: to have more space in the house and a yard so that young children could play without supervision, while parents spent more time with other children and adults. Forty percent of the wives and sixty-five percent of the husbands wanted to spend more time with their children in Levittown, and interestingly enough, all of the former city dwellers, as compared to half of the previous suburbanites and none of the small-towners, expressed this wish. Evidently, life in the suburbs deprives parents of time with their children less than that in the city. Because of the charge that suburbia encourages matriarchy, I was curious whether wives wanted their husbands to spend more time with the children; forty-five percent did, but almost the same number wished to be with their children more themselves. Again, former urban wives felt this need more often.

Levittown made it possible for these particular parents to achieve their wishes, for eighty-five percent of the wives and seventy-one percent of the husbands wanting more time with the children now had it. For the sample as a whole, about forty percent were with the children more frequently, but the remaining sixty percent reported no change. And all of the wives who wanted their husbands to devote themselves more to the children got what they wished. The new house was the cause, for the children and adults were around the house more, and they often worked together on the yard.

Moving to Levittown did not cut into the time available for family activities, for the journey to work, often alleged to have this effect, did not change significantly. But Levittowners did not share the critics' and the planners' distaste for commuting. Most said they like or do not mind a trip up to forty minutes; only a longer one garnered a significant number of dislikes. One-third of the Philadelphians said their commute was "wearing," and what made it so was not trip length but mode of travel, two-thirds of those taking the bus, thirty-seven percent of those driving and only twenty percent of car pool members reporting weariness after their journey. Indeed, for some people, the drive to and from work is one of the few moments of total privacy and may thus be a relaxing transition between the social demands of the job and the family.

Conversely, the car pool is a social experience, and in a community like Levittown, it becomes a substitute-on-wheels for all-male social clubs and neighborhood taverns. Even car pool trips of more than forty minutes were not found wearing. Indeed, women seem to be more affected by their husbands' journey to work than the men themselves, partly because the men cannot be with the children during the preparation of dinner and perhaps because the men take the strain of a long trip out on their wives.

Although suburbia is often described as a hotbed of adultery in popular fiction, this is an urban fantasy. Levittown is quite monogamous, and I am convinced that most suburbs are more so

## An Anatomy of Suburbia

than most cities. The desire for sexual relations with attractive neighbors may be ever-present, but when life is lived in a goldfish bowl, adultery is impossible to hide from the neighbors—even if there were motels in Levittown and baby-sitters could be found for both parties. Occasionally such episodes do take place, after which the people involved often run off together or leave the community.

There are also periodic stories of more bizarre sexual escapades, usually about community leaders. In one such story, a local politician was driving down the dark roads of the township in a sports car with a naked young woman while his wife thought he was at a political meeting. If there was any roadside adultery, however, it remained unreported, for no cases ever appeared on the police blotters during the two years I saw them.

The literature of suburban criticism abounds with references to suburban malaise and anomie, but it would be more correct to speak of suburban happiness, for most Levittowners experienced less depression, boredom and loneliness after the move. Even so, a minority, sometimes up to a third, report the opposite, particularly among the Philadelphians. Occasionally these feelings stem from being isolated in the community, but usually they reflect the more general problems of working- and lower-middle-class women in contemporary society. If there is malaise in Levittown, it is female but not suburban.

Thirty-six percent of the random sample spoke of improved morale after coming to Levittown and all but six percent of the remainder reported no change. Among the Philadelphians, however, only twenty-two percent reported a better disposition, and thirty-one percent a poorer one (among the women, the percentages were nineteen and thirty-eight)—one of the few instances in which change was more negative than positive. High- and low-status urbanites and people under 25 were unhappier now, and only those over 45 raised their morale significantly. In both samples, the improvement in morale could be traced mainly to the new house and yard, and the greater ease in rearing children, producing a feeling most often described as "relaxation." A Philadelphian said, "In the city, I'd have all that tension being out with my son. Here I can let him go, and if I want to do something I can putter in the garden. It is so quiet and serene here, it just makes you relax."

The people with poorer dispositions fall into four types. Young women who have become mothers in Levittown, particularly those who worked before, find it difficult to be full-time housekeepers and to cope with the children, and this is compounded by the feeling of being "stuck." Without a car or compatible neighbors, there is no respite or escape.

A second group, primarily working-class women, miss family and friends in the city and find it difficult to cut their ties to them. Among the random sample, more neighbor and couple visiting results in better morale, but among unhappy Philadelphians it does not help, even for women who have found a close friend in Levittown.

Third, some Jewish women, either more or less educated than the majority or with non-Jewish husbands, were now more unhappy. One, a working-class woman married to a Catholic, said, "Here you meet people only through organizations, churches, and clubs, but we are not organizational types and I don't care for organizational life." A better-educated one had the opposite problem: "I'd feel better if I could make friends with people, if the women here were more sincere. A lot of them here like to play cards and I don't and there are a lot of gossip-mongers and I don't believe in that."

Last, women with poor marriages and with husbands on the road or with long commutes suffer from poorer morale, although their prime reaction is loneliness.

The boredom in Levittown is shown in Table 1. Although

TABLE 1
AMOUNT OF BOREDOM IN LEVITTOWN*

| | Random sample | | | | | | Philadelphia sample | | |
| | First interview | | | Second interview | | | | | |
| Amount of boredom | W | M | All | W | M | All | W | M | All |
|---|---|---|---|---|---|---|---|---|---|
| "Almost every day" | 4% | 0% | 2% | 4% | 0% | 2% | 8% | 0% | 5% |
| "A few times a month" | 21 | 6 | 14 | 15 | 22 | 18 | 27 | 17 | 24 |
| "About once a month" | 21 | 28 | 24 | 27 | 6 | 18 | 27 | 11 | 22 |
| "Less often than that" | 21 | 11 | 17 | 23 | 17 | 21 | 11 | 5 | 9 |
| Never | 33 | 55 | 43 | 31 | 55 | 41 | 27 | 67 | 40 |
| Number | 24 | 18 | 42 | 26 | 18 | 44 | 37 | 18 | 55 |

* People were asked, "We all get bored every so often. How often do you find yourself feeling bored, having nothing to do, or nothing you want to do especially? Do you feel this way: almost every day, a few times a month, about once a month, or less often than that?" The "never" category was not read to the respondents.

## An Anatomy of Suburbia

people may under-report, forty percent (about a third of the women and more than half the men) are never bored and only a few women are constantly so. Boredom does not seem to be a serious problem in Levittown. Younger people experienced somewhat more boredom than older ones, but there was no pattern by class. Since former city dwellers reported as much boredom in their prior residence as suburban ones, the common idea that suburbanites are more bored than city dwellers is inaccurate.

If life in Levittown really produced boredom, one would expect an increase over time, but most respondents who had been bored when they first came to Levittown reported a decrease two years later, and only five and eight percent in the two samples reported an increase.

TABLE 2
AMOUNT OF LONELINESS IN LEVITTOWN, WOMEN ONLY*

| Amount of loneliness | Random sample† Second interview | Philadelphia sample |
|---|---|---|
| "Almost every day" | 0% | 3% |
| "A few times a week" | 4 | 5 |
| "A few times a month" | 15 | 16 |
| "About once a month" | 22 | 14 |
| "Less often than that" | 15 | 19 |
| Never | 44 | 43 |
| Number | 27 | 37 |

\* Respondents were asked, "In a new community, people sometimes feel lonely. How often would you say you feel lonely here?" All categories with the exception of "never" were read to them.

† In the first interview, the random sample respondents were asked only if they were lonely or not. Nineteen percent said they were lonely.

Loneliness is as rare in Levittown as boredom. Table 2 shows that only about twenty percent of the women are lonely at least a few times a month, and taking under-reporting into account, these can be thought "really lonely." Loneliness is roughly similar in amount to boredom, and the two also overlap, mainly because being stuck in the house can produce both feelings. Unlike boredom, however, loneliness strikes all kinds of Levittowners and does not vary with age, class, religion, or other characteristics. For example, twenty percent of blue-collar Philadelphians reported being lonely at least a few times a month, but so did twenty-five percent of professional ones.

The reason for this unexpected finding is that there are three types of loneliness: "social," which develops from lack of friends; "familial," which, at least in Levittown, is felt by women cut off from their parents and, more important, from husbands whose jobs require traveling, long hours, or such preoccupation with work that they have little time for their wives; and "chronic," a personal alienation above and beyond social and familial causes. The three types can strike the same person; indeed, when familial loneliness is not compensated for by social life, it may lead to the chronic variety.

Of the small number of really lonely in both samples, thirty-eight percent gave reasons which suggested social loneliness and fifty-four percent, familial. As might be expected, no one admitted chronic loneliness, but I would guess that not more than ten percent of Levittown's women were in this condition.

Almost half the random sample and twenty-two percent of the Philadelphians had been lonely in their former residence, and most seemed to have suffered from social loneliness. Levittown was a godsend for them, for seventy percent of the former and all of the letter reported less loneliness after the move. One Philadelphian said, "In the city, if I was alone, I stayed home. Here a neighbor comes over to talk. In the city, everyone worked and people didn't come out and talk."

Because so much loneliness is familial, it does not decrease with length of residence and, in fact, only becomes apparent after some time in Levittown. For example, of those not lonely after six months in Levittown, eighteen percent of the random sample and fifty-five percent of the Philadelphia sample were lonely by the second interview. Some had been seeing their families in the city or were busy venturing into new relationships in Levittown at first. Others were Jewish women, initially quite active, who realized after the organizational tasks had been taken care of and sociability became more important that they did not share prevailing group interests. Conversely, those whose initial loneliness was due to lack of social life reported that it had been dispelled after two years in the community.

Suburbia is purported to breed mental illness, but relevant data are hard to come by, especially in a new community without a hospital or a local psychiatrist. During the first two years of Levittown's existence, while three thousand families were arriving, I counted fourteen suicide attempts, fifteen families who appeared

## An Anatomy of Suburbia

more than once before the police on domestic conflict charges, an estimated fifty nervous breakdowns, an estimated hundred psychiatric referrals by doctors, a similar number of cases of pastoral counseling judged by the ministers to involve "serious" problems, and an estimated fifty juvenile delinquents in repeated difficulties with the police or the school. Comparisons to other communities are impossible because of the nature of the data and because of the difficulty of computing rates in a town just being occupied, but the figures do not seem alarming. I would judge there is no more mental illness, at least of the kind that surfaces into statistics, in Levittown than in other communities, and certainly less than in the cities.

More important, of sixteen case histories gathered from doctors, ministers, and the police, thirteen indicated similar emotional disturbances in former residences, and in no case was there any evidence that the problem had developed in or worsened in Levittown. Indeed, most of these people had come with the hope that a change of scenery might resolve their emotional problems. For example, two women, one married to an alcoholic, the other to a compulsive gambler, persuaded their husbands to move to Levittown, but once the novelty of the house and of home ownership wore off, the old problems returned, and eventually both families moved out.

Almost all emotional difficulties that came to light were experienced by women, and among these, two familiar types stand out: the working-class woman cut off from her parents and the wife whose husband is occupationally on the road.

The suggestion that mental illness has nothing to do with the suburbs may be surprising. It contradicts not only the critics but some English studies which found unexpectedly high rates of treated and untreated mental illness, of all degrees of seriousness, in new towns, and American research in suburbs and rapidly growing communities. These rates are sometimes attributed to the nature of suburban life—falsely, I think. The suburbs—like the English new towns—attract young, relatively sophisticated, and comparatively better educated people than established communities. As a result, they are physically healthier, and routine anxieties may express themselves through functional illnesses more often than organic ones. A sophisticated population is more aware of emotional problems and able to articulate them, and a new-town population will undoubtedly include disturbed people who came to the town to cure their problems or at least escape from the scene of previous disturbances. As a result, statistics of treated and untreated cases are likely to be higher than in established communities.

New suburbs also attract an unusually large number of socially mobile people. Downwardly mobile people have been shown by many studies to be troubled emotionally, and if they come to a new community with the false hope of improving their lot and find a majority of their neighbors upwardly mobile, their difficulties may only increase. Upwardly mobile people are occasionally beset by problems, too, and it is perhaps no coincidence that the more troubled Levittowners included working-class women who had married into the middle class or had left a cohesive ethnic enclave. Mobile people make considerable demands on community institutions which these cannot always satisfy; conversely, hyperactivity or social isolation may drive troubled people to the breaking point.

But the notion that suburban life is inherently stressful and dangerous for all its residents is simply inaccurate.

To test attitudes about the house, suburbia, and the city further, the random sample was asked to choose between its Levitt house and a hypothetical ideal row house resembling the Levitt house in a Levittown-like community: (a) if the community were only fifteen minutes from the husband's job; (b) if it were a similar distance from downtown Philadelphia; and (c) if it were cheaper. Although many planners argue that the row house is the answer to urban sprawl, and some predict it must become the major suburban building type during the next housing boom, most Levittowners were not interested. Altogether, twenty-two percent chose the row house at least once, but no one for the house itself. Nine percent picked it to reduce the man's journey to work—all of them women; seven percent, to be closer to downtown facilities; and fourteen percent, if it were at least $1,000 to $2,000 cheaper.

But most would not take the house at any price. "You'd have to give it to me," said one. "I figure I'm going to be 90 when I pay off this mortgage," said another, "and I might as well go first class." Even those who chose the row house said they did not want to live in one, and their choices really reflected dissatisfactions with Levittown. The common and almost universal objection was

## An Anatomy of Suburbia

lack of privacy. One Levittowner explained, "In a row house, you hear everybody's troubles. You are always hearing the other person's business and fighting about how much of the lawn and driveway is yours. You spend too much time with your car against the wall." Freedom from the supervision and judgment of adjacent neighbors (and from the temptation to judge them) is more important than easier access to job or city. Unless future row houses are designed to maximize privacy, and can also overcome their present low-status image, they will not be very popular with the next generation of home buyers.

The single most important source of Levittown's impact on people is undoubtedly the house, even though most of the changes it encouraged in the lives of Levittowners were intended. The house is both a physical structure and an owned property. Among its physical characteristics, space was the most significant source of change, providing easier child-rearing, more room for family activities, and greater privacy to its members, thereby reducing family friction and increasing contentment. Modernity encouraged improved housekeeping methods and allowed a bit more spare time for wives. Both house and yard offered opportunities for initial fixing and furnishing, and also for more lasting decorating hobbies, and other kinds of cultural self-expression. They also had unintended effects: more family cohesion and change in spare time and spare-time activity.

Contentment results principally from home ownership, particularly among men. Aside from the acquisition of property and its monetary value, ownership brings the freedom to do as one pleases and to indulge in forms of self-expression inside and outside the house that are not available to a tenant; it permits or encourages familial "settling down" and provides a public symbol of achievement, "something to show for all your years of living," as one Levittowner pointed out. Ownership also incorporates people into the block and gives some a feeling of community belongingness which may result in church, organizational, and political participation. These changes last only so long as people are satisfied with the house as a physical structure and with the community in which it sits, and, of course, they are most intense while the house and ownership are novel.

Generally speaking, the changes that could be assigned to the move from city to suburb alone were few. The city per se (and the leaving of it) had little impact on people's lives—and certainly not enough to encourage them to go back to it. The discovery that visiting may be preferable to "being out on the town" qualifies as a significant unintended change of suburban living and of community newness. Another consequence was the slowdown in the pace of living, noted primarily by former city dwellers and men. It follows from the ability to spend more time in the house and yard, activities for which one can set one's own pace; the increase in outdoor living, which may reduce the energy and desire to do other things; and the availability of friendly people nearby, which eliminates visiting that requires travel. The men, who report increased relaxation more than women, could avoid participation in disliked parental and in-law activities and escape urban congestion.

Many explanations have been offered for the intense desire for home ownership and the single-family, low-density house. One explanation proceeds from status: the popular desire for suburban home ownership imitates the fashion-setting upper and upper middle classes. The dream home of most Levittowners is not the Main Line or Westchester County suburban mansion, however, but "a bigger house with some acreage around it," a tiny farm (not to be farmed) with all the conveniences of urban and suburban living, including easy access to social life. This dream residence is not of recent origin, but is rooted in the cultures of most Americans, Protestant and Catholic, middle-class and working-class alike. Among middle-class Protestants, the home-ownership aspiration can be traced back to the rural and small-town heritage of eighteenth- and nineteenth-century America and England; among working-class Catholics, to the peasant settlements of continental Europe. Only the Jews did not share this rural heritage, and although acculturation has persuaded many to accept it, Jews are still more favorably inclined to city living than any other group.

The crucial difference between cities and suburbs is that they are often home for different kinds of people. If one is to understand their behavior, these differences are much more important than whether they reside inside or outside the city limits. Inner-city residential areas are home to the rich, the poor and the non-white, as well as the unmarried and the childless middle class. Their ways of life differ from those of suburbanites and people in the outer city, but because they are *not* young working- or lower- or upper-middle-class families.

## An Anatomy of Suburbia

My findings also question a related theory, espoused by city planners, that the community, especially its physical component, is a significant determinant of behavior. City planners overestimate the role of builders and designers as agents of change. City planners are geared to providing new opportunities, but usually those *they* find desirable, and without concern about how other people feel.

The attempt to induce behavior change through physical components is likely to fail, because it deals with spurious sources and agents. The policy-maker can increase contentment by providing sufficient internal and yard space to afford family members greater privacy and opportunities for more activity. And if his house planning is superior, people may be willing to accept innovations in the physical community, but if he suggests innovations at the price of an inferior house, he is sure to fail. If the policy-maker wants to increase neighborhood cohesion, however, physical solutions such as neighborhood schemes or the provision of plazas where neighbors can meet are irrelevant, for so long as neighbors have no reason to meet, they will not do so. Cohesion can only be increased by making the neighborhood a political unit, or by so altering the family that people will derive more satisfaction from being with neighbors than with spouse and children. Such policies are not likely to be popular or feasible.

So far, I have asked whether the planner *can* change behavior and aspirations, but have begged the question of whether or not he *should*. If Levittown were as harmful as the critics claim and as undesirable as the city planners believe, the answer would be obvious. Since this is not the case, however, the planner's decision about change should be governed by two assumptions: (a) in a pluralistic society, alternative ways of living—and community arrangements—are justified, provided they are not clearly antisocial or individually destructive; (b) the people for whom he is planning are on the whole the best judges of how they want to live. The planner may prefer urbanity, but unless he can prove other alternatives to be harmful, this preference only gives him the right to practice it himself.

# The Natural History of a Reluctant Suburb

WILLIAM M. DOBRINER

One of the most persistent mistakes in the flood of literature about suburbia is the tendency to lump together under the label of "suburban" all sorts of communities caught within the cultural and economic shadow of great cities. But in fact there is an enormous difference between an all-new suburb like Levittown and an established rural village invaded by suburbanites and turned into a reluctant suburb.

The internal problems of the mass-produced suburb and the sacked village are quite different. A Levittown has to create its institutions—its schools, its churches, its civic organization, shopping centers, "culture" groups, and the like. The invaded village, on the other hand, is a going concern before the suburban assault begins. It has evolved a social system that works for a population of a certain size. There are enough schools, churches, clubs, stores, streets, sewers, sidewalks, parking spaces, etc., to go around. But once the restless city discovers the little village and pumps a stream of suburbanites into its institutions, the social system soon develops a split personality. Where a Levittown is faced with the problem of creating a community from scratch, the sacked village has a community already, but it is soon divided between the pushy, progressive, and plastic world of the newcomers on the one hand, and the accustomed world of the old-timers—"the villagers"—on the other.

---

*Reprinted from* The Yale Review *49 (1960) © Yale University Press, by permission of the publisher and the author.*

## Natural History of a Reluctant Suburb

Wherever the suburban spearhead is pressing the rural village, the village has little hope of surviving unchanged, because the forces behind metropolitan expansion are irresistible. For a while the village may resist by elaborate zoning requirements or other legal barriers to invasion, but these are at best delaying actions. The tides of urbanism may be diverted for a decade or so, but what direct assault has failed to do a fifth column will accomplish. The city will seduce the young people of the village; they will go to urban colleges, take jobs in the metropolis, extend their range of contacts and eventually adopt an urban (suburban) way of life.

What it means for a long-established village to be suburbanized can be seen from the recent history of a community called here, for reasons of tact, "Old Harbor." It is a real place, in the general New England area, off the Atlantic Coast. Over three hundred years old, Old Harbor lies at the foot of a curving valley between two green necks of land stretching into the sea. Its history resembles that of many another New England village. In 1662, for example, a "morals committee" of six "respectable" citizens and hte minister carefully scrutinized all new settlers who arrived in the community. If the newcomers failed to pass the committee's standards of morality and respectability, they were asked to leave. So Old Harbor's tradition of skepticism and caution as to the worth of recent arrivals is anchored in over three hundred years of experience.

In its early years, Old Harbor served as the local nexus of an agrarian and colonial society. Its grist mills ground local grain into flour through the power of the impounded waters of the tide ponds and mill dams. The natural harbor drew shipping from all over the east coast. Whaling ships worked out of the home port, and coastal shipping from ports as far away as the West Indies unloaded hides, rum, cattle, cordwood, charcoal, etc., on Old Harbor's busy wharves. Over the years the farmers worked the land on the gently rolling slopes leading down to the water. The wheelwrights turned their wheels, the metal smiths pounded out their pewterware, the shipbuilders sent their vessels splashing into the bay, and the carpenters built the "saltbox" cottages down near the harbor. The village prospered but remained comparatively changeless in some fundamental ways—it continued to be a Yankee village of industrious merchants, seamen, farmers, and craftsmen.

Certain family names appear again and again in its records: the Rodgerses, the Platts, the Tituses, the Woodses, the Brushes, the Conklins, the Wickses, the Scudders, the Sopers, the Skidmores. In time more land was cleared, more ships were built, and small but vigorously independent men set up industries and crafts, farms and homes. Yet the essential "ethos" of the village remained constant—Yankee, Protestant, independent, cautious, shrewd, calculating, hard-working, and conservative.

Old Harbor figured in the American Revolution. One of its churches (still standing and functioning) served as headquarters for the local British forces. Eventually, George Washington came to Old Harbor and slept there. By the middle of the nineteenth century, in a society where so many persons, traditions, and things were new, Old Harbor had a lineage of two hundred years to look back upon. But change was imminent. In 1867 the railroad came to the village and became a serious competitor with marine transportation, and thereafter the harbor declined as a vital force in the village's economy. Even more ominous was the fact that 36.6 miles from the village lay the borders of a city. By today's standards, it was an urban infant, but even then it was showing a capacity for incredible growth and its influence was extending beyond its borders. Though it was still an entity apart and a universe removed from Old Harbor, some of the more perceptive villagers looked to "the city" with something more than casual Yankee curiosity and superiority. In writing to a relative in 1872, one villager noted, "There has been a very curious thing this summer, I must have seen fifteen or twenty strangers in town during July and August."

The first invaders of Old Harbor were members of the new industrial aristocracy who emerged in the decades after the Civil War. They were the first outsiders to discover the magical little coves and their verdant overcover, the unspoiled woodlands, the tiny village with so much history, and the green, gentle hills with the spectacular sweep of the sea. By the turn of the century, Old Harbor had become their carefully guarded preserve. They bought the old farms and cleared away acres for their summer playgrounds and gigantic estates. They fenced off two- and three-hundred-acre parcels and created separate dukedoms populated by communities of servants and laborers.

On the surface things had not changed much. The rolling hills, the snug harbor, the Yankee village with its saltbox cottages and

## Natural History of a Reluctant Suburb

local crafts, the busy farms, all remained the same. The estates were secluded behind acres of greenery and the new leisure class strove to protect "the colonial charm" of the village and its surroundings. The old inhabitants kept to themselves. They ran the village as they always had, but supplied the estates with provisions, ships, and such services as they were capable of providing. Though there was little basic understanding and compatibility between the "high society" of the nation and the "high society" of the village, the coming of the estates brought a new prosperity to Old Harbor and helped to take up the slack left by the decline of the fishing and whaling industries and the harbor in general. By the turn of the century, Old Harbor was passing into another stage of its life. By now the grist mills were great sway-backed structures rotting by the mill dams. The brick kilns, the tannery, and Ezra Prime's thimble factory were alive only in the memories of the very old. Children played sea games in the soft, pungent, peeling hulks of the whalers as they lay beached in the harbor marshes, their masts pointing like splayed fingers against the evening sky. And in the meantime, to the east, the urban goliath was yawning and stretching and looking fitfully about.

By the early 1920s, the township in which Old Harbor is located was undergoing rather intensive immigration from the metropolitan area. The city was going through one of its growth spasms, and the population was spilling over the city limits into the adjacent counties. Old Harbor was one county removed, but this was the decade in which the automobile drastically changed the character of American society and culture. Mass production had made Henry Ford's dream of a low-priced car for every family almost a reality. And a few miles to the south of the village, in "Old Harbor Station," the railroad terminus, a new and rather singular figure stood on the platform waiting for the 8:05 to the city: the commuter, the classic suburbanite, with his freshly pressed tight trousers, starched white collar, and morning paper folded neatly under his arm.

Now the automobile and the new concrete highways were bringing transient strangers to Old Harbor. The strangers were noisily evident on hot summer nights when a two-hour drive would carry them from the heat and congestion of the city to the beaches and cool valleys of Old Harbor. The character of Old Harbor weekends rudely changed as streams of cranky autos on spindly wheels rattled through the center of town and jammed up at traffic lights. Not only was Main Street becoming a thoroughfare for the beach traffic on weekends, but the city people intruded into the private bathing places along the waterfront. "Private Property" and "No Admittance" signs began to obliterate "the view." The number of both permanent residents and weekend transients, or, as the villagers called them, "shoe boxers," increased.

By the 1930s, the age of the palatial estates, begun seventy-five years earlier, was about over. The huge mansions in English Tudor, Renaissance, Baroque, Spanish, and various combinations had served their purpose. They had proclaimed the grandeur of American industrial growth and had bestowed calculated and lavish honor on those who built them. Now they were in the hands of the third generation or had been sold to second and third buyers, and each time a portion of the land had been sliced off in the transaction. In addition, government action unfriendly to the rich in the New Deal decade was making it difficult to maintain huge houses; income and inheritance taxes were forcing the estate holders to sell their property or simply to let the palaces go to seed. A few were given to educational institutions and one or two more were turned over to Old Harbor Township as museums or public parks. But there is little contemporary use for a decaying thirty-room castle with its entourage of outbuildings, so they waste away in their crabgrass kingdoms, the gargantuan headstones of an excessive age.

After the Second World War population that had been trapped in the city during the war years exploded into the county neighboring Old Harbor. In ten years, the number of people in this "rural" county passed a million and made it one of the most rapidly growing areas in the United States. Large numbers also spilled over into Old Harbor's county, whose sociological border by 1950 was well within the rural-urban fringe. In the ten years from 1945 to 1955, Old Harbor Township doubled its population, and the village itself has now absorbed between two and three times the numbers it had in 1940. In just ten years, a three-hundred-year-old village, with many of the descendants of the original founders still living there, underwent a social shock that wrenched it from whatever remained of the patterns of the past.

As Old Harbor soaks up the steady stream of suburban migrants,

## Natural History of a Reluctant Suburb

it has taken on a physical pattern quite different from the community of twenty years ago. Toward the center of town is the "old village," the nucleus of the "old-timer" community. There the streets are lined with aging oaks, elms, and maples, The houses are comparatively large and reflect the architectural trends of a hundred fifty years—authentic and carefully preserved saltboxes and Cape Cods, two-story clapboard or brick Colonials, straight and angular American Gothics, and prissy, frivolous Victorians. They stand fairly close to each other, but property lines are marked by mature hedges of privet, forsythia, and weigela. Each house proclaims an identity of its own. In front of an occasional Colonial or cottage a small sign will read "1782" or "1712." In the old village, even on a sunny day, there is shade and the scent of many carefully tended flowers. The sunlight filters through the great overhead branches and throws delicately filigreed shafts of yellow-green light on the clipped lawns, on the small barns and garages tucked behind backyard shrubbery, and on the hulls of old sailboats that will never again put to sea. The sidewalk slates are rippled by the massive roots below. Two elderly ladies, straight and thin, walk by with their market bags. There are few children. There is little noise. You sense that whatever these neighborhoods are now, the best in them has gone before.

Out along the periphery of the old village, up on what were farmlands five years ago, out along the land necks reaching toward the bay, down in the cove valleys, and up among the woody ridges, range the dwellings of suburbia. Here among the asbestos shingle or "hand-split shakes," the plastic and stainless steel, the thermopane and picture window, the two-car garages and pint-sized dining areas, the weathered wagon wheel and ersatz strawberry barrel, live the suburbanites in their multi-level reconstructions of Colonial America. It is impossible to avoid them. The signs strung along the highways point the way. "Butternut Hill—Turn Right." "This Way to Strawberry Farm Homes." This is no proletarian Levittown. "Peppermill Village" starts with a "minimum" house of "just" seven rooms and two baths for $22,500 and goes on up. But the architectural themes of all of the development are the same—antiquity, early American, "good taste." The Limited Dream finds a concretized expression of the past's myth in "Authentic Farmhouse Reconstructions" and the "Modernized New England Village."

Where the villagers live in comparative quiet against the steady but increasing hum of Main Street, the suburbanites live in sun and din. The Suburban Sound is a blend of children, dogs, doors, machines, and mothers. The bedlam of children at play is a universal sound, but the constant clatter of small machines and the ever-present yapping of frustrated dogs are uniquely suburban. In the summer months, the machines of suburbia are particularly vocal—the power lawn mowers (the grunt, click, and chug of the reel type serving as bass for the steady, high-powered whine of the rotary), the exhaust fans, the concrete mixers, the post-hole diggers, the tree cutters, the roto-tillers, the flooded-cellar pumpers, the hedge trimmers, and softly, in the distance, the growl and clink of the bulldozer steadily at work making more suburbs. Add to this the shouts of children, the cries of babies, the calls of mothers, and the muted tones of the dual tailpipes on the station wagon headed into the village, and the Suburban Sound is complete.

No longer is there enough space in Old Harbor. You can't park your car on Main Street anymore, there may not be room in church if you arrive late on Sunday, classrooms are "overcrowded," and you have to wait your turn for telephones to be installed in your new house. But these are simply the unsurprising results of sudden growth, and the Old Harborites are on their way to solving many of them. They have built schools and plan more. They are tearing down bits of the old village surrounding Main Street and are putting in parking lots. Some churches are adding wings or erecting new buildings. They have added policemen and fire engines, and have widened the critical streets. The physical problems, in general, are understood and are being coped with realistically.

The fundamental schism between the world of the old-timers and the world of the newcomers makes a problem that is less obvious but both more important and harder to cope with.

In their occupational characteristics, the old settlers range between the middle and upper-middle class. The majority are employed in Old Harbor as merchants, small manufacturers, and businessmen. They constitute the current rearguard of the entrepreneurs of the last century. The rest are mostly white-collar people of various persuasions who are employed either in Old Harbor or the neighboring, highly suburbanized county. Less than twenty percent commute into the central city.

The average villager is middle-aged, married, and probably has two children either finishing high school or going to college. As a group the old-timers' formal education did not go beyond high school, but they want their children to go to college and they will generally pick one of the better ones. About half of the old-timers are Protestant, a third are Catholic, and seven percent are Jewish. The Catholic and Jewish populations represent the changes in Old Harbor's ethnic or religious character that began at the turn of the century. The median family income for the old-timers in 1955 was about $6,700, roughly $2,300 over the national median for that year. Obviously not all old-timers in Old Harbor are high-school educated, regular church attendants and securely anchored in the white-collar occupations, but enough are to justify the image of the old-timer as localistic, Protestant, economically "comfortable," conservative, and middle class.

Some of the villagers trace their family lines back ten or twelve generations. Even those who arrived only fifteen or twenty years ago have spent enough time in Old Harbor to have become personally and deeply involved in the community. For them Old Harbor has become a "way of life" and an object of deep affection. When the old-timer thinks of himself, of his identity as a person, he also thinks of Old Harbor. The community, the social system, the institutions, the organizations, the friendships have become a part of his character. Whatever is the fate of the village has also become each old-timer's personal fate. An old-timer merchant put the matter this way: "I have traveled a lot in this country and I've been to Europe a couple of times too. But the biggest thrill in my life was when I got back from Europe and drove over Potter's Hill and saw the spire of Old First Church down in the valley. It was the most beautiful sight in the world. I really love this town—Old Harbor is the finest community in the United States."

The suburbanites are another story. They are a high-income group ($9,700 a year) of professional men and executives. Ninety-seven percent arrived in Old Harbor married and almost ninety-four percent bought houses there. They average about two grade-school children per family. Only a fourth are Roman Catholics; the great majority are Protestants, although a few more Jews have entered the community in recent years. Nearly four out of every ten of the newcomers were born outside the state. Two-thirds have been exposed to a college education. Close to half commute to the central city, and another third are employed in the county adjacent to the city.

Though the villagers are economically "comfortable," they are nonetheless rather stationary on the income ladder. They are pretty well frozen into an occupational cul-de-sac. The suburbanites, on the other hand, are upward bound—their jobs pay better and carry more prestige than the villagers'. For them the primary world is the metropolitan area. They work there, play there, and their most intimate friends live there. They tend to see in Old Harbor the familiar culture of the apartment house now spread into one-acre "country estates." To the villager, Old Harbor represents continuity between the generations, stability instead of the city's "chaos," and a place of permanence in a universe of bewildering change. The suburbanite sees in the village a weekend away from the advertising agency or the pilot's compartment. He experiences Old Harbor as a series of isolated, fragmented, unconnected social situations. Old Harbor is the family, a cocktail party, a bathing beach, a movie, a supermarket, a country club, a school, a church, a PTA meeting. It is a one-acre wooded retreat from all of the drive, bureaucracy, and anxiety of the city. But a weekend is enough for the necessary physical and psychological repairs; it's back to the city on Monday.

The temper of the suburbanite "community" may be summarized in the way the suburbanites talk about Old Harbor:

> I came to Old Harbor because there is still some green around here and yet I can get to the airport in forty-five nimutes. It's a nice place to live—the schools are good, and I like being near the water. It is hard to say how long we'll be here. I would like to be based further south, but as a place to live Old Harbor is fine.

> I can't think of Old Harbor as my town or anything like that. Most of my friends live closer to the city and I work there. I don't have any feeling of living in a small community or anything like that. I guess I sleep more of my time here than anything else, but it's a good place for the kids. I've got a lot of contacts and interests outside.

> I have to go pretty much where the company sends me. I was transferred up to the office over a year ago so we bought a place out here in Old Harbor. Probably be here for three or four years then most likely I'll be sent to South America. We like Old Harbor although the way it's building up it will be like the city in no time. Well, it doesn't bother me much; we won't be around here forever.

## Natural History of a Reluctant Suburb

But an old-timer says:

> They [the suburbanites] don't know what's going on around here. They don't care. But I do; this is my town. I used to fish down at the tide basin. Now they're talking of tearing it down. I went to school here. All my friends live around here. It's crazy what's happening. I can look out of my shop window and can't recognize forty-nine out of fifty faces I see. There was a time I knew everybody. It used to be our town. I don't know whose it is anymore.

For the villagers, Old Harbor is their community and they have a fierce sense of possession about it. It is a property that they share. And like any valuable property it is cared for and cherished. It must not be profanely or rudely used. This is the real issue that splits the suburbanite and villager communities apart. For the suburbanites, Old Harbor is another commodity; it is a product that can be consumed; it is a means by which they hope to achieve a complex series of personal goals. For the villagers, on the other hand, Old Harbor is not a means to anything; it is simply an end in itself.

The two communities inevitably brush against each other in the course of everyday life. They flow together on the central streets, in the movie houses, on the beaches, at graduation exercises, and in the stores and shops of Main Street. In their economic relationships, villager and suburbanite have struck a symbiotic truce. They need each other, the villager to sell and the suburbanite to buy. Suburbia has brought new prosperity to the villager. Traffic and congestion on Main Street mean crowds of buyers. Parking lots may be expensive, but they also mean customers. On the other hand, there are signs that increasing suburbanization will threaten the retailers of Main Street. The shiny "super shopping centers" to the south of the village, where a couple of thousand cars can park with ease, make the village shops seem dingy and dull. The discount stores and mechanized supermarkets of the shopping centers out along the highway augur a bleaker future along Main Street.

Perhaps the greatest single issue separating villager from suburbanite has been "the school problem." With the tripling of the school population, Old Harbor has been faced with an intensive building program. Since they are essentially realists in their village microcosm, the old-timers have reluctantly admitted the "need" for more schools. Enough of them have been eventually worn down in public meetings to cast an approving vote for new construction. For many a villager, however, it has seemed to mean money out of his pocket to pay for the schooling of other people's children. But the basic and decisive issue has not been whether to build more schools or not, but what kind of schools to build and what kind of education the children should have.

In their approach to this question, the villagers are traditionalists and conservative. They see a good education as including the basic skills taught by a dedicated but maidenly teacher in a plain school building. The suburbanites, on the other hand, are educational radicals; they are irrepressible spenders and cult-like in their dedication to the cause of modern education. It is an axiom among the old-timers that the more costly a pending proposition is the more the newcomers will take to it, and they are not entirely wrong. The newcomers appear willing to sacrifice all else to their "children's education." At PTA gatherings and public meetings of the school board, an ecstatic speaker can bring tears to sophisticated suburbanite eyes and justify the most outlandish cause by reminding his audience that "no expense is too great when it comes to our children's welfare. It will just cost the price of a few cartons of cigarettes a year to give our children this new gymnasium. Isn't our children's education, and clean, wholesome recreational facilities worth a few cents more a year? Is there any parent here who can deny their children this? Is there anyone here who will deny their children what America can offer . . . ?"

Everyone will be on his feet applauding, for the side of "the children" has won again, and every villager who voted against the plastic gymnasium or marble swimming pool will have to face the terrible question: "Do I really hate children?"

For the newcomers, anything that is educationally worthwhile must also be very expensive. "After all, you get what you pay for." The villagers, on the other hand, will battle the "frills" and "extravagances" and will turn down "excessive" curricular and building proposals. Eventually a compromise is worked out. But in the suburbias of the upper middle class, education is the cohesive issue around which a "consciousness of kind" develops for the newcomers. For many, education seems to have taken the place of religion.

While the newcomers have taken over the PTAs and infiltrated

## Natural History of a Reluctant Suburb

the school board, the villagers continue to control the churches. Suburbanites usually join the PTA before they become members of a church, though they swell the numbers of those attending religious services. But even in the ranks of the devout, there have been indications of a schism.

The villagers tend to look upon their churches as something more than formal religious centers. Over the years they have served as rallying points for a good deal of cooperative community activity, and they tend to stand for a morality and a traditionalism highly compatible with villager perspectives. One villager remarked that you can hardly keep from feeling a little possessive about a church you have helped to build. The minister of one Protestant church who rather reluctantly admitted that all was not harmony within his flock, pointed out that the "older residents" had finished paying off the church mortgage sometime around 1947, and a few years later the church had almost doubled its congregation. As the minister saw it, the villagers were indignant over the invasion of "their" church by "outsiders." They were especially smarting over the fact that, because of the devoted work of the old-timers, the newcomers had inherited a church free and clear of any financial encumbrance. The villagers felt that the solvency of their church had made it more attractive, and that the enthusiasm the suburbanites showed for it was not without crasser implications. As a consequence, the old-timers began to champion all church causes that were particularly expensive. It has been the villagers who have stoutly called for a new Sunday School building and a finer parish house. The villagers have been on the side of free and easy spending by the church ever since the suburban influx began.

This is not the whole story. A few years back, one of the most fashionable churches of Old Harbor made some sympathetic overtures to a purely newcomer religious group—Jews of the "Reformed" group who were conducting their services in an empty store on Main Street. The minister of this old Protestant church, which traces its origins back to the American Revolution and whose membership consists of the elect of Old Harbor society, offered the facilities of his church to the Jewish newcomers. The Jews happily accepted the offer. This not only brought the two worlds together but the Protestant and localistic villagers and the Jewish, cosmopolitan suburbanites even sponsored joint "functions" together. The differences between the villagers and suburbanites are not insurmountable, nor are the two separated by an impenetrable curtain of prejudice and ignorance.

The newcomers have largely ignored the formal political organizations of Old Harbor. Traditionally the community has been solidly Republican, and the upper-middle-class suburbanites have not threatened the political balance. There are a few more egghead Democrats in Old Harbor in recent years who write books or teach in a college, but they are regarded as odd and harmless, and no one pays much attention to them. This does not mean that the suburbanites are not politically active; they are, but they act outside political parties to do political things. Their means is the civic association. Each development or combination of developments has organized its own. As the Peppermill Village Civic Association, they lobby for sidewalks or against sidewalks, for street lights and sewers, or to keep out the sand and gravel contractor who wants to use the adjacent property for commercial purposes. Through the civic associations, the suburbanites engage in a series of running skirmishes with the villagers over local issues. Usually what they want costs more, so the villagers are against it.

The old-timers fill almost all the political offices, where they serve to balance the limited and self-interested objectives of the civic associations against the "broader needs" of the village and the township. But in this capacity the old-timers are more than old-timers; they are also politicians. Having learned that the suburbanites are amazingly perceptive on the level of neighborhood self-interest, the politicians will throw an occasional sop to the militant civic associations with an eye to the coming elections. Though the suburbanites are circumscribed in their interests, they are nonetheless organized, and can marshal massive political displeasure at the polls. As a consequence, the villager politicians must somehow walk a tightrope, balancing the political expediency of pleasing the newcomers against their own desire to keep the village what it was.

One wonders how many towns like Old Harbor are currently fighting to keep their identities in the industrializing South or in the rapidly growing Far West. How many Old Harbors are there all together? No one can even chance a guess. Each of the 168 great metropolitan centers of the nation is at present consuming a whole

## Natural History of a Reluctant Suburb

series of villages now within its sociological borders. And each village has a different history, a geography of its own and a set of institutions practiced by a population that is the same as nowhere else. Yet beneath the idiosyncratic surface, the villagers look with universal anxiety as the crush of metropolitanization proceeds. Everywhere the spirit of the small village suffers with the encroachment of urban anonymity and transiency. The Levittowns are fresh and naked, yet of a single character. The Old Harbors are split by the struggles of two communities to shape the prevailing character of the whole.

Yet the future lies with the metropolis and not the village. You can see it in the new super expressways that slice through Old Harbor's meadowlands. You sense the shift in internal balance in the village by the domination of the suburbanites at school board meetings. You know it on an autumn's evening in the crisp sea air, and in the deepening twilight around the mill pond. The great shuddering bulk of the mill squats in the hollow, intimidated by the headlights of the commuters as they race down and through the valley, dreary from the city and hungry for home. Pencils of light search into the gaping slats and crudely intrude upon the embarrassment of the mill's decay—the rusting gears, the splintered shaft, the rotting timbers, and marsh slop heaped up by the last high tide. And then with a rush the auto is gone, driving a little eddy of defiant leaves against the listless doors, leaving the old mill momentarily in shadows, huddled against the lowering sky. Through the empty windows, across the tide basin, and over the harbor, you can see the new shopping center bathed in neon and fluorescent light. There is a busyness about it. Up along the darkening necks the lights are going on in the new split-levels and "contemporaries" tucked into the ridges. The lights go on and off as the night rolls in. They seem to be winking at the senile mill as it sits and broods in the gathering darkness.

# Jewish-Gentile Relations in Lakeville

BENJAMIN B. RINGER

... We have attempted to study the relations between Jews and Gentiles in an established, traditionally Protestant community where Jews now form a significant part of the social environment, so that the modes of thought, feeling, and behavior with which members of the two faiths confront each other are conditioned by their daily circumstances of life as well as by their individual backgrounds and group ties. To do justice to these complex and changing relations, we have employed a comprehensive approach that relates the perceptions and responses of Jews to Gentiles, and vice versa, to various aspects of this social environment. Through it all, however, we have tried to keep two basic questions directly in view: *First*, what are the main sources of conflict and comity between Jews and Gentiles in Lakeville? *Second*, what are the chief forces and situations in the lives of individual Jews and Gentiles that bring them together, and how frequent and significant are these contacts?

Probably the single most important factor in Jewish–Gentile relations in Lakeville has been the recent influx of Jewish residents. This has shifted as well as expanded the population base, affected the traditional character of the community, and introduced immediate problems of municipal growth. Consequently it has placed the Jewish newcomer in a particularly vulnerable

*Chapter 14 of* The Edge of Friendliness, *by Benjamin B. Ringer, © 1967, by the American Jewish Committee, Basic Books, Inc., Publishers, New York. Reprinted by permission of the publisher and the author.*

## Jewish–Gentile Relations in Lakeville

position. He is the main scapegoat of the residents who disapprove of the cultural and political changes in Lakeville as well as of those who simply disapprove of Jews. The common image of the newcomers has been that of an aggressive and ethnocentric band of Jews who have only recently achieved the status which they seek to display and to confirm by living in Lakeville. Thus they are accused of trying to wield their newly obtained wealth to acquire social and even political power in the community. At the same time they are accused of clannishness, of lacking dignity and taste, of not knowing how to use their money, and of exaggerating its importance in their own lives and in their relations with others.

This image does not accurately represent the kind of Jew who has moved into Lakeville in recent years, since he is likely to be better educated and acculturated and to possess much more modest circumstances and status drives than the image implies; but it does serve important functions for different segments of the Gentile community. Those who appear to feel most threatened by the influx are long-time residents of moderate and low income. They worry that the traditions of Lakeville as a Christian community will be undermined, that the Jews will become politically potent in contrast to their own sense of powerlessness, and that the free-spending newcomers will continue to raise taxes, force up standards of living, and create new norms of status and conduct. Such complaints by this group of Gentiles take on a particular urgency because of their beliefs that their children are being exposed to the precocious *nouveau riche* behavior of the newcomers' children and will seek to emulate it. Thus the influence of the Jews will undermine the habits of modesty, frugality, and sobriety that they have sought to inculcate in their children. The main sphere of this danger is the local high school, since teen-agers are felt to be the most susceptible to the deviant manners and values of their peers. The wealthier old-guard Lakeville residents who have not followed many of their peers in moving out of the community are also disturbed by the waning of the genteel traditions of Lakeville which they attribute to the influence of new "Jewish" money and manners.

If the only Jews in Lakeville were newcomers and if all the newcomers were Jews, it seems likely that these concerns would increase the tensions between Jew and Gentile and result in a more openly expressed antagonism than we have observed. What modifies this situation is that some newcomers are Gentiles, who tend to look more favorably on the changes in the community and more favorably on the Jews as an enlightened, energetic, and civic-minded agent of progress in Lakeville.

The potential sharpness of the group conflict has also been modified by the presence of the long-time Jewish residents, who are viewed as an acceptable, even exemplary, group by their Gentile counterparts. Their image is that of a solidly established social and economic elite which has developed a style of life that is modest, tasteful, and proper. By virtue of his roots in the community and his adaptation to its prevailing mores and manners, the long-time Jewish resident is perceived to be a model of tact and deference who is willing to play a responsible role in the community without seeking to undermine its Christian traditions.

Thus there are three fairly distinct images of the Lakeville Jew, two of which are definitely positive in content. This diversity, however, is of small comfort to the Jewish newcomer, who is aware of the distaste, enmity, and invidious comparisons that he has evoked. He feels that he is being attacked from all sides, that his contribution to the community is not being given its due weight, and that his sensibilities are not being respected. Despite the justness of this reaction, which much of our data confirms, it is also apparent that the Jewish newcomer benefits from the fact that he has moved into a community where a small group of Jews was firmly established prior to his arrival. Thus he need not be a pioneer in making a place for himself in Lakeville. There are pathways of adjustment and acculturation that he can follow in adapting his behavior and values to the norms of the community and in aligning his identity as a Jew with his new situation as a mobile, middle-class suburbanite. That many of the Jewish newcomers are strongly motivated to follow these paths toward greater acceptance is suggested by their own life style as well as by their strong desire to dissociate themselves from behavior patterns which could be construed as aggressive, indecorous, clannish, or defensive.

## STYLE OF LIFE: SIMILARITIES AND DIFFERENCES

One of the major pathways of acculturation that Lakeville Jews—both newcomers and old-timers—have taken is clearly revealed in their leisure interests and activities. They have been particularly attracted to a model of leisure that reflects Lakeville's history as a summer colony of an elite Gentile group. Their favorite sport is golf; they are widely committed to the performing arts and are among the most avid supporters of Lakeville's own cultural traditions; and one of their favorite pastimes is playing bridge. So widely diffused are these preferences and interests among Jews that even those of moderate and low income, particularly among the women, have adopted them. Only the activities of men in the low-income bracket depart significantly from this model.

Among the Gentiles, however, this elite model tends to be confined to those of high income. And even in this stratum, the men show a marked attraction to another traditional model of leisure: that which reflects Lakeville's past as a home-centered small town in which a person, usually of relatively modest means, spends his leisure time in tinkering around the house and garden or in hunting and fishing.

Just as Jews and Gentiles differ in their attraction to the leisure traditions of Lakeville, so do they differ in the range of activities in which they become involved: Gentiles tend to specialize in their activities and Jews tend to generalize them. In other words, the average Gentile is intensively involved in a relatively few hobbies, games, or groups, while the average Jew extends his participation over a greater variety of them. For example, Jews typically participate in more sports and play more of the different games of cards than do Gentiles. This is due, in part, to the desire of the Jews to participate in a sport or card game (such as golf or bridge) that is characteristic of the community norms as well as in one more or less indigenous to their own background (such as handball and gin rummy). We have found a similar pattern in their organizational affiliations. The average Jew has many more affiliations than the average Gentile, though he does not devote appreciably more time to working in them. Thus, while youth-serving and health/welfare organizations are popular among both Jewish and Gentile women, only the former are likely to belong to both concurrently; the Gentile woman tends to move from one to the other in a sequence that follows her family cycle. Similarly, Jewish men are much more likely to belong to both occupational and fraternal groups than are Gentile men.

Finally, in keeping with these generalized and specialized patterns, we have observed that Jews are more likely than Gentiles to engage in activities regardless of whether they are personally interested in them. This is true of their participation in sports or in cultural activities such as concert-going. Similarly, Jews are more likely than Gentiles to belong to organizations that they do not participate in.

Why these seemingly consistent ethnic differences in the use of leisure recur is open to speculation. In part, they may be less a function of uniquely Jewish or Gentile group differences as such than of the composition of the two subcommunities. As we have already noted, the Jews of Lakeville are much more homogeneous than the Gentiles in age, income, and education. Given these similarities, we would expect greater consensus among Jews in their tastes and interests. In addition, many of them are relatively new to the community and are anxious to belong to it, which provides a further incentive for them to conform to the elite leisure mode even though they may not have a personal interest in its activities. Inversely, the Gentiles who are established at one stratum or another in the community experience less pressure to adapt to the elite model and are therefore more likely to do what they want to with their leisure time rather than what they perceive will gain them acceptance. All of which suggests that the distinctive orientation of the Jews, as well as their socio-economic composition, contributes to their patterns of leisure use. As we have further observed, Lakeville Jews in their twofold desire for integration on the one hand, and for maintaining group ties and interests on the other, are likely to involve themselves in both sectarian and nonsectarian activities and associations. Thus for this reason also they tend to distribute their affiliations over a broader range than Gentiles do. Though they may be unable to participate fully in more than a few of these groups, their membership in the others allows them to be identified with the two communities.

In sum, the extensiveness of the Jews' activities suggests that they are attracted more by certain extrinsic functions which these activities serve than by the activities themselves. Thus playing golf and bridge, for example, is likely to be viewed as a good way of getting together with people and of establishing one's claim to a desirable status in the community.

## CLIMATE OF OPINION AND MUTUAL ACCEPTANCE

Despite the many underlying differences and difficulties that mark Jewish–Gentile relations in Lakeville, overt group conflict is quite rare, and the general social atmosphere is usually characterized by tranquillity and tolerance. In part this is due to the passing of sufficient time for the initial impact of the population change to have spent itself, and for the municipal measures adopted to accommodate it to take effect. Also, in the intervening years the more bitterly hostile residents, particularly among the elite, have moved out of the community. At the same time, their need and desire to adapt to the prevailing social norms of the community and to participate in its daily life have made the Jewish newcomers more sophisticated in Lakeville terms; their presence has become less visible and objectionable. Some five years after the main influx, Jews and Gentiles in Lakeville today share many of the same interests in their homes, neighborhoods, schools, leisure activities, and so forth. Such common interests make the remaining differences between them less manifest and contribute to the tranquil surface of Lakeville society.

This process of "settling in" has also been abetted by the prevailing value systems of the Jewish and Gentile communities. Among Jews the basis of these values is clearly their strong desire for integration. Accordingly, few of them are willing to restrict their commitments and associations to their co-religionists and to the Jewish community. They are motivated to gear their behavior to Gentile standards, and though some of the newcomers may be willing to provoke group conflict in a matter such as Christmas celebrations in the schools, the general tendency is to avoid giving offense in the interests of being accepted.

Lakeville's Gentiles, of course, are in a different social position. Because of their dominance in the community and in the general society, they have little motivation to win the favor of the Jews. Consequently, their behavior is determined by how willing they are to accept Jews. In Lakeville, four out of five Gentiles say they are willing to live among Jews, though the degree and grounds of their tolerance vary in several respects. Some twenty-three percent say they would prefer to have only a minority of Jews: the figure they give averages just over twenty percent of the neighborhood population. A smaller group would allow at least as many

Jews as Gentiles. The rest, the substantial minority of forty-three percent, say they "don't care" how many Jews are in their neighborhood. By using our findings on the extent to which Jews, as a group, are perceived to be different from Gentiles, on the positive or negative evaluation of these differences, and on the number of Jews who are believed to exhibit these traits, we were able to classify the variety of Gentile attitudes into four general categories: the "exclusionist," the "exemptionist," the "pluralist," and the "egalitarian."

## THE CONTEXTS AND LIMITS OF FRIENDLINESS

Much of the interfaith tolerance in Lakeville is of the passive "live and let live" variety. It is unlikely, then, that Jewish–Gentile relations would develop much personal content without the community institutions and the individual pursuits that bring members of the two faiths together in some meaningful way. In the course of their daily lives Jews and Gentiles frequently find themselves in some sort of functional relationship where it is to their mutual advantage to work together amicably. Such functional relationships do more than cause Jew and Gentile to meet; they also provide a continuing context for them to get to know each other, to become friendly, and possibly to develop the strong ties of friendship. What is more, the separation of these functional relations from the more private spheres of life allows Jew and Gentile to participate in them without the usual inhibitions of class and ethnic factors.

Thus the necessity of making a living involves most Lakeville men in some economic or work relationship with people of the other faith. Such relationships often entail some social entertainment to promote business transactions or to improve cooperation within a work group or firm. Since these quasi-social arrangements have become widespread in the business and professional world, there is abundant opportunity for Jewish and Gentile men to get together in social situations.

In such situations each party understands that the motive of self-interest has brought them together, and therefore each takes in stride whatever socializing ensues as part of the rules and requirements of the economic game. But in the course of their transactions they may get to know a bit more about each other and to

## Jewish–Gentile Relations in Lakeville

like each other as individuals, so that the original relationship is transformed into personal friendship.

Indeed, the business and professional world is one of the most fertile grounds for our Jewish and Gentile respondents to cultivate significant interfaith relationships. Another is the organizations within Lakeville. Those organizations that provide most opportunities for Jews and Gentiles to come into friendly and meaningful contact are the youth-serving, neighborhood-community, and vocational groups—in other words, those designed to serve an "instrumental" rather than an "expressive" function.

The friendliness of the instrumental organizations derives from the personal relevance of the community of interest and needs that Jew and Gentile share. These extend beyond the organization itself and reflect the fact that many of Lakeville's Jews and Gentiles perform similar social roles and face similar social problems in child-rearing, home ownership, and their professional lives. In addition, the instrumental groups designed to serve these common interests and needs do not impinge upon the more private spheres of life. Thus relationships between Jew and Gentile in these associations do not compete directly with existing networks of friendship and do not involve status factors, both of which often inhibit Jews and Gentiles from relating to each other.

For our purposes, one of the significant features of these instrumental associations is that they provide a variety of opportunities for members to work together in small groups where they are joined by a specific common purpose and where the potential for personal contact and cooperative spirit is high. Thus committee work and the like provide settings where both parties can approach and work with each other as individuals and not merely as members of a group.

Once a basis of mutual acceptance and friendliness is derived from such contacts, it is unlikely that the relationship will be confined to these settings and functions. Instead it will usually take on more personal overtones and give rise to activities such as entertaining at home, sharing outside social engagements, and following other leisure activities that enable the relationship to develop a character of its own and to be sustained by the individuals themselves.

The third major ground of Jewish–Gentile contact in Lakeville is the neighborhood, and we have found that the neighborhood which best serves this purpose is the one where Gentiles remain in the majority. This finding is explained partly by the influence of certain demographic factors and group affiliations that affect the relative frequency and suitability of interfaith contacts. In a Gentile neighborhood, for example, the tendency of Jews to belong to the PTA makes more of them available in this organization than in the neighborhood itself and thereby enhances the effectiveness of the organization in bringing Jews and Gentiles together. In a Jewish neighborhood the PTA is less effective in this respect, because the selective recruitment to the organization makes it even more Jewish than the neighborhood is and reduces the possibility of Gentile participation. In addition, the age differences between Jews and Gentiles, which are relatively uniform in the various neighborhoods, create the probability that more of the younger Jews will find Gentile peers in a Gentile neighborhood rather than a Jewish one. Finally, we have observed that the neighborhood in which the Gentile occupies the majority status and the Jew the minority one more naturally fits the psychological orientation of each group toward the other, and thereby facilitates social intercourse.

So pervasive are the opportunities in Lakeville for Jews and Gentiles to come into contact with each other and to cultivate practical, cooperative relationships that the great majority of them report they have developed an identifiable friendship with at least one person of the other faith. In measuring the character and quality of this relationship, we found that it rarely matches in warmth, intimacy, interest, spontaneity, and trust the friendliest relationship that respondents have developed with someone of their own faith. Still, the best interfaith relationships are not casual or chance acquaintanceships, but have considerable personal content and significance. The level of intimacy they achieve tends to resemble that of the relations Gentiles and Jews develop with the friendliest neighbor of their own faith. However, few respondents who have both such relationships establish the same level of personal commitment in both; that is, they are more confiding and engaged with their friend than their neighbor, or vice versa. This finding indicates that the two relationships may be functional substitutes for each other.

To attain or to exceed the maximal standard set by neighborly intra-faith relations, friendships between Jews and Gentiles must go beyond the neighborhood context where they may have originated and must be pursued in and for themselves. The same requirement seems to be true of friendships that may have originated in voluntary associations within the community. Only those that have emerged from the context of work appear to be capable of transcending the neighborly standard whether they are pursued at work or elsewhere. Should a friendship between a Jew and a Gentile exceed the level of the neighborly, it often continues to grow until it is cherished by our respondents as one of the most meaningful relationships they possess, with Jew or Gentile alike.

## THE AURA OF UNREALITY

In the final analysis, though, despite the significant contacts between Jews and Gentiles and the benign atmosphere that prevails in Lakeville, an air of uncertainty and fantasy still characterizes their relations. In part, this results from the fact that their relationships rarely go beyond acquaintanceship to acquire the warmth and mutual trust of close friendships. As a result, few Jews and Gentiles appear to be in a position to gauge the feelings of the other with any accuracy, and thus they consult their own underlying anxiety or complacency, as the case may be.

Contributing even more significantly to this air of unreality is the very basis on which the Jew is accepted. He is judged as an individual and is accepted *if* he conforms to the standards set by a Gentile-dominated tradition. The orientation is essentially egalitarian in nature, and the goal is the assimilation of the Jew into the traditional mold of the community. The overall outlook is optimistic, for it is expected that in time even the Jewish newcomer will rid himself of his abrasive behavior and become fully acceptable.

But all Jews do not want to be cast into this mold; what this optimistic theory of acculturation and adaptation fails to confront is the Jewishness of the Jew. Most Gentiles in Lakeville are not concerned with the deeper meaning of Jewishness; they appear to treat it as just another barrier to the incorporation of the Jew into the community. In this they are joined by some Jews, particularly among the old-timers. However, to the majority of Jews in Lakeville the problem of being a Jew is not confined to that of integration into the community or the development of amicable relations between Jew and Gentile. While deeply favoring intergroup amity, they are also involved in a different and perhaps even more perplexing enterprise: that of working out their identity as Jews and developing a viable pattern of Jewish living. This desire for a religio-ethnic subcommunity which is simultaneously "Jewish" as well as compatible with and integrated into the larger structure of Lakeville and American society is as much a fact of life in present-day Lakeville as is its Gentile past. . . .

Despite the recent changes in Lakeville, most Gentiles and some Jews continue to press for uniformity with and conformity to an older version of the community. In effect, they refuse to legitimate the genuine diversity that already seems to characterize Lakeville. But until they do, or at least come to terms with it more effectively than they have, there will remain an air of fantasy and an undercurrent of unresolved tension between Jew and Gentile in the community.

# The Other Mayor Lee

### JOHN KRAMER

Mention "Mayor Lee" at a gathering of urban affairs specialists and you are apt to turn the conversation toward renewal and rehabilitation in New Haven, Connecticut. Richard C. Lee, New Haven's mayor since 1953, has achieved national stature for reversing, in that city, the ubiquitous trend toward urban blight and decay.

While Dick Lee justly earns his accolades, another Mayor Lee labors to transform a unique community deep in the Midwest. Without nationwide publicity, and with none of the indigenous resources available in New Haven, Mayor Clarence Lee of Kinloch, Missouri, works to eradicate substandard conditions and end the waste of human lives in his city of approximately eight thousand. Clarence Lee is black, and Kinloch has an all-black population.

In his most trying moments, New Haven's Lee never has to face the absolute problems that exist in Kinloch. Kinloch's Clarence Lee deals with acquiring the bare essentials of twentieth-century living. He fights for basics: indoor toilets, lighted streets, employment opportunities for his unskilled constituents, and rudimentary police protection.

### THE CITY

In population, Kinloch is second largest of the dozen self-governing black communities in the United States. It is not, as one

---

Reprinted from Focus/Midwest, vol. 5, 1967, with permission of Focus/Midwest Magazine, copyright Focus/Midwest Publishing Co., Inc.

might suspect, located just off Tobacco Road in some remote rural area. Instead, its 481 acres are locked solidly between two middle-class, white suburbs in the center of prosperous St. Louis County. Although Kinloch is ecologically suburban, six miles from the city limits of St. Louis, it hardly shares the affluence of its immediate neighbors.

With the exception of its center, where federal renewal funds have been used to erect one hundred row-type public housing units, Kinloch resembles a black residential area in some medium-sized Southern city. There are no tenements. The streets are lined with a variety of single-family dwellings. A few of the modest houses are well built and neatly kept, but most were hastily put together and now are in various stages of deterioration. Many of the roads are unpaved. Vacant lots are overgrown and littered. At high noon on any pleasant weekday, idle men sun themselves in front of taverns on Kinloch's main street.

The town totally lacks industry, and the few existing retail establishments are small, unattractive, and stocked for the most part with high-priced merchandise. Less than ten percent of the homes are served by sewers. Most rely on septic tanks, drainage fields, or what sanitation experts euphemistically call "direct flow." Kinloch's vital statistics are dismal. Some random examples: thirty-eight percent of the city's families receive some kind of state welfare assistance, the median family income is $3,075, forty-three percent of the residents over age 25 have less than eight years of education, and the adult male unemployment rate consistently hovers about ten percent, over twice the national average.

A series of natural and man-made barriers isolate the city. Indeed, Kinloch is so cut off from the surrounding white suburbs that the Peace Corps has used the town as a training site for its Liberia-bound volunteers.

To the east, the town of Ferguson maintains a one-foot strip of land along the Kinloch boundary. Roads through Ferguson stop at this easement, overgrown with brush, only to start again on the Kinloch side of the barrier.

To the north, residents of the City of Berkeley have fenced their back yards at the Kinloch city limits, creating a sort of "Kinloch Wall."

At the western edge of the city, a major commuter highway to

## The Other Mayor Lee

downtown St. Louis, and a fifty-yard-wide power-company right-of-way, effectively separate Kinlochians from those beyond.

Finally, at the southern edge of the town, a creek trickles along the dividing line. There is only one major road into Kinloch, and the few white motorists who wander in by mistake often experience a feeling akin to panic as they try to find an exit.

### THE HISTORY

There are varying accounts about the coming of the first blacks to Kinloch. One story suggests that the town once was a way-station on the pre–Civil War underground railroad, and a few escaping slaves remained to start small farms on the unused soil. Until 1937, the cities of Berkeley and Kinloch constituted a single quasi-community, an unincorporated area in St. Louis County, with whites in their section and the blacks in theirs. The entire district was known as Kinloch, after the Scottish Baron of Kinloch who first held title to the land.

In the mid-1930s, Kinloch's whites and blacks began to quarrel over the allocation of funds to the district's "separate but equal" schools. One of the blacks' complaints was the reluctance of the white-dominated school board to establish a black high school. With feelings running high, the whites' solution was to incorporate themselves as a separate city. They christened the gerrymandered municipality Berkeley, after the "Berkeley Orchard" subdivision in which most of them lived, and drew the boundaries to exclude blacks. Of course, most of the tax base went with the whites, and the blacks were left with little more than the community's original name.

From 1934 until 1948, Kinloch's blacks remained unincorporated. Necessary municipal services were provided by St. Louis County. Kinlochians who remember this period unanimously agree that county support was meager. They also agree that the county police force was made up largely of transplanted white Southerners, whose behavior toward blacks hardly produced love and affection. To gain some control over their community affairs, and to obtain what one long-time resident calls "something better than nothing," two thousand black citizens of Kinloch submitted their own incorporation petition in 1948. Missouri quickly granted their request for self-government and, on the first night of autonomy, Kinlochians celebrated with a mass prayer meeting to thank the Lord for deliverance.

Under Missouri laws, an incorporated city must provide for most of its own community needs. Hence, incorporation was a gamble for Kinloch. Local autonomy requires a financial capacity and, ideally, experienced leadership. Kinloch had neither. The new city's assessed property valuation in 1948 was slightly less than a million dollars, by far the least satisfactory tax base for any incorporated area in St. Louis County. The first mayor was a hod carrier, attempting to deal with the problems of an infant municipal government on a part-time basis.

The city almost succumbed before it reached its first birthday. In 1949 a group of Kinloch pragmatists, disturbed at such makeshift facilities as an all-volunteer police force operating without patrol cars, petitioned to disincorporate. A St. Louis County judge ordered disincorporation, but his decision was overruled on a technicality by the Missouri Supreme Court. The disincorporation petition, fought bitterly by Kinloch's first city officials, barely lacked sufficient signatures. Without the resources for another round in the courts, the disincorporation proponents decided not to make another try by petition, but to let the city fall of its own weight. Eighteen years later Kinloch remains incorporated, the cries for disincorporation are present but muted, and the weight is being lifted ever so slowly.

## MAYOR LEE

Clarence Lee is Kinloch's fifth mayor. He is tall, dark-skinned, and bears some resemblance to Jackie Robinson in the latter's thinner days. Within the community's ingrown society, where many residents take pride in tracing a three- or four-generation Kinloch ancestry, Lee is a relative newcomer. He was born in St. Louis in 1924, graduated from that city's then segregated Sumner High School, and moved to Kinloch in 1947 at the insistence of his new bride, a life-long Kinlochian who preferred suburban-style poverty to the kind offered by Lee's native urban ghetto.

Kinloch, in 1947, was beginning to stir with the notion it could govern itself, and Clarence Lee, working as a clerk by day and going to classes at St. Louis University at night, found himself

# The Other Mayor Lee

caught up in the fervor. Like many other residents of the new city, he attended regularly the bimonthly meetings of the Board of Aldermen. Within a year he joined Kinloch's incipient Young Democrats, a logical party affiliation after a boyhood spent in an apartment directly above Democratic headquarters on St. Louis's North Side. Using his tenure in the Young Democrats and his newly acquired position as vice-president of that organization as justification for a campaign based on personal political experience, Lee ran unsuccessfully for an aldermanic seat in 1955. He tried again in 1956, this time winning the first of what is now a string of six consecutive victories at the city's polls.

After five years as alderman, Lee was elected to his initial two-year term as mayor in 1961. His platform stressed the need for community self-sufficiency, and his ability to attain it. However, his 134-vote plurality—out of approximately three thousand votes cast—probably was earned largely by a promise aimed at the twenty-four church congregations in town. Lee pledged to end a pressing social evil: Sunday morning street parades held by Kinloch's more exuberant civic organizations.

Since taking office, Lee has had to face all of the problems, and more, that confronted his predecessors. Sunday sermons now can be held without accompaniment of outside fife-and-drum music, but Kinloch still lacks the resources to maintain adequate municipal services. Nevertheless, by combining personal stamina, an instinct for public relations, and some imaginative fiscal tactics, the mayor has managed to keep the city government operating. Above all, by aggressively pursuing funds made available through the federal government's War on Poverty, Lee has brought about some basic improvements in Kinloch's frustrating condition.

## THE MAYOR'S ROUTINE

The starting time of Lee's day is a matter of opinion. At midnight he begins his bread-and-butter job as a spray painter at nearby McDonnell Aircraft Corporation. Eight hours later he assumes his $50-a-month position as Mayor of Kinloch. Since the time demands on a mayor are open-ended, and often involve evening duties, Lee's workday often approaches twenty-four hours. His only routine pause comes when he smokes his ration of one cigarette a day. He catches sleep when he can. On no fixed schedule, but when time permits, Lee goes home to "toss around a little," and at midnight reports back to McDonnell.

Last summer, Lee started each day as mayor by assuming the role of milkman. To qualify for funds offered by some federal anti-poverty projects, Kinloch must contribute ten percent toward the total expenditure. The city is so lacking in financial resources that it cannot make the contribution in cash; instead Kinloch provides various services and is credited with dollar equivalents. Each morning shortly after eight Lee picked up two crates of milk cartons at the Kinloch High School and, in the course of the next hour, distributed them to the city's Head Start centers. Kinloch was credited with $50 a week for this service and Lee jokingly refers to himself as the "country's highest-paid milkman."

Head Start is one of a host of federal projects now functioning in Kinloch, and Lee does whatever he can to insure their effectiveness. On his milk rounds he carried a supply of hardware, and stopped to repair toys shaken apart by overenthusiastic youngsters. If on-the-spot maintenance was impossible, Lee carried the item home to his workshop and repaired it in his sparse free time. When Head Start supplies were received at Kinloch's post office, the mayor personally picked them up in his 1958 Chevrolet and delivered them to the centers. Time permitting, he accompanied classes on field trips, interceded for the teachers with higher authority, and checked the quality of the hot lunches delivered by an outside caterer.

Another Kinloch resident now makes Head Start's milk deliveries, allowing Lee to eat a quick breakfast at home before greeting his staff at City Hall at nine. Actually, morning greetings take little time because the staff, in Kinloch, consists only of a city clerk, a collector of taxes, a police matron who doubles as telephone operator, and the chief of police. In contrast to mayors of most other cities, Lee need not worry about the efficiency of his secretary. He has none.

City business is conducted in what once was Kinloch's leading funeral home, a building that probably could make any list of America's ten most inadequate city halls. Nevertheless, it is an improvement over Kinloch's first seat of government, evacuated in 1961 because rain water from an endless series of leaks threatened to wash city officials, records, and all into the street.

The mayor's minuscule office is at the end of a narrow corridor

The walls once were painted green but a good deal of peeling has taken place. Seated at a second-hand desk so small that he has difficulty fitting his legs underneath, Lee can gaze out his only window onto the uninspiring sight of an unpainted shanty next door. Along one office wall are two ancient wooden filing cabinets, also lacking paint. On another leans a black metal bookcase containing two telephone books and a four-year-old University of Missouri Extension publication entitled "Financing Missouri's Business." The starkness of the setting is illuminated by a bare fluorescent lamp attached to the ceiling.

A series of Kinloch citizens, on an infinitely varied set of errands, file into the mayor's chambers. Lee may act one instant as a marriage counselor, trying to settle a family argument, and the next as a job broker, attempting to place one of the town's chronically unemployed with an anti-poverty training project. No receptionist screens his callers and there are no eager assistants to whom he can refer their problems. Between visitors Lee answers his phone, opens the mail, and attends to the city problems that most urgently require his attention.

## LEE, THE GREAT SOCIETY, AND PRIVATE INVESTMENT

The mayors of some communities have resented the coming of Great Society programs, viewing the instigation of war-on-poverty activities as conflicting with their own interests. Clarence Lee of Kinloch welcomes all federal assistance projects with open arms, not only for the desperately needed financial relief they provide, but for the personnel that accompany them. With the almost $4 million in federal funds invested in Kinloch so far have come well-dressed and articulate people, most of them black, to provide professional services on a level heretofore unknown in the city. The Human Development Corporation, the local St. Louis agency responsible for administering Office of Economic Opportunity projects, has designated Kinloch a hard-core poverty area and has established a permanent neighborhood office. The facility is manned by a community coordinator and a growing staff of nearly two dozen. Specialists such as business consultants, family service counselors, health advisors, legal aid personnel, and home economists are initiating programs that the City of Kinloch could not dream of undertaking with its own funds. The immediate goal of the center's staff members is to inform the citizenry of various federally financed opportunities for self and community improvement. They encounter occasional resistance from Kinlochians who resent interference from outsiders, albeit blacks, but they get only encouragement from Lee. In his eyes, the center does not compete with City Hall; it is providing basic services the city should offer but cannot.

Lee's outstanding achievement in six years as mayor was the result of his active role in seeking federal help. Beyond the obvious aesthetic liabilities that accompany lack of sewers, Kinloch's primitive sanitation system has depressed the value of property and prevented the investment of outside capital in the community. Estimates for sewer construction in Kinloch ran as high as one million dollars, infinitely exceeding the city's capacity to tax or borrow. With the cooperation of executives of St. Louis's Metropolitan Sewer District, Lee aroused the interest of Missouri's two senators and the St. Louis area members of the House of Representatives, including those whose districts did not encompass Kinloch. Called to testify before the Senate Public Works Committee in March of 1964, Lee appeared armed with an up-to-date battery of Kinloch facts and figures which had been collected by the town's citizens on a volunteer basis. Documenting his case with these candid and distressing "self-surveys," Lee convinced the committee members of Kinloch's need for immediate assistance.

The result was the "Kinloch Amendment" to the Federal Housing Act of 1965. The amendment provided for a ninety percent federal grant for sewer construction in cities of less than 100,000 population, located in metropolitan areas, and suffering unemployment rates a hundred percent above the national average. Up to now, Kinloch is the only city to qualify. In February of 1966, Kinloch property owners in the sewerless sections of town approved a $100,000 bond issue to acquire the means for their ten percent contribution. The favorable vote was 1,112 to 12.

To take advantage of what Mayor Lee calls a "chance of a lifetime," Kinlochians virtually exhausted their city's bonding capacity. Therefore, revenue to meet Kinloch's remaining needs must be drawn from other sources. Hopefully, some of the money will come through private enterprise. Lee currently is negotiating with a nationally known garment concern, attempting to bring a three-hundred-job manufacturing plant to the city. In a community devoid of local industry, and with the traditionally restricted employment opportunities for blacks in St. Louis and St. Louis County, the garment factory would be a major breakthrough in Kinloch's battle for an adequate economic base. Then, with the prospective factory payroll as a lure, Lee hopes to develop a locally operated, if not locally owned, retail shopping complex.

Some outside capital already has come to Kinloch. Four subdivisions of modern single-family homes, selling from $9,000 to $30,000, are in the final stages of construction. The 115 new units will not solve Kinloch's housing problems, but they represent a start. The developers are having no difficulty selling their homes, most of them to Kinlochians seeking better living quarters. The sale of these new homes has been so brisk that independent contractors now plan to build another hundred or so, and there is also a more tentative proposal to build a set of two hundred garden-type apartments.

## EDUCATION IN KINLOCH

Some of Kinloch's ills, however, are not likely to be alleviated by private investment. The school system is a case in point. Various observers have termed Kinloch's schools the worst in St. Louis County. There are twenty-five school districts in the county, most of them enrolling pupils from more than one municipality. No one has come forward to consolidate their schools with Kinloch's, and the city must go it alone. One result is the highest school tax rate in the county ($4.23 per $100 of assessed valuation) and the lowest per pupil expenditure ($296.11 annually). Other consequences, predictably, are ramshackle and jammed facilities for the town's fifteen hundred pupils, totally inadequate school libraries, underpaid teachers generally offering inferior instruction, and a complete lack of specialists such as guidance counselors and remedial reading personnel. In past years, the Kinloch schools have had to ration such items as chalk, only to find some of the scarce sticks disappearing into the stomachs of hungry students.

When Clarence Lee assumed office in 1961, Kinloch's schools had reached their nadir. The superintendent, subsequently dismissed after eighteen years in that post, was under a St. Louis

County grand jury investigation for misappropriating the district's meager funds. The city's educational program was so deficient that the State refused to continue its accreditation. The quality of Kinloch's schools literally had fallen below the bottom of the rating scale.

It would be unfair to give Lee total credit for the changes that have taken place in the Kinloch school system since 1961. The town's elected six-member school board is an autonomous body with no direct ties to City Hall. However, it is a fact that the schools have begun to move forward under the Lee administration. A $155,000 bond issue in 1963 financed construction of a fourth school building, a nine-room junior high named after John F. Kennedy. Moreover, the city made a giant stride in education by replacing the former superintendent with an experienced professional administrator, Dr. Arthur Shropshire, formerly director of the Education Division at Langston University in Oklahoma.

Of course, Shropshire's initial programs, prescribing such essentials as kindergarten, the services of public health nurses to conduct routine health examination, and "in-service" projects to upgrade teachers' competence, all require funds which Kinloch cannot provide. The city's only recourse has been to request financial help from the federal government. Thus far, approximately $500,000 has been granted to Kinloch for improvements in its schools.

OPPOSITION TO LEE'S TACTICS

Despite obvious progress in Kinloch, and at least the long-range prospect of economic self-sufficiency, Mayor Lee is not without his detractors. The most vigorous anti-Lee voice in Kinloch belongs to William Petty, a 39-year-old brick contractor who occupies the second-ranking elective office in town as president of the ten-man Board of Aldermen. Running against Lee in the 1965 Mayoralty election, Petty was soundly defeated by a two-to-one margin. However, he easily maintains an aldermanic seat in his home ward and, hence, remains a potent voice of opposition. A friendly bear of a man, Petty matches Lee in personal determination but, until recently, has devoted most of his attention to his own business enterprise. Today, Petty has one of the highest incomes in Kinloch and is personally constructing what certainly will be the town's

## The Other Mayor Lee

finest residence, a ranch-style home that would do credit to the poshest white suburban neighborhood.

Although Lee and Petty have equivalent academic backgrounds —their two years of college place both at the top of Kinloch's educational elite—Petty is inclined to speak as a middle-class critic of an administration he sees employing lower-class political tactics. Preferring not to rely on the town's only newspaper, a biweekly which seems to criticize both the mayor and his opponent with equal fervor, Petty turns out a steady stream of scathing, but well-reasoned, newsletters to publicize his position.

An examination of some of Petty's political ammunition is revealing. Most of his criticisms of Lee are easily substantiated and, in another community, one acclimated to the conduct of government as it might be prescribed in a civics text, the mayor likely would find himself confronted by an outraged electorate. In Kinloch, Lee can roll with the punch.

Alderman Petty charges that Kinloch operates without an annual budget, in violation of Missouri law and contrary to any reasonable notion of proper city government. In fact, Petty's basic allegation is correct. Kinloch has not adopted a new budget since 1964. An independent audit of the city's records for that fiscal year, ordered by Petty from his position as alderman, revealed numerous shortcomings in bookkeeping. The auditors found that Kinloch did not maintain a general ledger, thus precluding an accurate statement of the town's assets and liabilities. Receipt and disbursement journals contained incorrectly added columns, and did not cross-balance. Records of many city transactions were missing entirely. However, the auditors found no actual cash shortages. Instead, they discovered an informal and virtually useless system of financial control.

Careful examination of the auditors' report confirms what most Kinlochians have known for years: the city's business is conducted on an ad hoc basis. Despite Petty's cries of outrage, this knowledge fails to excite Kinloch's voters, because it is generally agreed that any attempt to adhere to a systematic division of the town's inadequate income would result in overall devastation. Kinloch's property tax is within a nickel of Missouri's legal limit of 75 cents per $100 valuation, yet the municipality takes in only about $100,000 a year in revenue. Therefore, the mayor prefers to rob Peter to pay Paul, with Paul being the areas in which spending appears to be the most critically needed and Peter those programs lower in priority.

While such items as badly needed road repairs await additional revenue, Lee concentrates city funds on more basic endeavors. Kinloch recently spent $33,000 on a new fully equipped fire engine, replacing a 1941 museum piece. The modern pumper, and approximately forty new fire hydrants installed at a cost of $49 apiece, give the city adequate fire coverage for the first time. Street lights, costing $35 each, have been installed at nearly every corner, but local residents must organize their own "light clubs" to obtain illumination in the middle of a block. Purchase of a second-hand truck, coupled with federal funds to pay chronically unemployed men for work on "city beautification projects," is facilitating clearance of two pieces of city-owned property as park sites. Meanwhile, Lee prods representatives of the War on Poverty, pointing out the fine print in new legislation that might offer Kinloch additional financial relief.

### KINLOCH'S POLICE

A substantial portion of Kinloch's expenditures goes toward police protection, and herein lies Alderman Petty's main complaint. The days of volunteer foot patrolmen are over, but Petty and most other Kinlochians consider the police force woefully deficient. Petty claims that crime is rampant in the city, and that police laxity allows it to flourish. On the other hand, Kinloch reported only seventeen crimes to the county records center in 1965, and listed all seventeen as solved.

Petty probably is closer to the truth than is the official record but, again, the problem seems to be largely financial, and one of allocating priorities. The Kinloch force consists of one full-time officer per eight-hour shift, with assorted others, including the mayor, available for part-time duty. The department's equipment is reasonably modern, but two-way radio communication loses its effectiveness when the town's lone on-duty policeman is out of his car. When a backlog of calls develops, Kinlochians sometimes must wait hours until a policeman is available. Then, too, Kinloch has not yet been able to afford cells for the temporary hold-over of prisoners. When a Kinloch officer makes an arrest he often must decide whether to release the offender pending trial, or leave the

# The Other Mayor Lee

town entirely without protection while he makes the twenty-mile round trip to the county jail.

Shorthandedness, however, is only one of Kinloch's police problems. Members of the force lack any training except that obtained by practical experience. There are endless possibilities for malfeasance in a situation where police are underpaid and untrained. Indeed, it is difficult to find a Kinlochian who holds the city police in high esteem. A few of Lee's opponents have accused him of encouraging a corrupt department, in order to blackmail votes, if not money, in return for police immunity.

Alderman Petty has proposed the final solution to the police dilemma: abolish the Kinloch force and contract with the county for police protection. St. Louis County police have jurisdiction over unincorporated areas and, for a fee based on cost of operation, will assume responsibility for patrolling those county municipalities which prefer not to operate their own departments. In June of 1966 Petty, again from his position on the aldermanic board, asked the county police to estimate a yearly fee if the city decided to abolish its own force. A cost-finding study was designed, involving two weeks of experimental patrolling by county cars in Kinloch. Mayor Lee, citing Kinloch's pre-incorporation experiences with the county police, and expressing fear of the psychological effect that a sudden influx of white officers would have upon the populace of his all-black city, suggested the experiment might set off a "little Watts." The project was cancelled two days before it was to begin, when the county police commissioners officially claimed a sudden shortage of available manpower.

## KINLOCHIANS VERSUS THE POLICE

While Lee is reluctant to see Kinloch's black police force dissolved, its inadequacy has brought him his darkest hour. In September of 1962 one of the city's finest, a 74-year-old patrolman, shot to death a 20-year-old traffic offender while trying to serve him a summons. That evening, three hundred Kinlochians picketed the City Hall, demanding an end to "Jesse James law." Picketing soon turned to more dramatic forms of protest, such as a partially successful attempt to burn down the home of the police chief. As the disorder continued, youthful gangs of arsonists began setting fires indiscriminately. One blaze destroyed a portable frame addition to the already-crowded Kinloch elementary school. While Kinloch homeowners actually mounted armed guard over their properties, Mayor Lee requested help from the county and surrounding municipalities. A detachment of fifty white police arrived, some accompanied by police dogs. During the night, two county officers were wounded by shotgun blasts, although it never has been determined whether the shots were aimed at the men or the dogs. Sporadic shooting and arson continued for another seventy-two hours before the situation was brought completely under control.

After the unpleasantness, now referred to as a disturbance by Kinlochians and as a riot by most white county residents, the mayor promised to act upon the citizens' grievances. As a start, the elderly officer who had precipitated the whole affair was encouraged to offer his resignation. A study committee, made up of Lee and county officials, was convened to investigate ways of upgrading Kinloch's police. As expected, the committee's fundamental recommendations were for higher pay, better training, and the hiring of individuals with more suitable qualifications.

The mayor has been able to effect some increase in police salaries, which averaged only a dollar per hour at the time of the disorder, but Kinloch simply cannot afford adequate law enforcement. As a stopgap measure, three recruits recently were added to the force. If they survive probationary status, Kinloch will have two officers per shift. However, the situation is hardly healthy. The rookies will have to generate enough revenue through traffic fines to provide their own salaries.

Doubling Kinloch's meager corps of full-time patrolmen by no means exhausts Mayor Lee's fund of ideas on the subject. Scanning the horizon for federal assistance, Lee sees appropriations being made for training programs in various occupational categories. Why not extend the definition of one of these congressional bills to include training of the Kinloch police force, add the federal training stipends to the officers' present salaries, bring police wages to an attractive level, ask the county to conduct the training and have this credited as Kinloch's ten percent contribution, and thereby get training and financial assistance in the same package? Local anti-poverty administrators react to this scheme with some bewilderment, but after seeing the sewer amendment through to success, Lee views nothing as impossible.

## THE MORAL DILEMMA

While Clarence Lee struggles to bring a better way of life to a community almost totally lacking in indigenous resources, some observers question the morality of it all. They raise the issue, valid at least in the abstract, of the usefulness of an all-black city in an age of integration. Kinlochians, by and large, are too enthusiastic about the coming of indoor plumbing and about lighted streets to criticize these phenomena as strengthening a segregated status quo. They are accustomed to isolation and generally see no immediate prospect of closer ties with their reluctant county neighbors. Above integration, they desire immediate changes in their living conditions, even if these changes take place within the framework of an all-black society. Most blacks can understand this point of view, but it is not readily acceptable to a small number of liberal whites who occupy influential positions in the St. Louis area. These individuals tend to see Kinloch's attempts at self-sufficiency as insuring the city's continued existence as a black ghetto. Some recommend disincorporation, although they are unable to project any specific integration breakthroughs as a result. Others call for merger with Berkeley and/or Ferguson, forgetting that neither of Kinloch's immediate neighbors is remotely willing to absorb eight thousand blacks.

Lee answers the well-meaning moralists with a cliché: he hopes Kinloch will become a place where whites will want to live. Thus, instead of suggesting that Kinlochians integrate Berkeley or Ferguson, Lee speaks of integration coming to Kinloch. In the next breath, however, he talks of the likelihood of an influx of low-income black families from a half-dozen small unincorporated black communities in St. Louis County. He predicts almost a hundred percent increase in population in less than five years, estimating fifteen thousand residents, all of them black, by 1970. These individuals will come fleeing the outhouse-and-shanty style of living from which their own non-autonomous villages cannot escape. They will come to take advantage of a better way of life, in the only more attractive community that will readily accept them. If this wave of poverty-level blacks arrives, and all that seems to block them is the town's almost total lack of available rental accommodations, they will superimpose a new set of demands upon Kinloch's sputtering economy. Certainly, they will preclude white immigration in the foreseeable future, if for no other reason than that they will occupy all of the unused land.

Nevertheless, Kinloch probably will manage to cope with the problems posed by any new arrivals. Unlike Richard Lee of New Haven, Clarence Lee won't be able to pick up the telephone and call a brainstorming session of top city officials. Kinloch's mayor will have to develop his own strategy utilizing, perhaps, resources made available through some yet-to-be-passed federal legislation. But who is willing to wager that Kinloch, and its Mayor Lee, won't stave off municipal bankruptcy despite the odds? After all, who would have though in 1948, or even in 1961 when Lee took office, that Kinloch would survive into 1967?

# Mobile Homes: Instant Suburbia or Transportable Slums?

ROBERT MILLS FRENCH and JEFFREY K. HADDEN

In his best-selling book *Travels with Charlie*, John Steinbeck reported a surprising discovery he made while touring the nation. Everywhere he went, Steinbeck saw Americans living in a new type of housing—trailers, or mobile homes. Steinbeck's surprise was not only that so many people chose to live in houses on wheels, but also that trailers themselves had changed dramatically. No longer were trailers the cramped, semi-camping affairs which Steinbeck remembered from the World War II era when they were primarily emergency housing for defense-plant workers; the modern equivalent of the trailer had become a spacious and comfortable dwelling place.

The discovery which Steinbeck made parallels the discovery and acceptance of mobile housing by several million Americans. Since the end of World War II the growth of this type of housing has been phenomenal—increasing tenfold in just two decades. During this period the size and internal appearance of mobile homes has been dramatically changed, and their public image has been improved. The many beautifully landscaped mobile home parks available today contrast sharply to the crowded, mud-street "trailer towns" where a large proportion of mobile homes used to be parked. Even the name "mobile home" is a conscientious effort on behalf of the marketing experts of the industry to erase the negative image of the trailer. But behind the splendor of the new

---

Reprinted from Social Problems *16 (1968), pp. 219-226, by permission of the publisher, The American Sociological Association, and Robert Mills French.*

image linger some serious questions which no one at the moment seems to be asking. The potential impact of the rapid increase in mobile housing is of such magnitude as to raise serious questions as to society's ability to cope with the situation.

## GROWTH OF MOBILE HOUSING

In 1940 there were approximately 170,000 mobile homes (or trailers) in the U.S., representing less than one-half of one percent of all housing. By 1960 the number of mobile homes had increased to over three-quarters of a million and constituted just under one and one-half percent of all housing. Then during the first seven years of the 1960s the explosion occurred. In 1960 there were 104,000 mobile homes built. This figure jumped to 151,000 in 1963, and in 1965 the industry produced 216,000 mobile home units. During this seven-year period the total number of mobile homes more than doubled with the production of more than one million units. By the beginning of 1967 there were over one and three-quarter million mobile residences in the nation.

Assuming no significant increase in production during the next four years, another million mobile homes will be added to the housing market by 1970. This will represent approximately four percent of all housing. But the industry is not yet satisfied with its increasing share of the housing market. Last year the Mobile Home Manufacturers Association predicted annual production figures of 400,000 by the 1970s.

Examination of the market potential for relatively low-cost housing and the role that mobile homes have been playing in the current low-cost housing market would suggest that the manufacturers' projections may be quite realistic. In five years their share of total new housing doubled from seven percent in 1961 to nearly fourteen percent in 1966. Stated another way, one of every six single-family units started today is a mobile home. But the industry's share of the low-cost housing market is even more impressive. In 1965 mobile homes captured seventy-six percent of the market for homes valued at less than $12,500. For the next decade, at least, low-cost housing demands seem certain to continue to grow. Thus, unless the federal government becomes involved in low-cost housing construction in a big way, mobile homes seem destined to constitute more than ten percent of all housing by 1980.

## IMPLICATIONS OF THIS GROWTH

This rapid increase poses a whole host of important questions that must be faced by city planners, government officials, social scientists, and the industry itself. Who lives in mobile homes? Where are they located? How does the mobile home fit into the total community housing situation? Do mobile homes fulfill some unique needs, or are they competing with more conventional housing forms? What is the quality of mobile housing? Do mobile home dwellers carry their fair share of local taxes? Or are they located outside the incorporated city where they avoid taxes while creating unpredictable demands for local facilities? What about the residents' participation in local community affairs? Are they politically apathetic, or do they go to the polls and vote disproportionately in favor of programs that they are not likely to be around long enough to help pay for? In light of the rapid expansion of mobile housing, such questions take on enormous significance.

Historically, houses on wheels have been associated with lower-class elements of the population—gypsies, tinkers, and other transients who were not really a part of society. As recently as 1940 the Bureau of the Census lumped trailers into a category with railroad cars, tents, and shacks!

World War II and the period immediately thereafter saw trailers fulfill the role of emergency housing. It would have been easy to predict that trailers would subside into oblivion once the postwar housing emergency had been met. Far from collapsing, the industry began building larger, more homelike units while their marketing departments sought to expand sales via a new image. Although the cracker-box external appearance of the early trailers has remained, internal improvements and increased size have enhanced their appeal as housing. Due to increased size "mobile" homes have become increasingly immobile, thus limiting their usefulness for transient populations.

In the early 1950s the eight-foot-wide trailer was standard and accounted for the bulk of the market. The ten-foot-wide mobile home, which came into mass production in 1954, quickly replaced the eight-wides in popularity, and by 1961 were ninety-eight percent of all production. The still bigger twelve-wides appeared in 1962, and today the most popular size is twelve feet wide and sixty feet long. The trend to ever-larger units has led to double-wides (two connected twelve-wides) and expandables (which may be over twenty-four feet wide) that are capturing a sizable proportion of the market. In terms of internal space, the average new mobile home has increased in size from about three hundred square feet in 1956 to approximately six hundred square feet in 1965. The expandable and double-wide units currently run as high as fourteen hundred square feet and even larger models are predicted.

The increased size of mobile homes has permitted great internal changes—fully equipped modern kitchens with the latest advances in kitchen gadgetry, more and larger rooms, and much more storage space are some of the improvements which have been made. These "homelike" features, combined with the allure of something that is brand new, all add to the improved image and marketability of mobile homes.

All of this makes understandable the expansion in mobile home purchases, but it does not indicate where the market lies. Who buys these attractive homes on wheels? Where are they located? And how attractive will they be after the newness has worn off?

## CHARACTERISTICS OF MOBILE HOMES AND THEIR RESIDENTS

The 1960 Census of Housing provides the only systematic data on the characteristics and location of mobile homes.[1] These data do not begin to permit us to answer all the questions we have raised above, but they do provide some important clues and a basis for speculating about the potential consequences of this new form of housing.

The greatest proportion of mobile homes are found in the Western and Southern sections of the country, more often in and around cities than in the rural hinterland. Within Standard Metropolitan Statistical Areas, mobile homes tend to be located near the periphery, suggesting another form of suburbanization.

It has long been thought that military personnel, college students, construction workers, and retirees comprised the major market for mobile homes. Using rather crude ecological indicators

---

1. For a discussion of the census data see Mills and Hadden 1965, pp. 131–39. A more detailed discussion of the census data, along with a review of the literature concerning mobile housing, is available in French 1964.

it was possible to conclude that, while these groups comprise part of the market, the largest group consists of young married couples. The industry is well aware of this fact. Its spokesman, the Mobile Home Manufacturers Association (MHMA), has found that forty-three percent of mobile home households, as compared to twenty-four percent of all household heads, are in the 34-and-under age group. The MHMA predicts an increasing market potential among these "young marrieds" and points out that apartments, not permanent single-family dwellings, are the mobile homes' main competitor.

This information, coupled with the spatial location of mobile homes near the periphery of the city, suggests a trend toward *instant suburbia;* i.e., a low-cost means of escape from the inner city by young, striving middle-class families who cannot yet afford a suburban home. With one foot in suburbia via "wheel estate," they can now save for the day when they make a down payment on their dream home and enter suburbia in style.

## AN ALTERNATIVE TO THE "SUBURBIA" INTERPRETATION

While the model just presented seems plausible, its reality cannot be verified without systematic field surveys. In fact, the available evidence suggests that it is incorrect. In the first place, it implies that mobile home residents are likely to be young middle-class couples on their way up. That this is not the case is suggested by an industry survey which found only thirteen percent of mobile home residents employed in non-manual or "white collar" occupations. (Of the "white collar" group, almost one-fourth were sales workers, which is a peripheral middle-class occupation.) Over sixty percent of mobile home dwellers were engaged in some manual or "blue collar" occupation, with the remainder classified as retired or unemployed. These figures do not lend credence to the upwardly-mobile, young middle-class group interpretation.

Furthermore, the historical reasons for lower-class migrants to cluster in city centers have disappeared in the U.S. Around the turn of the century centralized industrialization combined with costly transportation from peripheral areas forced the immigrant laborer to live close to his job in crowded, substandard rental housing. With the advent of better roads and virtually universal auto ownership, today's in-migrant laborer does not have to live in the central city if he can find economical housing elsewhere.[2]

Today's in-migrants come from rural, generally Southern, areas. They need not cluster in the central city and may prefer, as rural persons, to stay on the outskirts rather than attempt a complete transformation of their life style. As they are probably WASPs (White Anglo-Saxon Protestants) they may also object to those ethnic groups, and particularly Negroes, who populate the central city areas. In short, rather than constructing housing for young middle-class families on the way up, mobile homes may be largely serving the needs of working-class families who are new urban residents from rural areas.

Additional factors suggest that mobile housing may be more desirable housing for blue-collar families. The lower cost of the mobile home (average $5,600) compared to the permanent home (average $16,200 for a minimum four-room frame home) may be an important consideration to working-class people who are not securely established in well-paying jobs. While they might hesitate to take on a twenty-year mortgage, a mobile home loan with an average maturity of five to seven years is short enough to seem reasonable.

Furthermore, the down payment required on a mobile home, fifteen to twenty-five percent, or $1,400 or less on the average unit, is small compared to the initial cost of permanent housing, which would be over $3,200 on a minimum standard house.

A unique feature of mobile home purchase is that the entire home including necessary furnishing and appliances is sold as a unit which can be financed in one transaction. This probably has greater appeal to the unsophisticated in-migrant who is baffled by matters of finance. In fact, the mobile home may be the only recourse for the young couple who wish to have their own home complete with all new household items but do not have good enough credit to contract for many purchases on the installment plan.

Moreover, as most mobile home dealers can readily arrange financing on the same basis as auto financing at high rates (up to

---

2. The Negro would be an obvious exception, for his choice of housing is often limited to the extent of the urban ghetto. Worth noting is the fact that virtually no Negroes live in mobile housing—in 1960 only 1.4 percent of all mobile housing was occupied by non-whites.

fourteen percent), they are not restricted by tight money conditions which restrict conventional housing loans to only the best risks. Since the dealer can easily repossess the unit and all its furnishings by hauling it away, normally poor risks might be financed to buy a mobile home.

If the low-down-payment, easily financed, complete package can be demonstrated to be a persuasive factor in mobile home buying, it might be an indicator of the type of person that would buy a mobile home, i.e., the low-income young person, tenuously established in his job and community standing, desirous of comfortable modern housing and furniture but unwilling to delay gratification of these wishes long enough to obtain permanent housing. These traits are more characteristic of lower-class persons than of the middle class.

Still, if the mobile home is less expensive than an apartment or permanent home, as is generally assumed, then purchase of a mobile home would eventually aid an aspiring couple to save for the future. Actually, on a monthly basis, little if anything is gained by living in a mobile home. In fact, mobile home living can be more expensive than apartment living. Rental of a parking space generally runs between $30 and $70; payments on the unit would be approximately $100 on the average unit. Additional expenses include gas, electricity, heating fuel, and licensing and/or personal property taxes in some states. It seems highly unlikely that the mobile home resident could pay any less than $100 per month for housing, and a more realistic estimate would be from $150 to $180 per month, with some units costing much more. Except for the very dregs of mobile housing, then, it seems hard to consider mobile homes lower-cost housing than much rental and even some self-owned housing.

Nor do mobile homes fit well into long-term middle-class housing plans as a potential down payment on a house. Due to their rapid rate of depreciation, mobile homes would not provide a substantial down payment. Inasmuch as they come complete with furniture of generally low quality, mobile homes would not provide middle-class couples with furniture for their dream homes. Restricted space combined with the necessity of taking a loss on disposal of the original furniture would prohibit gradually adding furniture for the future. In short, the very nature of the mobile home would tend to make it unsuitable, even temporarily, for the vast majority of middle-class families. Although manufacturers portray typically middle-class residents in their ads, these considerations suggest that upwardly mobile middle-class families do not constitute the majority of mobile home dwellers.

## POSSIBLE RAMIFICATIONS OF THE "WORKING-CLASS IN-MIGRANT" INTERPRETATION

If this analysis is correct, the ramifications for mobile housing are tremendous. Instead of being the residences of upwardly mobile persons desirous of entering suburbia via mobile home parks with attractive homes, well-kept lawns, etc., they may instead be attracting young, uneducated in-migrants from Appalachia and the South who cluster in "Hillbilly Havens" at the periphery of the city.

Given a mobile home population composed in large part of working-class in-migrants, the question arises: will these people inevitably create slum conditions? Not necessarily—but, as lower-class persons, they may continue old life styles of strewing about their belongings, failing to maintain lawn and garden, and generally violating the "niceties" of suburbia.

Even if our speculation regarding the current market for new mobile homes is incorrect, this does not negate the prospect that they will eventually become the residences of lower-class people. In fact, the quality of construction and the market value of used units strongly suggest that this is their inevitable destiny.

At present, the census data do not substantiate the prevalent stereotype of "trailers" as substandard housing. Mobile homes are predominantly owner-occupied, and the proportion that are reported as deteriorating or dilapidated is far below national figures for conventional housing. But this is obviously a function of the fact that most mobile homes are relatively new. More than seventy-five percent of all mobile units are less than ten years old.

How bright are future prospects of continued good condition? Partly this depends on the quality of individual brands, and while the MHMA claims to have quality control standards, the standards are minimal and do not appear to be rigidly enforced. The MHMA claims that mobile homes will last as long as conventional housing, but this seems highly doubtful.

The market value of mobile homes depreciates rapidly compared with conventional housing, which suggests something about the quality of the respective types. The simplicity of "trading up," i.e., trading a used model for a new, improved one, is stressed in advertisements, and the average mobile home dweller responds by trading his old unit every three years. Persons who view a residence as only temporary are less likely to make investments in upkeep than if they viewed the residence as permanent. The high depreciation would also seem to discourage upkeep. While it is perhaps too early to establish an average life for mobile homes, it seems fairly certain that this period will be considerably less than for conventional housing.

Like the dilapidated automobile, mobile homes may simply be scrapped when they deteriorate. The original low investment along with the possibility of trade-in makes this a very real possibility. If aged mobile homes are junked ("retired," in the jargon of the industry), will they be destroyed, or left to litter the countryside, or pile up in unsightly junkyards like automobiles?

While deteriorated mobile homes may very well be discarded, several factors may inhibit this development. Unlike autos which must at least run to be useful, mobile homes may be hopelessly run-down and still be used. Urban renewal in our cities has succeeded in reducing the total quantity of low-cost housing for the poor, and promises to reduce it even further. Add to this the possibility that if automation creates a larger proportion of the population that is permanently unemployed and unemployable, more low-cost housing will be needed. Deteriorated mobile homes may provide an inexpensive form of housing for this group.

Perhaps a more likely prospect that the desperately poor buying deteriorated mobile homes, is that they will be purchased by absentee landlords who will rent them to lower-class people. Thus, if mobile homes are destined to experience a rather rapid deterioration and are not disposed of as are deteriorated automobiles, it is altogether feasible that mobile home parks composed of old, run-down, rental units will become a new type of absentee-owned slum.

The census provides some indication that this problem might already exist on a small scale. In 1960, ninety percent of the mobile housing classified as in sound condition was owner-occupied, whereas only sixty-nine percent of mobile homes classified as deteriorating or dilapidated was owner-occupied. This might be attributed to the fact that pride of ownership keeps maintenance standards high, or merely that rental units are older and/or house poorer people. The speculation about older rental units is supported by the figures on median number of rooms per mobile home. Due to the recent trend to build larger units with more rooms, it follows that the older the unit, the fewer its rooms. In 1960, owner-occupied mobile homes had a median number of 3.2 rooms, as compared to 2.6 for renter-occupied units; thus, our speculation is supported. Heretofore, the number of rental units has been small and did not constitute a large enough population to have great effect even if they were slum-type substandard havens for lower-class people. With the increased numbers of new units each year, however, it would seem that as the life cycle of deterioration takes its course, an increasing number of units will become substandard rental units.

The market for deteriorating and dilapidated housing is potentially great. To the poor, cheap housing outside the corporate limits of the city would have many attractions. This would particularly be the case for the lower-class rural white from the South. Perplexed by the city and repelled by his inner-city residence beside ever-increasing proportions of Negroes, he might find a trailer camp at the edge of the city well suited to his temperament and income level. Here he could find kindred souls who share his frustration with city life. These "Hillbilly Havens" might become much like the *barridos* at the periphery of Latin American cities in which new migrants from the hinterland congregate with fellow kinsmen in villages. This pattern need not be restricted to whites. Negroes might also develop such enclaves. In any event, the potential problems of social control should be rather obvious.

This portrait may seem unduly alarmist, but the fact that the stage has already been set cannot be ignored. There are already over one and three-quarter million mobile homes, and it seems certain that the proportion of the total housing that they represent will continue to increase. Furthermore, while precise estimates are lacking, mobile homes will almost certainly deteriorate much more rapidly than conventional housing.

The problem would not be potentially as serious if these housing units were not on wheels. But there are few if any metropolitan areas in the country that currently have the political machinery to cope with the problem. As long as metropolitan governments must confine their jurisdiction to corporate city limits, the owners of "Hillbilly Havens" can always keep one jump ahead of annexation with their *transportable slums*. In the event that strict housing codes were enforced, the mobile slum, unlike traditional slums, could escape corrective measures by fleeing, in rag-taggle caravans, beyond the jurisdiction of the law.

Even if our speculation on the potential of mobile homes to become transportable slums is unwarranted, several factors remain which are not currently receiving adequate attention. Most important is the fact that mobile homes create unpredictable needs for public services. Large mobile home parks can be created almost overnight. Most cities have zoning areas which restrict mobile homes from some areas, but few cities have adequate codes and policies to permit systematic control and planning for this type of housing. Many cities lack the resources to prohibit the rapid emergence of a large mobile home park which would result in insufficient time and resources to plan for adequate school facilities. But even where such codes may exist, it is impossible to control and predict the composition of the residents of mobile home parks and their concomitant needs for public services. The increased size of mobile units creates greater flexibility in terms of the types of family units which may inhabit them. Thus, for example, a mobile home park which is largely inhabited by childless couples may undergo a very rapid transition in which the majority of the residents have children of school age, or vice versa.

Probably the most significant aspect of mobile homes is that we know so little about them. Since they tend to be at the fringes of cities in areas that are not zoned for conventional housing, they have remained relatively invisible. But the number of mobile homes is increasing too rapidly to ignore them or to rely on speculation as to how they fit into the overall housing scene in America. If our speculations are warranted, then local, state, and federal officials should begin to formulate public policies which will prevent the emergence of the problems this type of housing seems destined to create. To date, social scientists have virtually ignored this phenomenal housing development in American society. Obviously, the formulation of sound public policy will be aided by more careful study of mobile homes than has heretofore been the case.

## SUGGESTIONS FOR FURTHER READING

Those interested in "package" suburbs during their formative postwar years should read Herbert Gans, "Park Forest: Birth of a Jewish Community" (*Commentary*, vol. 21, April 1951, pp. 330-339). Another article providing insight into these enclaves, from the developer's point of view, is Alfred S. Levitt's "A Community Builder Looks at Community Planning" (*Journal of the American Institute of Planners*, vol. 17, Spring 1951, pp. 80-88). For a brief description of a postwar suburb's cultural ethos, fifteen years after its founding, see Lois Dean, *Five Towns: A Comparative Community Study* (New York: Random House, 1967).

Selection eleven is taken from *The Edge of Friendliness: A Study of Jewish-Gentile Relations* by Benjamin B. Ringer. This book is one of two volumes from the "Lakeville Studies" sponsored by The American Jewish Committee. The other is Marshall Sklare and Joseph Greenblum, *Jewish Identity on the Suburban Frontier: A Study of Group Survival in the Open Society* (New York: Basic Books, 1967). Ringer's book concentrates upon Jewish-Gentile relations. Sklare and Greenblum's work, in turn, focuses upon the religious and social behavior of Jews per se, and examines the effects of suburbia and affluence upon these practices.

The issue of blacks in the suburbs is one calling for further research, and the coming decade undoubtedly will produce a number of books and articles dealing with the black suburban experience. For a demographic overview of the situation (as of 1960) see Reynolds Farley, "The Changing Distribution of Negroes within Metropolitan Areas: The Emergence of Black Suburbs" (*The American Journal of Sociology*, vol. 75, January 1970, pp. 512-527). An exploratory study based upon interviews with the residents of six black suburban settlements outside of Philadelphia is reported by Leonard Blumberg and Michael Lalli in "Little Ghettoes: A Study of Negroes in the Suburbs" (*Phylon*, vol. 27, Summer 1966, pp. 117-131). Economic information about Kinloch, described in selection twelve, appears in Ingo Walter and John Kramer's "Political Autonomy and Economic Dependence in an All-Negro Municipality" (*American Journal of Economics and Sociology*, vol. 28, July 1969, pp. 225-248). Everett C. Ladd, Jr.'s *Ideology in America: Change and Response in a City, a Suburb, and a Small Town* (Ithaca, N.Y.: Cornell University Press, 1969) compares the prevailing political ideologies in three very different community settings in Connecticut. One of these communities is an essentially middle-class suburb—Bloomfield, outside of Hartford—where an influx of blacks from the central city currently is taking place. Ladd describes the town's uneasy accommodations to its new black residents and, in the process, provides one of the few detailed discussions of a racially mixed suburban milieu.

# PART IV: POLITICS IN SUBURBIA

# INTRODUCTION

Perhaps the most distinguishing institutional arrangement in suburbia is its political structure. Divided into innumerable local political jurisdictions, the suburbs of North America resemble, as political scientist Robert Wood has written, a collection of "republics in miniature." There are more than twenty-one thousand local governmental units in the suburban sectors of the United States' 243 Standard Metropolitan Statistical Areas.

In recent years, political scientists have begun to explore the social bases of politics in this immense collection of local governments. Three articles devoted to this task are reprinted here. Each in its own way, the three selections make the suburban myth obsolete. And, in the tradition of meaningful social research, each of them suggests questions requiring further investigation.

Frederick Wirt, in "The Political Sociology of American Suburbs: A Reinterpretation," confronts the suburban myth directly. Wirt was concerned with those portions of the myth which concede suburbia to the Republican Party. He gathered longitudinal election data from 154 highly diverse suburban municipalities. These data allowed him to determine if suburbia, in fact, was a Republican bastion (in 1960); if the Republican Party had enjoyed steady and overwhelming suburban voting majorities over time (from 1932 to 1960); and if the "political complexion" of suburban communities was associated with their socio-economic characteristics. On the first two counts the suburban myth was clearly in error. Wirt found the Democratic Party alive and well in suburbia and, from all indications, growing ever healthier. On the third count, also, the myth was deficient. Overall, Wirt's low-status communities were Democratic (even though these suburbs should have been Republican, according to the myth) while his high-status suburbs were Republican. Yet there was a socio-economic randomness to those suburbs with inter-party competition, a finding not explainable by the suburban myth nor by the axioms of political sociology. Indeed, the nature of political factualization in the suburbs is among the most significant questions now facing students of the suburban setting.

One of the few focused investigations of suburban inter-party competition is Dennis Ippolito's "Political Perspectives of Suburban Party Leaders," the second selection in part four. Ippolito interviewed eighty-five party executive committeemen (forty-seven of them Democrats and thirty-five Republicans) in Long Island's Nassay County. He found that the two sets of party leaders seemed to have similar socio-economic characteristics. But there were important demographic differences. The Democratic leaders were younger, more often Jewish and less often Protestant than their Republican counterparts, and had been residents of Nassau County for shorter periods of time. Apparently, these individuals were not being "converted" to Republicanism. Indeed, Ippolito's data indicate that these relatively recent suburban arrivals were the very people instrumental in making Nassau County's Democratic Party a viable political force. On ideological and evaluative grounds, too, there were differences between the two parties' leadership cadres. Partisan politics in suburbia, at least as it is practiced in Nassau County, obviously is more complex than is popularly assumed.

Of course, Nassau County is a vast terrain, situated in New York City's "inner ring" suburban sector. To study Nassau County as a whole is to study suburban diversity in its most pronounced form. What of the political structure in suburban communities which contain relatively homogeneous and high-status populations and, demographically at least, fit the popular imagery about suburbia? The third selection, "Political Participation in an Upper-Middle-Class Suburb," by Joseph Zikmund II and Robert Smith, explores this question.

The setting for Zikmund and Smith's research was Radnor Township, one of the thirty-eight townships comprising "mainline"

## Introduction

Montgomery County outside of Philadelphia. In Radnor, large numbers of males commute to the city. Research during the 1950s suggested that commuters play few active roles in local politics, leaving these tasks to women or to those men who both live and work in the suburban communities. Through mailed questionnaires to Radnor residents, Zikmund and Smith found that this township's male commuters were characterized, instead, by high levels of political participation, while the women of the area tended toward moderate activity or toward apathy. Furthermore, the authors suggest that the hard-core male apathetics in Radnor may well be the non-commuting "scientist-technicians" employed in nearby research facilities. Again, the need for additional research is clear.

At the conclusion of their study, Zikmund and Smith briefly argue *against* metropolitan government. As the selection by Daniel Grant in the next part indicates, Zikmund and Smith are swimming upstream, against the tide of most contemporary recommendations for reorganizing the metropolitan political system in the United States. No matter what the merits of their disputation, however, or the merits of Grant's more professionally conventional arguments, it is useful to realize that not all suburban study need produce (nor, in fact, does it produce) homogeneous recommendations for public policy.

# The Political Sociology of American Suburbia
## A Reinterpretation

### FREDERICK M. WIRT

Among the many consequences of American urbanism, the mass migration to the suburbs has been the most striking. These fringe towns orbit around a megalopolis, at once tied to it by gravitic bonds of commerce, transportation, and entertainment—and yet independent in many local affairs. A whole new literature has arisen about them, including a school of fiction depicting transplanted but rootless inhabitants who strive to find meaning in a life of metropolitan work, suburban civics, and newly adopted values. Non-fiction literature at the popular level has been of the whither-are-we-drifting variety, finding in these places a source of concern.

Social research into suburbs has dealt with their demographic characteristics, but surprisingly little depicts suburban political life. Lubell (1956) depicted the great Eisenhower support in suburbia in the 1950s. But he was uncertain that this was a permanent addition to the Republican party; rather it might be merely an expression of support of Eisenhower which other locales, such as core cities, were also showing.

Despite his cautions as to the future of suburban politics, much popular writing tended to see these places as predominantly Republican. This condition was explained by a simple theory. New immigrants and their children had realized vital aspirations through

---

*Reprinted from* **The Journal of Politics** *27 (1965), pp. 647–666, by permission of the publisher, The Southern Political Science Association, and the author. The author wishes to thank the Denison University Research Foundation and the Ohio Center for Education in Politics for financial aid.*

political attachment to the New Deal, and as one consequence of their prosperity moved to better surroundings, eventually to the suburbs. Here they tended to switch political loyalty to the Republican party. They did so for several reasons: partly to adapt to the immediate environment of these areas, but mostly because Republicanism was one characteristic of upper-class Americans. For the newcomer, voting Republican was an act of identification symbolizing his arrival. This thesis of suburban Republican growth is termed by Robert Wood as the "conversion" theory, although he did not necessarily accept its validity as an explanation of what had occurred. (Wood 1958, chap. 5; Greenstein and Wolfinger 1958; Manis and Stine 1958).

But this interpretation is somewhat heterodox. It assumes that party identification is a transient attitude, but the work of the Survey Research Center demonstrated very convincingly that party identification is a stable aspect of attitude structure, changing permanently only under the traumatic impact of war and depression. So a second explanation, which Wood calls "transplantation," is sometimes employed. This interpretation argues that the newcomers to suburbia were lifelong Republicans carrying their sense of affiliation with them as they migrated (1958, chap. 5).

Before we explain the facts, we had better make sure we have the facts straight. How Republican *are* these suburbs? That is, is the increased suburban vote for Eisenhower over Dewey in 1948 evidence of suburban Republicanism or of suburban support for Eisenhower? If it is only the latter, then it is fatuous to attempt to explain the inherent Republicanism of the suburbs, something assumed out of hand by *both* transplantation and conversion explanations.

Indeed, there is scattered evidence that indicates that suburbs are not as homogeneously Republican as assumed. Edson (1955) and Janosik (1956) in separate articles noticed surprising numbers of Democrats in St. Louis and Bucks County suburbs before 1960. Millett and Pittman (1958) found in two suburbs of Rochester, N.Y., no evidence of the conversion thesis. Even Lubell, in a curious footnote, had earlier noticed that "Some suburban returns I have analyzed point to a long-run trend to make the suburbs somewhat more Democratic, although not on any scale that would threaten Republican ascendancy in these communities" (1956, pp. 276–77).

What might have been written off as a series of local anomalies, became more difficult to explain away in 1960. Fully forty-nine percent of the suburban vote went for Kennedy. In only one metropolitan area (Kansas City) did Nixon's share of the suburban vote exceed Eisenhower's, while in seven areas Kennedy's share actually exceeded Nixon's (Boston, Detroit, Pittsburgh, St. Louis, St. Paul, San Francisco, and Washington) and in two the vote was even (Cleveland and Milwaukee).[1]

Another question not answered because not faced in both conversion and transplantation theses is: "How much of suburbia is upper middle class?" The key conceptual framework within which this question is explored here has been made explicit by two sociologists. William Dobriner puts it: "Perhaps one of the central theoretic problems growing out of suburbanization is the need to clarify . . . *the relationship between the suburb as an ecological variable and the elements of suburban organization and culture as class variables*" (1958, p. xxii; emphasis in original). Bennett Berger has pointed out the error of those scholars who, in equating suburbia with Republicanism, analyzed "the social and economic position and aspiration of white-collar people; their conclusions had to do with suburbs. To what extent these two variables are coextensive is precisely the question that has been ignored" (1960, p. 32).

Clearly, we need to re-examine notions about the pervasiveness of suburban Republicanism. This article shall probe beyond gross voting data to (1) explore whether there is variety in suburbia, both in electoral and socio-economic terms, and (2) to suggest some implications of suburban politics for the course of American politics, generally.

## SOURCES

The sources for this paper are aggregate data on election returns and census materials for 154 suburbs. These suburbs are from among the 260 so designated by Victor Jones and his associates in their extensive economic description of American cities (Jones, Forstall, and Colver 1963). The present author chose suburbs in the 10,000–25,000 population range in 1950 and employed 1960

---

1. *The 1960 Elections*, Republican National Committee (mimeo), 1961, pp. 18–20.

## TABLE 1
### COMPARISON OF THE MEANS OF RESPONDENT AND NON-RESPONDENT SUBURBS BY 1960 CENSUS INDICES

|  | Respondent Suburbs | Non-respondent Suburbs | Difference |
|---|---|---|---|
| % Non-white | 7.4 | 7.6 | 0.2 |
| % Under $3,000 income | 11.7 | 11.2 | 0.5 |
| Median age | 32.0 | 31.0 | 1.0 |
| % White collar | 49.0 | 50.2 | 1.2 |
| % Owner-occupied | 67.2 | 68.8 | 1.6 |
| Population (thousands) | 21.3 | 23.9 | 2.6 |
| % One-unit structures | 75.1 | 78.4 | 3.3 |
| Employment–residence ratio | 94.6 | 91.2 | 3.4 |
| Manufacturing % | 42.1 | 36.6 | 5.5 |
| % Homes built since 1950 | 26.0 | 34.1 | 8.1 |
| % Over $10,000 income | 45.5 | 25.8 | 19.7 |
| % Population change, 1950 | 35.9 | 57.2 | 21.3 |
| % Migrant | 48.4 | 19.3 | 29.1 |

census data (described later). My collection of electoral data began before 1960 and thus the 1950 population base was employed. But all census data analyzed below are drawn from Jones's post-1960 study. This population range was chosen because it constitutes the largest number of suburbs reported by Jones.

From these 260 suburbs[2] electoral data were received for 154 suburbs after four waves of mail questionnaires. These data covered the years 1932 and 1948–1960 for the offices of president, congressman, and mayor. Not all 154 suburb electoral results are complete; some municipalities were not legally in existence in 1932, some do not elect the mayor (all of California, for example), and some reported that no old records are kept. However, it was possible for any suburb to return complete data on twenty-one elections. The temporal span thereby provided could show a base in 1932 before the New Deal impact, the postwar changes (if any) and the post-Eisenhower changes (if any). Further, for any year, and across the years, one could determine the influence of the particular office upon party success. Finally, we may see the degree of party competition over the whole period.

Limitations on inferences drawn from mail polls are well-known. Thus, no level of confidence analysis is possible in this report: the conditions of random sampling cannot be met by a mail poll. However, Table 1 provides some basis for a belief that the

---

2. All Southern suburbs were omitted except two. It seemed likely when this study was begun that traditional Southern Democracy might operate in these suburbs and hence depress the national weight of suburban Republicanism.

returnees were not wildly different from the non-respondents.[3]

The last three measures do show a wide discrepancy. But by overweighting returns with high-income and high-migrant type suburbs, these data are those most relevant to the popular image of suburbia.

## SUBURBAN ELECTORAL PATTERNS

Because the assumption of suburban Republicanism underlies both the "conversion" and "transplantation" hypotheses, the first question is purely empirical: How Republican are American suburbs? Table 2 initiates the analysis.

TABLE 2
MEAN SUBURBAN GOP VOTE PERCENTAGE
FOR SELECTED OFFICES AND YEARS

|      | President % | N | Congress % | N | Mayor % | N |
|------|---|---|---|---|---|---|
| 1932 | 51.3 | 79  | 54.9 | 80  | 59.1 | 34 |
| 1948 | 52.4 | 143 | 52.4 | 138 | 57.9 | 55 |
| 1950 | —    | —   | 56.0 | 141 | 64.4 | 42 |
| 1952 | 56.4 | 152 | 55.6 | 146 | 58.9 | 59 |
| 1954 | —    | —   | 52.4 | 147 | 56.9 | 41 |
| 1956 | 60.0 | 152 | 54.1 | 151 | 54.0 | 57 |
| 1958 | —    | —   | 49.0 | 105 | 40.9 | 23 |
| 1960 | 47.3 | 110 | 48.9 | 109 | 46.0 | 24 |

Several conclusions are suggested here. Except at one or two points, these data do not reveal the high Republican percentages which suburbs are popularly thought to produce. The 1932–1948 comparison shows little Republican gain in the presidential vote in percentage terms; but it would loom larger naturally in absolute terms as suburban population had increased considerably over 1932. Although there is a rough picture here of a suburban Republican surge for Eisenhower, it will be recalled that outside suburbia there was also an Eisenhower surge. Further note that this Eisenhower increase in suburbia is accompanied by a parallel Republican *erosion* in the congressional and mayor vote, so that by

---

3. The usual criticism of the unreliability of mail polls lies in that the failure of the non-respondent to reply may reflect a factor systematically differentiating him from respondents. But here we were polling not individuals per se but representatives of political *units*. In four waves, mayors, city clerks, county election boards, and secretaries of state were solicited. There seems unlikely to be any variable associated with these official roles which would differentiate between responding and non-responding sources.

1960 the vote was split between the parties for all offices studied. Certainly these findings question whether the conversion theory is applicable if the assumption of Republican ascendancy cannot be factually sustained. Transplantation is still compatible with these data, although one possible inference, explored later, is that those coming to suburbia by the late 1950s were as much Democratic as Republican.

TABLE 3

FREQUENCY DISTRIBUTION OF REPUBLICAN SUBURBAN VOTE FOR SELECTED OFFICES AND YEARS BY PERCENTAGE

|  |  | N | 0-34% | 35-44% | 45-55% | 56-65% | 66-100% |
|---|---|---|---|---|---|---|---|
| President | 1932 | 79 | 14 | 24 | 18 | 19 | 25=100% |
|  | 1948 | 143 | 20 | 17 | 19 | 19 | 25 |
|  | 1952 | 152 | 11 | 18 | 20 | 18 | 33 |
|  | 1956 | 152 | 7 | 12 | 20 | 22 | 39 |
|  | 1960 | 110 | 20 | 24 | 22 | 25 | 10 |
| Congress | 1932 | 79 | 9 | 19 | 22 | 22 | 29 = 100% |
|  | 1948 | 138 | 22 | 15 | 20 | 15 | 28 |
|  | 1952 | 146 | 16 | 14 | 18 | 21 | 32 |
|  | 1956 | 151 | 19 | 11 | 17 | 23 | 30 |
|  | 1960 | 109 | 21 | 14 | 20 | 26 | 19 |
| Mayor | 1932 | 34 | 3 | 12 | 38 | 26 | 21 = 100% |
|  | 1948 | 55 | 9 | 13 | 25 | 27 | 25 |
|  | 1952 | 59 | 7 | 19 | 27 | 24 | 24 |
|  | 1956 | 57 | 11 | 14 | 39 | 19 | 18 |
|  | 1960 | 24 | 4 | 12 | 54 | 21 | 8 |

But such conclusions are gross, because the mean measures are deceptive. In order to reveal even more clearly the variation in suburban voting, Table 3 shows for each office and year the frequency distribution of Republican percentages. Such a schema permits scrutiny of a given year across offices or the reverse. Here "44-55%" constitutes a marginal range, a benchmark used by many practicing politicians. The two ranges either side of this middle position indicate a degree of party competition which may have different characteristics from the completely one-party system.

Examining this table by office, we find several conclusions available on suburban *presidential* voting. The share of presidential Democratic suburbs prior to Eisenhower paralleled that of the Republican suburbs, then dropped sharply in the fifties as the Republican share increased; but in 1960 the percent of Democratic suburbs rose again to exceed its pre-Eisenhower total as the Republican share dropped to its lowest point. Note that the weight of marginal suburbs remained roughly constant throughout, hovering around one-fifth. Turning to the *congressional* contests, a more stable picture appears. The Democratic share dropped somewhat during the Eisenhower elections as that of the Republicans increased, but in 1960 both parties had returned to the 1948 balance, with the Republican predominating, although not by a majority. Again, the weight represented by marginal suburbs remained constant, around one-fifth. Finally, in the *mayoralty* contests, what can be seen in the more limited data is a drop in both Republican and Democratic shares as that represented by marginal suburbs by the late fifties loomed largest of all three partisan possibilities; further, more marginal suburbs appear here than in the other two contests.

In contrast to the premise of both the "conversion" and "transplantation" hypothesis of suburban Republican growth, the data in Tables 2 and 3 raise serious questions about whether the Republican vote has grown. Eisenhower did make a visible impact upon the suburban vote as he did upon the urban and rural vote, but even in his best year, 1956, there remained a sizable minority of non-Republican suburbs, either marginal or heavily pro-Stevenson. The ephemeral nature of this vote is seen in the drastic Republican decrease in the 1960 election where the heavily Kennedy suburb predominated over the marginal or heavily Nixon suburb. Nor is suburban Republicanism overwhelming in congressional voting, for it actually shows a slight, gradual decrease since 1950. And even in the mayoralty contests, the former Republican predominance is also in decline, so that by the sixties the marginal contest may well predominate.

Table 2 shows that by the election of 1960, in electoral contests on all three levels there was no heavy national Republican suburban vote. By 1960, Republicans had a somewhat larger share of the suburbs in congressional votes and Democrats more in the presidential vote. However one chooses to explain it, the contours of the vote indicate that Republicans did not dominate the suburbs. It is likely therefore that the stereotype of the Republican suburb was built either by examining a few special suburbs (discussed later) or by equating the Eisenhower success of the fifties with a permanent Republican growth. Indeed, the data suggest that inter-party suburban competition is more lively and energetic than the literature contemplates.

## SUBURBAN INTER-PARTY COMPETITION

The measurement of party electoral competition can be as crude as examining the vote for one office for one year or as sophisticated and laborious as the scholar can construct.[4] I have utilized the Ranney-Kendall typology in which the discriminating variables are the percent of contests won by the second party and the size of that second party's vote (Ranney and Kendall 1956, pp. 161 ff.). For this, the second party in a suburb need but win twenty-six percent of the contests to be classified a "Two Party" suburb; of the remaining suburbs, some were classified "Modified One Party" if the second party won (*a*) over thirty percent of the vote in seventy percent of the elections, *and* (*b*) over forty percent of the vote in thirty percent of the elections. If suburbs fell below these minimum criteria of competition, they were designated "One Party." We thus arrive at five types of suburbs: One Party Democratic (OPD), Modified One Party Democratic (MOPD), Two Party (TP), Modified One Party Republican (MOPR) and One Party Republican (OPR).

The continuum thereby employed has certain limitations. Not all suburbs in the population range returned electoral results; those returning did not always provide complete results; the 1934–1946 elections are omitted; and no account of frequency of turnover is provided as some have suggested as an important measure (Schlesinger 1955). To the first two, one may merely comment that analysis must begin sometime and that Table 1 suggests a similarity in socio-economic base between sample and non-respondents. To the limitation of omission of the New Deal years, one may point out that inclusion of these (which would have cut down on the incidence of Republicanism) would distort changes, if any, in the postwar era.[5] To the limitation on providing no

---

4. Standing and Robinson (1958) provide a sophisticated measure and review other measures.

5. Key (1955) has shown that after the "critical election" of 1928, a partisan realignment took place which lasted at least up to 1952, so that by 1932 we deal with a crystallized partisan cleavage which forms a base for postwar comparison. Samuel Lubell (1952) earlier developed this thesis. Key (p. 9, fn. 7) cites evidence in Campbell et al. (1954), pp. 100–103, that some Republicans voted Democratic in 1932 and 1936, although later switching back; this lends weight to the present author's contention that post-1932 inclusion of New Deal voting would inflate the weight of Democracy in the suburbs. As constituted, the schema here employed gives a greater chance to demonstrate any postwar suburban Republican growth.

turnover measure, note that so few years are included here that such a measure would have a very flimsy empirical basis.

The degree of party competition in the Ranney-Kendall typology and in rough terms of percent of these contests won by Republicans is revealed in Table 4.

TABLE 4
FREQUENCY DISTRIBUTION OF SUBURBAN PARTY COMPETITION TYPES AND REPUBLICAN WINS

| Party Type | N | % | % GOP Wins |
|---|---|---|---|
| OPD | 27 | 17.5 | 5.0 |
| MOPD | 22 | 14.3 | 10.9 |
| TP | 25 | 16.2 | 48.2 |
| MOPR | 37 | 24.0 | 88.1 |
| OPR | 43 | 28.0 | 97.7 |
|  | 154 | 100.0 | 58.7 |

Table 4 shows the prevalence of Republican suburbs—roughly one-half of all suburbs here studied. Yet, there exists another half of this sample which does not fit the usual picture of suburban politics. Almost one-third are Democratic (one in six is OPD) and one-sixth TP. Put another way, in every six suburbs, three are Republican but two are Democratic and one is Two Party.

Other computations, not here included,[6] demonstrate that prior to 1960: Eisenhower received from each of the three party type areas (D, TP, R) an increasingly larger share of votes; most Republican gain for either congressional or presidential candidates came from the most Republican suburbs; the partisan suburbs tended strongly to support their own candidates most consistently (despite some Democratic suburbs being pulled toward Eisenhower) while the TP suburb shifted most—as befits a truly competitive area; and despite the foregoing evidence of change, if one compares 1948 with the big Eisenhower year of 1956, seventy percent of these suburbs appear in the same voting range. In short, there are surprisingly large numbers of non-Republican suburbs; in these there was some drift to Eisenhower; this Republican shift did not carry down strongly to congressional and mayoralty contests, and there are some suburbs that never moved Republican whether measured by winning contests or increasing percentage. With the

---
6. See the author's "Suburban Patterns in American Politics," a paper presented in the 1960 American Political Science Association Convention.

1960 election, this popularly exaggerated Republican suburban growth was reversed at all three offices.

## THE ECOLOGY OF SUBURBIA

Having isolated political differences among these suburbs and in so doing questioned the premise of monolithic Republicanism, we are now prepared to explore reasons for such differences. It is my contention that differences in suburban electoral behavior arise from differences in the socio-economic bases of these suburbs.

An approach to understanding these patterns may be found in introducing an ecological concept rarely treated in political analysis but quite familiar to sociology—the non-dormitory suburb. Political analysis has routinely treated the suburbs as though they were all similar. They are thought to be residential and peopled by middle-middle to upper-middle class or higher status; they contain only retail businesses, generally the hive-like shopping centers; the breadwinners leave *en masse* for the city in the morning and return to the split-level and dry martini in the evening. Readers of Whyte's *Organization Man* or almost any novel about suburbia will recognize these traits—or symptoms.

But there is another kind of suburb—the industrial. As early as 1925, H. Paul Douglass, writing on *The Suburban Trend*, recognized these two types, referring to the "suburb of consumption," the now familiar and publicized type, and the "suburb of production," the latter also lying adjacent to central cities but providing jobs for its own residents as well as others (1925, pp. 84-85). While the latter sends out goods and brings in persons, the suburb of consumption reverses this flow. This dichotomy received scant mention in the 1930s but was elaborated upon by C. D. Harris in a significant article a decade later (1943). During the fifties, sociologist Leo F. Schnore submitted the dichotomy to extensive analysis.[7]

Time does not permit here full treatment of Schnore's analysis, but a recapitulation of his findings is necessary. He relates a long history of these industrial suburbs; notes their presence in every part of the country; finds their identifying economic activity to be manufacturing (light or heavy), education and recreation,

---

7. Schnore 1956, 1957a, 1957b, 1958. Cf. also Martin 1957; Kish 1954. For some methodological problems in suburban study, cf. Duncan 1956, p. 5.

extraction (oil and mining) or governmental services; shows the residential suburb's rate of growth exceeded that of the industrial suburb (during the 1940s by almost twice, 31.9 percent to 17.0 percent); indicates that the former's increase is a function of better "housing opportunities," whereas the growth of regions and central cities is a function of more employment or economic opportunities; and concludes that as people will live where there are greater housing opportunities, preferring to drive to work or to nearby industrial suburbs or central city, the residential suburb will continue to grow at a higher rate than that of the industrial suburb.

As an initial approximation, the industrial-residential suburban dichotomy tells us that suburbs are not homogeneous. Dobriner, in his recent *Class in Suburbia*, exploring the bases of this heterogeneity, argues that:

> There is such a diversity of suburb forms it is misleading to label all suburbs 'homogeneous.' Suburbs differ greatly in the circumstances of their creation, in the price and use of their real estate, their degree of transiency, their size and institutional complexity, and the income, life style, occupation, and educational level of their residents. . . . Unfortunately, many of the quasi-empirical studies of suburbs which gave rise to the homogeneity myth focused on upper-middle-class areas around large central cities. *In fact, many suburbs are not essentially middle-class and accordingly do not exhibit those middle-class patterns too often mistaken as suburban patterns.* (1963, p. 13; emphasis added.)

It is Dobriner's contention that the variety of suburbs is a function of class characteristics, influenced primarily by "technological-economic" factors. "In the final analysis," Dobriner concludes, "suburbanites and city dwellers are joined together by common class bonds, and relatively few place factors separate them. It is unfortunate that the emphasis given to the few uniquely suburban situational features have blinded so many to this basic fact" (p. 59).

In the present study, we are not treating a "few uniquely suburban situational features" but 154 suburbs about which we have considerable electoral and socio-economic information. The previous part of this study has demonstrated political variety, both in electoral behavior and party competition. We are now ready to explore the bases of this variety.

## ECONOMIC CORRELATES OF SUBURBAN POLITICS

Voting studies almost without number, whether utilizing aggregate or survey data, have noted the relationship between economic indices and partisan voting. While the "party identification" thesis indicates that psychological factors can depress any one-to-one ratio between such economic factors as income and voting behavior, there still remains an association between such factors as high income and Republican voting. This association is not urged here as any sign of class conflict disguised as inter-party strife, but it is an association, and it has affected the behavior of party leaders in the conduct of campaigns.

The thesis now to be explored is that suburban political differences, like those of the core city, are associated with socio-economic differences. Suburbs which have the characteristics of upper middle class will be more Republican than those suburbs having lower-middle- and working-class characteristics; but suburbs which are most heterogeneous will show more inter-party competition. The socio-economic variables employed are drawn from the Jones materials in the *Municipal Year Book, 1963;* the brief definitions of these variables given below are expanded upon at that source (pp. 111–13).

The first analysis bearing on this proposition employs rough scales of limited categories. Figures 1 and 2 demonstrate the distribution of party competition types from Table 4 among three variables.[8]

The proposition that polar socio-economic characteristics will demonstrate polar electoral behavior is the subject of Figure 1, which combines OPD and MOPD into Democratic and OPR and

---

8. *Income Level* (IL) employs four quartile ranges computed from 1960 for all cities over 10,000 by Jones et al. with IL-1 the lowest and IL-4 the highest median family income. The *Rent Level* (RL) index relates the median gross monthly rent of a suburb to that of its SMA; RL-1 is $5 below the SMA median rent; RL-2 is in the range of ±$5 of the median, RL-3 $5 above, and RL-4 is more than twice the SMA median. *Functional Classification* distinguishes the proportions of different kinds of employment. Thus a manufacturing (Mm) suburb has over fifty percent of all employment in manufacturing and *less* than thirty percent in retail trade; Industrial (M) has over fifty percent in manufacturing but *more* than thirty percent in retail trade; Diversified Manufacturing (Mr) has more employment in manufacturing than in retail trade but less than fifty percent of the aggregate; Diversified Retailing (Rm) has more in retailing than in manufacturing but the latter is at least twenty percent of the aggregate; Retailing (Rr) has more employment in retailing than in any other form and manufacturing is less than twenty percent of the aggregate; and Other (O) covers places where other employment predominates.

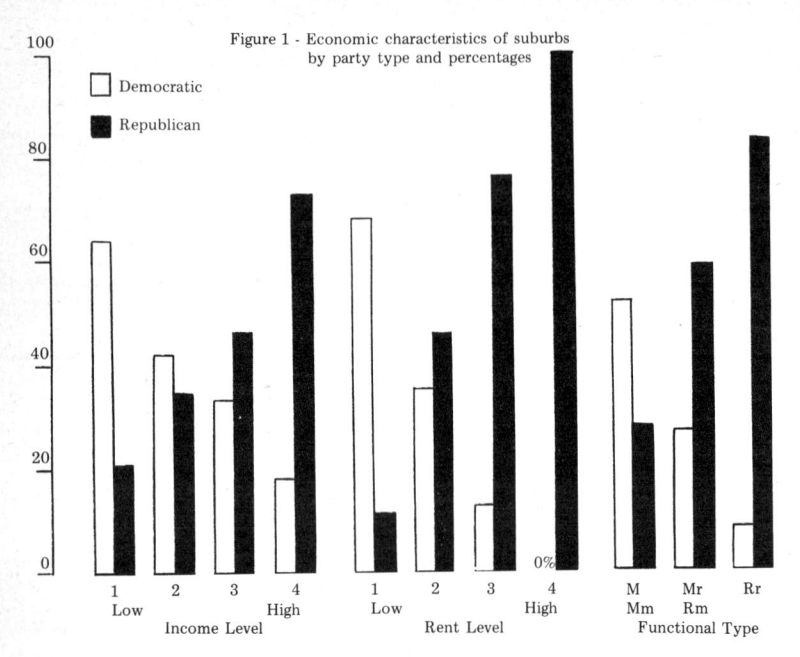

Figure 1 - Economic characteristics of suburbs by party type and percentages

MOPR into Republican. Democratic suburbs are indeed concentrated in low income, low rental, and high manufacturing type suburbs, while the Republican suburb has the opposite characteristics. As the economic structure changes, so does the political. Thus, as the Income Level increases, the proportion of Democratic suburb decreases regularly; almost two-thirds of the lowest income suburbs are Democratic (heavily OPD), while almost three-fourths of the highest income suburbs are Republican (heavily OPR).

If the thesis that economic and political homogeneity are associated seems borne out here, the thesis that economic heterogeneity produces greater inter-party competition is less supportable. Figure 2 combines TP with MOPD and MOPR to examine the thesis. To support the proposition it should reveal a greater amount of competitive suburbs in the middle ranges of these scales. But no such pattern emerges. In the first two scales the center ranges evidence the largest concentration (level 2 on both scales is average) as the thesis requires, but the differences are small, and in Functional Type we find no support. Here as in

Figure 2 - Economic characteristics of competitive suburbs by percentages

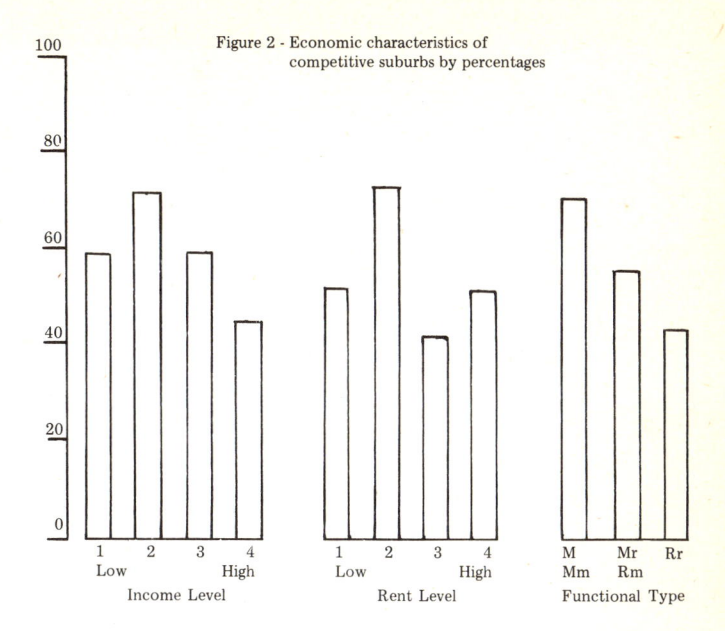

Figure 1 one finds suburbs falling opposite to the expected tendency. Thus one in five Republican suburbs falls in the lowest Income Level and one in ten in the lowest Rent Level, while eighteen percent of the Democratic suburbs are in highest Income Level.

In summary, these data show a rough association between the political complexion of suburbs and their economic characteristics. The more extreme the characteristics, the more likely the suburbs will have a similar political complexion; especially strong is this relationship between high economic indices and Republicanism. However, suburbs demonstrating intermediate economic characteristics are not associated mostly with inter-party competition, for such characteristics are spread among the various types of party competition. Figure 2 shows a somewhat stronger tendency for this combination to weigh most heavily among the average Rent and Income Levels, but this association is still not clearly established.

Several difficulties inhere in the nature of these three indices. First, the Income Level is based on *all* cities over 10,000 and not on suburbs in the range of our 154 suburbs. Further, the Income and Rent Level indices do not, by their natures, give us any indication of heterogeneity within any given suburb; any one of these suburbs at a given level might cover a wide variation in income or rent or it might have the same income or rent for all within it. Only Functional Classification permits us to determine heterogeneity. But this index, like the others (including Party Type), offers no fine discrimination in its scaling. What they do offer, however, is a first approximation that suburban political variety is related to variety in the suburban economic base.

## SUBURBAN POLITICS: IMAGE AND REALITY

This analysis raises serious doubts about the popular picture of suburbia and suggests that even the dichotomy of the industrial versus the residential suburb is an inadequate description. Not all suburbs by any means fit the popular description. Dobriner has identified the "images of suburbia penned by the commentators" with certain characteristic themes (1963, p. 6). Some of these themes are subject to testing by aggregate data such as this research employs. In Dobriner's terms, these are: warrens of young executives on the way up; uniformly middle class; homogeneous; political Jordans from which Democrats emerge Republicans.

*"Warrens of young executives on the way up."* Passing over the pejorative "warrens," what can we say of the age of suburbanites? In our sample, the median age was 32. Jones reports (Jones, Forstall, and Colver 1963, p. 105) a substantially smaller proportion of the elderly compared to "Central Cities" and "Independent Cities."[9] Age seems to have some correlation with suburban Republican voting, as known from studies of other locales, although this is not as strong as other variables (Campbell et al. 1960, pp. 161–67). When partial correlation analysis is conducted, holding certain variables constant (E/R, % Migrant, % White Collar, % under $3,000, % over $10,000) and varying median age, a coefficient for Age of .284 is obtained. As to "young executives,"

---

9. "Young" may be relative. Robert Wood shows that suburbanites are older than those in rural non-farm villages and independent cities but younger than those in the core city, based on 1950 census data (1958, pp. 314–15).

one can merely claim this from the data by inference. Age correlates with "% White Collar" at .338, with "% Migrant" at -.298, with "% over $10,000" at .335. These may be the attributes of "organization men."

*"Uniformly middle class . . . 'homogeneous.'"* These terms, as Dobriner goes to some pains to point out, are not self-defining and actually are popularly employed to group together quite disparate types of suburbs. As one sign, for example, Jones notes that "almost six out of ten recently incorporated suburbs have predominantly blue-collar labor forces (p. 104). Berger has written an entire book on a *Working-Class Suburb*, as noted. His suburban type appears also in my data, having middle or lower family income and rent levels, high manufacturing or industrial employment, low percentage of income over $10,000 and a high percentage under $3,000, etc. But certainly this should not be the only type. There may well fall out groups of blue-collar suburbs, high-income white-collar suburbs, and suburbs where these groups are amalgamated.[10]

*"Political Jordans from which Democrats emerge Republicans."* The material in the first part of this paper questioned this "conversion" theory by raising doubt about how Republican suburbs are. It is true that we cannot peer into psychological processes or value re-orientations with the unwieldy tools of aggregate voting and census data employed here. But these tools do have their uses in verifying the reality of two elements in the "conversion" thesis. Have our suburbs become more Republican? Electoral analysis of the traditional kind suggests an answer different than that usually given. All the more subtle measures of value re-orientation, found in survey work, have been possibly misled by a phenomenon of the 1950s—the massive support given Eisenhower. Far from being "political Jordans," American suburbs of the type here studied show no permanent effects in political socialization.

A second question about the "conversion" thesis is whether in studying one kind of suburb we have made judgments about all kinds of suburbs. But aggregate analysis suggests variety in suburbia. We have seen the political variety in terms of party competition. Linked to this is socio-economic variety, as Table 5 indicates.

---

10. The author is preparing from field work in the Cleveland SMSA a review of these model types.

TABLE 5
MEANS OF SOCIO-ECONOMIC FACTORS BY PARTY TYPES

| | % White Collar[1] | Median Age[1] | % Under $3,000 Income[1] | % Over $10,000 Income[1] | $E/R$[2] | % Mfg.[2] | % GOP Wins[3] |
|---|---|---|---|---|---|---|---|
| OPD | 39 | 29.8 | 15.8 | 46.1 | 111 | 54 | 5 |
| MOPD | 39 | 29.8 | 11.6 | 45.6 | 112 | 61 | 11 |
| TP | 44 | 31.0 | 12.8 | 45.0 | 92 | 51 | 48 |
| MOPR | 50 | 32.5 | 12.2 | 45.0 | 108 | 39 | 88 |
| OPR | 62 | 34.4 | 8.2 | 45.8 | 65 | 23 | 98 |

1. N is respectively 25, 22, 24, 37, 43.
2. N is respectively 27, 22, 24, 37, 43.
3. N is respectively 27, 22, 25, 37, 43.

When one isolates suburbs by their partisan characteristics, there emerge striking differences in their other characteristics, as in Table 5. These data suggest a suburbia of surprising variety, thereby questioning a basic assumption of the conversion thesis.

## INTERPRETATIONS

In the preceding, there seems substantial evidence that when we speak of "suburban" we must distinguish among different kinds of suburbia in socio-economic and partisan terms. Each kind represents a different life-style; as Berger notes of his working-class suburb, "Most of the features of life reportedly characteristic of Levittown, Park Forest, and other suburbs of their kind are notable by their absence" (1960, p. 23). He found auto workers retaining their life-style when moving to a tract suburb—carrying lunch pails, not belonging to organizations, attending church less than the middle class, and no Republican switching. Campbell and his associates in *The American Voter* go further with survey data (albeit limited) to show "the absence of a really unique change in political allegiance among ex-urbanites [which] further indicates that movement out of the metropolitan centers cannot stand as the factor responsible for changes in partisan loyalties that cut across non-movers as well" (1960, p. 459).[11] Instead of a mass conversion to Republicanism, a more discriminating process seems more likely.

---

11. The authors of this work did not treat suburbia as a special population category and thus "cannot accommodate in our analysis the crucially important qualitative differences among types of suburban communities" (p. 454, fn. 13).

## Political Sociology of Suburbia

Given the strength of partisan identifications, it seems possible that former city Democrats and Republicans carried their affiliations with them as they fled the city. Some sought suburbs of like-minded and like-situated people, and thus there developed working-class as well as elegant suburbs, each homogeneous in its distinctive party and economic contours. Other movers, with different partisan and economic backgrounds, came together in the same place to form a "mixed salad" suburb. From such combinations we can postulate a continuum of suburbs, ranged in terms of those factors here termed "life-style." Each life-style with its distinctive socio-economic syndrome is accompanied by a special partisan cast. At one end is Berger's working-class suburb of Democratic cast, at the other end is the suburb of elegance with its Republican cast, and in between lie different mixes of life-styles with less predictable partisanships.

Probably the basic error in confusing all suburbs with heavy Republicanism is the failure to realize that not only the upper middle class fled the city. The postwar world brought huge gains in income to all but the "one-third of a nation," now down to "one-fifth." Blue-collar and lower-middle-class citizens also achieved the economic potential for new homes, realtors appeared to cater to their potentials, and the pressure of urban Negroes upon white housing added yet another motive for departing. Upon arrival, they came with a life-style, some of which, such as partisan identification, erodes very slowly or is transformed only by such traumatic events as wars and depressions. What was there in the mere fact of a new locale to transform these deeply held views, particularly when some suburbs were so new? Place alone does not shape attitudes; it is the cultural milieu of a place that influences. But many suburbs were raw, new communities with no milieu yet formed, others offered a homogeneous culture which attracted the newcomer in the first place because it reflected his own life-style, and yet others were a mixed salad, offering few cultural directives that could influence uniformly the new arrival.

In other words, the exploding metropolis has created a suburban fall-out whose patterns in some respects duplicate those of the city. The city has known its working-class, "silk stocking," and mixed wards, its residential and industrial districts, and its heavily Democratic, heavily Republican and marginal areas. This varied pattern of life-styles and partisanships is not unlike what we have seen in the data of this paper. True, there is a more Republican than Democratic cast to suburbia as a whole—but not in the most recent years and not for all offices. But we also have working-class, elegant and mixed-salad suburbs whose constituents are revealed with differing socio-economic characteristics, whose ecology reveals other differences, and whose politics question severely the notion of suburbia as a "political Jordan" from whose waters Democrats emerge in the image of the compleat Republican.

As suburban developments extend their tendrils farther from metropolis—to contact at some future point the tendrils of other metropolises—we may expect this pattern of continual life-style reduplication to accompany them.[12] In terms of political socialization, however, those making the trek do not demonstrate any massive conversion, but instead show signs that in their covered station wagon they carry their already ingrained party affiliation. As the benefits of the affluent society spread even farther, there is a good likelihood that more Democrats will be in those wagons.[13]

---

12. Even the city Negro wards are appearing tentatively in suburbia, e.g., Ludlow in the Cleveland area.

13. 1964 Postscript——
Nothing in the 1964 returns challenged the previous findings of a renaissance of Democracy in suburbia; indeed these returns accentuate this movement. The Republican national decline in the 1964 election was even more sharp in the American suburban sample on which the preceding article was based.

Between 1960 and 1964, the median Republican vote for Goldwater in these suburbs fell to 33.8 percent (N=119 suburbs) while the Republican median for congressional voting declined slightly to 47.0 percent (N=119). Goldwater carried only sixteen of these suburbs (14.7 percent), while Republican congressional candidates were securing a majority in fifty-three (44.5 percent). The congressional changes from 1960 were possibly sharper than these measures reveal. Almost one-third (32 percent) remained roughly the same (±3 percent). But over one-half (56 percent) showed Republican congressional decreases greater than 3 percent; in at least one-quarter of these suburbs, Republican voting was 10 percent or more percentage points less. Only 12 percent of the suburbs produced a Republican congressional increase of over 3 percent in 1964.

Data are not yet available to determine whether the Republican suburban rate of decline in presidential voting varied from that in core city or outside-metropolitan areas. But the 16 percent suburban decline between 1960 and 1964 is certainly greater than the *national* decline for those years (11 percent). Work in progress comparing the weight of suburban, core city, and outside-metropolis votes in postwar presidential elections has produced a preliminary finding that of the three areas the suburban vote distribution has most nearly paralleled the national distribution. If this finding is reinforced in the 1964 election, it would seem to undergird the thesis that suburbia in its unsuspected variety is a mirror of multifaceted American politics.

# Political Perspectives of Suburban Party Leaders

DENNIS S. IPPOLITO

Within recent years, numerous studies have investigated the social, attitudinal, and behavioral characteristics of party leaders at the local level.[1] There remains, however, a relative paucity of data relating to political activists within suburban political organizations. Thus, while the political weight and importance of suburban areas have grown rapidly within the past two decades, first-hand knowledge of suburban political organization and party leadership is limited.

The present study adds to the substantive knowledge about local party personnel by reporting data which relate to the political perspectives of party leaders in a major suburban community—Nassau County, New York. In dealing with these perspectives, the major problem is that of relating leadership attitudes and orientations to the political system in which the party is operating. The question is one relating primarily to impact: what impact do certain types of party leaders have upon the party organization and how does the impact affect the operation of the party within its political environment? As Eldersveld stated in his Wayne County study:

---

1. Some of the more interesting work in this area includes: Bowman and Boynton 1966b; Eldersveld 1964; Hirschfield, Swanson, and Blank 1962; Marvick and Nixon 1961; Patterson 1963; Rossi and Cutright 1961.

---

Reprinted from The Social Science Quarterly 44 (1969), pp. 800-815, by permission of the publisher, the Southwest Social Science Association, and the author.

The party, in one sense, is what it believes—its attitudes and perspectives at all echelons. And what the party leaders believe may certainly determine in large part the image it communicates to the public and the success with which it mobilizes public support.[2]

The evidence presented here does not speak directly to this latter statement, but it does indicate that certain distinctive perspectives are exhibited by suburban party leaders and that these perspectives do constitute an important determinant for assessing the development and effect of political parties in suburban areas.

## METHODOLOGY AND LOCALE

In the period from September through October, 1966, interviews were conducted among executive committeemen of the Republican and Democratic county party organizations in Nassau County, New York. These party officials constitute, along with the county chairman and other county-wide officers, the highest level of party leadership within their respective county organizations. Nassau was chosen partially because of its socio-economic character—it is a heavily populated middle- to upper-middle-class suburb[3]—and also because the party organizations in Nassau are well organized and relatively competitive.[4]

From lists provided by the party organizations, a random, stratified sample was drawn from all executive committeemen in the two party organizations.[5] Within this sample, a structured personal

---

2. Eldersveld 1964, pp. 180–81. This study has drawn heavily upon the theoretical concepts developed by Eldersveld in his investigation of political perspectives in Part 2 of his Wayne County study.
3. Nassau County had a population of 1,300,171 in 1960 (est. 1966: 1,525,000) which represented a ninety-three percent increase since 1950. Income levels, occupational distributions, and education are among the highest in the New York Metropolitan Area. Median family income, for example, was $8,515 annually in Nassau in 1960, while the New York State average was $6,371 and the New York Metropolitan Region average was $6,548. Nassau is the richest and second largest (next to New York City) county in New York.
4. While there remains a Republican majority in Nassau, the Democratic gains of the past several years indicate the growing two-party character of the area. The Democrats now hold, for example, the county executive, which is the highest elective office in the county, two of the three Nassau seats in the House of Representatives, and four of the twelve state assembly seats. The Democratic averages for full-slate elections have increased from 21.3 percent to 40.3 percent of the total vote in the period from 1946 to 1966.
5. Within each party, the total number of sample units (fifty respondents per party) was apportioned among the three towns on the basis of each town's proportional representation on the executive committee. Thus, for example, Hempstead, which accounts for slightly more than half of the executive committeemen in each party, was apportioned a

interview, averaging about one hour in length, was administered to eighty-five party leaders. The response rate, slightly higher among Democrats, was eighty-five percent.[6]

In dealing with the data in this study, a number of general propositions, drawn from the literature on local party activism, have been used as a general framework. Their applicability or non-applicability to suburban party activism provides a readily available means for assessing the comparative nature of suburban party leadership.

1. Within an area characterized by substantial inter-party competition and a relatively high degree of socio-economic homogeneity, class or status differences between the party leaderships are minimal (Althoff and Patterson 1966, p. 40; Hirschfield et al. 1962, pp. 491, 505). The parties can, however, exhibit differential group representation in terms of such factors as age, religion, and residential mobility (Hirschfield et al. 1962, pp. 494-98; Wilson 1962, pp. 9-16).

2. The party leaderships are differentiated in terms of ideology; ideology is the major determinant of party affiliation (Hirschfield et al. 1962, p. 491; McClosky, Hoffman, and O'Hara 1960, pp. 406-27).

3. The political party offers a number of incentives to its activists. Group- and society-related incentives, however, are becoming increasingly relevant for the contemporary activist (Marvick and Nixon 1961, p. 208; Hirschfield et al. p. 491; Eldersveld 1964, pp. 273-303).

4. In terms of the role definitions of its leaders, the majority party in a given area tends to be organizationally oriented (Patterson 1963, pp. 348-52; Althoff and Patterson 1966, pp. 46-50). For the minority party, electoral activities are the predominant concern of the leadership.[7]

---

corresponding number of sample items in each party. The reason for this stratification is that there are variations in the demographic distributions, particularly income, for the three towns. Hempstead, with the largest population, is the "poorest" of the three towns, while North Hempstead, with the smallest population, is the "richest." Thus, by stratifying the sample, it was hoped to make it more representative.

6. While a larger sample would have been desirable, time and other problems militated against it. Since all of the interviews were conducted by the author, the problems which Nassau presents in terms of size and the availability of party leaders were extremely acute.

7. Althoff and Patterson 1966. The categorization and analysis used in this paper follows that set forth in Bowman and Boynton 1966a.

5. Party leaders are not uniformly conscious of the party's role as a power group; substantial numbers of local leaders define party goals in idealistic and/or modified power terms (Eldersveld 1964, p. 242). Further, the tendency to minimize the power goal of the party is more pronounced within the minority party (ibid.).

These propositions, and the research from which they are drawn, evidence the increasing concern of political scientists with developing meaningful insights relating to the structure and character of local parties and their personnel. If these and other hypotheses are to be relevant in developing a general theory of the political party, however, they must inevitably apply to parties and to party activists in differing types of locales. In the following sections, the data from this study will be measured against these propositions in order to test their applicability for a given level of party leadership in a specific type of locale.

## THE SOCIAL CORRELATES OF PARTY LEADERS

The party leaderships in Nassau County exhibit differential group representation. The contrasts in this case, however, are not related to socio-economic status or class. While the Democratic leadership is characterized by extremely high levels of education, income and occupational status are similar for both leadership groups.

There are, however, some important differences between the parties. The Democrats tend to be younger, better educated, and more status-mobile than the Republicans. They are also, in the main, a product of the post–World War II migration into the county, particularly from New York City. The Republican leadership, as might be expected given the extent of previous Republican dominance, is primarily "home-grown," and, in terms of tenure in party office, it is essentially an old-guard leadership.

That the two leaderships represent different political backgrounds as well as different political generations is shown by the fact that eighty-two percent of the Democrats who have moved into Nassau within the past twenty years (which amounts to about two-thirds of all Democrats) spent most of their lives in New York City.

TABLE 1
SOCIAL CORRELATES OF PARTY LEADERS
IN NASSAU COUNTY, 1966

|  | Democrat | Republican |
|---|---|---|
| Income |  |  |
| $5,000-$9,999 | 6% | 3% |
| $10,000-$14,999 | 20 | 18 |
| $15,000 or more | 74 | 79 |
|  | 100% | 100% |
| N = | (46) | (39) |
| Education |  |  |
| High school or less | 8% | 26% |
| High school plus noncollege | 0 | 13 |
| Some college | 11 | 18 |
| College graduate | 22 | 13 |
| College plus graduate or professional | 59 | 30 |
|  | 100% | 100% |
| N = | (46) | (39) |
| Occupation |  |  |
| Professional, technical, etc. | 70% | 62% |
| Business, managerial, etc. | 26 | 35 |
| Clerical and sales | 2 | 0 |
| Craftsmen, foremen, etc. | 2 | 0 |
| NA | 0 | 3 |
|  | 100% | 100% |
| N = | (46) | (39) |
| Age |  |  |
| 20-39 | 35% | 8% |
| 40-49 | 46 | 26 |
| 50-59 | 17 | 38 |
| 60 or over | 2 | 25 |
| NA | 0 | 3 |
|  | 100% | 100% |
| N = | (46) | (39) |
| Religion |  |  |
| Jewish | 59% | 12% |
| Catholic | 35 | 41 |
| Protestant | 2 | 44 |
| Other | 4 | 3 |
|  | 100% | 100% |
| N = | (46) | (39) |

In terms of religion, moreover, leadership representation of certain groups tends to parallel a party's electoral support among these same groups. A 1962 survey of party identification among Nassau voters, for example, indicated that Jewish and Protestant support was sharply divided among the two parties (Silverman and Campbell 1962). Only seven percent of the Jewish voters identified as Republicans, as opposed to fifty-four percent of the Protestants.

Conversely, only eighteen percent of the Protestants identified as Democrats, as opposed to sixty-six percent of the Jewish voters. Among Catholic voters, support for the two parties was almost equally divided—thirty-three percent identified as Republicans and forty percent as Democrats. As Table 1 indicates, leadership representation of these religious groups tends to reflect their patterns of electoral support.

Neither the competitive position of the parties nor their ideological stance—the Republican party is both the majority and the more conservative party—appears to have any decided effect upon the social class of the leaders whom the parties recruit. It is clear, however, that within a given socio-economic stratum, the parties do have differential appeals to certain types of groups.

In the case of the Democratic leadership, the social correlates examined above (including the degree of Jewish representation which has added significance in the context of New York politics) resemble to some degree the profile of the amateur activist as outlined by Hirschfield et al., Wilson, Carney, and others.[8] Among Democrats, for example, lawyers account for only sixty percent of those with graduate or professional training, so that there is substantial representation of engineers, businessmen, teachers, and other professionals. Within the Republican leadership, on the other hand, all Republicans in the highest educational category are lawyers. This indicates that at least within the Democratic party a much broader base for citizen participation is being utilized.

## IDEOLOGY AND POLITICAL ACTIVISM

Some of the differences between the Democratic and Republican leaderships in terms of social group representation might appear to be related to factors such as party dominance. The age patterns and career origins of Democratic leaders, for example, could be in part a function of the relative openness of leadership posts within the party as it has developed within the past two decades. The parties are, however, also distinguished by the policy attitudes of their leaderships.

Democratic leaders are much more liberal than Republican

---
8. See, for example, Carney 1958.

## Table 2
## RESIDENCY PATTERNS AND CAREER ORIGINS OF PARTY LEADERS

|  | Democrat | Republican |
|---|---|---|
| **Residency in Nassau** | | |
| Born in county | 5% | 41% |
| More than 20 years | 15 | 33 |
| 15–19 years | 24 | 13 |
| 10–14 years | 28 | 10 |
| Less than 10 years | 28 | 3 |
|  | 100% | 100% |
| N = | (46) | (39) |
| **Career origin*** | | |
| Pre-1940 | 9% | 39% |
| 1940–1950 | 20 | 41 |
| 1951–1955 | 26 | 15 |
| 1956–1960 | 30 | 5 |
| 1961–1966 | 15 | 0 |
|  | 100% | 100% |
| N = | (46) | (39) |

* This refers to when the leader first held an official position in the party.

leaders in their attitudes on certain policy issues.[9] Nearly three-fourths of the Democrats (seventy-four percent) took a liberal position on all six policy issues, as opposed to five percent of the Republicans. Further, no Democrat was consistently conservative, and only nine percent gave as many as two conservative responses.

As Table 3 indicates, the differences between the parties in terms of a liberal-conservative distinction are substantial on most issues. The domestic policy questions show the greatest contrasts,

---

. The items which were utilized included: (1) "The government ought to help people get doctors and hospital care at low cost," (2) "If Negroes are not getting fair treatment in jobs and housing, the government in Washington should see that they do," (3) "If the cities and towns around the country need help in building schools, the government in Washington should give them the help they need," (4) "The government in Washington should see to it that everybody who wants to work can find a job," (5) "The United States should continue to give economic aid to countries that need it," and (6) "The United States should continue to work to strengthen the United Nations." The categorization was as follows:

    Agrees strongly—strong liberal
    Agrees—liberal
    Disagrees—conservative
    Disagrees strongly—strong conservative.

Strictly speaking, the two items relating to foreign policy should be on an internationalist-isolationist scale, but for the sake of simplicity, liberal will be equated to internationalist and conservative to isolationist. There are, of course, obvious problems involved in using these questions to speak to "ideology," but they are useful if their implicit limitations are recognized.

TABLE 3
PROGRAMMATIC DIFFERENCES BETWEEN PARTY LEADERSHIPS

|  | Percent Liberal Democrat | Republican |
|---|---|---|
| Issue |  |  |
| Medical aid | 93 | 46 |
| Civil rights | 96 | 46 |
| Aid to education | 91 | 36 |
| Job aid | 93 | 59 |
| Foreign aid | 92 | 69 |
| United Nations | 100 | 82 |
| N = | (46) | (39) |

TABLE 4
IDEOLOGICAL DIRECTION OF LEADERSHIP ATTITUDES

|  | Percentage of Group Strong Liberal ||| Percentage of Group Strong Conservative |||
|---|---|---|---|---|---|---|
|  | Democrat | Republican | Percent Difference | Democrat | Republican | Percent Difference |
| Issue |  |  |  |  |  |  |
| Medical aid | 65 | 20 | 45 | 5 | 28 | 23 |
| Civil rights | 76 | 18 | 58 | 2 | 23 | 21 |
| Aid to education | 54 | 10 | 44 | 2 | 38 | 36 |
| Job aid | 67 | 18 | 49 | 2 | 23 | 21 |
| Foreign aid | 59 | 18 | 41 | 2 | 10 | 8 |
| United Nations | 96 | 51 | 45 | 0 | 10 | 10 |
| N = | (46) | (39) |  | (46) | (39) |  |

with somewhat lesser contrasts on foreign policy (the Republicans tend to be more liberal on the foreign policy issues than they are on domestic issues).[10] While these distributions are indicative of the general orientation of the competing leaderships, they do not fully reflect the degree of inter-party differences.

In Table 4, data are shown for the leaders who take the most liberal and the most conservative positions on each issue. A majority of Democrats, ranging from fifty-four percent to ninety-six percent, take the most liberal position on all issues. The degree of difference between the parties is relatively uniform, and it indicates that real ideological distinctiveness exists, at least at the liberal end of the spectrum.

A majority of leaders in both parties also perceived issue-related differences between the parties, although there was a more

---

10. It is probable that greater distinctiveness will occur for domestic, as opposed to foreign policy, issues at upper leadership levels. See, for example, Eldersveld 1964, chap. 8, especially p. 185.

TABLE 5
THE SALIENCE OF IDEOLOGY FOR PARTY LEADERS

|  | Democrat | Republican |
|---|---|---|
| Parties different<br>Issue terms | 78% | 57% |
| Parties different<br>Non-issue terms | 7 | 15 |
| Parties similar or only slight difference | 15 | 28 |
|  | 100% | 100% |
| N = | (46) | (39) |

pronounced tendency among Democrats to articulate differences in these terms. Thus, if the party leaderships do reflect to some extent their organizations and electoral supporters of their organizations, the parties in Nassau County are not operating within an ideological vacuum.

It appears, then, that ideology is a party-related phenomenon. The liberals and strong liberals are Democrats, and religion, education, age, or career origin has very little effect upon the degree of liberalism. Among Republicans, the only factor which has any consistent effect is religion. Republican Catholics are substantially more conservative than Republican Protestants. Indeed, Catholics in both parties appear to be ideologically distinctive. Democratic Catholics are, if only to a slight extent, more liberal than Democratic Jews.[11] Thus, while ideological congruence within the Democratic party is decidedly higher than that within the Republican leadership group, each party could take a stand on an issue which reflects the attitudes of most, if not all, of its leaders and still present a definite contrast to the opposing party.

## INCENTIVES AND PARTY LEADERS

The expressed, perceived motivations which executive committeemen had for seeking and continuing in party office indicate that majorities in both parties emphasize "group- and society-related" incentives.[12] As might be expected, there are some substantial

---

11. The average extreme liberal score for Democratic Catholics on all six issues is .5 percent above the party average; for Jewish Democrats it is .5 percent below the party average. The difference here, of course, is insignificant, but it does point up the distinctiveness of Catholic leaders. Republican Catholics, for example, are 9.5 percent above the extreme conservative average for the party and Republican Protestants 9.0 percent below it.

12. This categorization follows that set forth in Eldersveld 1964, p. 278.

TABLE 6
INITIAL AND CURRENT INCENTIVES FOR PARTY WORK*

|  | Democrat Initial | Democrat Current | Republican Initial | Republican Current |
|---|---|---|---|---|
| Personally instrumental | | | | |
|   Social contacts | 7% | 2% | 5% | 3% |
|   Political fun, enjoyment, etc. | 2 | 20 | 16 | 10 |
|   Business, economic, and political gain | 4 | 7 | 15 | 16 |
| Group- and society-related | | | | |
|   Ideological, philosophical, and issue concerns | 49 | 43 | 11 | 8 |
|   Community obligation | 9 | 17 | 33 | 28 |
|   Party attachment | 22 | 11 | 20 | 32 |
| Other | 7 | 0 | 0 | 3 |
| | 100% | 100% | 100% | 100% |
| N = | (46) | (46) | (39) | (39) |

* In response to the questions: "What was the most important reason for your becoming a party official?"; "What is the most important reason for your doing party work now?"

TABLE 7
GOVERNMENT POSITIONS HELD BY PARTY LEADERS*

|  | Democrat | Republican |
|---|---|---|
| None | 50% | 23% |
| Appointive position only | 48 | 57 |
| Elective position only | 2 | 5 |
| Appointive and elective positions | 0 | 15 |
| | 100% | 100% |
| N = | (46) | (39) |

* These are exclusive of honorary or nonpartisan positions.

differences between initial and current incentives, and these tend to mute some of the more marked disparities between the two leaderships. Such factors as party attachment and community obligation, however, still distinguish the Republican activist from his Democratic counterpart. And while ideological or issue concerns have decreased slightly among Democrats, they are still the most important incentives for almost half of the Democratic leadership.

Few leaders in either party, then, are in politics for the express purpose of some sort of personal gain. It is clear, however, that traditional incentives, such as patronage and political advancement, have been used by both parties. As Table 7 indicates, a substantial number of leaders in both parties hold or have held appointive or patronage posts. For Republicans in particular, patronage posts have been important career offices, with more than three-fourths of the Republicans who hold such posts having been in them for over ten years. Tenure among Democrats is considerably shorter, with most having held a position for less than five years, but the party has had such positions at its disposal only recently.

There has been, however, one important difference in the manner in which the parties have used patronage. For the Republicans, patronage has apparently been an accepted and expected reward for party work over the years. Among Democrats, however, the use of patronage has evoked considerable debate within the party. The county chairmen and others, who hoped to use the talent available in the executive committee to establish some degree of partisan control over the county administration inherited by the party in 1961, have frequently had to convince party leaders to take such posts. There has been a tendency for the appeal to be phrased in terms of party loyalty on the one hand and the opportunity to influence public policy on the other. The resistance among executive committeemen to take these jobs has been occasioned first by the pejorative implication which many of them associate with patronage and second by the financial sacrifice which many have had to undergo to take what some might consider to be financially lucrative jobs.[13]

But if the Democratic leaders have been unattracted by patronage, a number of them are characterized by political ambitions. A majority of Democrats, as well as slightly less than a majority of Republicans, would like to run for public office.[14] Elective office, as opposed to appointive office, is apparently more compatible with their ideologically oriented approach to politics.

The vocational aspect of politics, then, has been considerably more important for Republican leaders than for their Democratic counterparts. Nevertheless, a considerable number of Democrats look upon politics as much more than a transient or avocational matter.

---

13. The normative objections to patronage discussed here are not atypical. See, for example, Wilson 1962, chap. 7.
14. Fifty-two percent of the Democrats expressed a desire to run for public office and would seriously consider doing so, while forty-six percent are non-aspirants. Among Republicans, twenty-one percent either held office or were running for office, and another twenty percent expressed a desire to run and had some expectation of doing so.

TABLE 8
THE MOST IMPORTANT ACTIVITY OF THE PARTY LEADER*

| Orientation of Activity | Democrat | Republican |
|---|---|---|
| Campaign-related | (31%) | (38%) |
| General campaign work | 11% | 20% |
| Voter drives, registration, etc. | 13 | 10 |
| Fund-raising | 2 | 5 |
| Public relations | 5 | 3 |
| Party organizational | (43%) | (28%) |
| General organizational oversight and leadership | 26% | 15% |
| Recruiting and organizing committeemen | 15 | 8 |
| Liaison between county organization and committeemen | 2 | 5 |
| Representational | (4%) | (18%) |
| Act as representative for local area and residents | 4 | 18 |
| Patronage, favors, etc. | 0 | 0 |
| Ideological | (15%) | (8%) |
| Policy-making | 7% | 8% |
| Educating voters | 8 | 0 |
| Nominating | (7%) | (8%) |
| Recruitment and nomination of candidates | 7% | 8% |
|  | 100% | 100% |
| N = | (46) | (39) |

* These are ranked according to ratings assigned by the respondent.

## POLITICAL ROLES AND PARTY GOALS

It has been hypothesized that the role definitions of leaders within a majority party in a given area tend to be organizationally oriented, while those of the minority party are inclined toward campaign-oriented roles. In Nassau County, however, these role definitions are reversed.

While the differences are not great, Democratic leaders emphasize campaign-related activities to a lesser extent than do Republican leaders. Conversely, there is a substantially higher number of Democrats (forty-three percent) than Republicans (twenty-eight percent) who view organizational activities as paramount. A plausible hypothesis which explains this distinctiveness is that Democrats are still involved in the building of an organization which can challenge the Republicans at all levels in the county. In order to maximize their competitive position, the Democrats must necessarily devote more time to recruiting, organizing, and overseeing their committeemen and local organizations. The Republican organization is probably better established (as exemplified by the tenure for leaders in our sample), and it can possibly count on its greater numbers to provide the necessary replenishments of personnel at lower levels. Moreover, the increase in Democratic strength may have induced a greater emphasis upon campaign activities among Republicans.

As might be expected, ideological functions are more important for Democrats than for Republicans. The difference, however, is slight (only seven percent), and it relates not to policy-making but rather to voter education. This could indicate that even the most liberal Democrats do not concern themselves to any great extent with the direct formulation of party policy. This does not mean that they are oblivious to these policies. Rather, it appears that most Democratic leaders are, in general, satisfied with the position which the party takes on most issues. Even when they have the opportunity to do so (and a substantial number of Democrats stressed that this was often), Democratic leaders do not find it necessary to engage in an inordinate number of ideological crusades within the party. The party's policies and candidates tend to reflect quite accurately the ideological tenor of the leadership, so that efforts along this line are, for the most part, minimal. The situation would probably be very different if these same Democrats were insurgents trying to influence or to capture a conservative organization.

It is necessary to emphasize that the relatively low figures for the nominating, ideological, and representational tasks (designating them as "most important") do not mean that leaders in both parties do not perform these functions or that they consider them to be unimportant. Thirty-nine percent of the Democrats and thirty-three percent of the Republicans, for example, did mention activities relating to the recruitment and nomination of candidates as among their important activities, but relatively few consider them to be their most important activities.

Within particular subgroups in each party, moreover, there is a substantial degree of variation in role interpretation. This does not, however, appear to be associated with any given recruitment, career, incentive, or ideological factor. There appears to be some degree of individuality and autonomy within both parties in the taking on and defining of leadership roles, and much of this could be a function of the operational requirements of a leader's local organization, such as a zone or assembly district.

*Electoral Focus.* In addition, the electoral considerations of both party leaderships are similar. Leaders in both parties are mainly concerned with elections involving candidates who are directly related to their organizations. The electoral division which is most relevant for them is not that between national, state, and local elections. Rather, the major distinction is between elections involving local or locally based candidates—that is, candidates elected solely from the county, including those in town, county, state legislative, and U.S. House races[15]—and those involving candidates at the state and national level.

TABLE 9

VARIATIONS IN EFFORTS OF PARTY LEADERS
BY TYPE OF CANDIDATE

|  | Democrat | Republican |
|---|---|---|
| Candidates receiving greatest effort |  |  |
| Presidential | 2% | 6% |
| Local and locally based* | 78 | 71 |
| Equal for all | 15 | 23 |
| DK | 5 | 0 |
|  | 100% | 100% |
| N = | (46) | (39) |

* This includes all candidates elected solely within the county.

As Table 9 indicates, both leaderships direct their efforts primarily toward elections involving local and locally based candidates. This is true for about three-fourths of all leaders. Very few direct the major part of their efforts toward presidential candidates, and none toward statewide candidates, although a number of Republicans—twenty-three percent—and some Democrats—fifteen percent—state that they work equally hard for all candidates.

The focus on certain types of candidates appears to result from several factors. First, candidates elected solely within the county are nominated by the county parties. If either party is to be influential outside the county, particularly in terms of nominating statewide candidates, it must necessarily be able to show strength

---

15. Most of the local or village races are nonpartisan. Thus, the partisan "local" elections are for the town councils, the town supervisors—who sit on the County Board of Supervisors—and posts such as town clerk, receiver of taxes, and superintendent of highways. Posts other than the county executive are also elective at the county level, including the county clerk, district attorney, and the chairman of the Board of Assessors.

within the county. Second, as many leaders mentioned, there is usually very little they can do in the presidential, gubernatorial, and U.S. senatorial campaigns. These races are directed from outside the county, they tend to generate their own enthusiasm, and much of the campaigning is done through the mass media. Third, volunteer organizations usually spring up during the gubernatorial and presidential races, and these groups do much of the work which the regular organizations would otherwise be required to perform. In addition, it is easier for the parties to get volunteers for the major races, while they often have to scrape up people to ring doorbells or put up posters for an assembly or councilmanic candidate. It is, therefore, part interest and part necessity which encourages the party leader to focus his attention on the candidates who are closest to home.

The leaderships in both parties, then, have quite similar perceptions of their roles and of the duties associated with these roles. Further, there is a generally uniform consensus within each party on the relative priority of given activities. If there is confusion in this respect, it affects both parties, and it occurs in a highly personal context.

## VIEWS ON PARTY GOALS

Another important factor which relates to the political activist is his perception and evaluation of party goals. Are the leaders in both parties highly power-oriented, or do they attach differing importance to electoral success? It is, of course, difficult to assess with any real accuracy the power orientation of the activist. There is no research technique which has been widely tested in this particular context. Nevertheless, certain questions can be employed which will provide at least a partial evaluation of the importance of power-winning considerations.[16]

---

16. The questions used here were: (1) "Would you favor a strong stand on such civil rights issues as open housing and fair employment practices for your party even if it means the loss of some votes?" Ninety percent of the Democrats and twenty-six percent of the Republicans answered this in the affirmative. Twenty-eight percent of the Republicans said "no," and thirty-eight percent of the Republicans and six percent of the Democrats said they didn't support the policies anyway. (2) "As far as your party is concerned, what type of candidate would you like to see nominated in 1968 (for the presidency) and why?" Fifty-six percent of the Republicans and seventeen percent of the Democrats answered in terms of the ability of the candidate to win. All of the rest

Within the limits of the questions used here, the party's goal as a "power group" is recognized, in certain circumstances, by both leaderships. There are, however, other considerations relating to party goals which are also relevant for many leaders. For Democrats, the party's programmatic and ideological functions—in terms of the policies which it supports and the candidates that it nominates—are considered to be important. No Democrat who supports open housing and fair employment laws (and this accounts for ninety percent of the leadership) believes that the party should neglect or be ambiguous about these policies even at the risk of losing votes. Of Republicans who support these policies, however, slightly more than half feel that the party should not sacrifice votes on these issues alone. Similarly, when asked about the primary attribute of their party's next presidential candidate, eighty-three percent of the Democrats answered in terms of the issues or particular abilities of a candidate, while a majority of Republicans (fifty-six percent) concentrated upon a candidate's ability to win. The views on ticket-splitting of both parties are fairly similar, with a substantial majority in either party favoring, or at least not objecting to, ticket-splitting. Only about a third of the Republicans and a fifth of the Democrats disapproved of ticket-splitting under any circumstances. The idea that ticket-splitting forces the parties to nominate better candidates, for example, finds rather wide support within both parties.

Thus, while the Democratic leadership is power-oriented in some respects, power or electoral success is not the only party goal which it recognizes. The Republican leadership, perhaps because it represents a traditional majority party and because it is more diverse ideologically, is more power-oriented than the Democratic leadership on questions relating to issues and candidates. But there are substantial segments of the Republican leadership which place a great deal of emphasis upon goals other than power.

---

(except three percent Republican DK) articulated their answers in terms of policies or candidate abilities. (3) "Was there ever a time when you thought that your party's supporters would have been justified in splitting their ballots? Under what circumstances do you feel that this would be justified?" Twenty percent of the Democrats and thirty-three percent of the Republicans objected to ticket-splitting under any circumstances. Fifty percent of the Democrats and forty-eight percent of the Republicans approved of it only under certain conditions (such as policy disagreements or poor candidates). Twenty percent of the Democrats and eighteen percent of the Republicans approved of ticket-splitting as a good practice in general.

## SUMMARY AND CONCLUSIONS

Several of the hypotheses that were set forth at the beginning of this paper can be answered in the affirmative. The socio-economic character of Nassau County and its degree of inter-party competition are complemented by high status levels in the party leadership. Further, there are a number of marked similarities in the status attributes of the two leaderships. The parties do draw from different groups within certain economic strata, however, and representations of these groups in the leadership appears to be associated with electoral support and leadership ideology.

While the ideological "analysis" employed in this study is severely limited, it does reinforce an already impressive body of data relating to the ideological distinctiveness of party leaderships at the local level. The suburban political activist shares certain policy attitudes with other members of his party, perceives important differences between the parties, and is, to some extent, reinforced by his policy and issue concerns to enter and to continue party work.

The motivational basis of political activism certainly comprehends a greater diversity of social, environmental, and personality factors than those noted here. Nevertheless, it is clear that the perceived motivations or incentives for the suburban political activist tend to deal, in the main, with the substance of politics rather than with politics as a mere channel for personal gain.

The suburban party leaders also define their roles in a manner which does relate to the electoral success of the party.[17] But substantial numbers of leaders, particularly within the Democratic party, view party goals as somewhat more complex than the single electoral imperative.

Within the party leaderships in Nassau County, then, there are a

---

17. The distribution noted here suggests that the relationship between the functional requirements of the party organization and leadership role definitions should not be overlooked. In much of the literature concerning party leadership roles, little attention has been given to the environmental and organizational conditions which might require competing leaderships to assume these differing roles. It may be that effective organization is more necessary for electoral success in some locales than in others; therefore, a developing party might have to invest more of its resources in organization building than the majority party would. This is apparently the case in Nassau. The Democratic organization has to be particularly effective in order to get the Democratic vote to the polls. The Republicans, who enjoy a substantial registration edge and who have an established organization, can direct their efforts toward the campaign itself.

number of analogies with the political activist types portrayed in the literature. In terms of the "amateur" vs. "professional" model of activism, our data appear to denote different "centers of gravity" within each party.[18] The Democratic leadership, for the most part, resembles in some important ways the amateur model. Ideology is highly liberal, idealistic rationales in political action are frequently referred to, party regularity and party attachment are not approached as religious tenets, and widespread civic participation—at least in terms of occupations within a given status group—is evidenced. Among Republican leaders, one finds greater evidence of professionally-oriented perspectives. There is a higher degree of ideological diversity and a somewhat lesser degree of ideological salience than among Democrats, and the electoral success of the party and personal attachment to the party are also relatively higher.

But while there is a different center within each party, neither party leadership can be classified so neatly. While Democrats may not accept patronage as a personally relevant goal, a substantial number do have political ambitions. While these ambitions probably reflect some interest in bringing ideological commitment to public office, they also require that the party continue to improve its competitive position up to or beyond parity. Among Republicans, however, there has apparently been some "amateurization." Given the one-party character of Nassau up until as recently as ten years ago, it is possible that a substantial number of Republican leaders entered politics with a somewhat greater anticipation of personal gain than they now admit or which they now find relevant.[19]

---

18. For analyses of the amateur and professional models, see Wilson 1962, especially chap. 1; and Salisbury 1965.

19. One research possibility would be to investigate changes in a given leadership through time. This would be particularly interesting in an area where one of the parties appears to be developing but where its electoral prospects in the short run are bright. It would, for example, be valuable to know how the leaders of the two parties view politics today as opposed to the way they (and here is meant for the most part the same leaders) viewed it twenty years ago, with the focus upon many of the questions that have been examined here. The amateur may become more professional with years in the party, while the professional, who has received his pay-off and had a long career in the party, may find the time to start worrying about party policies and other concerns relevant to the amateur. In addition, the suggestion here, that perceptions of the past do change, makes those perceptions no less relevant or important. The use of recall data is essentially to uncover an individual's perceptions of the past, so that "inaccuracy," in the normal sense in which it applies, is not an overriding problem.

If the admittedly limited data presented here reflect trends in other suburban areas (and, indeed, in other areas) political activism at the local level may involve greater citizen participation, greater policy orientation, and, in general, a more functionally complete type of politics than it has in the past. There is a definite base for a suburban politics which is more than "trivial."

# Political Participation in an Upper-Middle-Class Suburb

JOSEPH ZIKMUND II and ROBERT SMITH

In the United States, political participation is directly related to social status and a person's own feelings of competence and self-confidence (i.e., political efficacy).[1] The usual consequence of these patterns in most local areas is the existence of a political elite or leadership group composed of the "better sorts" and, perhaps, some representatives of the "less advantaged" peoples in the community. Recent studies seem to indicate that this arrangement holds in suburbs, just as it does in other kinds of localities.[2] However, virtually all of the research on participation in suburbia has been directed either to suburbs generally or to the working-class suburbs in the United States. To date, we have left unanswered the question: What are the patterns of political participation in suburban communities where almost everyone has a college education, a high salary, and a managerial, professional, or white-collar job? Put somewhat differently, when everyone has the basic social characteristics usually associated with political leadership, who is active in local affairs and who is not?

---

1. For general discussions of political participation, see Milbrath 1965; and Lane 1959.
2. Gilbert 1967, pp. 270-71; Gans 1967, pp. 26-27. Somewhat contradictory evidence appears in Williams et al. 1965, pp. 226-30. It must be added that while both the Gilbert and Williams books touch upon participation in the community discussed in this article, neither makes it a primary concern.

---

"Political Participation in an Upper-Middle-Class Suburb" by Joseph Zikmund II and Robert Smith is reprinted from Urban Affairs Quarterly, vol. 4, no. 4 (June 1969), pp. 443-458, by permission of the publisher, Sage Publications, Inc., and Joseph Zikmund II.

The literature on suburbia provides two suggestions for what might be considered partial answers to these questions. First, W. T. Martin, in his article "The Structuring of Social Relationships Engendered by Suburban Residence" (1956), argues that in the suburbs, where a large portion of the male residents are gone from the area during the day and return home late in the evening after a long commuter ride, the women of the community become the political activists. Second, Scott Greer, in his more recent article "The Social Structure and Political Process of Suburbia" (1960), suggests that local involvement factors such as membership in local, nonpolitical organizations, general social conviviality, and readership of local newspapers are highly related to political participation in suburbs.[3]

The purpose of this study is to test both the general propositions that relate participation to social status and to feelings of self-efficacy, and these more specific propositions by Martin and by Greer in a somewhat unique community composed almost entirely of upper- or upper-middle-class residents—a community that is peculiar precisely because it *does* fit the so-called suburban image or myth.[4] The particular hypotheses to be tested are:

1. Local political participation is directly related to age, education, income, and occupation (from Lane and Milbrath).
2. Local political participation is directly related to feelings of self-efficacy (also from Lane and Milbrath).
3. Women participate more than men, and
4. Commuters tend to have relatively low rates of participation (both from Martin).
5. Local political participation is directly related to general attachment and involvement in the community (from Greer).

The community chosen for study was Radnor Township, Delaware County, Pennsylvania,[5] a respectable, old suburban area on

---

3. Greer 1960, pp. 514-26. See also Greer's follow-up article, "The Social Structure and Political Process of Suburbia: An Empirical Test" (1963).

4. The "myth of suburbia" probably can be traced back to William H. Whyte's *The Organization Man* (1956). This overgeneralized image has been justly attacked by several writers; among those not previously mentioned are: Berger 1960; Schnore 1965, pp. 203-21; Wood 1958, pp. 114-21; and Zikmund 1968. However, students of suburbia must be aware that, just as the "suburban myth" does not apply to all suburbs, it is equally dangerous to believe that there are no suburbs which fit the "myth."

5. Local politics in Radnor are primarily on the township level. There are no towns, villages, or other incorporated places within the township boundaries which conduct any significant, official, public business.

TABLE 1
CHARACTERISTICS OF RADNOR RESIDENTS

|  | 1960 Census | Study Sample | League of Women Voters Sample[a] |
|---|---|---|---|
| *Age* | | | |
| 20–29 | 21[b] | 11 | |
| 30–39 | 19 | 16 | |
| 40–49 | 20 | 27 | |
| 50–59 | 18 | 19 | |
| 60 and over | 22 | 27 | |
| *Education* | | | |
| None | 1 | 0 | |
| Elementary | 18 | 2 | |
| High school | 40 | 20 | |
| College | 41 | 77 | |
| *Income* | | | |
| $0–4,999 | 16 | 6 | 7 |
| $5,000–9,999 | 35 | 17 | 15 |
| $10,000 or more | 48 | 76 | 78 |
| *Religion* | | | |
| Protestant | | 71 | |
| Catholic | | 23 | |
| Jewish | | 2 | |
| None or other | | 4 | |
| *Marital Status[c]* | | | |
| Single | | 8 | |
| Married | | 79 | |
| Widowed or divorced | | 13 | |
| *Residence* | | | |
| Own home | 65 | 74 | |
| Rent or other | 35 | 26 | |
| *Political Affiliation* | | | |
| Republican | | 79 | |
| Democrat | | 11 | |
| Independent | | 10 | |
| | | (N=239) | |

a. These data were obtained from an unpublished study of Radnor completed in 1965 by the local League of Women Voters. The League's data were based on interviews in 318 homes drawn from a random probability sample. Income data are the only material available for comparison with the present study.

b. Each cell is the percent of the adult Radnor population or of the sample.

c. Marital status cannot be compared between the census and the sample used in this study because the sample tapped only adults (21 or over), while the census question concerned with marital status involves people over 14 years of age.

the Philadelphia Main Line. A social-economic portrait of Radnor residents as recorded by the 1960 census appears on Table 1.[6] Respondents for this study were selected on a random basis from the local telephone directory. This list of residents was used only

---

6. Compare these data to William M. Dobriner's description of the "suburban myth" (1963, p. 6).

## TABLE 2
### POLITICAL ACTIVITY IN RADNOR BY KINDS OF ACTIVITIES (QUESTIONNAIRE)

| | Percent Responding "Yes" |
|---|---|
| | (N=239) |
| Have you ever been asked to vote for a candidate in a local election in Radnor? | 86 |
| Has anyone ever asked you to support his or her candidacy in a local election in Radnor? | 76 |
| In the past year or so have you had any written or spoken contact with political or governmental officials in Radnor? | 58 |
| Have you given money or done other things to help in campaigns for local political office in Radnor? | 38 |
| Do you talk to people during political campaigns and try to show them why they should vote for one of the candidates in elections for Township Commissioners in Radnor or Justice of the Peace? | 36 |
| Do you go to political meetings, rallies, dinners, or things like that in respect to local elections in Radnor? | 33 |
| Have you ever been asked to serve in any organization in Radnor? | 27 |
| During the past year or so have you yourself done anything actively in connection with some local issue or problem, political or non-political? | 27 |
| Did you ever try to get someone to run for office in Radnor or encourage a person to run? | 18 |
| Have you ever held an office or had a job in a political party? | 8 |
| Have you ever held public office? | 5 |
| Have you ever been asked to serve on a Township Commission or Board? | 4 |

after assurance from the Pennsylvania Bell Telephone Company that ninety-five percent of the people in this area have telephones, and that the types of people having unlisted numbers match the population as a whole to such an extent as not to bias a random draw from the directory.[7] A total of 704 names was chosen. From these, 238 usable questionnaires were returned by mail in time for the final analysis.[8] A comparison of the social composition of the sample, as reflected in the returned questionnaires, with the 1960 census and with another recent survey of Radnor also appears on Table 1.

For reasons of convenience, and at least some small measure of comparability, the questions used to test political participation

---

[7]. This information comes from a survey by Bell Telephone of telephone users in the suburban areas surrounding Philadelphia (Mr. G. Lodge, Director of Marketing Research, Bell Telephone Company of Pennsylvania, September 18, 1967).

[8]. On the use of mail questionnaires see: Moser 1958, pp. 127-44, 175-84; McDonagh and Rosenblum 1965; Mayer and Pratt 1966.

were borrowed directly from Aaron Wildavsky's (1964) study of Oberlin, Ohio, and the responses to these twelve questions were collapsed into Wildavsky's very useful three-part classification scheme of "Active Participants," "Voter Observers," and "Apathetics" (Wildavsky 1964, pp. 15-16). Table 2 presents the percentage of "yes" responses to the twelve questions and describes the general levels of political participation evident among Radnor residents. As compared to Wildavsky's (1964) Oberlin data, for example, Radnorites are very active in local affairs. While the proportion of Radnor residents who have held public office is not high, they are hyperactive with regard to most of the other variables such as voting, contacting public officials, doing campaign work, etc. As is evident from Table 3, this high level of political activity is directly related to the social-economic status of Radnor residents.

However, the first, and perhaps most important, finding to be derived from this table is that, contrary to Martin's assertions, Radnor women appear significantly[9] less in the Active Participant category than do the men of the community, 31 to 49 percent respectively. While the proportion of women who may be identified as Active Participants is certainly not low, more of the Radnor homemakers fall into the Voter Observer group (44 percent). The proportion of Apathetics was about even between men and women, 22 and 15 percent respectively.

When we turn to age as a factor related to participation, we find that the youngest citizens, as would be expected, have the lowest rate of Active Participants (15 percent) and the highest rate of Apathetics (50 percent). However, participation increases very rapidly after people leave their twenties. Active Participation is 56 percent for those in the 30-39 age bracket, drops somewhat (to 42 percent) for those in their forties, climbs back to 49 percent for the 50-59 age group, and then tapers off to 34 percent among those citizens 60 years or older. Once the barrier of 30 is reached, the proportion of people who fall into the Voter Observer category steadily increases with age, while those in the Apathetic grouping gradually decrease in number.

---

9. The use of the word "significant" or "significantly" at all times in this article means: statistically significant at the 0.05 level. These judgments have been made from a standard table found in Cuthbert (1940).

## TABLE 3
### RELATIONSHIP BETWEEN DEMOGRAPHIC CHARACTERISTICS OF RADNOR RESIDENTS AND LEVELS OF POLITICAL PARTICIPATION

| Demographic Level | Active Participants | Voter Observers | Apathetics | |
|---|---|---|---|---|
| Male | 49[a] | 29 | 22 | (130)[b] |
| Female | 31 | 44 | 25 | (108) |
| *Age* | | | | |
| 20–29 | 15 | 35 | 50 | (26) |
| 30–39 | 56 | 18 | 26 | (39) |
| 40–49 | 42 | 33 | 25 | (64) |
| 50–59 | 49 | 38 | 13 | (45) |
| 60 and over | 34 | 50 | 16 | (64) |
| *Education* | | | | |
| High school or less | 27 | 50 | 23 | (52) |
| Some college | 36 | 43 | 21 | (42) |
| College degree | 53 | 27 | 20 | (79) |
| Postgraduate | 40 | 32 | 28 | (65) |
| *Income* | | | | |
| Less than $10,000 | 26 | 48 | 26 | (54) |
| $10,000–15,000 | 31 | 24 | 45 | (55) |
| Over $15,000 | 52 | 27 | 21 | (128) |
| *Occupation*[c] | | | | |
| Professional | 47 | 24 | 29 | (34) |
| Managerial | 57 | 26 | 17 | (35) |
| White collar | 49 | 28 | 23 | (57) |
| Laboring | 25 | 46 | 29 | (24) |
| Housewife | 35 | 43 | 22 | (58) |
| Retired | 23 | 57 | 20 | (30) |

a. Figure in each cell is the percent of the Radnor sample. Rows total to 100 percent.
b. 238 respondents answered the political participation questions. When the number of respondents for any set of responses does not total 238, the difference (in parentheses) indicates the number of respondents who did not answer the particular social or opinion question.
c. Occupation of respondent, not head of household.

Education also appears to be directly related to participation. Considering for the moment only those people with no postgraduate college work, two distinct trends are evident: first, Active Participation increases as education increases while, second, the proportion of Voter Observers tends to decrease. However, it is interesting to note that Active Participation among those with a postgraduate education is considerably lower than among those with only four years of college, and that this is also the group with the highest portion of political Apathetics.

In addition, political activity is also related to the incomes and occupations of Radnor residents. The only surprise with regard to the factor of income is that the middle-income category ($10,000–$15,000) contained a significantly larger portion of Apathetics when compared to people earning either more or less than these amounts, 45 percent versus 21 and 26 percent, respectively. The several occupational types formed a predictable hierarchy in terms of Active Participation. The managerial people clearly topped the list, followed by white-collar and professional types, housewives, and then the laboring and retired residents. The only interesting discovery here was that professionals shared with laborers the highest proportion of Apathetics (29 percent).

In a community as rich as Radnor it is not surprising that Republicans predominate. For as long as records have been kept, township government has been controlled by the Republican Party. Typical of other kinds of one-party areas,[10] Active Participation in Radnor seems to be reserved primarily for supporters of the majority party. By contrast, Democrats had a very low rate of Active Participation and a very high proportion of Apathetics (see Table 4).

Table 5 indicates the relationship between the responses to general questions regarding a sense of civic obligation, self-confidence, and political efficacy on the one hand, and levels of political participation on the other. In each case the responses indicate a high level of civic obligation[11] and political and social efficacy on the part of most Radnor residents. In addition, the more self-confident or efficacious the response, the more likely it is that the person is politically active. However, it should be noted that participation is high even among those who feel no sense of civic obligation, feel ill at ease in social conversation, or doubt the basic democratic assumptions concerning the responsiveness of government and the capacity of the common man to understand the workings of government. Whether a concern to protect one's interests in the public arena or the pressure of a general climate of participation for its own sake lies behind these findings, we cannot say. The fact remains that in Radnor even the confused and the unconvinced take part in local affairs.

---

10. See, for example, Heard 1952, chaps. 3–8.
11. A methodological note. Given the very high sense of civic obligation among Radnor residents, we must keep in mind that respondents may have felt that they ought to participate in local politics and, thus, reported that they did participate, when in fact they did not. In other words, when we interpret the levels of participation of Radnorites—Table 2—it is possible that these values are somewhat inflated.

## TABLE 4
### RELATIONSHIP OF POLITICAL IDENTIFICATION AND PAST PARTISAN ELECTORAL SUPPORT WITH POLITICAL PARTICIPATION

| Partisanship | Active Participants | Voter Observers | Apathetics | |
|---|---|---|---|---|
| *Political Identification* | | | | |
| Republican | 45[a] | 36 | 19 | (188)[b] |
| Independent | 33 | 46 | 21 | (24) |
| Democrat | 19 | 31 | 50 | (26) |
| *Presidential Vote in 1964* | | | | |
| Goldwater | 46 | 38 | 16 | (125) |
| Johnson | 36 | 37 | 27 | (86) |
| No vote | 23 | 27 | 50 | (22) |

a, b. See footnotes to Table 3.

## TABLE 5
### RELATIONSHIP OF CIVIC OBLIGATION AND SELF-EFFICACY WITH POLITICAL PARTICIPATION

| | Active Participants | Voter Observers | Apathetics | |
|---|---|---|---|---|
| *Civic Obligation* | | | | |
| "... a person ought to take part in community affairs." | | | | |
| Agree* | 46[a] | 35 | 19 | (154)[b] |
| Neutral | 29 | 39 | 32 | (41) |
| Disagree | 31 | 38 | 31 | (42) |
| *General Self-Confidence and Political Efficacy* | | | | |
| "In social conversation I frequently have definite ideas and try to convince others." | | | | |
| Agree* | 46 | 35 | 19 | (138) |
| Neutral | 38 | 44 | 18 | (55) |
| Disagree | 28 | 30 | 42 | (43) |
| "Public officials do not care much what people like me think." | | | | |
| Agree | 25 | 50 | 25 | (44) |
| Neutral | 32 | 39 | 29 | (38) |
| Disagree* | 47 | 31 | 22 | (151) |
| "Sometimes politics and government seem so complicated that people like me can't really understand what is going on." | | | | |
| Agree | 35 | 38 | 27 | (78) |
| Neutral | 44 | 41 | 15 | (27) |
| Disagree* | 44 | 34 | 23 | (133) |

a, b. See footnotes to Table 3.
* Asterisks indicate a position of civic obligation or self-confidence and political efficacy.

## TABLE 6
### RELATIONSHIP OF OPINIONS REGARDING RADNOR POLITICS WITH POLITICAL PARTICIPATION

| | Political Participation Level | | | |
|---|---|---|---|---|
| | Active Participants | Voter Observers | Apathetics | |
| "Anyone in Radnor who wants to, gets a chance to have his say about important issues." | | | | |
| Agree* | 53[a] | 34 | 13 | (137)[b] |
| Neutral | 17 | 36 | 47 | (59) |
| Disagree | 38 | 42 | 20 | (40) |
| "Participation in government and politics raises a person's prestige in Radnor." | | | | |
| Agree | 42 | 38 | 20 | (92) |
| Neutral | 38 | 31 | 31 | (99) |
| Disagree | 41 | 45 | 14 | (44) |
| "A person might lose friends if he gets too involved in community issues." | | | | |
| Agree | 54 | 23 | 23 | (83) |
| Neutral | 41 | 41 | 18 | (37) |
| Disagree | 32 | 43 | 25 | (116) |
| "Most decisions in Radnor are made by a small group that pretty well runs this township." | | | | |
| Agree | 46 | 38 | 16 | (143) |
| Neutral | 19 | 33 | 48 | (57) |
| Disagree* | 56 | 32 | 12 | (34) |

a, b. See footnotes to Table 3.
\* Asterisks indicate the most efficacious position on the related questions.

Probably the most varied and least predictable results come from the questions which seek to elicit views on the conduct and consequences of local politics in Radnor (Table 6). The responses seem to be less a measure of the psychic factors which lead to participation than a gauge of the political realism of Radnorites. While a majority of residents "agree" that anyone can have his say, an even larger portion "agree" that most Radnor decisions are made by a small group that runs the township. Similarly, while participation is somewhat higher among those who take the more efficacious position on these two questions (marked by an asterisk) than among those who have given the opposite response, the real difference occurs between those who take one of the polar extremes ("agree" or "disagree") and those who respond "neutral." In each case the "neutrals" had a very high rate of political apathy. Oddly enough, the question concerning loss of personal friends from political participation indicates that the lowest rate of participation occurs among those who "disagree" and the highest rate

*Political Participation* 265

### TABLE 7
### RELATIONSHIP OF FACTORS CONCERNING ATTACHMENT TO THE RADNOR COMMUNITY WITH LEVELS OF POLITICAL PARTICIPATION

| Attachment Factor | Active Participants | Voter Observers | Apathetics | |
|---|---|---|---|---|
| *Type of residence* | | | | |
| Own home | 49[a] | 37 | 14 | (177)[b] |
| Rent | 15 | 36 | 49 | (58) |
| *Plans for next year* | | | | |
| Remain in Radnor | 42 | 37 | 21 | (213) |
| Move from Radnor | 29 | 29 | 42 | (24) |
| *Length of residence* | | | | |
| Less than 3 years | 11 | 22 | 67 | (55) |
| 3-7 years | 51 | 32 | 17 | (59) |
| 8-17 years | 52 | 41 | 7 | (61) |
| 18 or more years | 46 | 48 | 6 | (63) |
| *Organizational memberships* | | | | |
| None | 22 | 41 | 37 | (109) |
| Some | 57 | 32 | 11 | (129) |
| *Place where respondent grew up* | | | | |
| Radnor | 64 | 27 | 9 | (11) |
| Other Philadelphia suburbs | 57 | 25 | 18 | (51) |
| Philadelphia | 39 | 42 | 19 | (31) |
| Cities other than Philadelphia | 37 | 32 | 31 | (59) |
| Miscellaneous others | 32 | 46 | 22 | (82) |
| *"Most of my friends live here in Radnor"* | | | | |
| Agree | 56 | 33 | 11 | (46) |
| Neutral | 58 | 37 | 5 | (19) |
| Disagree | 34 | 37 | 29 | (172) |
| *Read local newspaper* | | | | |
| Frequently | 52 | 35 | 13 | (132) |
| Less frequently | 27 | 37 | 36 | (105) |
| *Place of employment of head of household* | | | | |
| Radnor | 43 | 26 | 31 | (61) |
| Philadelphia | 57 | 27 | 16 | (77) |
| Other | 32 | 41 | 27 | (59) |
| Retired | 19 | 62 | 19 | (41) |

*a, b.* See footnotes to Table 3.

among citizens who "agree." The question regarding personal prestige and political participation fails to discriminate among rates of Active Participation; however, those who respond "neutral" again have the highest incidence of Apathetics. Once more, we suggest that the questions concerning Radnor politics itself may tap the feelings of those who are active and who thus know very well what the consequences of participation can be.

The several factors presented on Table 7 are all intended to give some indication of the personal and social attachments of Radnor residents to their local community. Most of these factors, including home ownership, plans to stay in Radnor, length of residence, organizational memberships, local upbringing, local friends, and readership of the local newspaper, show strong relationships with the incidence of Active Participation. The one exception—place of employment—however, is very important, for contrary to Martin's suggestion that commuters would have low rates of Active Participation, in Radnor they have the highest. Even compared to people who work in Radnor itself (local businessmen, etc.) the difference is quite great.[12] This, of course, parallels the previous finding that Radnor men are more politically active than the local housewives.

We began with five hypotheses concerning political participation; they have been tested, and the results are now evident. The data from Radnor indicate that the general assertions relating political activity to social rank and to feelings of self-efficacy hold in this rather unique community. Similarly, Scott Greer's findings that participation correlates with the several local-attachment factors are upheld. However, Martin's suggestions that in suburbia the commuter is not politically active and that the women take his place in local affairs are called into serious question. At the same time we learn that identification with the local majority party is directly related to high rates of Active Participation, while personal evaluations of the character and consequences of local politics seem to play little role in encouraging or discouraging local involvement. The picture which emerges is one of a well-educated, well-to-do, Republican, white-collar commuter with strong financial and personal attachments to the local area, who, at one and the same time, performs his civic duty and looks after his own interests through Active Participation in community affairs. See the participation figures for persons in Category A on Table 8. There are, of course, the Democrats, the newcomers, the renters, the people under 30, but each of these represents a clear minority of the Radnor population, and they are all likely to remain minorities for a long time to come. The overall Radnor tradition of high

---

12. This supports Williams's finding that in upper social-rank suburbs, a majority of local leaders work in the center city (Williams 1965, p. 227). Williams and his colleagues suggest that since a majority of workers in white-collar suburbs commute to the center city, the reason that a high portion of the leaders of these suburbs also commute is simply a function of statistical probability and is without substantive importance (1965, pp. 228–29). We think this begs the question.

## TABLE 8
### PARTICIPATION OF SELECTED, SOCIAL-ECONOMIC CATEGORICAL GROUPINGS IN RADNOR TOWNSHIP

|  | Political Participation Level | | |
|---|---|---|---|
|  | Active Participants | Voter Observers | Apathetics |
| Category A[a] | 30[b] | 4 | 0   (34)[c] |
| Category B[d] | 3 | 7 | 8   (18) |

a. Category A is composed of those Radnorites who meet all of the following criteria:
   Age—over 30 but less than 60
   One or more years of college education
   Earn more than $15,000
   Own their own home
   Lived in Radnor more than three years
   Belong to some local organizations
   Work in Philadelphia (i.e., commuters)
   Identify with the Republican party
b. See footnote a on Table 3.
c. See footnote b on Table 3.
d. Category B is composed of those Radnorites who meet both of the following criteria:
   Have some postgraduate college education
   Either (1) work in Radnor, or (2) work someplace other than Philadelphia, but not in Radnor.

political participation is not threatened by these kinds of people.

However, the majority pattern may be endangered by another segment of the local population—the noncommuting scientist-technician. Although there is no way to isolate these people on the basis of occupational classification, for some may be involved in management and others in more professional kinds of research and development, we suggest that many of them will have some kind of postgraduate college education.[13] While the number of respondents does become very small when the culling process is completed, the results can be suggestive, even if not a conclusive demonstration (see Category B on Table 8). Participation by the eighteen respondents in Category B is very low (only 17 percent being Active Participants) as compared with 27 percent for all people with just a high school education or less, 36 percent for those with some college training, 53 percent for college graduates, and 40 percent for all people with some postgraduate schooling (see again Table 3). If, as Herbert J. Gans argues, industrial decentralization is accompanied by the further decentralization of

---

13. This would also apply to local lawyers, doctors, and dentists. However, the findings are important even if the sample breakdown on the bases of work and level of education does not provide a totally pure type—the noncommuting scientist-technician.

offices and research facilities (Gans 1967, p. 421) then the portion of noncommuting scientist-technicians living in suburbs like Radnor is likely to increase. Already Radnor is providing living space for scientist-technicians employed at nearby research installations such as the General Electric Space Center, the Burroughs office-machine plant, and a number of smaller research and engineering companies. Perhaps it is a "scientific" posture of uninvolvement, or the transient character of their jobs, or the long hours they often are expected to work, which prevents more Active Participation from these people. Unfortunately for suburban communities like Radnor, the scientist-technician is drawn to these places because they provide good schools and a pleasant environment for the family, but the scientist-technician may not be willing to pay the price of involvement necessary to maintain the very advantages that bring him to these communities. If true, and if the proportion of scientist-technicians continues to grow in suburbia without a marked change in their participation patterns, then the tradition of civic activity in Radnor and similar communities may, indeed, be weakened.

Two general points are worth noting in conclusion. First, Radnor and other suburbs of this type exhibit a very strong commitment to the goals of popular democracy, both in theory and in practice. Here you have the highest achievement of the fundamental ideal of citizen participation. The environment or tradition of civic activity must have some influence on newcomers who move into the community, and many ex-Radnorites who move to other areas must carry away some sense of the Radnor political style. Thus, it is quite possible that the communities like Radnor materially contribute to the overall functioning of the democratic system by actually demonstrating that competent citizen participation can be maintained over time and can be made to grapple responsibly with the persistent problems of local government.

At the same time, it is quite likely that metropolitan integration poses the greatest threat to the preservation of this democratic tradition. We suggest that any attempt to integrate Radnor politically into one single, metropolitan governing unit would be not only extremely difficult, but politically disastrous as well.[14] While it is readily apparent that it will be necessary for suburbs to share

---

14. Other authors have reached much the same conclusion for quite different reasons (Williams 1965, pp. 289–312).

the costs of the core areas, the attempt to achieve this financial cooperation through assimilation will probably eliminate this kind of suburb as an essential component of the democratic society. We contend that living and participating in Radnor can make democratic ideals seem a reality, at least at the local level. The data presented in Table 7 indicate the strong relationship between local attachment and local identity on the one hand and Active Participation on the other. Were this localized focus destroyed through political assimilation and the social homogenization that could follow, it is quite possible that political alienation would replace political efficacy and the tradition of citizen participation would soon disappear. The solution to the problems of the city does not lie in highly centralized, regional government. If the federal principle applies for the country as a whole, it also should apply in the metropolitan sprawl.

## SUGGESTIONS FOR FURTHER READING

The classic book about suburban politics in North America is Robert Wood's *Suburbia: Its People and Their Politics* (Boston: Houghton-Mifflin, 1958). Wood's major thesis is that the suburbanites' fondness for small, local government creates a series of difficult social and political dilemmas. A later book by Wood, *1400 Governments* (Cambridge: Harvard University Press, 1961) explores the workings of the "ridiculously fragmented" political structure of the New York City metropolitan region. Another important book-length treatment of suburban politics is Oliver P. Williams, Harold Herman, Charles S. Liebman, and Thomas R. Dye's *Suburban Differences and Metropolitan Policies: A Philadelphia Story* (Philadelphia: University of Pennsylvania Press, 1965). This volume examines the relationship between the population and land-use characteristics of Philadelphia suburbs and the fiscal policies of these suburbs' local governments.

Thus far, only a few sociologists have attempted to link the political processes in the various kinds of suburbs with these localities' other institutional arrangements. Foremost among these few is Scott Greer. In "The Social Structure and Political Process of Suburbia" (*American Sociological Review*, vol. 25, August 1960, pp. 514-526) Greer constructs a taxonomy of "organizational types"—ranging from "multi-level participators" to "isolates" and then derives seventy-four hypotheses dealing for the most part with suburban political participation. In a subsequent article, "The Social Structure and Political Process of Suburbia: An Empirical Test" (*Rural Sociology*, vol. 27, December 1962, pp. 438-459), Greer tests elements of his theoretical formulation with data drawn from St. Louis County, Missouri. For expanded treatments of suburban politics, in the broad context of metropolitan social organization, see two of Greer's best known books: *The Emerging City* (New York: The Free Press, 1962) and *Governing the Metropolis* (New York: Wiley, 1962).

In recent years the growing interest of political scientists in suburban political behavior has resulted in a number of excellent articles. Among these are: Charles G. Bell's "A New Suburban Politics" (*Social Forces*, vol. 47, March 1969, pp. 282-288); Bryron Downes's "Issue Conflict, Functionalism, and Consensus in Suburban City Councils" (*Urban Affairs Quarterly*, vol. 4, June 1969, pp. 477-497); Thomas Dye's "Popular Images of Decision-Making in Suburban Communities" (*Sociology and Social Research*, vol. 47, October 1962, pp. 75-83); and Joseph Zikmund II's "Suburban Voting in Presidential Elections: 1948-1964" (*Midwest Journal of Political Science*, vol. 12, May 1968, pp. 239-258).

# PART V: TOWARD SUBURBIA'S FUTURE

# INTRODUCTION

One of the major premises of contemporary suburban study is that suburban North America is evolving into an urban area. However, the pace of this suburban to urban evolution and the precise form that suburban society will take in the future are not easily predicted. Thus far, most suburban development has been "natural"—that is, it represents the normal processes of metropolitan deconcentration made rampant by technology, affluence, and an economic system that encourages new housing construction along with commercial and industrial expansion. Yet man has the capacity to influence (or regulate) suburban growth, to alter some of the forms of suburban social organization, and thereby influence the level and the content of suburban diversity. The three selections in this final part deal with aspects of planned suburban change.

In "The Metropolitan Government Approach: Should, Can, and Will It Prevail?" political scientist Daniel R. Grant concisely reviews the pressing issue of government consolidation in North America's metropolitan areas. If metropolitan government can be achieved in more than the handful of areas where it now functions, it will be possible to bring about sorely needed programs of metro-wide service and planning coordination. There is opposition, however, from both cities and suburbs, and the likelihood of widespread metropolitan government is dim. As Grant points out, there are greater prospects for "special districts" and other ad hoc problem-solving schemes which will involve coordination between discrete sets of metropolitan political jurisdictions.

The second selection, "Suburban Action: Advocate Planning for an Open Society," contains an explicit call for the opening of suburbia to more low-income families (primarily blacks). It also contains a formula for social action. The authors, Paul and Linda Davidoff and Neil Newton Gold, prescribe both formal and informal methods of "advocacy," some of which require legal experience and extensive funds, but some of which require no more than individual motivation and energy. The authors employ broad functionalistic arguments to support their case. They point to the consequences of isolating a vast poverty-level population in the cities while employment opportunities are fast decentralizing into suburbia. But much of the opposition to open housing in the suburbs is likely to be parochial and emotional. Many suburban whites view the idea in a narrow racial frame of reference and, recently, the thrust of some black political thought has been directed toward building "community control" within the inner-city itself. Despite the formidable opposition, metropolitan planners are increasingly accepting the premise that there is a "need for regional and national approaches to planning for the needs of the black and the poor." In the coming decades the issue of open housing in the suburbs is certain to become a major source of political controversy.

No matter what the future political structure of our urban regions, or their socio-economic and racial configurations, the metropolitan areas of North America are certain to increase in population. Predictions for the growth of the United States population run as high as 100 million by the year 2000 ("the third 100 million"), and it is likely that most of these new citizens will reside in urban regions. Heretofore, suburban development has been spurred by the notion that life is best led upon a relatively open terrain. Thus the spread of single-family suburban homes far from the city limits, and the concomitant denuding of millions of acres of fertile and sometimes scenic land. As the metropolitan population of North America continues to grow, the question of suburban sprawl becomes crucial. Should the suburbs continue to push into the rural areas, or should metropolitan planning attempt to contain our spreading cities by creating new kinds of living arrangements, at high levels of population density, within the existing metropolitan setting?

# Introduction

The final selection is from *The Last Landscape* by William H. Whyte. This is the same William H. Whyte who was instrumental (albeit unintentionally) in making the "suburban myth" a major component of American social thought. Since his forays into postwar suburbia, Whyte has become one of America's leading conservationists. *The Last Landscape* addresses itself to the ways "our metropolitan areas look and the ways they might look." Reprinted here is chapter twenty, "The Case for Crowding," in which Whyte deals with the question of population density in the metropolis.

Whyte avoids the conventional argument that we are running out of space. That argument is invalid. Instead, he contends that an eternally spreading metropolitan expanse is simply inefficient and dull. Continued deconcentration, says Whyte, "would go against the grain of all the forces that give a metropolis its vitality." Far better, then, to increase population densities within metropolitan territories, halt the relentless extension of suburbia into the hinterland, and by judicious use of metropolitan space produce a more livable environment in both cities and suburbs.

Whyte's thesis is not entirely novel. Other urban commentators have observed that population density in itself is not inherently evil, and the notion that suburban sprawl must be halted is generally accepted. But it is unlikely that many suburbanites, or city dwellers, will enthusiastically embrace Whyte's ideas about "crowding." Clearly, the strategies for limiting the physical size of our metropolitan areas, while at the same time housing greater numbers of metropolitan residents, are matters for urgent debate. And clearly, too, the future of our cities and suburbs alike rests upon the debate's outcome.

# The Metropolitan Government Approach
## Should, Can, and Will It Prevail?

DANIEL R. GRANT

There are three important questions concerning the "metropolitan government approach" to the problems of the urban regions: (1) *Should* the metropolitan community govern itself? (2) *Can* the metropolitan community govern itself? (3) *Will* it govern itself? It is important to note that the question is not "Can a given *segment* of the metropolis govern itself?" or "Can the *national* or *state government* govern the metropolis?" These are interesting and significant questions, but the concern of the following discussion is on the specific questions of whether or not the whole metropolis should, can, and will govern itself.

It should be noted also that these are three different kinds of questions, and there is reason for doubting whether a political scientist, *as such*, should, can, or will answer them. Any question which begins with "should" is usually a value-loaded question and is perhaps more appropriately tackled by a political philosopher or simply a citizen stating his own value preferences. The second question is more manageable, since it relates to the description, observation, and analysis of governmental experience in various situations where the metropolitan government approach has been attempted. The third question is very hazardous indeed, because it involves the task of political prediction or forecast, and it is hardly

---

*"The Metropolitan Government Approach: Should, Can, and Will It Prevail?" by Daniel R. Grant is reprinted from* Urban Affairs Quarterly, *vol. 3, no. 3 (March 1968), pp. 103-110, by permission of the publisher, Sage Publications, Inc., and the author.*

news that the batting average of political scientists still falls considerably short of perfection in this arena. The attempted answers should therefore be taken with these preliminary disclaimers in mind.

At the risk of being accused of establishing the case by carefully adopting a special set of definitions, it is important to begin by explaining what is meant by "the metropolitan community governing itself." This would involve a governmental structure and process in which the whole metropolitan community—core city and suburbs together—participates not only in area-wide planning, but in area-wide policy-making and policy-execution for those problems which are obviously area-wide in scope and character. By this definition it should be clear that few if any of the 212 metropolitan areas in the United States are actually governing themselves, because of the extreme fragmentation of government units.

But *should* the whole metropolitan community govern itself? The case for it may be expressed in many ways, but the simplest way is to use the well-worn cliché—in unity there is strength, and in fragmentation, competition, confusion, and disunity there is weakness. Four kinds of unity or coordination are of vital importance to the future of the metropolitan community.

1. Coordination of effort is needed between different geographic parts of the metropolitan area. Failure to have such geographic coordination tends to result in streets that do not meet, land uses that are incompatible, sewage from one area polluting the water of another, unvaccinated dogs from one section menacing another, and the duplicate purchasing of expensive equipment and facilities. If geographic coordination is impossible at the metropolitan community level, there will be inevitable pressure to achieve it at the state or national level.

2. Coordination of effort is needed between different functions and services. Failure to achieve such functional coordination tends to isolate the education of the child from the health of the child, tends to inhibit the cooperative location and operation of parks, recreation programs, and schools, and tends to place additional obstacles in the already difficult path of urban renewal cooperation with public works, welfare, and education programs, to name only a few. If coordination between functions and services is impossible at the metropolitan community level, there will certainly be pressure to achieve it at the state or national level.

3. Area-wide coordination of financial resources is needed. Failure to coordinate financial resources frequently means that the area with the lowest personal incomes must finance schools for the greatest number of children, that the most badly blighted areas may have the lowest tax resources with which to finance the elimination of blight, and that the area with the most expensive problem of sewage disposal and treatment may have the least resources to accomplish the job. If a pooling of financial resources is not possible at the metropolitan community level, there will be strong pressure for state or national action to achieve this result.

4. Area-wide coordination of the human resources of the metropolitan community is needed and may ultimately be the most serious need of all. By this is meant the coordination of the most able, highly specialized, and professional administrative personnel, the most able civic and political leadership, and the interest and participation of voters and citizens as a whole. Failure to coordinate these human resources of the metropolis tends to segregate the most able leaders in separate political entities—frequently suburbs—and to isolate them from the core city's problems. Such a political structure tends to encourage an irresponsible attitude by citizens in high-income suburbs—"We in Azalea Heights solve our own slum problems; why don't you in Gutter City solve yours?" Furthermore, the fragmented governmental structure of the metropolis tends to make the fixing of responsibility by citizens an impossible task. If the essence of democracy is fixing responsibility and holding governmental officials accountable, the fragmented structure constitutes a very real obstacle to democracy in the metropolis. If responsibility cannot be pinpointed at the metropolitan level, there will certainly be pressure to move the decision-making to the state or national level.

## CAN THE METROPOLITAN COMMUNITY GOVERN ITSELF?

Is it really possible to make and carry out public policy in the metropolis on an area-wide basis? A comparative study of three "metro" systems of government in Toronto, Miami, and Nashville indicates that it is possible. Each of these three metropolitan areas has an ongoing, working government whose boundary lines encompass the bulk of the metropolitan community and whose authority

## The Metropolitan Government Approach

is adequate for most of the more obvious area-wide problems. None of these three is a panacea; each still has most of the typical problems of urban government except one—it is legally capable of grappling with area-wide problems on an area-wide basis.

Each of the three metro governments follows a different approach to the common goal of area-wide policy formation and administration. *Toronto*'s is a metropolitan federation of cities— originally thirteen cities when established in 1953, but consolidated to six in 1967 (five boroughs plus the city of Toronto). The upper level of the federation is given responsibility for a considerable number of area-wide functions, with certain others being reserved for the local units. *Metropolitan Miami* has a two-tier form of government, but it is not a federation of cities because almost one-half of the population lives in unincorporated portions served directly by Dade County Metro. Although the twenty-seven cities under Dade County continue to perform a large number of functions—many of them alleged to be properly area-wide by advocates of consolidation—the charter actually gives Metro the power to take over such functions if they fall below an adequate standard of performance. *Nashville* has a single metropolitan government for the entire city and county area of 533 square miles, which was achieved by consolidating the city of Nashville with Davidson County. The single government has two service areas with two different tax rates, one for an expandable urban services area of some seventy-five square miles, and the other for the total area, including the urban core.

Within the limitations of this discussion it would be impossible to give a detailed appraisal of the experience of these three areas as they seek to govern themselves on a metropolitan-community basis. It is possible, however, to mention a few achievements by each, and to temper these with a few caution signals. *Toronto*, for example, has compiled a tremendous record of public works accomplishments with respect to subways, expressways, sewer and water lines, and arterial streets. A conservative estimate of the ten-year savings on the interest rates on bond issues is fifty million dollars, due to the lower interest rates the area-wide government was able to obtain. *Miami*'s achievements have been less spectacular, but area-wide planning, traffic regulation, and traffic courts are among the more noteworthy achievements, and it is generally conceded by the opponents of Metro that the threat of further consolidation has kept the twenty-seven cities on their toes. Schools in Dade County had already been consolidated, prior to the adoption of Metro.

*Nashville*'s Metro is the youngest of the three, having been inaugurated in 1963, and it was immediately saddled with the job of extending urban services to some fifty square miles of annexed suburbs. A sizable list of accomplishments can already be cited, however, including equalizing and upgrading the quality of public schools, extending and expediting the racial integration of pupils and faculty throughout the entire area, some rather dramatic cases of cooperative action by park and school authorities in acquisition and development of land on a multi-purpose basis, improved police coordination and professionalization, elimination of duplicate functions such as tax assessment, and the area-wide planning and construction of expanded sewer and water services. One of the most commonly cited achievements of metropolitan government in Nashville and Davidson County is the encouragement of an area-wide view of problems, as distinguished from a narrow segmental view, by officials and citizens alike.

Informed observers in all three areas generally contend that these and other achievements of metropolitan government have been made without the loss of small-community pride and participation, and without any loss of a sense of political access by minority groups to government officials.

It should not be concluded that Metro is a panacea, however, or that there are no critics of the Toronto, Miami, and Nashville systems of metropolitan government. In Toronto, for example, many have criticized Metro for too much emphasis on the physical aspects of urban problems—for focusing attention on public works to the neglect of social services. Dade County Metro has been criticized for its fiscal incapacity, its inability to move ahead on major area-wide functions as aggressively as Toronto has done, and for its problems of political instability (the first two Metro managers were fired, and frequent charter amendment proposals kept the Metro proponents fighting for its life during the first few years of its existence). In both Nashville and Toronto there has been no overall reduction in taxes, and informed observers are divided on whether taxes have increased at a lower rate than would have been required without the new form of government, or, as some believe, there actually has been a net increase in taxes. There is some evidence to support the latter position, the argument being that the bright, new, shiny image of a much publicized invention in effective metropolitan government tends to generate a revolution of rising expectations among citizens and interest groups. The result seems to be irresistible pressures for new and improved services that can be met only with increased taxes. The experience of two of these three cities seems clearly to indicate that Metro is more an instrument for getting things done than it is for reducing taxes.

## WILL THE METROPOLITAN COMMUNITY GOVERN ITSELF?

The final question is whether or not the 212 metropolitan areas in the United States will actually adopt governmental structures to permit public policy to be made and carried out on an area-wide basis. It would be possible, and even commonplace, to "beg the question" by answering that "it all depends. . . ." However, the evidence at hand points toward a more specific (and more pessimistic) answer. Regardless of the strength of the rational case which can be made for metropolitan government, and of the strong value-preferences of the writer, the answer seems to be in the negative for the great majority of metropolitan areas. It is possible that there might be a few additional metropolitan governments created in the next two or three decades, perhaps even a baker's dozen or so, but the political obstacles to their creation are so great that most efforts seem to be doomed to failure. Some of the chief reasons are summarized below:

1. The strong mutual distrust of the suburbs and core cities of each other militates against political union. In the suburbs the core city image is one of corrupt city machines, graft, high taxes, heavy debt, the "great unwashed masses," and the "wrong side of the tracks." In the core city the suburban image is one of wealthy, overprivileged, lily-white, anti-Negro people who enjoy a free ride on all the city services without paying taxes.

2. Political party cleavage between Democratic core cities and many Republican suburbs almost guarantees the opposition of at least one group of party leaders to metropolitan merger proposals.

3. The American tradition of a guaranteed veto power for all units of government—core city and suburb alike—stacks the cards

heavily against the adoption of area-wide government. This is particularly true when all cities, no matter how small, are given the veto against overwhelming popular majorities. It does not seem likely that many states, even with reapportioned legislatures, will take the metropolitan bull by the horns as the Canadian provincial government of Ontario has done, and impose a rational local government structure upon a metropolitan community by fiat. Without such state initiative in reorganization, the local veto tradition will continue to block reorganization efforts.

4. The popular fear of "big government" and the tendency to equate the metropolitan government concept with big government place two strikes against any proposal for area-wide government, regardless of how careful the proponents are to guarantee the continuation of all existing local governments. The argument that the creation of some kind of metropolitan community decision-making structure is the only way to avoid centralization of decision-making at the state or national level is a rather sophisticated argument which is not easy to translate into votes from the masses in a referendum. The "metro-monster" charges are much easier to relate to popular fears of big government.

5. One other deterrent to the adoption of area-wide government for metropolitan communities is the failure of political scientists, for the most part, to distinguish between the problems of the older, larger, more complex metropolis, and that of the newer, smaller, less complex metropolis. In recent years the better-known political scientists writing in the field of metropolitan politics seem to be in general agreement that area-wide metropolitan government is either politically impossible to attain or that it is inappropriate, even if it could be attained. This may well be true for the ten or twenty largest metropolitan areas in the United States, although the recent reorganization of greater London was apparently based on a rejection of this assumption. Nevertheless, it is this writer's personal opinion that it is not yet too late to adopt effective area-wide government for the small- and medium-sized metropolitan areas in the United States. The tendency of many writers to imply that their conclusions concerning the very large metropolis are generalizations applicable to all 212 U.S. metropolitan areas has probably had a greater "wet-blanket" effect in the smaller areas than is commonly realized. One can understand the pessimism of the better-known political scientists when it is

remembered that most of them are attached to universities in the largest metropolitan areas and have observed firsthand the near hopelessness of efforts to integrate the fragmented local government structures in "megalopolis." But their pessimism, reflected in textbooks, books of readings, articles, and speeches, is having a strong influence on the students and researchers in the smaller metropolitan areas. Their message seems to be "Don't waste your time on Metro."

In summary, it may be said that metropolitan communities should and can govern themselves, but that the great majority of them probably will not. That is, they probably will not adopt a governmental structure which makes possible area-wide decision-making and area-wide execution of decisions at a sub-state or sub-national level. The vacuum caused by a metropolitan society without metropolitan government will undoubtedly be filled during the next two or three decades by a growing nationally directed functional federalism, in cooperation with a variety of limited-purpose special districts and limited-area cities, towns, townships, and counties. The metropolitan government approach would be far more rational, but the "intergovernmental megalopolity," with its myriad vertical and horizontal relationships, is a far more realistic prediction.

# Suburban Action
## Advocate Planning for an Open Society

PAUL and LINDA DAVIDOFF
and NEIL NEWTON GOLD

Advocate planning has been defined as the exercise of the planning function on behalf of specified individuals and groups, rather than on behalf of a broadly defined "public interest." From its beginning, the movement toward advocacy planning has stressed the need to plan with, and in the interests of, the formerly unrepresented groups in the planning process—the poor, the black, and the underprivileged. In many cases, this form of advocacy has involved planners working with neighborhood organizations of the poor and the black in order to create alternate plans for renewal, relocation, Model Cities, or highway location. In the process of working for and with these neighborhood groups, advocates have often become aware of the difficulty of solving many of their clients' problems with planning that is limited to neighborhood physical areas. Out of this awareness has grown a sense of the need for region-wide and national approaches to planning for the needs of the black and the poor.

From the beginnings of advocacy planning it has been recognized that *ideological advocacy* in which the advocate represented his own point of view, rather than that of a client, could play an important role in the planning process. This article describes an ideological advocacy agency created to promote the use

---

Reprinted from the Journal of the American Institute of Planners 36 (1970), pp. 12-21, by permission of the publisher, the American Institute of Planners, and Neil Newton Gold.

of suburban resources for solving metropolitan problems of race and poverty.

## GHETTOS AND PUBLIC POLICY

Present efforts to solve the "urban crisis" tend to restrict solutions to inner-city ghetto areas. Ghetto and poverty areas have been the locus of nearly all the research and action programs undertaken by both public agencies and private nonprofit groups as part of the war on urban poverty and discrimination. Job programs have concentrated on finding employment opportunities for ghetto youth in declining areas. Industrial development programs have concentrated on bringing industry into the ghettos. Housing programs have tried to rehabilitate obsolete slum apartments or "renew" ghetto neighborhoods. The Model Cities program, while aimed at improving the lives of disadvantaged residents, has tended to restirct chances for such improvements to Model Cities areas.

What these programs have in common is an underlying strategy based on a false assumption: the assumption that because the problems of race and poverty are found in the ghettos of urban America, the solutions to these problems must also be found there. These ghetto-oriented programs largely ignore the geographic distribution of resources through the metropolitan regions. The resources needed to solve the urban poverty problem—land, money, and jobs—are presently in scarce supply in the inner cities. They exist in substantial supply in suburban areas but are not being utilized to solve inner-city problems or combat poverty and discrimination. As a result, ghetto residents are denied the income gains and improvements in housing quality that would result from freer access to suburban jobs and land.

The cities must create new opportunities in the ghettos; and they must create decent environments in areas that are now slums. But these goals cannot be achieved until there is effective utilization of all resources in metropolitan regions.

## THE SUBURBAN SHIFT

One of the most striking aspects of American economic growth over the last two decades is the fact that eighty percent of the new jobs created in the nation's large metropolitan areas have been located in their suburban rings. The central cities of these metropolitan areas have not only failed to win a significant share of new urban employment, but, in some cases, they have experienced a net outflow of jobs.

In the tri-state New York area, for example, the central city gained only 111,000 new jobs between 1952 and 1966, compared with a gain of 888,000 jobs for the region as a whole. In the St. Louis area, employment in the central city actually declined in this period—by 50,000—compared with an employment increase of 193,500 in the St. Louis suburbs. In Philadelphia, central city employment also declined in this period; from 773,622 jobs in 1952 to 758,925 jobs in 1966. The Philadelphia suburbs, on the other hand, gained a total of 249,433 new jobs in these years. In San Francisco, to take a final example, the central city gained nearly 25,000 new jobs in this fifteen-year period, roughly one-eighth of the employment increase that took place in the San Francisco suburbs (202,000).

In the face of the concentration of public attention on the urban crises, it is important that policy-makers understand that this remarkable shift in the location of urban growth has taken place and that the process of industrial and commercial decentralization has had a transforming impact on the distribution of opportunities and rewards within urban areas.

Better known than the shift in location of new metropolitan employment is the shift in location of population growth within metropolitan areas. Here, too, the results are striking, and fateful, in their implications for urban policy. Between 1950 and 1966, the population of the nation's central cities increased by 7,400,000. In the same period, the population of their suburban rings increased by 36,500,000. By 1966, more Americans lived outside of central cities in our urban configurations, than inside central cities.

Not only have central cities been on the short end of urban population growth, but their share of future growth is destined to decline still further. According to the most reliable estimates of the distribution of future population growth, nearly all of the one hundred million additional persons who will live in the United States by the year 2000 will live in suburban areas. There will be little if any growth in central city (or rural) population during this period. In some central cities, in fact, the prognosis is for sustained population outflow to the suburban rings, depending upon availability of sufficient housing opportunities.

The nation's suburbs, then, have been the locus of the bulk of new jobs and new population growth in metropolitan areas. Not surprisingly, suburban areas also have experienced the greatest share of all new housing starts in urban areas, increasing from sixty percent in the 1950s to seventy percent and above in the 1960s. In some of the largest metropolitan areas such as St. Louis, Philadelphia, Detroit, the District of Columbia, Cleveland, Boston, and Baltimore, nearly eighty percent of new residential construction is taking place outside the central city.

Underlying the movement of jobs, housing, and population from central cities to their surrounding suburbs is the availability of a relatively vast supply of vacant land outside of central cities. Indeed, in the nation's twenty largest urban areas, ninety-nine percent of the vacant land lies outside of core cities. The unavailability of vacant land within central cities necessarily sets reasonably firm limitations on the employment and population capacities of these areas. Conversely, the existence of a seemingly limitless supply of vacant land on the urban periphery practically insures that future urban growth will take place in the fringe areas.

In sum, the suburbs of the United States have become the New America of the twentieth century: the growth area of private economy, the locus of most of the nation's new jobs, housing, and population.

## SUBURBAN DISCRIMINATION

Blacks and other minority groups have not moved out of central cities to the surrounding suburbs. Only the white population has benefited from the availability of suburban job and housing opportunities. By 1966, as a result of the suburbanization of the white population, only forty-two percent of urban whites remained in central cities. Among non-whites, on the other hand, more than eighty-two percent lived in central cities in 1966—a higher proportion than in 1950.

Still more significant, as an indication of recent demographic trends, is the fact that between 1960 and 1966, one hundred percent of the urban white population growth of 10,152,000 occurred in the suburbs. The central cities lost white population during these years. Conversely, during the same period, ninety percent of the non-white population gain of 2,757,000 took place in central cities.

A striking piece of evidence from our preliminary research regards the movement of population between 1960 and 1965 in the northern section of suburban Westchester County, New York. The section studied comprises sixty-eight percent of the county's area. In 1965, it contained fourteen percent of the county's population and four percent of the county's non-white population. This area—most of the vacant land in Westchester—is zoned almost exclusively for large-lot single-family development. Between 1960 and 1965, the white population in this area increased by 20,000, the non-white population by one.

These remarkable population shifts have resulted in severely imbalanced population distribution in our metropolitan areas. The cities of the United States are rapidly becoming ghettos of the poor and the black, while the suburbs appear likely to remain affluent and white. We are well on our way to becoming the two nations: "one black, one white—separate and unequal," described in the Kerner Commission report. This growing separation of white and black in U.S. metropolitan areas is a direct result of the nation's acknowledged failure to insure that all social and racial groups are able to gain access to suburban land.

A second, and equally baleful, consequence of the decentralization of American economic life and the outward movement of population from central cities, is the maldistribution of jobs and workers in our urban areas. For nearly two decades, rural refugees, mainly black, Mexican-American, and Puerto Rican, have been arriving in the great cities of the nation to find that the jobs they were looking for have been disappearing—in part, because they have been relocated in the suburbs. While the suburban communities to which these jobs have been moved welcome new tax-paying industrial and commercial facilities, they are unwilling to permit their vacant land to be used for housing for employees who work in the new facilities. In effect, blacks and other minorities are unable to follow their jobs to the suburbs. Thus, these rural migrants are piling up in the overcrowded central cities, without jobs, without access to jobs, without access to information about suburban job opportunities, without decent housing, and without any prospect of overcoming their condition by further migration. At the same time, as if to mock the policies that have created our present crisis, suburban job opportunities remain unfilled for lack of adequate manpower.

Although no data are available on the number of unfilled jobs in suburban areas, census publications, particularly *County, Business Patterns*, and *Census of Manufacturers*, show clearly that in suburban areas many new unfilled jobs are in blue-collar occupations and at unskilled and semiskilled levels. For this reason—and in light of the fact that if present trends continue, eighty percent of future urban employment growth in large metropolitan areas will take place in the suburbs—appropriate linkages connecting the central city labor force and areas of expanding job opportunities must be created.

In lieu of governmental action to enable central city workers to compete for job openings in the suburbs, the private sector, in its own interest, prevailed upon the federal government to create the urban mass transit demonstration program to experiment with methods of aiding workers to get to suburban plant sites. In so doing, the private sector, particularly that portion in durable goods manufacturing, acknowledged that the present distribution of jobs and workers in urban areas constituted a significant drain on the nation's productive capacity and human resources.

Regrettably, interim results from the various urban mass transit demonstrations strongly suggest that transportation linkages are insufficient to overcome the barriers that separate the unemployed in central cities from suburban job areas. It seems clear that more substantial linkages must be created if the suburbs are to enter fully into the mainstream of American life. Pre-eminent among these connections is the creation, reasonably close to suburban job sites, of a supply of widely dispersed moderate-cost housing for working-class families. This is the challenge now confronting both government agencies and the private sector.

Restrictive zoning and land use controls in suburban areas constitute the principal barrier preventing development of job-linked moderate-cost housing in the suburbs. Among the specific devices that suburban governments have used to prevent construction of such housing are: minimum lot size requirements, minimum house size requirements, restrictive subdivision regulations, and unduly expensive building standards. In addition to these devices, many suburban communities have adopted zoning ordinances that prohibit all forms of multifamily housing within their jurisdiction. Taken together, these restrictive zoning and land use controls have been remarkably effective in preventing low- and moderate-income families from penetrating suburban housing and land markets, in greatly limiting the matching of jobs and workers in urban areas, and in raising the cost of new housing in the suburbs to all home-seeking families. If this nation is to provide for the housing and job needs of its minority citizens, the power of government must be used to break the land use barriers erected by suburban communities. This challenge may soon be recognized as the new frontier of the civil rights movement.

POLICY ISSUES

A basic policy must be decided before the nation can embark upon a program of affirmative action in the suburbs. The issue is whether the expenditure of billions of dollars of public funds to rehabilitate the substandard housing stock of central cities and to encourage industry to locate within central cities—particularly, within the slums and ghettos of central cities—is justified in the face of the overwhelming trend toward decentralization in American economic life.

A corollary issue is whether problems and solutions in urban areas are place-limited; that is, whether the fact that the urban crisis is concentrated in the central city slums and ghettos requires that solutions to the urban crisis be limited in their geographic focus to these same slums and ghettos.

Decentralization and Public Policy

The facts of suburbanization have long been recognized by planners, demographers, developers, and the general public. What has begun to change is the public policy stance adopted toward these facts. In the early 1950s, recognition of the decline of the central city led to a concern with stemming it and with "bringing back" the fleeing middle-class family to live in renewed and rehabilitated downtown neighborhoods. In the mid-1950s, the failures of the renewal program—its displacement of black and poor families, its failure to provide adequate relocation housing—brought a shift in policy toward rebuilding the ghettos for the benefit of their residents. This may be termed the "keep back" theory for ghetto residents.

Now there is a growing recognition that both the "bring back" and the "keep back" theories are inadequate efforts to stem the tide of movement to the suburbs. Urban development policy is moving toward acceptance of suburbanization. Seen in this context, urban development policy is not a set of demands for rearranging general trends of population movement. Instead, it is a set of demands for structural change in the society set against the backdrop of these movements.

In our view, the decentralizing forces of American economic life are not reversible. The absence of vacant land within central cities, coupled with the existence of an enormous supply of vacant land on the urban periphery, will not permit a major expansion of the employment capacity of central cities. Public programs that seek only to rebuild the central city housing stock and to encourage industry to locate within central cities and within ghettos run counter to the movement of the private economy.

While isolated examples of in-city plant location will occur, as in the case of the IBM plant in Bedford Stuyvesant,[1] the private sector will continue to locate the bulk of its new plants and equipment outside central cities. In the same year in which IBM created three hundred jobs in Bedford-Stuyvesant, the company created three thousand jobs in the New York region as a whole. The blacks of Bedford-Stuyvesant did not have access to these three thousand jobs.

The bulk of the central city substandard housing stock is found in areas considered ripe for urban renewal. These areas contain most of the non-white population of central cities. Increasingly, they are the locus of central city unemployment and underemployment. Land prices in central-city urban renewal areas have been rising even more rapidly than have suburban land prices. This is occurring in spite of the fact that the level of land prices in suburban areas is markedly lower than the level of land prices in central-city urban renewal areas.

The convergence of these factors gives some indication of the added cost involved in building low- and moderate-cost housing

---

1. See Schrank and Stein (1969).

on developed land in areas characterized by a declining blue-collar job market. They suggest that substantial housing cost savings can be achieved by locating the bulk of new low- and moderate-cost housing stock outside central cities.

### The "Urban Crisis" and Public Policy

The second major public policy decision is whether the "urban crisis" is in fact an "urban" crisis, or a crisis of class and race in the nation as a whole. Public policy has tended to see the problems of slums and ghettos as problems of "renewal areas," "project areas," and "Model City neighborhoods." It is our view that the problems to be found in these areas are not problems of areas, but problems of allocation of public and private resources, and that their remedy is to be found in the reallocation of resources. Public policy to aid ghetto and slum residents should be tested in terms of its ability to enlarge opportunities for blacks and for the poor. This recasting of policy does not imply ending planned improvement of urban spatial and structural conditions; rather, it makes these conditions the means for serving human needs. If neighborhoods are to be rebuilt in central-city ghetto areas, it will be necessary in many cases for the population density in these areas to be reduced. Rebuilding at present densities raises impossible problems of cost and residential amenity. To renew the neighborhoods, we must open opportunities for out-migration to new, decent housing outside the ghetto. Once densities have been reduced in this way, clearance of dilapidated structures can take place without creating insoluble problems of relocation or temporary relocation while reconstruction goes forward.

In recent months we have seen a growing awareness, on the part of public and private groups, of the negative consequences of exclusive concern with the ghetto as the place for ending poverty. For example, three presidential commissions have reported on the need to fashion metropolitan area–wide solutions to urban poverty and blight.

In its December 1968 report, the President's Committee on Urban Housing (Kaiser Commission) concluded that:

> The location of one's place of residence determines the accessibility and quality of many everyday advantages taken for granted by the mainstream of American society. Among these commonplace advantages are public educational facilities for a family's children, adequate police and

fire protection, and a decent surrounding environment. In any case, a family should have the choice of living as close as economically possible to the breadwinner's place of employment.

It makes little sense for federally subsidized housing to be concentrated in and around the central cities' slums where social and environmental disadvantages can negate the uplifting qualities of decent housing.[2]

The 1968 Report of the National Advisory Commission on Civil Disorders (Kerner Commission) presented the nation with three choices:

We can maintain present policies, continuing both the proportion of the nation's resources now allocated to programs for the unemployed and the disadvantaged and the inadequate and failing effort to achieve an integrated society.

We can adopt a policy of "enrichment" aimed at improving dramatically the quality of ghetto life while abandoning integration as a goal.

We can pursue integration by combining ghetto "enrichment" with policies which will encourage Negro movement out of central city areas. . . .

To continue present policies is to make permanent the division of our country into two societies: one, largely Negro and poor, located in the central cities; the other, predominantly white and affluent, located in the suburbs and in outlying areas.

The second choice, ghetto enrichment coupled with abandonment of integration, is also unacceptable. It is another way of choosing a permanently divided country. Moreover, equality cannot be achieved under conditions of nearly complete separation. In a country where the economy, and particularly the resources of employment, are predominantly white, a policy of separation can only relegate Negroes to a permanently inferior economic status.

We believe that the only possible choice for America is the third—a policy which combines ghetto enrichment with programs designed to encourage integration of substantial numbers of Negroes into the society outside the ghetto.[3]

The December 1968 report of the National Commission on Urban Problems (Douglas Commission) stressed the costs of maintaining large inner-city ghettos both in terms of actual costs to governments of providing services to the ghetto populations and in terms of the socially explosive character of the ghettos. In discussing the employment problems of ghetto residents the commission noted that:

---

2. The Report of the President's Committee on Urban Housing, *A Decent Home* (Washington, D.C.: U.S. Government Printing Office, 1969), p. 13.

3. *Report of the National Advisory Commission on Civil Disorders* (New York: Bantam, 1968), p. 22.

Available employment of the type for which slum adults might qualify is generally not available in the slum. In a recent year, sixty-three percent of all construction permits for industrial buildings were issued for locations outside central cities. On the other hand, seventy-three percent of office building construction permits were issued inside central cities. Central cities increasingly are becoming white-collar employment centers while the suburbs are becoming the job employment areas for new blue-collar workers. This is ironical in view of the fact that low-paid blue-collar workers, especially if they are Negroes, live in the central cities while the white-collar workers are increasingly living in the suburbs. Traveling to work becomes increasingly difficult for both.[4]

Edward Logue, president of the New York State Urban Development Corporation, writing in *Look* magazine, said that:

> As the inner-city housing crisis worsens, we persist in the notion that the central city *by itself* must provide for the housing needs of ill-housed low-income families. We cling to this fallacy despite the reality that the central cities no longer have significant amounts of vacant land and no large supply of decent, available, low-cost relocation housing. We have, in short, adopted an approach to the city housing problem that is guaranteed to fail. But there are answers.
>
> There is an ample supply of vacant land suitable for housing low-income families in a ten-mile-wide belt around just about every one of our cities, except possibly New York and Los Angeles, where it may be necessary to go twenty miles or farther. Yet access to this land . . . has been denied to low-income families.[5] (Italics in original.)

The Center for Community Change in Washington, directed by former Industrial Union Department director Jack Conway, is discussing the possibility of suburban development of housing opportunities in the Detroit area. The Regional Plan Association and National Committee Against Discrimination in Housing are studying the job and housing opportunities in the New York suburbs. Other research programs are beginning to study the implications of the Kerner Commission's challenge to create a "single society," rather than to perpetuate the walls between the ghetto and the society at large. *As yet, however, programs to implement this concern have not moved from study to action. We still do not have viable strategies for expanding the role of the suburbs in developing solutions to problems of race and poverty.*

---

4. Report of the National Commission on Urban Problems, *Building the American City* (Washington, D.C.: U.S. Government Printing Office, 1969), p. 3.
5. *Look,* April 1, 1969, p. 70.

## THE OBJECTIVES OF SUBURBAN ACTION

The availability of new jobs and vacant land in the suburbs makes it apparent that the suburbs can contribute greatly to creation of a society in which resources can be shared more equitably among all classes of the population. However, as we view the actions and policies of public agencies in the nation and, in particular, the New York region, we believe that the potential of the suburbs for solving national problems has not yet been grasped by public and private agencies, nor by the majority of the public.

A number of agencies concerned with issues of urban development have recently begun to support more concerted use of suburban resources to solve metropolitan problems of race and poverty. The National Committee Against Discrimination in Housing, with a long and distinguished record in the housing discrimination field, is now studying means to overcome restrictive zoning measures and to utilize the growing number of jobs in suburban areas to solve unemployment and underemployment problems. The Regional Plan Association of New York has significantly contributed to public understanding of the suburban potential. More recently a large number of citizens' organizations and religious associations have taken the lead in attempting to develop non-profit moderate- and low-income housing in the suburbs. Additionally, many of these same groups have led inquiries into the nature of white racism to find ways to overcome the very hostile attitudes toward social change that exist within many suburban communities. We believe that until public opinion and public agencies favor significant change in suburban practices, it will be necessary for voluntary associations to take the lead in demonstrating the reasonableness of a new approach to the relationship of suburbs to the solution of race and poverty problems.

As one organization dedicated to altering the imbalance in current urban policy regarding use of suburban resources, Suburban Action has set the following goals for its work:

1. Assisting in opening suburban land and housing to low- and moderate-income and non-white families, by eliminating restrictive and discriminatory land use barriers.
2. Creating new opportunities for linking suburban jobs and

unemployed and underemployed residents of central city and suburban low-income areas.
3. Assisting actions preventing suburban ghettos from enlarging through the creation of adequate housing and employment opportunities for residents of those areas throughout the suburbs.
4. Promoting widespread discussion and analysis of alternatives to the real property tax. In doing this, stressing the need for tax reform in order to reduce the disparities in public services, most notably in education, between cities and suburbs and between rich and poor suburban communities.[6]

Suburban Action's list of objectives excludes mention of education, health, recreation, and other important topics that must be addressed if racial and economic disparities are to be reduced. The exclusions are less related to a sense of priorities than they are to the current abilities of the agency.

## SUBURBAN ACTION'S PROGRAM

To move toward achievement of its objectives, Suburban Action has a set of programs covering the areas of housing, employment, taxation, and land use. The agency is based in White Plains, New York (suburban Westchester County), and is directing its programs toward conditions within the New York region and toward policy formulation at all levels of government.

### Housing

Throughout suburban areas, organizations have been formed to work for fair housing (nondiscriminatory housing) and for construction of low- and moderate-cost housing units. In many cases the housing that can be developed within suburban communities offers only token solutions to regional housing needs. Frequently voluntary agencies may spend a number of years seeking to persuade public officials that their community should address housing needs both inside and outside the jurisdiction. Where successful, these groups may be empowered to build twenty to fifty units of nonprofit housing. The results are significant for the communities since they often represent a significant change in housing policy,

---
6. See Netzer (1968).

but the sum of projects constructed as a result of these private efforts is very small.

We hope that one result of regional organization of fair housing and other interested groups would be expanding the interest of such associations. We would like to see such organizations take a more active role in combating restrictive zoning measures. Fair zoning may be as important as fair housing to achieve a significant increase in the supply of moderate- and low-income housing. Additionally, we think it of the utmost importance that local housing groups begin to demand housing not only to meet the needs of local residents, but also to meet the needs of the region's population. We have run up against strong opposition on this issue.

Many activists concerned with housing conditions in their suburban communities believe that their first obligation is to build units that will satisfy the demands of neighbors who are inadequately housed. They do not wish to become involved in the more abstract question of assisting in solving the housing problems of the vast number of indecently housed inner-city residents.

It might be argued that limited local needs should be met first before larger regional issues are tackled. We do not think this is the case. We believe that a program to meet regional needs is of far greater magnitude and requires an immediate start. Very different programs will be involved. Thus, we think that the regional need for housing will provide the most important evidence in the constitutional attacks we hope to initiate against restrictive zoning.

In attempting to educate some of the public about regional housing needs, we are seeking to induce development of associations that will present programs capable of meeting these needs. To achieve this end, one of Suburban Action's first products will be publication of a housing program for Westchester County. This publication will be aimed at exciting interest in the housing question in the midst of an election year when candidates for county and local office may be asked to respond to the questions on housing problems. We recognize that the program we will publish will not be acceptable to most politicians, but we do believe that by making the housing issue an important topic for discussion, we may begin to generate the possibilities for effective coalitions among different classes having a common interest in improved housing.

One of the most important groups we hope to persuade to join in the struggle for a massive regional housing program is private industry. The shortage of both white-collar and blue-collar workers constitutes a serious constraint on the efficient function of large suburban-based corporations, particularly on their capacity to expand their plants and equipment. For this reason we are hopeful that these corporations will enter the housing field, through development of job-linked housing on sites owned by them or on sites susceptible to their influence.

Employment Programs

Suburban Action's employment programs seek to make more efficient use of manpower resources of metropolitan areas by creating links between jobless and underemployed workers in disadvantaged communities and available or pending employment opportunities in the suburbs. This will involve monitoring the location of new employment growth in the region, particularly manufacturing and construction employment. It will involve arranging for contacts between inner-city employees and suburban employers who would benefit from an expanded labor supply. It will also involve creation of demonstration projects that connect inner-city Model Cities communities and suburban job centers.

Emphasis in this program will be on the creation of relatively highly paid jobs for employees presently working at hourly rates of about $2. We have found that many community action programs concerned with manpower development receive notices only of jobs paying low wages. There may be a presumption on the part of employers that community action programs are concerned only with individuals deemed incapable of holding other than low-wage positions. Nevertheless, our initial work indicates that a significant number of suburban jobs paying over $3.50 an hour are open and that private industry will cooperate with interested parties in making these jobs available to low-income persons willing to give up their present positions to take on higher-paying jobs.

Suburban Action will also look toward the creation of opportunities for black and Puerto Rican businessmen to invest their resources in the affluent suburbs, as a necessary corrective to current programs that confine opportunities for minority group businessmen solely to declining slum and ghetto neighborhoods.

## Municipal Taxation Programs

Present suburban taxing methods are an inducement to fiscal zoning. Even without race or class bias on the part of inhabitants of suburban communities, there would still be strong antipathy to new families who did not "pay their way." Families who move into a suburban community and constitute a drain on a community's tax base are unwelcome neighbors. Suburban Action's programs in public finance will promote discussion about alternatives to the real property tax.

Community growth is expensive. Residents of growing suburban towns often strongly resent changes that will require further increases in their perceived "already too high taxes." There is no way of measuring whether or not their perception is correct, but what we do know is that the present form of raising local revenues gives strong support to tendencies to evaluate new families in terms of their tax-paying abilities. We submit that such abilities do not provide a sound basis for community judgments regarding the right of an individual to reside within a particular community.

If suburban communities are to be more welcoming to those who cannot afford to pay their own way, it will be necessary to redesign the local revenue system to make the tax-paying ability of an individual a matter of relative indifference. For example, if local revenues resulted from a federal income tax reimbursement to a locality, the amount being a function of the community's population and, perhaps, the needs of the community, then the tax-paying ability of a potential resident would become a matter of relative indifference. That individual's wealth would not alter the overall revenue receipts of the community.

A similar system could be created with a state or county income tax. But whatever the system, so long as the members of a community were not compelled to take restrictive action against a potential newcomer because of his financial status, such a system would represent a marked improvement over the present condition. We also believe that a strong case can be made against the real property tax as a major source of local income. The real property tax is unfair to families on stable or declining incomes. It fails in such cases to adequately account for the tax-paying ability of a family.

The public must be persuaded that the quality of services

offered by a local government unit should not depend upon the wealth of its inhabitants. The children of a poor community deserve as decent an education as the children of a wealthy community. Further, if all parts of a region—and particularly the relatively underdeveloped portions—are to assume a fair share of the burden of providing decent housing, jobs, and education for the region's population, then we must develop a program for relieving the financial pressures on the community subjected to rapid growth. If growth is not to be viewed as unwanted on the grounds that it is too costly, perhaps the costs of new service facilities required to meet the demands of a rapidly increasing population should be met by higher levels of government.

Land Use Programs

Suburban Action's land use programs will seek to eliminate restrictive and discriminatory policies and practices in zoning, subdivision requirements, and building codes that effectively exclude low- and moderate-income families from access to the region's vacant land. Programs will be designed to foster public discussion about the need to open this supply of vacant land to builders and developers who will build housing for disadvantaged groups now confined to central cities. Land use issues will be broadly defined to include questions related to transportation design and planning and their impact on site selection for new residential and commercial-industrial development.

Suburban Action will initiate a series of legal cases challenging the constitutionality of state planning and zoning enabling legislation and the constitutionality of local laws that bar multifamily housing from their jurisdictions. There is, perhaps, no more important task confronting those of us who would have suburban areas serve all classes of the population than defeating the ability of suburban localities to zone out all but the very small portion of the population that can afford to pay the high entrance charge (purchase of a house on an acre or more of land) so many of these localities have established.

On the basis of Douglas Commission findings and the position taken by many experts within the field, we are confident the court will be far more receptive than in the recent past to challenges to the propriety of local restrictive zoning controls. We think that Suburban Action, along with a number of other organization agencies now vitally concerned with overthrowing exclusionary zoning practices, will be able to effectively demonstrate that both acreage zoning requirements and exclusion of multifamily dwellings deny access to new housing to an overwhelming majority of metropolitan residents.

Zoning Test Case

The test case we seek to initiate will be based on a set of assumptions about where an attack on zoning can be most successfully made and on a set of arguments regarding the deleterious consequences of certain forms of zoning. The case will be brought in a jurisdiction that excludes all forms of multifamily housing. It will be brought by a nonprofit developer who has gone to the expense of preparing building plans for substantial numbers of multifamily housing units and who has attempted to have these plans approved by the municipal planning agency and by the municipal building department. To file such plans the developer must own, or have an option on land suitable for development within the municipality. Since the municipality prohibits all multifamily housing, the developer's plans *must* be rejected. It is this rejection which will set the stage for judicial examination of the constitutionality of zoning ordinances prohibiting all multifamily units.

To create the proper constitutional issue, the developer must select an area that is characterized by:

1. Proximity to a large central city containing substantial numbers of unemployed and underemployed workers of Negro and other minority group extraction.
2. An employment base that is growing very rapidly and that contains a substantial number of unfilled jobs requiring unskilled and semiskilled workers.
3. An absence of vacant low- and moderate-cost units within a reasonable commuting distance from the employment centers.
4. A work force that is compelled to travel long distances in journeying to work.
5. An existing supply of multifamily housing built before the introduction of the ordinance prohibiting all new multifamily housing.

6. Restrictions requiring new single-family homes to be constructed on lots of an acre or more.

The argument will be that prohibition of multifamily housing, by establishing a de facto minimum new housing cost of $30,000 within the community, effectively excludes all persons who cannot afford to spend $30,000 for a house, or who may not need the kind of space characteristic of single-family housing. The exclusion of such persons, among whom must be numbered the bulk of the Negro and minority communities, will be said to constitute a denial of the equal protection of the laws contrary to the Fourteenth Amendment of the United States Constitution. Plaintiff's brief will lay out the legal claims and then proceed, in the Brandeis tradition, to establish beyond doubt that the social and economic consequences of exclusion adversely affect those individuals and families who could find jobs in the community provided housing opportunities were available. The brief will show that less than fifteen percent of the household population in the United States can afford housing at $30,000 and that none of the unemployed and underemployed, who need the kind of jobs available in the municipality, are able to purchase such housing. The brief will then examine the social, political, and economic consequences of sustained unemployment on minority group workers and their families, and it will show the interrelationship between unemployment in central cities and the rising tide of welfare, violence, and social disorganization that has come to characterize ever larger segments of the ghetto population. Finally, the brief will point out the impact of the artificial concentration of minority group families in central cities on the tax base. Decreasing the tax base decreases the ability of cities to provide the kind of public services needed to deal with problems of poverty and social disorganization and to sustain the loyalty of the diminishing middle class, both white and black.

## THE WHITE ADVOCATE IN SUBURBIA

Early discussions of the advocate planner's role stressed efforts on behalf of the black and the poor in central cities (Davidoff 1965). Later variations on this theme included the discussion of the advocate role every planner plays in speaking for the interests

## Suburban Action: Advocate Planning

of a client. Lisa Peattie (1968) and others have noted that only a narrow line exists between representation of a client's interests and attempted imposition of the planner's values on his client when he acts as organizer as well as technician in advocate projects in the ghetto.

In Suburban Action's efforts, we assume the role of advocate for an interest that is otherwise unrepresented in suburban planning debates—unrepresented not because it is unorganized, fearful, or voiceless, but unrepresented because it is not there. Consequently, we are speaking for what *we* regard as our clients' interests—in fact, we are speaking for ourselves as white planners who want to see changes in suburban economic, political, social, and physical structure.

Suburban Action represents the institutionalization of a concept concerning one form of advocate planning. This concept emphasizes the role of the planner as a proponent of goals, as an actor concerned with the purposes of the system for which he plans. This view stems from a theory of planning that suggests that at least some planners should more actively espouse purposes than means. It is not a denial of the importance of the planner's technical role where he details effective ways to accomplish given goals. But it does rest on the belief that an essential part of the planning process is the determination of appropriate sets of ends for a system.

A planner concerned with formulation of goals may work to satisfy the needs of his client. As an advocate of his client's interests, he may seek to understand his client's objectives and to put forth as goals his translation of what he believes to be the objectives of his client.

An alternate view of a planner concerned with formulation of goals is one that shows the planner presenting his own ideas in regard to goals. Here the planner is acting to see that a certain social situation is achieved. He does this because he believes it important for one or more reasons, but he does not propose goals in order to satisfy a client. In fact, in this case he has no client other than his own ideology.

Terms of the Suburban Debate

Most educated suburban citizens are aware of the national trends toward suburbanization of population and employment.

They are also aware of the pressures of population movement on their own communities. The level of public debate on issues of land development in the suburbs, however, falls far below any broad recognition of these trends and their implications for local public policy. Debate on issues of job and housing development in the suburbs revolves almost exclusively around two issues: local taxes, especially school taxes; and racial integration of the existing housing stock.

The tax issue for the local community is invariably increasing the size of the tax base by inviting in industrial development versus increasing the taxpayers' burden by inviting in additional households with children. Where possible, the solution is to preserve the "character" of the community by inviting in neither jobs nor housing. Next, in order of preference, is bringing in industrial development of the nuisance-free variety. Last on the list is construction of housing for families with children, who must be educated at local expense. The racial issue is the question of whether a Negro homeseeker, looking for a house in a given community, should be permitted equal access with whites to houses on the market.

These debates take place within a purely local, intellectual framework. Each locality assumes that its behavior affects only its own residents. Each local government assumes the burden of protecting the rights and privileges of its own residents only. Unwritten local rules of debate preclude even the mention of the name of the central city in whose metropolitan hinterland the debate is taking place. The farthest afield a liberal discussant can go is to the neighboring suburban community or, at the remotest extension, to the suburban county of which both communities are a part.

A remarkable absence of generalization, abstraction, and recognition of large-scale trends characterizes the tone of public debate in suburban communities. Each citizen is assumed to be competent to discuss the whole range of his town's affairs; every citizen can exercise his voting rights to control the destiny of his community; each citizen is an intimate and valued part of the body politic. In many ways, the suburbanite has achieved the democratic ideal of direct participation in community affairs, of citizen rule, of community control.

### Support for Suburban Innovation

In this situation, the voice of the advocate for metropolitan-wide interests of the poor and the black strikes a jarring note. He speaks for "outsiders," the nemesis of the close-knit community. He speaks against the immediate economic interests of the community. He threatens to tear apart the fabric of local society by including alien elements. Escalating the controversial proposals of local open-housing advocates, he calls for opening not only the existing housing stock but also additional units of low-cost housing, and not only to the black middle-class homeseeker but also to lower-class renters, white or black, and the unemployed. He speaks in opposition to local concerns for protecting the value of property and keeping tax rates down.

Consequently, in suburbia, the white advocate who addresses himself to changing the beliefs and practices of the white community must look hard to find a local base of support. He can find it in several places: the suburban church; builders and housing developers; some groups within the fair housing movement; and suburban employers of low- and moderately-skilled workers. These often uncomfortable bedfellows each support certain aspects of Suburban Action's work. Substantial support for the work of the suburban advocate will also come from the foundations, who, like the advocates themselves, have only themselves and their interpretations of the public interest as clients.

We believe that ideological advocate planning that seeks to introduce alternatives in the formulation of policy is a role that many planners should play. Advocacy of this variety can stimulate discussion about politics and programs in ways that public planning agencies, for a variety of reasons, cannot.

# The Case for Crowding

WILLIAM H. WHYTE

The net of what I have been saying about landscape action is that we are going to have to work with a much tighter pattern of spaces and development, and that our environment may be the better for it. This somewhat optimistic view rests on the premise that densities are going to increase and that it is not altogether a bad thing that they do. It is a premise many would dispute. Our official land policy is dead set against higher densities. It is decentralist, like official policies in most other countries. The primary thrust of it is to move people outward; reduce densities, loosen up the metropolis, and reconstitute its parts in new enclaves on the fringe.

I do not think it is going to work out this way. Certainly, outward movement will continue, but if our population continues to grow, the best way to accommodate the growth will be by a more concentrated and efficient use of the land within the area. The big "if" is whether or not intensity or use will be coupled with efficiency of use. It may not be. But it can be. Europe is the proof of this. Many of those who ask why we cannot take care of the landscape like Europeans do fail to realize that these landscapes, both urban and rural, accommodate far more people per acre than do ours. The disparity is not due primarily to our averages being weighted by the vast open spaces of the West. Even in our most

---

Reprinted from The Last Landscape by William H. Whyte. Copyright © 1968 by William H. Whyte. Reprinted by permission of Doubleday and Company, Inc., and the author.

## The Case for Crowding

urban states the metropolitan areas average out to lower densities than their counterparts in Europe—indeed, to some entire European countries.

The case for higher densities cannot rest on a shortage of land. There is none. It is true that top-grade agricultural lands are being overrun by urban expansion, that open space in the right places is increasingly difficult to save. The fact remains, however, that if we wish to go the expansion route, there is room for it. Expand the diameter of a metropolitan area by only a few miles and enough land will be encompassed to take care of a very large population increase. This may be a poor way to do it, but the option exists.

Nor are our cities running into each other. Metropolitan areas are being linked more tightly, but this is not the same thing as collision. Consider, for example, the great belt of urban areas along the Eastern Seaboard from Boston to Norfolk. It is well that we are paying more attention to the continuities of this megalopolis, as Jean Gottman has done so well, but to call it a "strip city," as many are doing, is misleading.

There is no such city, and the proposition can be easily tested. Fly from Boston to Washington and look out the window. Here and there one suburbia flows into another—between Baltimore and Washington, for example—but the cities retain their identities. This is especially apparent at night when the lights beneath simplify the structure so vividly; the brilliantly lit downtowns, the shopping centers, the cloverleafs, the spine of freeways that connect it all. But just as striking is what is dark—the forests of Massachusetts and Connecticut, the pine barrens of New Jersey, the farmlands of the Eastern Shore, the tidewater of Virginia. For many miles along the great urban route you can look down and see only the scattered lights of farms and small towns.

Urbanized sectors in other parts of the country—excepting, always, Los Angeles—show much the same characteristics. They are systems of cities, tied by high-speed rail and road networks, but they have not yet congealed into an undifferentiated mass. There is room outside them for expansion. There is room inside them. Whichever way is best, a measure of choice is still open to us.

The choice is by no means an either-or one, for there are forces working in both directions, and there is only so much we can do by planning and public policy to shape these forces to our liking. But this margin is important. Our government programs for transportation, for new housing and urban development have a great leverage, and a shift of emphasis one way or the other could have a considerable effect on the metropolis of not too many years hence.

Decentralize or concentrate? Most of the prescriptions for the ideal metropolis opt for decentralization. Expansion of the metropolis is to continue, only this time the expansion will be orderly. Instead of a sprawl of subdivisions, new development is to be channeled into planned new communities, with rapid transit linking them and green belts separating them. Some proposals would place the new communities outside the metropolitan areas altogether.

Obviously, the limits of suburbia are going to expand some in any event, and obviously there are going to be new communities. But the main show is not going to be out on the perimeter. Outward expansion looks easiest, but it is the least efficient way of taking care of an increased population. As development moves further outward from the core, returns diminish and costs increase, and at an accelerating rate. Water distribution is an example. If you double the population within a given area, you can service it by enlarging the diameter of the present pipe system; if you try to take care of the population by doubling the area, however, you not only have to enlarge the present pipes, you have to lay down a prodigious amount of new ones, and as they poke out into the low density areas costs become progressively steeper. The new residents may be charged an extra sum to help foot these capital costs, but the rest of the community bears most of it.

The same is true with mass transit and other utilities and services. A disproportionate amount of capital investment is needed to provide urban services for people out in the low density areas out on the periphery, but because of the rate structures that usually apply to these services, the fact is masked that other people have to pay more than they should to make up the difference. The other people are the ones in the high density areas that are easiest and most profitable to serve. We have made utilities, economist Mason Gaffney observes, "an agency for milking the center to feed the border, thus subsidizing decentralization."

## The Case for Crowding

Concentration provides efficiency; for the same reason it provides maximum access to what people want. This is what cities are all about. People come together in cities because this is the best way to make the most of opportunities, and the more accessible the core, the more choice of opportunities there is, the more access to skills, specialized services and goods, and to jobs. By subsidizing new freeways and peripheral beltways we can make it easier for people to move about within the outer area, but vigorous centers are not the less vital for this but the more, and a policy for dispersing their functions will fail.

Business and industry talk decentralization but while firms may be dispersing their production units, they have been centralizing their office and managerial operations more than before. As I have noted earlier, the British tried to reverse this trend by doing everything possible to stop commercial growth in London and make it go somewhere else. Despite the constraints, commercial growth expanded mightily, and an office building boom of spectacular proportions took place.

For a while we also entertained notions of a commercial exodus. Right after the war it was widely predicted that corporations would be moving their headquarters to campus-like retreats in the suburbs, and there was much favorable publicity when several firms in New York did so. Executives, it was said, would be able to think more; the office force would be closer to home, and more content; space would cost less; the surroundings would be more pleasant in every way. But the movement never quite came off, and several firms who had moved quietly repatriated. New office buildings went up, and on the highest-cost land in the center of the city. Before long, in what seemed almost a frenzy of centralization, whole blocks of big buildings on Park Avenue were being torn down to put up bigger buildings.

The center of things attracts because it is the center of things. What the decentralists would like to do is to cut down the number of things, or, rather, put them somewhere else. They are for urban renewal, but at much lower density. They want to open up the center, disperse as many of its functions as possible, and reassemble them in subcenters out in the hinterland where, in miniature, will be all the advantages of the city—art, music, commerce, universities, urban excitement—but without the disadvantages.

A dull metropolis it would be. This kind of decentralization would not only be a very inefficient way to accommodate growth, it would go against the grain of all the forces that give a metropolis its vitality. Rather than pursue this ill-conceived provincialism, we must look inward as well as outward, to the strengths of the metropolis, and seek a much more intensive and efficient use of the land already within it.

One way is to raise housing densities—both by putting more people on acres developed for housing and by bringing into use acres now wasted or underused. Densities are, of course, relative. What would be considered a very high density for suburbia—twenty people to the acre—would be low for the core, and densities will probably always tend to diminish as the distance from the city grows. At almost any point, however, there could be some increase in density without a lowering of living standards. In some cases the standards would be higher if there was an increase.

This is particularly true in the city. The decentralists who bewail its insensate concentrations talk as though cities are bad because we have been compressing more and more people into them. But we have not been. The populations of our cities have remained static or have decreased. One of the big problems of the gray areas of the cities, indeed, si that they do not have a sufficiently large or varied population to support an urban concentration of services and stores. Instead of cutting down the densities still further, it would make more sense to raise them.

In the city, English architect Theo Crosby points out, high densities are needed for a high level of amenity. Transportation, for example. "The typical planners' compromise—between 100 and 200 people per acre," says Crosby, "makes the vehicle-pedestrian dilemma insoluble. It is only at reasonably high densities (200-300 people per acre is the minimum) that the car is downgraded to the status of a luxury. At this density you can choose to use a car; you don't have to use it. Such a density also means that the network of public transport can be afforded, for it is only at high densities that rapid-transit systems make economic sense."

Density also has an important bearing on the look and feel of a neighborhood. If it is urban it ought to be urban. Most of our redevelopment projects are too loose in fabric. They would look better, as well as being more economic, if the scale were tightened up. This is true even of one of the best, the Southwest

# The Case for Crowding

redevelopment area in Washington. Some of the architects involved believe that there would be more life and style to it if they had been able to pull the components closer together.

This does not mean putting everybody up in towers. Unfortunately, the arguments for and against high density are usually presented in terms of towers versus anything else—either spread out or go up in the air.[1] But this is a false choice. A well-knit pattern of low buildings can house a great many people, and often quite amenably. So, obviously, can towers; on any one acre, the maximum possible. But there are other acres to be counted. When towers are spaced out in rows, as in the conventional urban project, the density figures for the over-all project can be surprisingly low.

The usual redevelopment or public housing project generally houses fewer people per acre than the neighborhood that was torn down to make way for it. The design formulas call for lots of space, almost to a suburban scale, and a big point is made of how little ground is taken for the buildings themselves. The projects of the New York City Public Housing Authority, for example, cover some two thousand acres, an area almost a seventh the size of Manhattan Island. The Housing Authority proudly points out that only sixteen percent of the area is used for buildings.

What is gained? Open space, it is said. But the open space is drab and institutional and much of it is forbidden to human trespass. The open space is for the architects, so they can have enough ground to put up towers. But to what end? The design does not pursue its logic. The towers are put up, presumably, for density's sake—to make up for the housing that was not built on the open space. But the net density remains low, and not just by slum standards. In the standard public housing project the number of people per net acre is lower than in many middle-class neighborhoods of three- and four-story houses.

---

1. Philosophically, the most influential exponent of low-density housing has been Britain's Town and Country Planning Association. It equates high-density housing with standard high-rise projects. It detests them, with good reason, and has been berating the authorities for continuing to build them. People do not like living in them as well as in low-rise housing, the Association argues, and they especially miss having private gardens of their own. This is a strong case, but in arguing it the Association gives short shrift to the possibility of designing the more human scale low-rise housing to higher densities. To do so, it warns, would be to court the delusion that "skill can create a new Utopia by cleverer compression." This polarizes the case much too much. Utopia, no, but surely there is a middle ground between high-density towers and low-density garden towns. People who want to build only towers like to have the argument thus polarized. Just goes to prove, they say, that they have no reasonable alternative.

This is an inefficient use of high-cost land, and if we are to continue it, we ought to have some strong social reason for doing so. The stock justification is that lower densities mean healthier living, and planners of this persuasion make much of the correlation between the number of people per acre and the rate of crime and disease in slum neighborhoods. There is a correlation. But is it cause and effect? There is a distinction to be made between overcrowding—that is, too many people per room—and a high number of people per acre. Overcrowding does make for an unhealthy environment; high density may or it may not.

A lot of nonsense is heard these days about the psychological effects of living too close together in cities, or of living in cities at all for that matter. Many of the stock criticisms are quite ancient—filing-cabinet apartments producing filing-cabinet minds, neuroses, tenseness, conformity, and so on. But now the accusations are being made more scientifically. There is a rash of studies under way designed to uncover the bad consequences of overcrowding. This is all very well as far as it goes, but it only goes in one direction. What about undercrowding? The researchers would be a lot more objective if they paid as much attention to the possible effects on people of relative isolation and lack of propinquity. Maybe some of those rats they study get lonely too.[2]

If we study the way people themselves live, we will find strong empirical evidence that they can do quite well in high-density areas. It depends on the area. Some neighborhoods with relatively low densities have high disease and crime rates. Conversely, some neighborhoods with higher densities have low disease and crime rates. Obviously, other factors are the determining ones. (Hong Kong, one of the most densely populated cities in the world, with up to twenty-eight hundred people per acre, has relatively low

---

2. One phenomenon they might look into is the way people often jam up in groups when they do not have to. Cocktail parties, for example. People who go to them habitually complain about the crowding, the noise, and the smoke. But notice how they behave. They do not like too much room. They bunch together and towards the end of the party they will have themselves all jammed into one corner of an otherwise empty room.

The way people behave in the out-of-doors is not totally dissimilar. In a trenchant study of national parks, Noel Eichorn and Frank Fraser Darling comment on the curious psychology of the camp ground: "To some of us [it is] quite a baffling phenomenon. Mr. Lon Garrison told us of his study in Yosemite in the 1930s when he found that many people apparently like being crowded in camp grounds. At least, when the density of occupation of camp grounds decreased after Labor Day, there was a general movement from the outliers to the center, where the density consequently remained high." (*Man and Nature in the National Parks,* Washington: The Conservation Foundation, 1967.)

disease and crime rates compared to congested areas in the U.S.)

Why is it, furthermore, that so many of our high-density neighborhoods are the most sought after? This is not just a matter of high-rise luxury apartments; in New York some of the tree-lined blocks of four- and five-story brownstones with interior gardens have net densities higher than nearby public housing projects. The latter average about two hundred fifty people per acre. Remodeled brownstone areas run from about one hundred eighty people to as high as three hundred fifty people per acre.

Brooklyn Heights is an example. The fine old homes there (which are about twenty-five feet wide by fifty feet deep, plus a fifty-foot garden) have been lovingly rehabilitated into a neighborhood of outstanding charm. But densities are high. For each gross acre (including streets) there are about thirteen houses, and, on the average, they provide a total of sixty-five units. The number of people per unit averages between three and three and a half, giving an over all density of about two hundred people per gross acre. On the basis of land use efficiency, let alone amenity, this beats many a high-rise collective.

Other attractive examples can be found in Washington, Chicago, San Francisco, and many other cities; areas that by orthodox planning standards should be hopelessly congested are among the most pleasant, and sought after, in the city. Too much should not be made of the correlation, but surely something is wrong with a planning policy which calls for density standards so out of whack with the marketplace.

The standards are the legacy of a utopian concept which was never originally intended for the city. It is the garden city ideal: difficult enough to achieve in suburbia, and wholly inapplicable to the city.

In some aspects the original model was more realistic in its specifications than the current standards. Ebenezer Howard's ideal garden city called for somewhere between seventy and one hundred people per acre and this was to be out in the country. For rebuilding of our cities some planning standards call for densities not much greater—about a hundred people per acre for ideal neighborhoods, rarely more than a hundred fifty people.

To do away with congestion, these plans would do away with concentration. But concentration is the genius of the city, its reason for being. What it needs is not fewer people, but more, and if this means more density we have no need to feel guilty about it. The ultimate justification for building to higher densities is not that it is more efficient in land costs, but that it can make a better city.

There are now prototypes to prove that this can be so. For years many people have been arguing that the conventional project design, with its towers and malls, ought to be abandoned. In its stead they proposed a flexible approach that would combine high rise and low buildings; such projects would fit existing neighborhoods, would provide economically high densities, and in the form of stepped terraces and enclosed gardens the kind of amenity—and privacy—not found in the lower density tower projects. There was nothing particularly new about the idea—it is essentially a modern adaptation of the residential square—but it was objected to as being too visionary. Even if it was desirable, some housing people said, it would not be possible to get such designs through the mills of the lending institutions and government agencies. But a few did get through the mill—the redevelopment of Washington's Southwest area, for example—and then came a few more. They worked. They were economic. People like them. Lately even more imaginative approaches have been demonstrated—most notably the design of Montreal's Expo '67 Habitat. I would wager that they are going to work too.

Public housing people are testing new approaches. To the delight of locals, the New York City Housing Authority has commissioned a series of "vest pocket" projects under the Model Cities demonstration program, and it has picked some really good architects to design them. These projects will be small—some will take up only part of a block—and none will look quite like the others. The buildings will be low, mostly of four stories. The ground coverage will be higher than in the conventional tower projects, but though there will be proportionately less open space, it will be put to much more effective use. The open space will be enclosed by the buildings; instead of being dribbled on the streetside, it will be massed in the interior and all of it will be for people.

Because these projects are to so human a scale, some people have surmised that the densities have necessarily been set too low to make them truly economic. This is not the case. Architect Norval White, who is coordinating the work of the various architects, believes that the *apparent* density will be low—as it is in

Brooklyn Heights. But the actual density will be high, averaging around three hundred people per acre.

Further out, densities will continue to be relatively low, and on the outer edge of suburbia fairly large lots will probably continue to be the rule for many years to come. Over-all, however, there is bound to be an increase in the number of people housed in a given area, and much of this increase will be concentrated in pockets of high-density housing.

So far, cluster has not been used to increase density, but the efficiency with which it can house more people per acre is so great that inevitably it is going to be used for that purpose. Developers already have this in mind, as local governments are only too aware; their density zoning ordinances, roughly translated, mean no more density. For the moment developers are not pushing too hard to up the allowable quota of houses; they are getting enough in return in construction savings to be content. But this happy coincidence of self-interests is too good to last much longer. The next big drive of the developers will be cluster *and* more houses, and if the population increase continues they are going to win.

Another rich source of suburban controversy will be apartments. Most suburbs do not want them, and at rezoning hearings the opposition, often the best people in town, will offer statistical proof that apartment people breed too many children, get more out of community taxes than they pay, have little allegiance to the place, and are in general not the element one would want. But the apartments have been going up just the same. Too many people need apartments, and the pressures have been translated into land prices of compelling force. If a plot can be rezoned from one-family residential to garden apartments, the market price per acre vaults immediately, and if the change is to high rise, it can leap as much as $250,000 an acre. The possibility of this profit overspill will prompt other local citizens to argue that apartment people have to live somewhere; breed few children, move to houses when the children are school age, are above average in education and income, and are highly desirable in every respect.

But a zoning variance is almost always necessary. Despite the clear warning of the marketplace, most suburbs are not anticipating apartments; they have their zoning so set that no new apartments will ever get built without a zoning change. They are playing

Canute. There will be changes, just as in the density in density zoning. All in all, suburban zoning boards are in for a rough time.

There are other ways to raise the carrying capacity of our urban land than having more people per acre. We can also increase the number of effective acres, and this can be done without pushing farther out into the country to find them. Within the metropolitan area there is a considerable amount of land that is not used at all, and an appalling amount that is used wastefully.

Parking space is the greatest wastage. Even with our present parking technology, backward as it is, we are allocating much more space for cars than is necessary. A study by the Urban Land Institute of a cross-section of shopping centers indicates that from a purely economic point of view the best rule of thumb would be 5.5 spaces per 1000 feet of shopping space. Most shopping centers far exceed this average—an under-use of high-cost land that would be more functional for the environment if it were used for almost any other purpose, including plain grass.

Industry is profligate, too. The trend to the one-story, horizontal plant has good reasons behind it. Aesthetically, the new plants are built to a considerably higher standard than most new subdivisions. But they, too, consume a great amount of space, and as with shopping centers more of it is given over to parking than to the primary activity. Industrial parks pool space more efficiently, and they require no more land for buffering or landscaping than one isolated plant. If industrial expansion continues, it would seem inevitable that land costs would induce more of this kind of concentration. But might there not also be something of a reversal in the trend to the horizontal? Within a decade we may be hearing of the revolutionary new concept of a vertical stacking of manufacturing space, with improved materials handling making it possible to have factories four and five stories high.[3]

Utility rights-of-way should be tightened up too. High tension lines are so unsightly our eye tends to blank them out, and few people realize what a considerable swath they cut through our

---

3. Another possibility is a high-rise shopping center. This would concentrate on one acre what now is spread over many. The goods and services would be grouped by category, stacked in floors one above the other, with vertical transportation systems tying in with mass transit lines underground. No cars or parking spaces would be necessary. The entire complex would be enclosed and kept at constant temperature and humidity. It could be termed a department store.

urban land. This single-purpose use of land is unnecessarily wasteful, and as I noted earlier, the rights-of-way can be put to good use as connective and recreational space.

Nor does so much land have to be taken. The most striking thing about a utility map of an area is the duplication of effort by different kinds of utilities. Oil pipelines, water conduits, and electric lines angle this way and that along separate rights-of-way, except, as in the central city, where they have been forced into joint routes. Why could they not be pooled? Several new high-voltage transmission lines have been laid down over railroad tracks. The kind of right-of-way that has been greediest of space, the super highway, offers similar potentials. The New York Thruway Authority is now merchandising to utilities the idea of leasing space in a strip along its right-of-way. In Pennsylvania a "utilities corridor" bill has been introduced which encourages the same kind of pooling along any new highway.

Bridges can be made to do more duty. Instead of putting up massive towers for a new river crossing, utilities can put electric lines, even oil pipelines, on the underside of existing bridges. Most bridges are forbidden to such uses, but where they have been permitted the lines or pipelines have proved compatible. The bridge authority gets revenue it otherwise would not, the utility saves a great deal by not having to build the towers, and the public does not have to look at them.

Such efficiency, to repeat a point, makes for good aesthetics, and in some cases it is the aesthetic argument which has tipped the scales. But the most compelling factor is economic, and that is why with some optimism we can look forward to more of such measures for better land use.

Some kinds of under-use will not be so easily resolved. For planners, the most frustrating open spaces to contemplate are the cemeteries of the city. Together, they take up a large amount of space—in some areas, like Queens in New York—they form the bulk of the urban open space. Many a planner has toyed with the thought of all the good things that could be done with the land were there a relocation effort. Those who are wise have kept the idea to themselves. Title problems are immense, and the whole subject politically explosive.

Reservoir and watershed lands of private and municipal water companies are in many states restricted to any use except the gathering of rain. Pressure for recreational use has been mounting—particularly from sportsmen—and in time it would seem inevitable that these lands will be opened up to multiple use. The delaying action is strong, however, and in one respect it has been quite beneficial. The fact these lands have been unavailable as usable open space has made it easier to get public support for acquisition of other open space.

In the city, perhaps the most exciting potential for gaining extra space is the use of air rights. Railroads are old hands at leasing these out; the New York Central's Park Avenue operation, started in 1913, is still the prime example. For good and financial reasons, railroads have recently been doing a lot more to get their freight yards and tracks decked over with revenue-producing projects. Railroads in the Chicago area have been particularly active, and many of the most striking new buildings there have been going over tracks.

City-owned land has great capabilities too. In New York City, for example, subway freight yards, together with railroad tracks, total some 9641 acres. These are probably the dreariest acres to look at in the city, and development over top of them could greatly improve the looks of the city as well as its finances. A few starts have been made. Two new public schools are being built over subway storage yards. Since school buildings are customarily low and flat-roofed, in some cases it would make sense to go a step further and lease the air rights over the schools for yet another structure. In a project for one new high school in New York, part of the air rights are to be used for the construction of an apartment tower. The lease payments will pay a substantial portion of the interest on the school construction bonds.

City-owned reservoirs can be decked over too. Philadelphia is now considering the proposal of a developer to build a commercial and shopping complex over a city reservoir. The city's planners and engineers like the idea; in addition to the income, the structure would keep the sun off the water in summer and there would be much less loss through evaporation.

Expressways and streets are going to be exploited more vigorously. Back in 1961 Governor Nelson A. Rockefeller's Committee for Urban Middle Income Housing proposed a large-scale program for housing one million persons in New York City in developments using air rights, many of them over streets. At the time, the proposal was deemed much too visionary, but now a number of specific projects along this line are being given serious consideration. One is a "Linear City" that would group schools, low- and middle-income housing, stores, and community facilities of private and public uses over a stretch of expressway.

There are problems, of course, in this kind of construction. An apartment project built several years ago atop the Manhattan approaches to the George Washington Bridge, for example, has run into difficulties because of the great amount of noise and air pollution the high concentration of cars beneath sends up. But the technical challenge is not too difficult. The real problem, as the *New York Times'* Ada Louise Huxtable has pointed out, is governmental. "In the city," she notes, "the municipal pipeline is jammed with simple projects unable to clear the hurdles of requests, reviews, and multi-departmental jurisdiction. A proposal of the scope and size of Linear City must cut across all city departments and agencies. A design breakthrough is not enough. An administrative breakthrough is equally necessary."

But ways will be found. There is revenue pressure to find them. Highway departments are an example. Not so many years ago most would have recoiled at the thought of buildings over their rights-of-way. Now they have become very open-minded about such projects and in some cases vigorously opportunistic. The New York State Thruway Authority has been circularizing developers with a brochure *Fashion Your Future Out of Thin Air* and lists the acreages in various urban areas that it thinks would be excellent for commercial development. (In response to a query from the City of Yonkers, it said it would make air rights available free of charge for municipal projects; if any federal money became available for municipal purchase of air rights, however, the authority said it would want to be paid.) The Massachusetts Turnpike Authority has leased air space in the Boston area for the construction of a supermarket and is promoting the development of other segments. By all indications, there is going to be a lot more of this kind of double development in all the states, and for all kinds of highways.[4]

---

4. Toll road authorities have been in the forefront because they are exempt from many of the restrictions to regular highway projects and they are by nature quite promotion minded. But now the road is open for air rights development on the interstate highways. The Federal Aid Highway Act of 1961 authorized the use of air space above, and below, interstate highways for almost any purpose that would not conflict with the highway.

Let me turn from the techniques of compression to the matter of whether or not it is justified. In bespeaking a more intensive use of the land I have been accepting the fact of growth. But is it inevitable? And is it good? A number of ecologists and conservationists think not. They are horrified by the specter of a growing population devouring the resources we have left. Space is finite, and thus any rate of growth must at some time finally fill up that space. The Malthusians believe we are very close to that time. Unless nature or catastrophe intervenes, they hold, we must find a way to limit the growth ourselves.

They even see a danger in planning measures to make better use of the land. Only a palliative, they say. Writing in *Science* (July 1965) geographer George Macinko puts the case thus: "The operating assumption that a continuing demand for space can be met by ingenuity in allocation of space is untenable for a limited space subject to a continuing demand. Such space allocation is a delaying or rearguard action that slows down the ultimate confrontation. It does not 'solve the problem' and may in the long run have adverse effects. By appearing to be a solution, it temporarily hides one of the most pressing reasons for public concern—the fact that open land is in danger of becoming exceedingly short in supply."

Malthusians argue that planners can no longer make sensible plans unless they face up to the issue of population control, and as a minimum, demonstrate to the public the choices involved. They point out that in almost all of the alternative regional design plans growth is assumed; in the worst alternative presented, "unplanned growth," the bad word is "unplanned." Why not, critics ask, a "planned no-growth" alternative? The planners could say to people, look, we've shown you different ways we can handle a growing population; now we'd like to show you what a job we could do if the population doesn't grow, or if we find ways to deliberately restrict it. The Malthusians have little doubt that this would be the best of the alternatives.

I wonder. On the face of it, it would seem easier for land planners to cope with growth if there were not any, or, at least, much less. But there is a challenge and response equation involved. When growth pressures were less we wasted land and abused it. And were there respite we might be as bad as ever. We are, of course, still enormously wasteful, but we are beginning to feel guilty enough about it to try and mend our ways a bit. Events have forced us to, and it is quite doubtful if we would be now adopting better land-use measures except for the pressures of growth.

It is a shame so much land had to be sacrificed to force the recognition, but the blight seems a necessary stimulant (it is not by accident that so many of the new approaches have been tried first in California). We have to have our noses rubbed in it. Whether or not, as the Malthusians hope, the discipline leads us to the further step of population control, we are being goaded to a more effective use of space, now, and the process is hardly a palliative.

It is a necessity. Perhaps, in time, people will have far fewer babies than they are having now. They have been cutting down the rate, certainly, and if they continue to our estimates for the year 2000 may be well over the mark. For the years immediately ahead, however, we are bound to have a bigger population, and on the basis of the future parents already born, for at least the next twenty years we are going to have to house a lot more people than we have now. This means higher densities and we should do the best job we can to cope with the fact.

## SUGGESTIONS FOR FURTHER READING

The volume of literature espousing one or another form of metropolitan-wide government is enormous. Two articles which can provide a starting point for further reading on the subject are H. Paul Friesema's "The Metropolis and the Maze of Local Government" (*Urban Affairs Quarterly*, vol. 2, December 1966, pp. 68-90) and John Rehfuss's "Metropolitan Government: Four Views" (*Urban Affairs Quarterly*, vol. 3, June 1968, pp. 91-111). For a reasonably brief but very readable case-study account of the failure of a referendum calling for a limited form of metro-government see Henry J. Schmandt, Paul G. Steinbicker, and George D. Wendel's *Metropolitan Reform in St. Louis* (New York: Holt, Rinehart, and Winston, 1961).

The attempt to open the suburbs for low-income residents, especially blacks, is an issue so current that the most likely sources of information are the daily newspapers and weekly newsmagazines. Perhaps the best background reading is provided by the speeches of Senator Abraham Ribicoff of Connecticut, who has introduced two pieces of legislation toward this purpose. Senator Ribicoff's floor statements when submitting these bills (S.4545 and S.4546—Introduction of The Urban Education Improvement Act of 1970 and The Government Facilities Location Act of 1970) are particularly instructive. They may be found in *The Congressional Record* (vol. 116, November 30, 1970).

The problem of metropolitan sprawl, like metropolitan government, has a vast bibliography. One of the best-known works on the subject is Jean Gottman's *Megalopolis: The Urbanized Northeast Seaboard of the United States* (New York: The Twentieth Century Fund, 1961). For undergraduate reading, Gottman's work has been synthesized and illustrated in Wolf Von Eckardt's *The Challenge of Megalopolis* (New York: The Twentieth Century Fund, 1964). Another book about the geographical extension of metropolitan areas is *Soil, Water, and Suburbia* (Washington, D.C.: U.S. Government Printing Office, 1968). This volume is a report of the proceedings of the National Conference on Soil, Water, and Suburbia held in June 1967 and sponsored by the United States Department of Agriculture and the United States Department of Housing and Urban Development. It contains a wide-ranging series of expert statements treating the natural and social ecological implications of suburban expansion.

# REFERENCES

Althoff, Phillip, and Patterson, Samuel C. 1966. Political activism in a rural county. *Midwest Journal of Political Science*, vol. 10, February, p. 40.
Axelrod, Morris. 1956. Urban structure and social participation. *American Sociological Review*, vol. 21, February, pp. 13-18.
Bell, Charles G. 1969. A new suburban politics. *Social Forces*, vol. 47, March, pp. 282-288.
Bell, Wendell, 1958. Social choice, life styles and suburban residence. In *The Suburban Community*, ed. William M. Dobriner, pp. 225-247. New York: G. P. Putnam's Sons.
Bell, Wendell, and Force, Maryanne T. 1956. Urban neighborhood types and participation in formal associations. *American Sociological Review*, vol. 21, February, pp. 25-34.
Benedict, Ruth F. 1934. *Patterns of Culture*. Boston: Houghton Mifflin.
Berger, Bennett M. 1960. *Working-Class Suburb: A Study of Auto Workers in Suburbia*. Berkeley and Los Angeles: University of California Press.
Birch, David L. 1970. *The Economic Future of City and Suburbs*. New York: Committee for Economic Development, CED Supplementary Paper Number 30.
Blumberg, Leonard, and Lalli, Michael. 1966. Little ghettoes: a study of Negroes in the suburbs. *Phylon*, vol. 27, Summer, pp. 117-131.
Bogue, D. J., and Kitagawa, E. M. 1954. *Suburbanization of Manufacturing Activities*. Oxford, Ohio: Scripps Foundation.
Bowman, Lewis, and Boynton, G. R. 1966a. Activities and role definitions of grassroots party officials. *Journal of Politics*, vol. 28, February, pp. 121-143.
———. 1966b. Recruitment patterns among local party officials: a model and some preliminary findings in selected locales; *American Political Science Review*, vol. 60, September, pp. 667-676.
Bridenbaugh, C. 1955. *Cities in Revolt*. New York: Knopf.
Campbell, Angus, et al. 1954. *The Voter Decides*. Evanston, Ill.: Row, Peterson.
———. 1960. *The American Voter*. New York: John Wiley & Sons.
Carney, Francis. 1958. *The Rise of the Democratic Clubs in California*. New York: Henry Holt & Co.

Cuthbert, Daniel. 1940. Statistically significant differences in observed per cents. *Journal of Applied Psychology*, vol. 24, December, pp. 826-830.

Davidoff, Paul. 1965. Advocacy and pluralism in planning. *Journal of the American Institute of Planners*, vol. 31, November, pp. 331-338.

Davis, Richard Harding. 1894. Our suburban friends. *Harpers*, vol. 89, June, pp. 155-157.

Dean, Lois. 1967. *Five Towns: A Comparative Community Study*. New York: Random House.

Dewey, Richard. 1960. The rural-urban continuum: real but relatively unimportant. *American Journal of Sociology*, vol. 66, July, pp. 60-66.

Dobriner, William M. 1958. Introduction: theory and research in the sociology of the suburbs. In *The Suburban Community*, ed. William M. Dobriner, pp. xiii-xxviii. New York: G. P. Putnam's Sons.

———. 1963. *Class in Suburbia*. Englewood Cliffs, N.J.: Prentice-Hall.

Donaldson, Scott. 1969. *The Suburban Myth*. New York: Columbia University Press.

Dornbusch, S. 1952. *A Typology of Suburban Communities*. Chicago: Chicago Community Inventory.

Douglass, Harlan Paul. 1925. *The Suburban Trend*. New York and London: Century Co.

———. 1934. Suburbs. In *The Encyclopaedia of the Social Sciences*, vol. 14, pp. 433-435. New York: Macmillan.

Downes, Bryron. 1969. Issue conflict, functionalism, and consensus in suburban city councils. *Urban Affairs Quarterly*, vol. 4, June, pp. 477-497.

Duhl, Leonard J. 1956. Mental health and community planning. In *Planning 1955*, pp. 31-39. Chicago: American Society of Planning Officials.

Duncan, Otis D., 1956. Research on metropolitan population: evaluation of data. *Journal of the American Statistical Association*, December, p. 5.

Duncan, Otis D., and Duncan, B. 1955. Residential distribution and occupational stratification. *American Journal of Sociology*, vol. 60, March, p. 494.

Duncan, Otis D., and Reiss, Albert J., Jr. 1956. *Social Characteristics of Rural and Urban Communities, 1950*. New York: John Wiley & Sons.

Duncan, Otis D., and Schnore, Leo F. 1959. Cultural, behavioral and ecological perspectives in the study of social organization. *American Journal of Sociology*, vol. 65, September, pp. 132-155.

Dye, Thomas. 1962. Popular images of decision-making in suburban communities. *Sociology and Social Research*, vol. 47, October, pp. 75-83.

Edson, Charles. 1955. *The Suburban Vote*. Senior Thesis, Harvard University. Quoted in Robert C. Wood, *Suburbia: Its People and Their Politics*, pp. 144-45. Boston: Houghton Mifflin, 1958.

Eldersveld, Samuel J. 1964. *Political Parties: A Behavioral Analysis*. Chicago: Rand McNally.

Enders, John. Undated. *Profile of the Theater Market*. New York: Playbill.

# References

Farley, Reynolds. 1970. The changing distribution of Negroes within metropolitan areas: the emergence of black suburbs. *American Journal of Sociology*, vol. 75, January, pp. 512-527.

Fava, Sylvia Fleis. 1958. Contrasts in neighboring: New York City and a suburban community. In *The Suburban Community*, ed. William M. Dobriner, pp. 122-131. New York: G. P. Putnam's Sons.

Foley, Donald L. 1957. The use of local facilities in a metropolis. In *Cities and Society*, ed. Paul Hatt and Albert J. Reiss, Jr., pp. 237-247. Glencoe, Ill.: The Free Press.

Form, William H., et al. 1954. The compatibility of alternative approaches to the delimitation of urban sub-areas. *American Sociological Review*, vol. 19, August, pp. 434-440.

French, Robert Mills. 1964. *An Analysis of Trailers in America*. Unpublished M.A. thesis, University of Wisconsin.

French, Robert Mills, and Hadden, Jeffrey K. 1965. An analysis of the distribution and characteristics of mobile homes in America. *Land Economics*, vol. 41, May, pp. 131-139.

Friesema, H. Paul. 1966. The metropolis and the maze of local government. *Urban Affairs Quarterly*, vol. 2, December, pp. 68-90.

Fromm, Erich. 1955. *The Sane Society*. New York: Rinehart & Co.

Gans, Herbert J. 1951. Park Forest: birth of a Jewish community. *Commentary*, vol. 21, pp. 330-339.

———. 1959. *The Urban Villagers: A Study of the Second Generation Italians in the West End of Boston*. Boston: Center for Community Studies (December) (mimeographed).

———. 1961. Planning and social life: an evaluation of friendship and neighbor relations in suburban communities. *Journal of the American Institute of Planners*, vol. 27, May, pp. 134-140.

———. 1967. *The Levittowners*. New York: Pantheon.

Gilbert, Charles E. 1967. *Governing the Suburbs*. Bloomington: Indiana University Press.

Goldstein, S. 1963. Some economic consequences of suburbanization in the Copenhagen metropolitan area. *American Journal of Sociology*, vol. 68, March.

Gottman, Jean. 1961. *Megalopolis: The Urbanized Northeast Seaboard of the United States*. New York: Twentieth Century Fund.

Greenstein, Fred I., and Wolfinger, Raymond E. 1958. The suburbs and shifting party loyalties. *Public Opinion Quarterly*, Winter 1958-59, pp. 473-482.

Greer, Scott. 1956. Urbanism reconsidered: a comparative study of local areas in a metropolis. *American Sociological Review*, vol. 21, February, pp. 19-25.

———. 1960. The social structure and political process of suburbia. *American Sociological Review*, vol. 25, August, pp. 514-526.

———. 1962a. *The Emerging City*. New York: Free Press.

———. 1962b. *Governing the Metropolis*. New York: John Wiley & Sons.

———. 1963. The social structure and political process of suburbia: an empirical test. *Rural Sociology*, vol. 27, December, pp. 438-459.

Greer, Scott, and Kube, Ella. 1959. Urbanism and social structure: a Los Angeles study. In *Community Structure and Analysis*, ed. Marvin B. Sussman, pp. 93-112. New York: Thomas Y. Crowell Co.

Hallowell, A. I. 1943. The nature and function of property as a social institution. *Journal of Legal and Political Sociology*, vol. 1, pp. 115-138.

Harris, Chauncy D. 1943. Suburbs. *American Journal of Sociology*, vol. 49, May, p. 6.

Hawley, Amos H., 1956. *The Changing Shape of Metropolitan America: Deconcentration since 1920*. Glencoe, Ill.: Free Press.

Heard, Alexander. 1952. *A Two-Party South*. Chapel Hill: University of North Carolina Press.

Hirschfield, Robert S.; Swanson, Bert E.; and Blank, Blanche D. 1962. A profile of political activists in Manhattan. *Western Political Quarterly*, vol. 15, September, pp. 489-506.

Hoover, E. M., and Vernon, R. 1959. *Anatomy of a Metropolis*. Cambridge, Mass.: Harvard University Press.

Janosik, G. E. 1956. The new suburbia. *Current History*, vol. 31, August, pp. 91-95.

Janowitz, Morris. 1952. *The Community Press in an Urban Setting*. Glencoe, Ill.: Free Press.

Jonassen, Christen T. 1955. *The Shopping Center versus Downtown*. Columbus, Ohio: Bureau of Business Research, Ohio State University.

Jones, Victor, and Collver, Andrew. 1959. Economic classification of cities and metropolitan areas. In *The Municipal Yearbook, 1959*, ed. Orin F. Nolting and David S. Arnold, p. 72. Chicago: International City Managers' Association.

Jones, Victor; Forstall, Richard L.; and Collver, Andrew. 1963. Economic and social characteristics of cities. In *Municipal Year Book, 1963*, pp. 85-157. Chicago: International City Managers' Association.

Kasahara, Yoshiko. 1968. A profile of Canada's metropolitan centres. In *Canadian Society Sociological Perspectives*, ed. Bernard R. Bilshen et al. Toronto: MacMillan of Canada.

Key, V. O. 1955. A theory of critical elections. *Journal of Politics*, vol. 17, February, pp. 3-18.

Kish, Leslie. 1954. Differentiation in metropolitan areas. *American Sociological Review*, vol. 19, August, pp. 388-398.

Ktsanes, Thomas, and Reissman, Leonard. 1959. Suburbia: new homes for old values. *Social Problems*, vol. 7, Winter, pp. 187-194.

Kurtz, Richard, and Eicher, Joanna B. 1958. Fringe and suburb: a confusion of concepts. *Social Forces*, vol. 37, October, pp. 32-37.

Ladd, Everett C., Jr. 1969. *Ideology in America: Change and Response in a City, a Suburb, and a Small Town*. Ithaca, N.Y.: Cornell University Press.

Lane, Robert E. 1959. *Political Life*. Glencoe, Ill.: Free Press.

Levitt, Alfred S. 1951. A community builder looks at community planning. *Journal of the American Institute of Planners*, vol. 17, Spring, pp. 80-88.

# References

Lewis, C. 1946. *Children of the Cumberland*. New York: Columbia University Press.
Lubell, Samuel. 1952. *The Future of American Politics*. New York: Harper & Bros.
———. 1956. *Revolt of the Moderates*. New York: Harper & Bros.
Manis, Jerome G., and Stine, Leo C. 1958. Suburban residence and political behavior. *Public Opinion Quarterly*, Winter 1958-1959, pp. 483-489.
Martin, Walter T. 1956. The structuring of social relationships engendered by suburban residence. *American Sociological Review*, vol. 21, August, pp. 446-453.
———. 1957. Ecological change in satellite rural areas. *American Sociological Review*, vol. 22, April, pp. 171-183.
Marvick, Dwaine, and Nixon, Charles. 1961. Recruitment contrasts in rival campaign groups. In *Political Decision-Makers*, ed. Dwaine Marvick, pp. 193-217. New York: Free Press.
Mayer, Charles S., and Pratt, R. W., Jr. 1966. A note of non-response in mail survey. *Public Opinion Quarterly*, vol. 30, Winter 1966-1967, pp. 637-646.
McClosky, Herbert; Hoffman, Paul J.; and O'Hara, Rosemary. 1960. Issue conflict and consensus in American party leaders and followers. *American Political Science Review*, vol. 54, June, pp. 406-427.
McDonagh, E. C., and Rosenblum, A. L. 1965. A comparison of mailed questionnaires and subsequent structured interviews. *Public Opinion Quarterly*, vol. 29, pp. 131-136.
McKenzie, R. D. 1934. *The Metropolitan Community*. New York: McGraw-Hill.
Milbrath, Lester W. 1965. *Political Participation*. Chicago: Rand McNally.
Millett, John, and Pittman, David. 1958. The new suburban voter: a case study in electoral behavior. *Southwestern Social Science Quarterly*, vol. 40, June, pp. 33-42.
Moser, C. A. 1958. *Survey Methods in Social Investigation*. London: Heinemann.
Moses, Robert. 1956. *Working for the People: Promise and Performance in Public Service*. New York: Harpers.
Murphy, Raymond E. 1966. *The American City*. New York: McGraw-Hill.
Netzer, Dick. 1968. *The Economics of Suburban Growth*. Stonybrook: State of New York.
Ogburn, W. F. 1937. *Social Characteristics of Cities*. Chicago: International City Managers' Association.
Park, R. E.; Burgess, E. W.; and McKenzie, R. D. 1925. *The City*. Chicago: University of Chicago Press.
Patterson, Samuel C. 1963. Characteristics of party leaders. *Western Political Quarterly*, vol. 16, June, pp. 332-352.
Peattie, Lisa R. 1968. Reflections on advocacy planning. *Journal of the American Institute of Planners*, vol. 34, March, pp. 80-88.
Pinkerton, James R. 1969. City-suburban residential patterns by social class. *Urban Affairs Quarterly*, vol. 4, June, pp. 499-519.
Pryor, Robin. 1968. Defining the rural-urban fringe. *Social Forces*, vol. 47, December, pp. 202-215.

Ranney, Austin, and Kendall, Wilmore. 1956. *Democracy and the American Party System.* New York: Harcourt, Brace.

Rehfuss, John. 1968. Metropolitan government: four views. *Urban Affairs Quarterly*, vol. 3, June, pp. 91-111.

Reiss, Albert J., Jr. 1955. An analysis of urban phenomena. In *The Metropolis in Modern Life*, ed. Robert M. Fisher, pp. 41-49. Garden City, N.Y.: Doubleday & Co.

———. 1959. Rural-urban and status differences in interpersonal contacts. *American Journal of Sociology*, vol. 65, September, pp. 182-195.

Riesman, David. 1957. The suburban dislocation. *Annals of the American Academy of Political and Social Science*, vol. 314, November, p. 125.

———. 1958. The suburban sadness. In *The Suburban Community*, ed. William M. Dobriner, pp. 375-408. New York: G. P. Putnam's Sons.

Ringer, Benjamin B. 1967. *The Edge of Friendliness: A Study of Jewish-Gentile Relations.* New York: Basic Books.

Rose, Arnold M. 1947. Living arrangements of unattached persons. *American Sociological Review*, vol. 12, August, pp. 429-435.

Rosenwaike, Ira. 1970. A critical examination of the designation of standard metropolitan statistical areas. *Social Forces*, vol. 48, March, pp. 322-333.

Rossi, Peter H., and Cutright, Phillips. 1961. The impact of party organization in an industrial setting. In *Community Political Systems*, ed. Morris Janowitz, pp. 81-116. Glencoe, Ill.: Free Press.

Salisbury, Robert H. 1965. The urban party organization member. *Public Opinion Quarterly*, vol. 29, Winter 1965-1966, pp. 350-364.

Schauffler, M. 1941. *The Suburbs of Cleveland.* Unpublished Ph.D. dissertation, University of Chicago, Department of Sociology.

Schlesinger, Joseph A. 1955. A two-dimensional scheme for classifying the states according to degree of inter-party competition. *American Political Science Review*, vol. 49, December, pp. 1120-1128.

Schmandt, Henry J.; Steinbicker, Paul G.; and Wendel, George D. 1961. *Metropolitan Reform in St. Louis.* New York: Holt, Rinehart, and Winston.

Schnore, Leo F. 1956. The functions of metropolitan suburbs. *American Journal of Sociology*, vol. 61, March, pp. 453-458.

———. 1957a. The growth of metropolitan suburbs. *American Sociological Review*, vol. 22, April, pp. 165-173.

———. 1957b. Satellites and suburbs. *Social Forces*, vol. 36, December, pp. 121-127.

———. 1958. Components of population change in large metropolitan suburbs. *American Sociological Review*, vol. 23, October, pp. 570-573.

———. 1962. Municipal annexations and the growth of metropolitan suburbs, 1950-60. *American Journal of Sociology*, vol. 67, January, pp. 406-417.

———. 1963. The socio-economic status of cities and suburbs. *American Sociological Review*, vol. 28, August, p. 84.

———. 1965. *The Urban Scene.* New York: Free Press.

# References

Schrank, Robert, and Stein, Susan. 1969. Industry in the black community: IBM in Bedford-Stuyvesant. *Journal of the American Institute of Planners*, vol. 35, September, pp. 348-351.

Seeley, John R. 1959. The slum: its nature, use and users. *Journal of the American Institute of Planners*, vol. 25, February, pp. 7-14.

Seeley, John R.; Sim, R. Alexander; and Loosley, Elizabeth W. 1956. *Crestwood Heights: A North American Suburb*. Toronto: University of Toronto Press. Also published as *Crestwood Heights: The Culture of Suburban Life*. New York: Basic Books, 1956.

Silverman, Corinne, and Campbell, Alan K. 1962. *Nassau '62: A Survey of Party Strength and Voters' Opinion*. New York: Metro Consultants.

Sklare, Marshall, and Greenblum, Joseph. 1967. *Jewish Identity on the Suburban Frontier: A Study of Group Survival in the Open Society*. New York: Basic Books.

Smith, Joel. 1970. Another look at socioeconomic status distributions in urbanized areas. *Urban Affairs Quarterly*, vol. 5, June, pp. 423-453.

Smith, Joel; Form, William; and Stone, Gregory. 1954. Local intimacy in a middle-sized city. *American Journal of Sociology*, vol. 60, November, pp. 276-284.

Spectorsky, A. C. 1955. *The Exurbanites*. Philadelphia: J. B. Lippincott Co.

Standing, William H., and Robinson, James A. 1958. Inter-party competition and primary contesting: the case of Indiana. *American Political Science Review*, vol. 52, December, pp. 1066-1077.

Stauber, Richard. 1965. The swampy science of suburbia: a case for the sociology of knowledge. *Kansas Journal of Sociology*, vol. 1, pp. 137-154.

Stone, Gregory P. 1954. City shoppers and urban identification: observations on the social psychology of city life. *American Journal of Sociology*, vol. 60, July, pp. 36-45.

Strauss, Anselm. 1960. The changing imagery of American city and suburb. *Sociological Quarterly*, vol. 1, January, pp. 15-24.

Taylor, Graham R. 1915. *Satellite Cities*. New York and London: D. Appleton.

Vernon, Raymond. 1959. *The Changing Economic Function of the Central City*. New York: Committee on Economic Development, Supplementary Paper No. 1. January.

Vidich, Arthur J., and Bensman, Joseph. 1958. *Small Town in Mass Society: Class, Power and Religion in a Rural Community*. Princeton, N.J.: Princeton University Press.

Von Eckardt, Wolf. 1964. *The Challenge of Megalopolis*. New York: Twentieth Century Fund.

Walter, Ingo, and Kramer, John. 1969. Political autonomy and economic dependence in an all-Negro municipality. *American Journal of Economics and Sociology*, vol. 28, July, pp. 225-248.

Warner, Sam B. 1962. *Streetcar Suburbs*. Cambridge, Mass.: Harvard University Press and M.I.T. Press.

Wattell, Harold. 1958. Levittown: a suburban community. In *The Suburban Community*, ed. William M. Dobriner, pp. 287-313. New York: G. P. Putnam's Sons.

Weber, A. F. 1899. *The Growth of Cities in the Nineteenth Century.* New York: Macmillan.
White, T. H. 1961. *The Making of the President, 1960.* New York: Atheneum.
Whyte, William F., Jr. 1955. *Street Corner Society.* Chicago: University of Chicago Press.
Whyte, William H. 1956. *The Organization Man.* New York: Simon & Schuster.
Wildavsky, Aaron. 1964. *Leadership in a Small Town.* Totawa, N.J.; Bedminster.
Wilensky, Harold L. 1961. Life cycle, work situation, and participation in formal associations. In *Aging and Leisure: Research Perspectives on the Meaningful Use of Time*, ed. Robert W. Kleemeier et al., chap. 8. New York: Oxford University Press.
Wilensky, Harold L., and Lebeaux, Charles. 1958. *Industrial Society and Social Welfare.* New York: Russell Sage Foundation.
Williams, Oliver P., et al. 1965. *Suburban Differences and Metropolitan Policies: A Philadelphia Story.* Philadelphia: University of Pennsylvania Press.
Wilson, James Q. 1962. *The Amateur Democrat.* Chicago: University of Chicago Press.
Wirth, Louis. 1928. *The Ghetto.* Chicago: University of Chicago Press.
———. 1938. Urbanism as a way of life. *American Journal of Sociology*, vol. 44, July, pp. 1-24. Reprinted in *Cities and Society*, ed. Paul K. Hatt and Albert J. Reiss, Jr., pp. 46-64. Glencoe, Ill: Free Press, 1957. [All page references are to this reprinting of the article.]
Wood, Robert C. 1958. *Suburbia: Its People and Their Politics.* Boston: Houghton Mifflin.
———. 1961. *1400 Governments.* Cambridge, Mass.: Harvard University Press.
Woodbury, Coleman. 1955. Suburbanization and suburbia. *American Journal of Public Health*, vol. 45, January, p. 2.
Wrong, Dennis. 1967. Suburbs and myths of suburbia. In *Readings in Introductory Sociology*, ed. Dennis Wrong and Harry Gracey. New York: Macmillan.
Young, Michael, and Willmott, Peter. 1957. *Family and Kinship in East London.* London: Routledge & Kegan Paul, Ltd.
Zikmund, Joseph II. 1968. Suburban voting in presidential elections: 1948-1964. *Midwest Journal of Political Science*, vol. 12, May, pp. 239-258.